Historical Legacies of Communism in Russia and Eastern Europe

This book takes stock of arguments about the historical legacies of communism that have become common within the study of Russia and Eastern Europe more than two decades after communism's demise and elaborates an empirical approach to the study of historical legacies revolving around relationships and mechanisms rather than correlation and outward similarities. Eleven chapters by a distinguished group of scholars assess whether postcommunist developments in specific areas continue to be shaped by the experience of communism or, alternatively, by fundamental divergences produced before or after communism. Chapters deal with the variable impact of the communist experience on postcommunist societies in such areas as regime trajectories and democratic political values; patterns of regional and sectoral economic development; property ownership within the energy sector; the functioning of the executive branch of government, the police, and courts; the relationship of religion to the state; government language policies; and informal relationships and practices.

Mark R. Beissinger is Henry W. Putnam Professor of Politics at Princeton University and director of the Princeton Institute for International and Regional Studies. He previously served on the faculties of Harvard University and the University of Wisconsin-Madison. Beissinger is the author or editor of four books and numerous journal articles. His book *Nationalist Mobilization and the Collapse of the Soviet State* (Cambridge, 2002) won several awards, including the 2003 Woodrow Wilson Foundation Award from the American Political Science Association.

Stephen Kotkin is the John P. Birkelund '52 Professor in History and International Affairs at Princeton University, where he has also served as vice dean of the Woodrow Wilson School and director of Princeton's Program in Russian and Eurasian Studies. He is the author of numerous books and publications, including *Magnetic Mountain: Stalinism as a Civilization* (1995); *Armageddon Averted: The Soviet Collapse, 1970–2000* (2001); and *Uncivil Society: 1989 and the Implosion of Communist Establishments* (2009).

Advance Praise

"Mark R. Beissinger and Stephen Kotkin have assembled a who's-who of scholars on Eastern Europe and Eurasia, many of whom made their careers in the era after the end of communist rule. The authors are therefore particularly adept at separating 'historical legacies' from plain history – examining the precise ways in which the habits of the past may (and may not) matter in such diverse areas as policing, property rights, and economic performance. This book reminds us why edited volumes – carefully crafted around a common theme – are still indispensable vehicles of scholarly communication."

– Charles King, Georgetown University, author of *Extreme Politics: Nationalism, Violence, and the End of Eastern Europe*

"Total system state socialism is gone, but polities across Eurasia continue to contend with Leninist legacies. And no wonder: state socialism was an earth-changing experiment in social engineering. *Historical Legacies of Communism in Russia and Eastern Europe* takes careful stock of how these legacies matter (and, alternatively, how they fade from significance). Representing the best of historically informed social science, this book is conceptually innovative, empirically grounded, contextually sensitive, and intellectually provocative. Its wide range of cases invites serious thinking about how the socialist period will continue to shape our world."

– Edward Schatz, University of Toronto

Historical Legacies of Communism in Russia and Eastern Europe

Edited by

MARK R. BEISSINGER
Princeton University

STEPHEN KOTKIN
Princeton University

CAMBRIDGE
UNIVERSITY PRESS

32 Avenue of the Americas, New York, NY 10013-2473, USA

Cambridge University Press is part of the University of Cambridge.

It furthers the University's mission by disseminating knowledge in the pursuit of education, learning, and research at the highest international levels of excellence.

www.cambridge.org
Information on this title: www.cambridge.org/9781107054172

© Cambridge University Press 2014

This publication is in copyright. Subject to statutory exception and to the provisions of relevant collective licensing agreements, no reproduction of any part may take place without the written permission of Cambridge University Press.

First published 2014

Printed in the United States of America

A catalog record for this publication is available from the British Library.

Library of Congress Cataloging in Publication data
Historical legacies of communism in Russia and Eastern Europe / edited by Mark R. Beissinger, Stephen Kotkin.
 pages cm
Includes bibliographical references and index.
ISBN 978-1-107-05417-2 (hardback)
 1. Post-communism – Economic aspects – Europe, Eastern. 2. Post-communism – Economic aspects – Russia (Federation) 3. Europe, Eastern – Economic policy – 1989– 4. Russia (Federation) – Economic policy – 1991– 5. Europe, Eastern – Politics and government – 1989– 6. Russia (Federation) – Politics and government – 1991– I. Beissinger, Mark R., editor of compilation. II. Kotkin, Stephen, editor of compilation.
HC244.H554 2014
330.947–dc23   2014002030

ISBN 978-1-107-05417-2 Hardback

Cambridge University Press has no responsibility for the persistence or accuracy of URLs for external or third-party Internet Web sites referred to in this publication and does not guarantee that any content on such Web sites is, or will remain, accurate or appropriate.

Contents

List of Contributors		*page* vii
Acknowledgments		ix
1.	The Historical Legacies of Communism: An Empirical Agenda *Stephen Kotkin and Mark R. Beissinger*	1
2.	Communist Development and the Postcommunist Democratic Deficit *Grigore Pop-Eleches*	28
3.	Room for Error: The Economic Legacy of Soviet Spatial Misallocation *Clifford G. Gaddy*	52
4.	Legacies of Industrialization and Paths of Transnational Integration after Socialism *Béla Greskovits*	68
5.	The Limits of Legacies: Property Rights in Russian Energy *Timothy Frye*	90
6.	Legacies and Departures in the Russian State Executive *Eugene Huskey*	111
7.	From Police State to Police State? Legacies and Law Enforcement in Russia *Brian D. Taylor*	128
8.	How Judges Arrest and Acquit: Soviet Legacies in Postcommunist Criminal Justice *Alexei Trochev*	152
9.	Historical Roots of Religious Influence on Postcommunist Democratic Politics *Anna Grzymala-Busse*	179

10. Soviet Nationalities Policies and the Discrepancy between
    Ethnocultural Identification and Language Practice in Ukraine   202
    Volodymyr Kulyk
11. *Pokazukha* and Cardiologist Khrenov: Soviet Legacies, Legacy
    Theater, and a Usable Past   222
    Jessica Pisano

Index   243

Contributors

Mark R. Beissinger is the Henry W. Putnam Professor of Politics at Princeton University.

Timothy Frye is the Marshall D. Shulman Professor of Political Science at Columbia University.

Clifford G. Gaddy is senior Fellow at the Brookings Institution in Washington, DC.

Béla Greskovits is professor of international relations and European studies at Central European University in Budapest, Hungary.

Anna Grzymala-Busse is the Ronald and Eileen Weiser Professor of European and Eurasian Studies in the department of political science at the University of Michigan.

Eugene Huskey is the William R. Kenan, Jr., Professor of Political Science at Stetson University.

Stephen Kotkin is the John P. Birkelund '52 Professor in History and International Affairs at Princeton University.

Volodymyr Kulyk is a leading research Fellow at the I. F. Kuras Institute of Political and Ethnic Studies of the National Academy of Sciences of Ukraine in Kyiv, Ukraine.

Jessica Pisano is associate professor of politics at the New School for Social Research.

Grigore Pop-Eleches is associate professor of politics and international affairs at Princeton University.

Brian D. Taylor is associate professor of political science at Syracuse University.

Alexei Trochev is associate professor in the School of Humanities and Social Sciences at Nazarbayev University in Astana, Kazakhstan.

Acknowledgments

The editors would like to thank the following Princeton University programs for their financial support of this project: the Princeton Institute for International and Regional Studies; the Program in Law and Public Affairs of the Woodrow Wilson School of Public and International Affairs; the Shelby Cullom Davis Center for Historical Studies; and the Mamdouha S. Bobst Center for Peace and Justice. We would also like to thank the following individuals who are not authors in this volume but who contributed in significant ways to the discussions underlying these chapters: Valerie Bunce, Keith Darden, Rasma Karklins, George Khelashvili, Jeff Kopstein, Bruce Parrott, Peter Rutland, Kim Scheppele, and Jason Wittenberg. Finally, we would like to thank Ms. Patricia Zimmer for her outstanding organizational support for the workshops that helped to produce these chapters, as well as Brittany Holom for her help with indexing.

1

The Historical Legacies of Communism: An Empirical Agenda

Stephen Kotkin and Mark R. Beissinger

Writing in the early 1990s, social scientist Ken Jowitt famously argued that "whatever the results of the current turmoil in Eastern Europe, one thing is clear: the new institutional patterns will be shaped by the 'inheritance' and legacy of forty years of Leninist rule" (Jowitt 1992, 285). Many would now agree. And yet, over the past two decades, the pace of change within most postcommunist societies has been tremendous, leading some to wonder whether the notions of "postcommunist" or "post-Soviet" retain any substance at all (Humphrey 2002). Property has been redistributed, societies have been opened to the world, and open political competition to varying degrees has been introduced. Many of the postcommunist states – including three that were once part of the Soviet Union – have joined the European Union and NATO. As Russian journalist Masha Lipman noted a decade after Jowitt made his observation, "In just over a decade as independent states, the various former Soviet republics have gone their separate ways so fast and so far that it's hard to believe they were once parts of the same empire" (Lipman 2003).

Here we have a genuine (and largely unacknowledged) puzzle within the study of the former communist countries: As the world approaches the twenty-fifth anniversary of the fall of the Berlin Wall (November 2014), has communism been largely transcended, or do communist legacies remain operative? Such a question may seem surprising to some. But that the historical experience of communism continues to act as a powerful undercurrent shaping the long-term trajectories of postcommunist development is not an assumption to be taken for granted. If it does continue to affect postcommunist development, in what ways does it do so specifically, and can such assertions be demonstrated with any degree of confidence? Perhaps trajectories have been shaped instead by fundamental divergences produced after communism, or even by precommunist historical developments. More fundamentally, what is a historical legacy, and how should it be identified? How do we actually know when historical legacies are at work? And what would we need to know to falsify such assertions? In short, can legacy arguments, like that Jowitt posited two decades ago, be specified and tested in any rigorous way? And what major lessons do variations in the transcendence or reproduction of practices and institutions from the communist era hold for social scientific understanding and for public policy?

Answers to many of these questions would seem to depend to an uncanny degree on geography. If someone fell asleep during the 1970s in, say, Minsk, Moscow, or Tashkent and suddenly awoke today, what would they think? That person would not know the details of the Soviet collapse or of the so-called reforms of the 1990s (let alone the vast literature purporting to explain what happened). But they would know a great deal about Brezhnev-era political machines across Soviet Eurasia. Would the broader picture of governance across Eurasia today come as a complete shock, or would it seem eerily familiar? If one took Brezhnev-era machines, added some multi-candidate elections and legalized private property, then shook very hard, what would come out? Conversely, anyone who fell asleep during the 1970s and awoke today in, say, Tallinn, Warsaw, or Prague might well be thoroughly astonished by what they saw.

In fact, most analysts draw a sharp line between the twelve former union republics of the Soviet Union whose incorporation into the USSR was internationally recognized, on the one hand, and the Baltic states and Eastern Europe, on the other. But how great are the differences across these two sets of cases, and what accounts for them? Are there realms of activity in which a communist legacy has persisted irrespective of geographic location? Why have some aspects of the communist experience been shed more easily than others have? And what is it, anyway, that geography represents – the impact of precommunist historical experiences? The influence of different versions of communism? Critical decisions made by leaders or different forms and degrees of external influence in the wake of communism's demise? In fact, arguments have been made on behalf of each of these interpretations. What were the relative impacts of domestic processes versus the effects of neighborhood and diffusion? Were democratization efforts by outsiders consequential (helpful, harmful) or inconsequential? Was European Union accession decisive, as some claim? To what extent did EU influence, when it did occur, depend on the presence of conditions laid down before or during communism for its effects? And was deepened globalization a cause as well as an outcome of the differentiated paths of development in the wake of communism? In short, any argument about the historical legacies of communism raises broader questions about the main linkages explaining convergent and divergent patterns of postcommunist development.

The fundamental idea underlying this volume is to confront empirically the historical legacy arguments that have now become commonplace in the study of former communist countries. The very definition of postcommunism as a political and social phenomenon implies the continued presence of distinctive communist legacies – at least in some critical realms of activity – without which the postcommunist moniker would otherwise be meaningless. Certainly, for many analysts of the Eurasian and Eastern European regions, communism continues to be understood as a defining historical experience, much like colonialism was for much of the developing world.[1] Like colonialism, Soviet-style systems involved a fundamental reordering of political, legal, economic, and social relations and are often said to have produced certain cultural attitudes and ways of behaving that have proven difficult to change. But this most certainly is not uniformly so. Moreover, as with colonialism, one might expect the influence of the communist experience to decay gradually over time in many areas, as new factors and experiences arise that shape developmental trajectories. Now, more than two decades after the collapse, it seems natural to ask what has been the long-term impact of communism on political, social, and economic development of the formerly communist states.

Our approach has been to define clearly notions of historical legacies and to ask a group of knowledgeable experts in particular spheres of activity to subject claims of legacies to rigorous examination. We do not seek to assert a *comprehensive* framework for explaining how past legacies cause present institutions and practices in the postcommunist world (and beyond). That is because, at this stage, we do not think a comprehensive framework is needed (let alone possible on the basis of current research). On the contrary, this volume urges that historical legacies be thought about empirically, contextually, and with greater rigor. The lack of a comprehensive approach to the subject, therefore, amounts to a conscious methodological choice, reflecting an understanding of how the study of historical legacies should be approached (rigor over comprehensiveness, at least until we know more). Thus, we seek to understand why, given patterns of late communism, certain institutional forms, ways of thinking, and modes of behavior appear to have persisted more than two decades after the demise of communism, finding new purpose, while others have fallen by the wayside. We seek to understand why this occurred in some contexts and not in others. We also aim to focus some attention on the variable formation of communist legacies in realms that have at times received less attention in the scholarly literature but that nevertheless remain critical to an understanding of the politics of the region (for instance, state institutions, property redistribution, law, and the global context).

In this introduction, we lay out some of the fundamental issues that subsequent chapters pursue in more depth, provide common definitions, and offer some guidelines for how we believe the study of historical legacies should be approached – steps that we believe could be just as easily used for understanding historical legacies in other parts of the world or involving other historical eras.[2] As will be evident, demonstrating the salience of historical legacies proves considerably harder than it looks.

Replacing Transitions with Legacies?

For many years after the collapse of communism, scholars of postcommunist politics highlighted "transitions" from communism (especially in the realm of institutional change) rather than manifest persistence in politics and economics. But by the late 1990s, it had become evident that the transition model had run its course, even among most of its proponents (Carothers 2002). At this time, many scholars began to rediscover deeper historical patterns that were thought to have shaped developmental trajectories. This in turn led to the emergence of an enormous variety of legacy arguments, particularly among political scientists. Occasionally there have been attempts to connect these social science appeals to the work of historians and vice versa, but that dialogue remains highly underdeveloped.[3]

Uses of the concept of legacy have been broad and varied. One study, for instance, pinpointed several "models" of communist rule that defined the nature of center-periphery interactions in the non-Russian republics in the aftermath of communism: a "most-favored-lord" model pushing gradual assimilation; a colonial model, uprooting local society but establishing barriers to full assimilation; an integral model, in which local society was ruled over but retained a strong sense of autonomy and cohesion vis-à-vis metropolitan authority (Laitin 1998). Other studies reminded us that the various outcomes of postcommunist party systems in Eastern Europe did not emerge from a tabula rasa, but were influenced by the variety of forms of state-society relationships that had already materialized under communism (or in some accounts, immediately prior to the onset of communism) (Kitschelt et al. 1999; Grzymala-Busse 2002; Wittenberg 2006). Inevitably, scholars pushed legacy arguments back still further in time, arguing that the timing of literacy's arrival in Eastern Europe and Eurasia (whether it occurred prior to or under communism) functioned as the critical juncture determining patterns of postcommunist political and institutional development (Darden and Grzymala-Busse 2006). Thus, on the eve of the twentieth anniversary of the Soviet collapse, a growing social science literature had formed around legacy arguments, provoking questions about the meaning of legacy itself.[4]

Taking this shift to legacy approaches as our point of departure, we invited a group of scholars of the contemporary postcommunist world with a historical bent to reexamine what we think we know about postcommunist political development and to think broadly and unsentimentally about the historical legacies of communism. We developed a framing paper that provided them with a common set of definitions and questions and that laid out a common framework for analyzing historical legacies. The group met twice – once in advance of writing their papers to define an agenda for the papers and to discuss the framing concepts, and a second time to discuss in detail the first drafts of the papers that they had prepared. Our interest in putting together this project was not only in elaborating a better understanding of what one means by a historical legacy, but also to encourage scholars to engage empirically with how one might prove or disprove a legacy's existence and what kinds of argumentation and evidence would be necessary to demonstrate or undermine a legacy argument convincingly. We believe such an exercise is necessary because legacy arguments can be, and have been, easily abused, both by their practitioners and their detractors (for critiques, see Kopstein 2003; Pop-Eleches 2007; LaPorte and Lussier 2011).

Legacy arguments have often been made at a high level of generality, sometimes assume that correlation or similarity is sufficient evidence of a legacy, and frequently fail to trace the actual mechanisms connecting past and present that are implied within them. Tellingly, legacy studies often contradict one another, raising the issue of how one should sort out the validity of their various claims. It may seem obvious that the past conditions the present and always lies embedded within it. It is just as obvious that the present is not the past, and that one never steps in the same river twice. But how does one think about the deeper structural connections between past and present without trivializing the enormous ruptures with the past that have occurred? Rather than simply substituting "legacy" for "transition," we seek to turn the discussion toward a deeper understanding of what constitutes a legacy and of the particular logics and mechanisms that would allow us to give substance to an otherwise mercurial concept.

We also encouraged our authors to draw attention to a number of areas for which we believe the connections between the communist past and the postcommunist present deserve better specification. For example, attention to the executive branch within the literature on postcommunist societies since 1991 has not kept pace with the study of postcommunist voting patterns and public opinion, as scholars have taken advantage of new opportunities to apply survey techniques in postcommunist countries while access to information about government bureaucracies often remained difficult.[5] While ample attention has been paid to the choice of economic reform strategies in the 1990s, far fewer people studied long-term patterns of investment and employment or the implications of inherited economic infrastructure that might shape postcommunist political and economic development (and vice versa).[6] Scholars have analyzed extensively the massive redistribution of property that followed the end of communism (Frye 2000; Volkov 2002; Verdery 2003; Dunn 2004; Hedlund 2005; Ledeneva 2006; Allina-Pisano 2008). But the extent to which these patterns of postcommunist political economy remain connected to the past or have instead been shaped by new dynamics remains uncertain. There are also excellent studies of the transformation of postcommunist judiciaries and court systems (Solomon 1995; Hendley 1999; Trochev 2008), but the linkages between the trajectories of the courts and what was inherited from the past are not always clearly specified. While the social ramifications that flowed from the upheaval of communist collapse have been studied in great detail (Shlapentokh 1996; Webber 2000; Humphrey 2002; Taylor 2003), the role of the outside world has often remained a blank spot or has been reduced to a focus on democracy promotion efforts. Relatively few scholars, for instance, have examined how postcommunist societies have been shaped (or not shaped) by globalization and the world economy: the impact of world energy markets, foreign investment, trade, global cultural currents, or the role of possible models for emulation (for exceptions, see Segbers 2001; Wallander 2007; Pickles and Jenkins 2008).

It bears keeping in mind that any social science recourse to history must also take into account specific historical junctures. To take one example, a variety of explanations have been put forward to explain economic success, often taking Britain and the European continent as key case studies, but the post–World War II East Asia development story unfolded at a time when the United States was the global economic power and championed an open global economy – a situation that did not exist when the first industrial revolution occurred. Communism collapsed during a specific historical moment, a time of pronounced ascendancy of markets over the public sphere, a trend that the collapse itself epitomized. But perhaps more consequentially, even before communism was collapsing in Europe and Eurasia, East Asia was fast becoming a global manufacturing base that competed with anything the bloc could produce or might hope to produce. At the same time, the American market was largely closed to the former Soviet countries. Such a specific globalization conjuncture may have profoundly shaped the possibilities and limits for how the turn away from central planning unfolded.

We believe that in examining linkages between the past and present there is also a need to move beyond the self-imposed normative boundaries that have at times limited inquiry about the postcommunist region. In much of the literature on the legacies of communism, legacies are understood largely as burdens from the past – bloated bureaucracies, alienation from politics and parties, social distrust – a kind of negative inheritance marshaled to explain the disappointing outcomes of transition (Volgyes 1995). We are not concerned with this kind of a liabilities and (more rarely) assets approach to the past, or what David Lane has felicitously called the "footprint" of Sovietism as a limit on change (Lane 2011, 3). Lane and his co-contributors largely treat legacies as a fetter on the transition to markets, law, and pluralism, although they credit some countries (Poland, Hungary) with "traditions" that facilitated transition to a Western model. Nor are we fundamentally concerned with what is broadly called "political culture," which Stephen White refers to in the postcommunist context as "the revenge of the superstructure" (traditions of collectivism, patriotism, and social justice versus shallow roots of a liberal order) (White 2011, 65). We encouraged our authors not to measure developments by holistic yardsticks or by some abstract conception of what kind of societies these places *should* have become, but by what kinds of relationships they actually have. We asked them, for instance, to pay attention to such questions as who owns property, how can there be private property in the absence of the rule of

The Historical Legacies of Communism

law, how do these patterns and outcomes relate or do not relate to what was inherited from late communism, and so on. We asked them not to focus on how these places ought to be governed – as the transitions literature sometimes suggested – but how they are actually governed and how this might or might not be concretely related to the communist past.

Finally, let us underscore that the editors of this volume are agnostic about the significance of the communist experience for former communist countries. In designing this project, we fully expected to find considerable variation in the extent to which the communist experience continues to matter, whether across particular countries (and within them) or across particular spheres of activity (and within them).[7] Legacies, if they exist, might not include all parts of the former communist bloc or even all parts of the Soviet Union. The communist experience is also not the only significant historical experience that might exert legacy effects, and multiple legacies could well be at work, whether precommunist (Russian imperial, Habsburg, Ottoman), pan-communist, or exclusive to the Soviet Union. Moreover, other logics of causation completely unrelated to the past are most certainly at work. We asked our authors to assess all these possibilities empirically in this volume, putting the claims of various legacy arguments associated with the communist experience to the test. We fully understand that important differences existed among communist countries even within Eastern Europe, let alone between the communist bloc and the Soviet Union. The inclusion of both Eastern Europe and the Soviet Union in the analysis should help clarify what legacies might be specific to particular communist experiences (as evidenced, for instance, in Anna Grzymala-Busse's chapter on the relationship between religion and postcommunist states) and what might be the result of communist experiences more generally (for example, Grigore Pop-Eleches's chapter on the effect of communist education and urbanization on postcommunist political values). We believe that the important question is not whether historical legacies of communism exist, but rather where, in what spheres, in what manner, and why they do or do not manifest themselves. In this sense, we see our tasks as outlining an empirical agenda and providing an approach for answering questions rather than providing a definitive answer to the question of what are the historical legacies of communism.

What Is a Historical Legacy?

By a "legacy," we mean a durable causal relationship between past institutions and policies on subsequent practices or beliefs, long beyond the life of the regimes, institutions, and policies that gave birth to them. In this respect, we would differentiate legacy arguments from other forms of nondisruptive continuities sometimes found within the historical (and even historical institutionalist) literature. Past and present are obviously interwoven in every society. But for us, broad continuity in and of itself does not qualify as a historical legacy. Rather, legacy arguments only fit situations when there has been a significant rupture between past and present – an end to one order and the beginning of another – that the legacy is supposed to straddle. In this respect, legacies are characteristic of a peculiar set of historical circumstances: specifically, macrohistorical ruptures such as revolutions, state collapse, decolonization, or major incidents of regime change. Here, there is overlap with the historical discipline (and with the historical institutionalist literature) to the extent that scholars elaborate the mechanisms by which broadly similar practices are observed across instances of major historical change, and these practices remain relatively durable over the long term. Thus, not all "critical juncture" arguments qualify as historical legacy arguments as we understand the term. Rather, legacy arguments for us are not about what remains the same so much as about what enables particular practices or beliefs to endure (and sometimes, to reemerge) – often in new form and to new purpose – in the context of large-scale macrohistorical change.

We also want to differentiate legacy arguments from the kinds of behaviors that result from structural isomorphism or functionalisms that carry over across historical divides. Andrew Janos (2000), for example, offers a grimly brilliant portrait of long-standing international hierarchies in Eastern Europe, showing Eastern Europe's stubbornly persistent economic lag behind Western Europe and the ensuing envy of Western European prosperity, especially among elites. For him, this persisting international hierarchy produces continuity in the politics of backwardness. Janos writes not in terms of legacy, but rather in terms of fate. His is not a story of the embedded and durable impact of regimes, institutions, or policies, but rather of continuity in structural position.

In a sense, the type of causality involved in a legacy relationship is "genetic," in that legacy arguments assume that particular practices or beliefs became embedded by a deep and formative historical experience that no longer exists (much like a gene might be passed on by a parent to a child and remain potentially influential in a child's development beyond the life of the parent). In a legacy relationship, these "genetic" attributes grow salient in the life of the offspring society through a variety of causal mechanisms, some of which might come into play only in interaction with the environment of subsequent historical experience. As we know, not all of an individual's genetic makeup affects a person's behavior, individuals contain multiple sets of genes that might offset one another, genes often gain effect only in interaction with environmental causes, and most everyday behavior seems to be more affected by context and environment than by genetic background. Moreover, widespread debate is taking place over how "determinative" of behavior genes can be. Yet few would argue that genes have no effect on behavior. We think of historical legacies in much the same way: not all deeply embedded historical experiences affect subsequent behavior; legacies – to be effective – usually interact with other causal mechanisms and processes; multiple legacies might reinforce or contradict one another; most everyday behavior may have more to do with context than with legacies; and the extent to which legacies, even when operative, are "determinative" is subject to variation and investigation. By making this analogy, we in no way mean to imply that societies have a "genetic code" that determines their behavior; on the contrary, our attention to mechanisms, to the influence of other causal processes, and to variability in legacies precludes that type of thinking. Rather, we merely mean to turn attention to the process by which deeply embedded historical experiences might or might not form durable relationships over the long run.

To talk about the legacies of a prior order there need not be a total institutional collapse or dissolution; some organizational and institutional continuity is likely even during periods of major political upheaval or regime change. For example, the end of communist regimes did not, at least initially, lead to much change in the operation of educational institutions in most postcommunist states (Eklof et al. 2005) (though some changes eventually were introduced). Similarly, as Eugene Huskey points out in this volume, some executive institutions in Russia carried over directly across the initial regime-change divide. But even in these cases of organizational inertia there was no mere continuation of the past, as old institutional forms needed to adapt to a radically different political, economic, and societal environment. The changeover from central planning to a market economy would seem as great a rupture as could possibly be imagined. But equally momentous were the end of the political monopoly of the Communist Party and its network of institutions, the breakup of three states of the region into twenty-four states, the opening of the former communist lands to the outside world, the introduction of various degrees of political competition, and the easing of political regulation of societal development. In this sense, a legacy involves the persisting influence of the past within a broader context of large-scale macrohistorical change.

A quintessential example might be Alexis de Tocqueville's analysis *The Old Regime and the French Revolution*, written in 1856 (a half century after the events of the revolution), which argued that the centralized character of French absolutist monarchy fundamentally shaped post-1789 state institutions and political culture, notwithstanding the revolutionaries' intentions to achieve a decisive rupture with the past, primarily because the revolutionaries kept the strong old regime state as their main instrument to smash everything (Tocqueville 1955). As the Tocquevillean example suggests, for a legacy to be evident with some degree of certainty there must be some significant time gap between the past and present in question, so that the purported relationship cannot be considered a temporary state of affairs. This is what we mean by the "durable" element of an historical legacy.[8] Thus, we differentiate between short-term effects that might be evident immediately after a macrohistorical rupture (and that soon fade) and the more lasting, long-term effects that rightfully belong to the realm of historical legacies.

To put the matter another way, it might have been possible to anticipate in the immediate years after communism's collapse (when Jowitt, for instance, was writing) that some legacies of communism would be important going forward, but impossible to pinpoint accurately which specific legacies of the communist experience would endure. Precisely when the more enduring manifestations of communist legacies were first identifiable can be debated. Some would argue that two decades after the collapse, patterns of development have grown clearer, and in many spheres relative equilibria have been reached, so that one can begin to assess communism's legacies.[9] Others would argue that two decades is still too early to identify the long-term impact of the communist experience on postcommunist development, leading to the likelihood of what statisticians call Type I errors (identifying the presence of a legacy when in fact the phenomenon in question is only temporary). Ultimately, assessing legacies can only be accomplished through future examinations over an extended period of time. In this respect, the chapters of this volume might best be construed as one cut at identifying some of the possible historical legacies of communism, but ultimately whether they are correct in their assessments can only be determined over the *longue durée*.

One would expect the magnitude of the rupture (the extent to which it involves a disruption to ongoing societal relationships) to vary considerably across geographic, policy, and behavioral spheres and to exercise an independent effect on the degree to which old regime practices and beliefs might endure. Whether regime change occurs through a "handing over of the keys" to entrenched local elites (as occurred in Soviet Central Asia) or through extensive mass mobilization (as occurred in parts of the Soviet Union and Eastern Europe) should also influence whether and how legacies materialize. But it is also true that not all regimes and political orders leave significant legacies behind them. The effects of some are relatively fleeting, while others leave consequences that last for decades and even centuries beyond their demise. In theory, one should expect that the length and depth of a historical experience should be related to how broad a legacy it generates in its wake.[10] In this respect, Eurasian and Eastern European communism was a relatively brief but deep experience. In those regions where it lasted longest (Russia, Central Asia, the Caucasus, Belarus, and most of Ukraine), it endured for a little more than seventy years, extending across three generations; elsewhere in the Balkans, Central Europe, and the Baltic, it persisted for slightly more than forty years (two generations). Indeed, as noted earlier, much scholarship has pointed to this difference as critical in determining the impact of communism's historical legacies. But while brief, Eurasian and Eastern European communism also thoroughly transformed these societies; it totally reordered social structures, functioned as a modernizing device, and imposed similar political and economic institutions across an enormous variety of cultures. In this way communism may have exercised some kinds of homogenizing effects on the societies that experienced it, creating some elements of a distinctive culture that shared certain features irrespective of the specific cultural milieu in which it appeared (for example, the substitution of central planning for the market fostered analogous informal practices and shortages wherever it occurred – practices and circumstances that were as easily recognizable to a resident of the Baltic or Poland as to someone from the Caucasus or Central Asia). By contrast, some have suggested that while communism certainly involved extensive societal engineering and transformation, its lasting impact may be relatively ephemeral compared to other civilizations, largely because many of the changes it introduced were forced or impractical, impoverished societies or impeded their development, or isolated societies from (noncommunist) global change, and therefore could be more easily and quickly jettisoned in the wake of communism's demise. Still, even as we debate the depth of communism's impact, the sheer scope of the changes associated with the communist experience also stands out, affecting not only politics, but also such spheres as the economy, language use and identities, demography, law, religion, and public attitudes and beliefs. All of these are subjects the authors cover in this volume.

Forms of Legacy Relationships

As we have defined the term, a legacy involves a durable causal relationship between earlier institutions and practices and those of the present in the wake of a macrohistorical rupture. We focus specifically on a legacy as a *relationship* rather than a correlation or similarity (isomorphism) for three reasons: 1) because we wish to emphasize the causal interconnections and mechanisms that link past and present rather than formal appearances; 2) because similar-looking things may come about for reasons other than a historical legacy (for example, because of functionalism or spurious correlation); and 3) because legacy relationships often involve the creation of something new out of something old in a way that sometimes only vaguely resembles the old or that applies the old to new spheres of activity. We by no means exclude correlation as one piece of evidence in support of a legacy effect. But correlation is usually insufficient on its own as evidence of a legacy for a number of reasons. For one thing, quantitative studies of historical legacies, because they rely on measurements across extensive periods of time, quite often rely on weak and unreliable measures and are highly vulnerable to omitted variable bias. Indeed, much of the historically oriented social science literature has pointed out that correlation alone is unlikely to clarify the mechanisms at work in a legacy relationship – what we consider the most important part of a legacy argument.[11] And because legacy relationships often involve the creation of something new out of something old or put old practices to use in new spheres of activity, focusing solely on correlation can be quite misleading. Thus, correlational evidence alone risks both Type I (identifying the presence of a legacy when the phenomenon is not there) and Type II (failing to identify the presence of a legacy when it is there) errors. The most common problem with legacy arguments as they currently exist within the literature is the failure to identify the mechanisms that connect past with present. Too heavy a reliance on correlation as the key criterion for identifying a historical legacy thus leads to legacy arguments that are loose, unsubstantiated, and ultimately unconvincing.

We acknowledge that our conception of legacies differs from a number of other understandings. Jason Wittenberg, for instance, in a wide-ranging and stimulating essay on the nature of historical legacies, places primary emphasis on correlation and sameness as essential aspects of a legacy, though he allows for a number of different criteria by which sameness might be established – among them, "literal unchangingness, stability of key features, unbroken existence, or pragmatic comparison of what counts as the phenomenon in each period"(2011, 15). We postulate that legacies can assume a wide variety of patterns of similitude, with a number of different ways the past might be implicated in the present. But we argue that legacies are not the same phenomena as those to which they are related in the past, and almost always involve something new that combines past with present or applies the past in a different way. We therefore place less emphasis on similarity than on mechanisms and interconnections between past and present.

As part of this project, we identified a number of different types of legacy relationships based on the existing literature on historical legacies that represent different logics of durable connection between past and present – what we refer to in this volume as *fragmentation, translation, bricolage, parameter setting*, and *cultural schemata*. We asked our authors, if they make an argument in support of a legacy effect, that they specify which type or types of relationship were operative. In doing this, we did not mean to confine our authors to this list, but instead merely sought to compel them to specify the nature of the legacy relationship more clearly than has often been the case within the literature on the historical legacies of communism.

Under fragmentation (what Eugene Huskey in this volume calls a "thin" legacy relationship, because its existence is never seriously challenged), "new" units are created out of an institutional rupture that are merely fragments or remnants of old institutions, and therefore closely resemble the parent unit. They may even be the same institution or organization operating under different circumstances or in an altered environment. As a number of scholars have noted, fragmentation in this sense occurred, for instance, in the wake of decolonization in many African states, as formerly colonial bureaucracies came to function after independence as the bureaucracies of newly independent states (Young 1994). A good example from the postcommunist region is the National Security Committee (KNB) of Kazakhstan, which was established as a fragment of the KGB shortly after the breakup of the USSR – with almost entirely the same staff, much the same operating rules, and the same organizational culture; the main difference between the two organizations was largely a single letter (N for G), indicating the nationalization of the organization and its subordination to republican (rather than all-union) goals and authority. In Belarus, as Brian Taylor notes in this volume, the regime did not even bother to change the KGB's name, though much the same transition occurred.

In his chapter, Alexei Trochev points to courts in Belarus and Turkmenistan as examples of fragmentation, observing that "the old guard remains in charge: courts have been renamed, and the word 'socialist' no longer precedes 'legality,' but the essential task of judges in criminal cases remains the same: to support the procuracy." These types of fragmentation legacies tend to be the products of relatively weak ruptures (handing over the keys to local elites) and organizational inertia, but ultimately their continued reproduction across time depends on the ways these old forms are harnessed for new advantages.

A second form of legacy relationship we refer to as translation – a notion we draw from the historical institutionalist literature (see Campbell 2010). Translation denotes a situation in which an old practice finds new purpose and is redeployed in a different way than was true at the time in which the practice originated, but still resembles in some fundamental respects the earlier practice in the modes of action involved or the meanings attached to them. An example of translation in the postcommunist region might be the relationship between propaganda against political opponents in the communist period and *chernyi piar* (black public relations) in postcommunist Russia and Ukraine (Wilson 2005; Ledeneva 2006). Postcommunist Russia and Ukraine gave birth to a different information environment from that of communism, one involving media competition, which transformed the salience of subtler forms of media manipulation, such as the planting of rumors and false information in the media about people in order to discredit them. As Andrew Wilson (2005, 1–32) has noted, in both communist and postcommunist environments, the use of manipulative, heavy-handed informational practices that play loose with the truth to manufacture public consensus and the use of disinformation and "active measures" to undermine opponents bear broad resemblances. Indeed, the techniques of *chernyi piar* owe their origins less to borrowings from Madison Avenue than to the propaganda departments that once blanketed these countries and to the ways the communist secret police attempted to discredit political dissidents. At the same time, the dirty tricks of the new "political technologists" (as they are called) in postcommunist Russia and Ukraine have become a full-fledged and remunerative industry – one that serves not an ideology or even a system, but specific individuals and commercial interests.

In this volume, Brian Taylor cites what he calls the "elite Chekist legacy" in Russia as an example of translation. The myth of the secret police as uncorrupted patriots serving the interests of the state and recruited from the nation's best and brightest was widely promoted during the Soviet period. In the postcommunist context, these same ideas were used to legitimate the central role of the FSB within domestic politics and the Putin presidency, allowing top-level police officials, still known as *Chekisty*, to translate status into political power and economic gain. Another example of translation is cited in Eugene Huskey's examination of the Russian presidency, in which he shows how the Kremlin's business office maintained an extensive set of services for the political elite on both sides of the regime-change divide, but under conditions of marketization it began to operate as a business in the private sector and to sell its services to the public on a commercial basis – for example, coming to operate a series of luxury hotels. The extensive political influence of Catholic churches that Anna Grzymala-Busse sees as characteristic of some East Central European polities is the result of a translation legacy in which churches utilized their critical roles as guarantors of social peace during the late communist period to gain unusual institutional access over policy making in the postcommunist period, translating this "fusion of national and religious identities" into sway over education and social policy. Translation clearly relies on some element of inventiveness on the part of agents, who take advantage of new opportunities presented under conditions of macropolitical change and the widespread presence of prior practices, resources, conditions, or beliefs from the old order to establish new patterns of behavior.

In a third type of legacy relationship, bricolage, elements of the past become thoroughly intermixed and interpenetrated with the present, creating something completely new that only vaguely resembles the old, but that still profoundly bears its imprint (Campbell 2010). In particular, property ownership in many postcommunist societies has been described as following this kind of syncretic and hybridized pattern, involving a recombination of units formed out of the socialist experience (at a time when large-scale private property did not exist) into new and powerful financial, industrial, and commercial private companies (Stark 1996). In this volume, Béla Greskovits uses the notion of bricolage to explain why, among those countries that inherited complex manufacturing infrastructures from socialism, some East Central European countries were able to use these as the building blocks for establishing new export-oriented "manufacturing miracles" after socialism, while in other countries these industries essentially died. He argues that foreign corporations decided to invest in the inherited manufacturing sectors of particular countries because of the reform infrastructure and special incentive packages provided by host governments, but also because of the ways that these governments sought to promote or undermine their industrial inheritance from socialism. The extensive hybridization characteristic of bricolage is the product of agents "making do with 'whatever is at hand,'" as Levi-Strauss (1966, 17) famously put it, to craft together disparate elements from existing repertoires to form something completely new.

A fourth form of legacy relationship – parameter setting – places limits on how individuals think and behave, so that the legacy relationship involves the existence of limits on what can occur rather than what actually does occur. As scholars have noted in the institutional economics literature, these limits may be imposed by the inertia of past practices or institutions that prove, through mechanisms of sunk costs, increasing returns, or other logics of convenience, resistant to change (North 1990; Collier and Collier 1991; Pierson 2000; Mahoney 2002). Alternatively, they may have origins in thick social norms or cultural beliefs that make inherited structures and ways of doing things sticky

(Hanson 1995, 312–13; Nunn and Wantchekon 2011). An oft-cited example of this kind of parameter-setting legacy are the political boundaries of the post-Soviet states, which, like boundaries in postcolonial Latin America and Africa, have for the most part been accepted without revision despite historical claims, or (where challenged) have been extremely difficult to alter. There was a political rupture – states in a union became independent – but logics of convenience intersected with the prevailing norms and interests of the international system to establish strong disincentives to boundary change. In this volume, Clifford Gaddy writes of Soviet policies of Siberian development as a gnarled tree that cannot be easily straightened out, despite the huge costs that climate and distance entail, because of how "the amount, the nature, or the disposition of the inherited assets constrains future reallocation." As Gaddy describes the dilemma, the geographic location of Russia's inherited physical assets as a result of Soviet development policies produced a spatial misallocation of resources that continues to weigh heavily on the country's development in postcommunist circumstances. Volodymyr Kulyk describes another example of a parameter-setting legacy in which Soviet nationalities policies bred a growing disjunct between language use and ethnic identity in Ukraine, a legacy that has persisted in the post-Soviet era despite a radically altered relationship between the state and Ukrainian culture and identity. Here, the sunk costs of language acquisition, combined with the geographic concentration of language communities, fears of the resistance that imposed language requirements might evince, pressure from international minority rights organizations and from Russia, and economic opportunities have limited the degree to which language practice has tipped toward Ukrainian, even while individuals, now freed from the constraints of Soviet passport nationality, feel no pressing need to bring ethnic identities into line with language use or vice versa.

Finally, legacies may take the form of cultural schemata – embedded ways of thinking and behaving that originate from socialization experiences under the prior political order but persist long beyond the macropolitical rupture. These may be the products of particular formal socialization experiences that endure beyond the rupture and are reproduced in subsequent generations, or may represent the kind of "feel for the game" that Bourdieu (1990, 66) places under the rubric of habitus, by which people interpret and anticipate the actions of others through the lens of personal or historical experience. A yearning among many Russians to regain a superpower status once enjoyed by the Soviet state or an instinctive mistrust of Russian motives among Balts, Georgians, and Western Ukrainians (both well documented in public opinion surveys) have much to do with cultural schemata that were produced out of the experience of Soviet power (and in some instances, out of experiences with tsarist authority that predated Soviet power) (Beissinger 1995). In his essay in this volume, Grigore Pop-Eleches provides a legacy argument based on cultural schemata in explaining what he identifies as the postcommunist democratic deficit – that is, the fact that former communist countries are significantly less democratic than one would expect on the basis of their levels of socioeconomic development. In particular, he shows that in former communist countries, education has a much weaker democratizing impact (and is not as closely connected at the individual level to democratic values and modes of participation) than elsewhere in the world. He ascribes these effects to two specific features of communist education – the heavy emphases on ideological indoctrination and technical education. These forms of socialization, he argues, failed to produce the kinds of values and ways of thinking typically associated with a prodemocracy middle class.

To sum up the five handles we proposed to our authors: *fragmentation* involves inheritance of whole parts of institutions directly from an old regime; *translation* entails utilizing old institutions or practices for completely new purposes; *bricolage* means welding together bits of old and new institutions into something entirely new; *parameter setting* signifies the foreclosing of particular institutional or policy options because of constraints left over from the past; and *cultural schemata* refer to mental frames generated by past regime practices that make certain sorts of conduct seem normal and others unthinkable, foreign, or bizarre. There is, of course, overlap here, and the production of a historical legacy may undoubtedly involve multiple mechanisms. More research will bring further additions and refinement.

Indeed, several of our authors point to an additional form that may or may not qualify as a historical legacy: revivals. Here, a particular practice associated with the past is brought back to life after having been previously eliminated for some period of time. Eugene Huskey gives a good example in his chapter on Russian government: the revival of the cadres reserve system. This system of creating a pool of potential replacements for key offices was an invention of the late communist period, but then disappeared in the 1990s, only to be revived a decade later by Putin as a tool for centralizing control over the Russian state bureaucracy. As Huskey notes, there were of course strategic and functional reasons for choosing to reestablish the cadres reserve system. Yet, as he argues, it is also clear in this case that the past "framed the alternatives," so that elites in other parts of the world would have been unlikely to have considered such an option. Huskey argues that the ability of revivals to resurface after having once been jettisoned "is a testament to their potency and tenacity." Yet the real question may be how durable the cadres reserve system remains. If the cadres reserve system persists and becomes a permanent part of the Russian administrative landscape, we may well want to consider it a form of legacy, even though it disappeared for a period of time in the immediate wake of communism. Yet we might not want to broaden the notion of legacies to encompass all of the ways the past might frame decision making and function merely as a pool of experience that decision makers rely on in dealing with the present. In short, for revivals to be considered legacies, a researcher needs to specify why revivals are not simply functional responses to similar problems experienced across the regime divide (Huskey in fact does a good job of this), and why the revival is more than just the lessons decision makers learn from history.

Toward More Robust Legacy Arguments

Part of the rationale for this volume is a frustration with the proliferation of assertions about legacies within the postcommunist field, in particular with the looseness with which the notion of legacy has often been deployed in everyday discourse. We profoundly believe that there are long-term historical legacies of communism that have already become apparent and that will become more apparent over time. We also profoundly believe that the notion of legacy has at times been used inappropriately and is easily abused. Indeed, in his chapter in this volume, Timothy Frye raises cautions about how legacy arguments have sometimes been used to explain postcommunist political economy. He argues that the Soviet legacy of central planning has actually exercised minimal impact on the regime of property rights in the Russian oil and gas industries, which has instead been predominantly shaped by functional influences from the marketplace and particular decisions by postcommunist governments. He rightfully raises the danger that with legacy arguments one can always "rummage around in the institutional legacy and find some features of the past that 'fit' the data." As a suggested remedy for this, he suggests that we adopt the approach of reasoning forward, starting with the past and looking for how it did or did not project ahead, rather than reasoning backward, loosely searching for the lineages of the present in the past.

Jessica Pisano also sounds strong cautions against the ways legacy arguments can be easily abused in her chapter on a particular, well-publicized incident in Russia of political window dressing or *pokazukha*. Observers often view the prevalence of *pokazukha* in post-Soviet Russia as a legacy rooted in the ways society went about subverting and tricking tsarist and Soviet power. But Pisano warns against relying too heavily on "phenotypical similarities" between past and present as the basis for deciding the presence of legacies. Not only do similar forms of fakery appear in other contexts around the world, but there is also a great deal of complexity in the motives underlying how similarly labeled phenomena appear on both sides of macro-historical divides. As she puts it, "Interpreting elements of the past or formal similitude as persistence, we risk misreading actors' intentions: we may see people as simply repeating the past, even as they incorporate new practices in the service of entirely novel aims." She argues that there are different ways the past is still with us in the present, not all of which can be reduced to the notion of "legacy." In particular, she introduces two alternative ways the past might be implicated in the present: what she calls "legacy theater" (efforts to stage elements of the past that deliberately create an impression of continuity but for distinctly contemporary aims); and what she refers to as "a usable past" (social and linguistic repertoires from the past that contemporary actors deliberately draw on, often to critique the present). Through the multiple layers of reality that she unpeels in the particular example of *pokazukha* she has chosen, she demonstrates that it is often difficult to untangle what we understand as historical legacies from other ways actors use the past for contemporary purposes.

Indeed, as these chapters suggest, there should be a high bar for making a credible legacy argument. A robust legacy argument must establish the legacy's scope conditions (the spatial and functional spheres in which it manifests itself), and explain why the legacy manifested itself in these spheres in particular; it must demonstrate that the legacy is related to policies and practices that occurred prior to a macrohistorical rupture, and that these policies and practices were unique to a particular historical experience; it must elucidate the type of legacy relationship involved and the actual mechanisms underlying the enduring effects of the past beyond the original context that gave rise to them; and it must eliminate (or at least raise serious doubts about) possible alternative explanations for the phenomenon in question.

Much of the purpose of this project was to inspire our authors to lead the way toward making more robust legacy arguments. Too often legacy arguments have been made at too high a level of abstraction, attempting to explain broad, compound phenomena (such as levels of democracy, varieties of capitalism, or the rule of law) that are made up of a variety of relationships. However, if the study of legacies is to move away from a focus solely on formal, outward similarities and toward a greater appreciation of relationships and mechanisms, legacy arguments cannot be made in general terms, but rather need to drill down to explain the specific linkages between past and present within concrete spheres of activity – spheres that have consequences for how compound phenomena such as democracy, capitalism, or the rule of law ultimately function. Indeed, historical change always involves different degrees and ways the past is intertwined with the present. In this respect, historical legacies need to be bounded by the particulars of place and functional sphere of activity, with significant differences in the degree to which they operate across different functional and spatial realms. For instance, in his chapter on the legacies of communism in the legal sphere, Alexei Trochev notes the ways the dominance of procurators over judges in the spheres of detentions and acquittals has survived the postcommunist transition in practically all postcommunist contexts, despite other far-reaching changes in postcommunist legal systems. But he also notes that the mechanisms underlying this survival have been different in different postcommunist countries. In this respect, specifying the scope conditions for a legacy is a necessary step if legacies are to be examined in a genuinely empirical way.

A robust legacy argument also necessarily involves a historical argument that identifies the defining historical experience originally responsible for the practices and beliefs in question. Legacy arguments obviously need to get their history right. But getting one's history right turns out to be a significantly more complicated affair than many social scientists realize. Historians, as Ian Lustick (1996) once reminded us, differ not just on interpretations, but also on the facts.[12] That creates multiple historical records from which social scientists can and do "select" the information that supports their theories (historical sociologist John Goldthorpe (1991, 225) once described this as the "delightful freedom to play 'pick-and-mix' in history's sweatshops"). One solution would be for social scientists to carry out their own historical research in the primary documentation for each case they are adducing, but this would obviously be impractical. Lustick suggests that because "selection biases" cannot be eliminated, choices about which past matters need to be made explicit and defended. He proposes four "strategies" for the social scientist dipping into history: identify the particular historiographical school or approach being drawn from; explain the variance in the historiography; triangulate among narratives; bring to light alternate narratives to the one being used, perhaps in discursive footnotes.

However welcome Lustick's suggested approach would be, for legacy arguments it would still not eliminate the existence of multiple pasts that vie for any explanation for the persistence of particular practices or beliefs across a macrohistorical rupture. Obviously, history did not begin or end with communism. Determining what constitutes a "defining" historical experience is thus hardly a simple issue (Brown 1966; Kopstein 2003; Pop-Eleches 2007; Detrez and Segeart 2008). A significant number of scholars (for example, Wittenberg 2006; Ekiert and Ziblatt 2013) argue that precommunist histories have been more consequential for explaining patterns of behavior in the former communist countries than communism itself (though the mechanisms underlying these relationships are not always well specified). Certainly, legacies are sometimes cumulative, involving a mixture or overlapping of pasts rather than experiences from any single historical era. Brian Taylor raises this question specifically with respect to the organizational structures, general functions, and standard practices of Russia's law enforcement agencies – all of which have roots in both tsarist and Soviet pasts. Thus, a legacy argument places a particular onus on the researcher to elucidate the nature of these pasts, to specify their relationship to one another and to the phenomenon in question, and to identify what was unique or distinctive about them and why they should have exercised a critical impact on subsequent behavior in a particular sphere.

Most important, as we have emphasized in this chapter, a convincing legacy argument requires elaboration of the particular causal mechanisms that account for why elements of practices or beliefs persist beyond the life of the institutions or policies that gave birth to them. As noted earlier, legacies necessarily involve processes of reproduction, recombination, resurrection, and redeployment through which practices and beliefs embedded by an earlier regime find new or renewed meaning over the long term, within a different macrohistorical context. Within the study of institutions specifically, historical institutionalism has identified a variety of mechanisms of "path dependency" through which actors gain increasing returns for behaving in ways that are consistent with how they behaved in the past, such as: the large start-up costs involved in creating new institutions; the rules and accompanying incentives often built into institutions that are deliberately intended to immunize them from challenge and change; the growing familiarity with institutions over time and accumulation of knowledge about how to work them; the ways those who benefit from particular institutional arrangements may act to block change; or how rules and behaviors are normally taken for granted and are, under most circumstances, not subjected to conscious reflection.[13] Still others focus on how institutions endure as a result of an ongoing political contestation in which institutions that outlive their founding coalitions find new purposes in the hands of different sets of actors. Such arguments suggest the presence of multiple "critical junctures" for any legacy to persist beyond its original moment of institutionalization (Thelen 2004, 31). Indeed, in line with this argument, Eugene Huskey argues in this volume that confidence in the presence of a legacy is increased when particular practices or beliefs associated with the old order endure despite repeated efforts to eliminate them.

Finally, a convincing legacy argument requires that the investigator seriously address the validity and weight of alternative explanations. To what extent can the phenomenon in question be ascribed instead to institutional choices, functional factors, external influences, or global trends? And what can be traced uniquely to the historical experience in question? A number of the chapters in this volume indeed demonstrate that relationships that have sometimes been interpreted as historical legacies of communism are in fact due to other causes. In his chapter in this volume, Timothy Frye shows that the structure of Russia's oil and gas industries is more precisely the product of institutional choices, external market forces, and global trends than it is a historical legacy. Frye underlines the critical role that comparison plays in an effective legacy argument, for to demonstrate the ways a historical experience has uniquely influenced developments, one must demonstrate that those contexts that underwent a different historical experience have not adopted similar forms or practices. Brian Taylor also raises the point that many aspects of the behavior of Russian police and secret police persist not "because they are legacies, but because they are functional for law enforcement agencies more generally." As Taylor shows, a number of features of the Russian police and secret police that probably do qualify as historical legacies also had functional dimensions to their adoption. Thus, sometimes the persistence of a particular practice across a macrohistorical rupture may be due to multiple mechanisms – some functional, some historical – that intertwine, making the effect of a historical legacy difficult to assess.

Organization of the Volume

Our empirical chapters begin with Pop-Eleches's wide-ranging comparative chapter, which examines the relationship between communist modernization and democratic values. Using cross-national time-series data, he shows that former communist countries are less democratic than their levels of socioeconomic development would have predicted. He provides evidence from individual-level surveys that the problem lies to a large extent in communist education, suggesting that its emphasis on technical training and ideological indoctrination resulted in the emergence of middle classes that place lower emphasis on democratic values and are less politically active than their counterparts in noncommunist countries.

The chapters that follow are by and large organized around common spheres of activity, with the idea of presenting readers with the various ways historical legacies have or have not materialized within these spheres and how different authors approach the study of legacies within analogous spheres of activity. Three chapters engage various dimensions of the economic legacies of communism. Clifford Gaddy makes the case for a legacy of spatial misallocation that emerged out of Soviet central planning, which pushed populations into far colder climates than likely would have been the case under market conditions. Béla Greskovits focuses on the sectoral legacies of communist development, and how in particular the establishment of complex manufacturing sectors under socialism variably fared when intersecting with postsocialist policy choices and global economic forces. Finally, Timothy Frye evaluates the validity of legacy-based arguments as explanations for the property structure of the Russian energy sector, making several important methodological points about legacy-based arguments in the process.

The three subsequent chapters examine legacies in the realm of political and legal institutions. Eugene Huskey examines the tsarist and Soviet legacies in the organization and operation of the Russian executive branch of power. Brian Taylor points to the organizational, cultural, and behavioral legacies of Soviet police and law enforcement agencies on successor organizations in post-Soviet Russia, as well as the limits of such arguments. And Alexei Trochev focuses on the persistence of two attributes of communist legal systems in the postcommunist period – the practice of pretrial detentions and the avoidance of acquittals – showing how postcommunist judges remain junior partners relative to prosecutors and police within the criminal justice system.

This book's last three chapters explore various aspects of the cultural dimensions of historical legacies. Anna Grzymala-Busse dissects variations in the political influence of churches in postcommunist Eastern Europe and how national and religious identities became fused in some cases but not others. She shows that, rather than a simple reflection of deep historical legacies, these outcomes were largely produced during the late communist period and grew reinforced by postcommunist developments. Volodymyr Kulyk's chapter examines the legacies of Soviet nationalities policies in Ukraine – in particular, the discrepancy between language use and ethnic self-identification – and why this discrepancy has persisted long after the demise of Soviet power. Finally, through a detailed examination of a single episode, Jessica Pisano shows how actors sometimes evoke continuity with the past to disguise new aims (what she calls "legacy theater") or draw on social and linguistic repertoires from the past to frame the present (what she refers to as a "usable past"). In both practices, the notion of legacy functions more as cultural frame than as objective reality.

In the end, we hope that this collection of empirical studies on the historical legacies of communism encourages a deeper understanding of the processes of change at work in the Eurasian region over the past two decades. We also hope that these examples of how to study legacy issues inspire further systematic research on historical legacies along the lines of that presented here, both within the study of former communist states and in other contexts. The issue of why some institutional forms, modes of behavior, or ways of thinking durably persist across historical divides, finding new purpose beyond the life of the institutions and policies that give birth to them even while others fall by the wayside, is an abiding question of social scientific inquiry.

Notes

1. See, for instance, Beissinger and Young (2002). For a forceful anti-legacy argument covering postcolonial Africa, see Herbst (2000). For the opposite view, see Young (1994).
2. The issue of historical legacies of the Tsarist period for communism has been the subject of a number of excellent studies. See, for instance, Rigby (1979) and Hirsch (2005).
3. Some scholars anticipated the subsequent recourse to longer time frames. See Poznański (1996) and Kotkin (2001).
4. Further examples of legacy arguments abound: Janos (1994); Crawford and Lijphart (1997); Panagiatou (2001); Ekiert and Hanson (2003); Bunce (2005); Karklins (2005).
5. Notable exceptions include McAuley (1997) and Huskey (1999). For a critique of how this has shaped our knowledge of postcommunist societies, see Goode (2010).
6. For some of the few examples of such works, see Gaddy (1996); Greskovits (2003a); and Greskovits (2003b).
7. For a similar point within the historical institutionalist literature concerning "critical junctures," see Capoccia and Kelemen (2007, 349).
8. Capoccia and Kelemen (2007, 360) refer to this as the "temporal leverage" of a critical juncture, although they measure it relative to the length of time of the "critical juncture" itself. By contrast, we do not accept the notion that a legacy is any more of a legacy if the historical experience that sets it in motion is brief.
9. Perhaps the most influential argument concerning equilibria in postcommunist politics was made in the mid-1990s and focused on stalled or partial economic reform. See Hellman (1998). Hellman's argument, however, was not a legacy argument at all, but instead revolved around the economic interests of early winners.
10. Contrary to our argument here, much of the historical institutionalist literature views "critical junctures" as relatively short periods of time involving heightened contingency and choice (Capoccia and Kelemen 2007, 348).
11. Mahoney, Kimball, and Koivu (2009). For an example of a quantitative legacy study that does an excellent job of providing correlational evidence but whose

credibility, without process tracing or case study evidence, is subject to question, see Acemoglu, Johnson, and Robinson (2001). For critiques of Acemoglu, Johnson, and Robinson for unreliable and inappropriate measures, a misleading sampling frame, and omitted variable bias, see McArthur and Sachs (2001); Mahoney (2010, 18–19); Albouy (2012).

12 "The facts of history," Carl Becker wrote, only partly in jest, "come in the end to seem like something solid, something substantial like physical matter, something possessing definite shape and clear, persistent outline – like bricks and scantlings; so that we can easily picture the historian as he stumbles about in the past, stubbing his toe on the hard facts if he doesn't watch out" (cited in Barnes 1937, 266).

13 For an excellent review of the literature and the variety of explanations for institutional persistence, see Campbell (2010).

References

Acemoglu, Daron, Simon Johnson, and James A. Robinson. 2001. "The Colonial Origins of Comparative Development: An Empirical Investigation." *American Economic Review* 91: 1369–1401.

Albouy, David Y. 2012. "The Colonial Origins of Comparative Development: An Empirical Investigation: Comment." *American Economic Review* 102, 6: 3059–76.

Allina-Pisano, Jessica. 2008. *The Post-Soviet Potemkin Village: Politics and Property Rights in the Black Earth.* New York: Cambridge University Press.

Barnes, Elmer. 1937. *A History of Historical Writing.* Norman: University of Oklahoma Press.

Beissinger, Mark R. 1995. "The Persisting Ambiguity of Empire." *Post-Soviet Affairs*, 11/2: 149–84.

Beissinger, Mark R. and Crawford Young. 2002. "Convergence to Crisis: Pre-Independence State Legacies and Post-Independence State Breakdown in Africa and Eurasia." In Mark R. Beissinger and Crawford Young, eds., *Beyond State Crisis?: Postcolonial Africa and Post-Soviet Eurasia Compared.* Baltimore, MD: Johns Hopkins University Press: 19–50.

Bourdieu, Pierre. 1990. *The Logic of Practice.* Stanford, CA: Stanford University Press.

Brown, L. Carl, ed. 1966. *Imperial Legacy: The Ottoman Imprint on the Balkans and the Middle East.* New York: Columbia University Press.

Bunce, Valerie. 2005. "The National Idea: Imperial Legacies and Post-Communist Pathways in Eastern Europe." *East European Politics and Societies* 19/3: 406–42.

Campbell, John L. 2010. "Institutional Reproduction and Change." In Glenn Morgan et al., eds., *The Oxford Handbook of Comparative Institutional Analysis.* Oxford: Oxford University Press: 87–116.

Capoccia, Giovanni and R. Daniel Kelemen. 2007. "The Study of Critical Junctures: Theory, Narrative, and Counterfactuals in Historical Institutionalism." *World Politics* 59, 3 (April): 341–69.

Carothers, Thomas. 2002. "The End of the Transition Paradigm." *Journal of Democracy* 13: 5–21.

Collier, Ruth Berins and David Collier. 1991. *Shaping the Political Arena.* Princeton, NJ: Princeton University Press.

Crawford, Beverly and Arend Lijphart, eds. 1997. *Liberalization and Leninist Legacies: Comparative Perspectives on Democratic Transitions*. Berkeley, CA: International and Area Studies.
Darden, Keith and Anna Grzymala-Busse. 2006. "The Great Divide: Literacy, Nationalism, and the Communist Collapse." *World Politics* 59: 83–115.
Detrez, Raymond and Barbara Segeart, eds. 2008. *Europe and the Historical Legacies in the Balkans*. New York: Peter Lang.
Dunn, Elizabeth C. 2004. *Privatizing Poland: Baby Food, Big Business, and the Remaking of Labor*. Ithaca, NY: Cornell University Press.
Ekiert, Grzegorz and Stephen Hanson, eds. 2003. *Capitalism and Democracy in Eastern and Central Europe: Assessing the Legacy of the Communist Past*. New York: Cambridge University Press.
Ekiert, Grzegorz and Daniel Ziblatt. 2013. "Democracy in Central and Eastern Europe 100 years On." *East European Politics and Societies* 27, 1 (February): 88–105.
Eklof, Ben et al., eds. 2005. *Educational Reform in Post-Soviet Russia: Legacies and Prospects*. New York: F. Cass.
Frye, Timothy. 2000. *Brokers and Bureaucrats: Building Market Institutions in Russia*. Ann Arbor: University of Michigan Press.
Gaddy, Clifford G. 1996. *The Price of the Past: Russia's Struggle with the Legacy of a Militarized Economy*. Washington, DC: Brookings.
Goldthorpe, John H. 1991. "The Uses of History in Sociology: Reflections on Some Recent Tendencies," *British Journal of Sociology* 42: 211–30.
Goode, Paul J. 2010. "Redefining Russia: Hybrid Regimes, Fieldwork, and Russian Politics." *Perspectives on Politics* 8, 4: 1055–75.
Greskovits, Béla. 2003a. "Beyond Transition: The Variety of Post-Socialist Development." In Ronald Dworkin et al., eds., *From Liberal Values to Democratic Transition*. Budapest: Central European University Press, 201–25.
  2003b. "Sectors, States, and the Paths of Post-Socialist Development." In Nauro Campos and Jan Fidrmuc, eds., *Political Economy of Transition and Development: Institutions, Politics and Policies*. Dordrecht: Kluwer Academic Publishers, 99–120.
Grzymala-Busse, Anna. 2002. *Redeeming the Communist Past: The Regeneration of Communist Parties in East Central Europe*. New York: Cambridge University Press.
Hanson, Stephen E. 1995. "The Leninist Legacy and Institutional Change." *Comparative Political Studies* 28, 2: 306–14.
Hedlund, Stefan. 2005. *Russian Path Dependence*. New York: Routledge.
Hellman, Joel. 1998. "Winners Take All: The Politics of Partial Reform in Postcommunist Transitions." *World Politics* 50/2: 203–34.
Hendley, Kathryn. 1999. "The Demand for Law." *East European Constitutional Review* 8/4: 89–95.
Herbst, Jeffrey. 2000. *States and Power in Africa: Comparative Lessons in Authority and Control*. Princeton, NJ: Princeton University Press.
Hirsch, Francine. 2005. *Empire of Nations: Ethnographic Knowledge and the Making of the Soviet Union*. Ithaca, NY: Cornell University Press.
Humphrey, Caroline. 2002. "Does the Category 'Postsocialist' Still Make Sense?" in C. Hann, ed., *Postsocialism: Ideals, Ideologies, and Practices in Eurasia*. New York: Routledge: 12–15.

2002. *The Unmaking of Soviet Life: Everyday Economies after Socialism.* Ithaca, NY: Cornell University Press.
Huskey, Eugene. 1999. *Presidential Power in Russia.* Armonk, NY: M. E. Sharpe.
Janos, Andrew C. 1994. "Continuity and Change in Eastern-Europe – Strategies of Post-communist Politics." *East European Politics and Societies* 8/1: 1–31.
Janos, Andrew. 2000. *East Central Europe in the Modern World: The Politics of the Borderlands from Pre- to Postcommunism.* Stanford, CA: Stanford University Press.
Jowitt, Ken. 1992. *The New World Disorder: The Leninist Extinction.* Berkeley, CA: University of California Press.
Karklins, Rasma. 2005. *The System Made Me Do It: Corruption in the Post-Communist Region.* Armonk, NY: M. E. Sharpe.
Kitschelt, Herbert, et al. 1999. *Post-Communist Party Systems: Competition, Representation, and Inter-Party Cooperation.* Cambridge: Cambridge University Press.
Kopstein, Jeffrey. 2003. "Postcommunist Democracy: Legacies and Outcomes." *Comparative Politics* 35/2: 231–50.
Kotkin, Stephen. 2001, 2008. *Armageddon Averted: The Soviet Collapse 1970–2000.* New York: Oxford University Press.
Laitin, David D. 1998. *Identity in Formation: The Russian-Speaking Populations in the Near-Abroad.* Ithaca, NY: Cornell University Press.
Lane, David Stuart. 2011. "Trajectories of Transformation: Theories, Legacies, Outcomes." In David Lane, ed., *The Legacy of State Socialism and the Future of Transformation.* Lanham, MD: Rowman and Littlefield, 3–30.
LaPorte, Jody and Danielle N. Lussier. 2011. "What Is the Leninist Legacy? Assessing Twenty Years of Scholarship." *Slavic Review* 70, 3 (Fall): 637–54.
Ledeneva, Elena V. 2006. *How Russia Really Works: The Informal Practices that Shaped Post-Soviet Politics and Business.* Ithaca, NY: Cornell University Press.
Levi-Strauss, Claude. 1966. *The Savage Mind.* Chicago, IL: University of Chicago Press.
Lipman, Masha. 2003. "Turkmenistan: Following in Stalin's Footsteps," *St. Petersburg Times,* February 11: 14, at http://www.sptimes.ru/archive/pdf/842.pdf (accessed on July 3, 2013).
Lustick, Ian S. 1996. "History, Historiography, and Political Science: Multiple Historical Records and the Problem of Selection Bias." *American Political Science Review* 90/3: 605–18.
Mahoney, James. 2002. *The Legacies of Liberalism: Path Dependence and Political Regimes in Central America.* Baltimore, MD: Johns Hopkins University Press.
  2010. *Colonialism and Post-Colonial Development: Spanish America in Comparative Perspective.* Cambridge: Cambridge University Press.
Mahoney, James, Erin Kimball, and Kendra L. Koivu. 2009. "The Logic of Historical Explanation in the Social Sciences." *Comparative Political Studies* 42, 1: 114–46.
McArthur, John W. and Jeffrey D. Sachs. 2001. "Institutions and Geography: Comment on Acemoglu, Johnson and Robinson (2000)." *NBER Working Paper Series,* Working Paper 8144 (accessed at http://www.nber.org/papers/w8114).
McAuley, Mary. 1997. *Russia's Politics of Uncertainty.* New York: Cambridge University Press.
Nunn, Nathan and Leonard Wantchekon. 2011. "The Slave Trade and the Origins of Mistrust in Africa." *American Economic Review* 101 (December): 3221–52.

North, Douglass. 1990. *Institutions, Institutional Change and Economic Performance.* Cambridge: Cambridge University Press.
Panagiatou, R. A. 2001. "Estonia's Success: Prescription or Legacy?" *Communist and Post-Communist Studies* 34/2: 261–77.
Pickles, John and Robert M. Jenkins, eds. 2008. *Globalization and Regionalization in Post-Socialist Economies: Common Economic Spaces of Europe.* New York: Palgrave Macmillan.
Pierson, Paul. 2000. "Increasing Returns, Path Dependence, and the Study of Politics." *American Political Science Review* 94, 2: 251–67.
Pop-Eleches, Grigore. 2007. "Historical Legacies and Post-Communist Regime Change." *Journal of Politics* 69/4: 908–26.
Poznański, Kazimierz Z. 1996. *Poland's Protracted Transition: Institutional Change and Economic Growth 1970–1994.* New York: Cambridge University Press.
Rigby, T. H. 1979. *Lenin's Government: Sovnarkom, 1917–1922.* Cambridge: Cambridge University Press.
Segbers, Klaus, ed. 2001. *Explaining Post-Soviet Patchworks*, 3 vols. Aldershot, England and Burlington, VT: Ashgate.
Shlapentokh, Vladimir. 1996. "Russia: Privatization and Illegalization of Social and Political Life." *Washington Quarterly* 19/1: 65–85.
Solomon, Peter H. Jr. 1995. "The Limits of Legal Order in Russia." *Post-Soviet Affairs* 11/2: 89–114.
Stark, David. 1996. "Recombinant Property in East European Capitalism." *American Journal of Sociology* 101/1: 993–1011.
Taylor, Brian D. 2003. *Politics and the Russian Army: Civil-Military Relations, 1689–2000.* New York: Cambridge University Press.
Thelen, Kathleen. 2004. *How Institutions Evolve: The Political Economy of Skills in Germany, Britain, the United States, and Japan.* New York: Cambridge University Press.
Tocqueville, Alexis de. 1955. *The Ancien Régime and the French Revolution.* Garden City, NY: Doubleday.
Trochev, Alexei. 2008. *Judging Russia: Constitutional Court in Russian Politics, 1990–2006.* New York: Cambridge University Press.
Verdery, Katherine. 2003. *The Vanishing Hectare: Property and Value in Postsocialist Transylvania.* Ithaca, NY: Cornell University Press.
Volkov, Vadim. 2002. *Violent Entrepreneurs: The Use of Force in the Making of Russian Capitalism.* Ithaca, NY: Cornell University Press.
Volgyes, Ivan. 1995. "The Legacies of Communism: An Introductory Essay." In Zoltan Barany and Ivan Volgyes, eds., *The Legacies of Communism in Eastern Europe.* Baltimore, MD: Johns Hopkins University Press, 1–22.
Wallander, Celeste A. 2007. "Global Challenges and Russian Foreign Policy." In Robert Legvold, ed., *Russian Foreign Policy in the 21st Century and the Shadow of the Past.* New York: Columbia University Press: 443–97.
Webber, Stephen L. 2000. *School, Reform, and Society in the New Russia.* New York: St. Martin's Press.
White, Stephen. 2011. "Russia: the Revenge of the Superstructure." In David Lane, ed., *The Legacy of State Socialism and the Future of Transformation.* Lanham, MD: Rowman and Littlefield: 53–68.

Wilson, Andrew. 2005. *Virtual Politics: Faking Democracy in the Post-Soviet World*. New Haven, CT: Yale University Press.
Wittenberg, Jason. 2006. *Crucibles of Political Loyalty: Church Institutions and Electoral Continuity in Hungary*. Cambridge: Cambridge University Press.
  2011. "What Is a Historical Legacy?" unpublished paper, available at http://witty.berkeley.edu/Legacies.pdf.
Young, Crawford. 1994. *The African Colonial State in Comparative Perspective*. New Haven, CT: Yale University Press.

2

Communist Development and the Postcommunist Democratic Deficit

Grigore Pop-Eleches

This chapter addresses the question of how the regime trajectories of Eastern European and Eurasian countries were shaped by the legacies of the communist developmental and political project in the two decades since the collapse of communist one-party states. I start out by documenting a significant and persistent democratic deficit among the former communist countries and then focus on the theoretical challenge that this deficit poses for our understanding of the link between socioeconomic development and democratization: Why did the fairly significant developmental achievements of communist regimes yield such modest democratic dividends, and, related, why are the regime repercussions of communist education and urbanization so different from those of development policies in noncommunist countries?

While the roots of the postcommunist democratic deficit obviously include institutional legacies involving both fragmentation and translation dynamics, in this chapter I focus primarily on legacies operating at the individual level, which can be conceptualized along the lines of the *cultural schemata* and *parameter-setting legacies* discussed in the introduction to this volume. Thus, I argue that the peculiar nature of communist development policies affected the extent to which the modernization process produced the types of mobilized prodemocratic individuals who make up the constituencies that have generally been seen as the link between development and democracy. In particular, I argue that the emphasis on technical/hard science training and the heavy reliance on ideological indoctrination in communist education systems resulted in the emergence of middle classes that placed lower emphasis on democratic values and were less politically active than their counterparts in noncommunist countries.

This work was supported by a grant of the Romanian National Authority for Scientific Research, CNCS – UEFISCDI, project number PN-II-ID-PCE-2011-3-0669.

This chapter contributes to the debates about the link between historical legacies and postcommunist political trajectories in two ways. First, to the best of my knowledge, it is the first systematic analysis of the postcommunist democratic deficit, and therefore complements earlier studies that focused primarily on legacy-based political differences between ex-communist countries (Kurtz and Barnes 2002; Darden and Grzymala-Busse 2006; Pop-Eleches 2007). Second, this chapter tries to bridge the gap between macro-analyses of regime trajectories and a small but growing group of studies that analyze the impact of communist legacies on postcommunist political attitudes and behavior (Bernhard and Karakoc 2007; Pop-Eleches and Tucker 2013a, 2013b).

In addition to contributing to a better understanding of the role of legacies in shaping both individual attitudes/behavior and aggregate political outcomes, this study poses a significant theoretical challenge to the newly resurgent literature about the link between development and democracy.[1] The postcommunist regime transformations provide an interesting testing ground for these debates because the twenty-eight countries that emerged after the dissolution of the Soviet bloc shared important developmental legacies after several decades of communist rule, but also displayed significant and consequential differences (Horowitz 2003; Pop-Eleches 2007). Moreover, the abrupt "Leninist extinction" (Jowitt 1992) meant that the timing of the transition away from communist one-party rule was fairly exogenous, in the sense that the threat of Soviet intervention to prop up communist regimes was removed at roughly the same time for all the countries of the former Soviet bloc.

However, so far this theoretical promise has not been sufficiently fulfilled. Much of the cross-national statistical research on the drivers of democratization either used pre-1990 data (Przeworski and Limongi 1997; Barro 1999; Boix and Stokes 2003), and therefore obviously ignores the postcommunist experience, or includes ex-communist countries as part of a global sample but does not explore the potential causal heterogeneity because of the inclusion of a set of countries with such unique economic and political development trajectories (Epstein et al. 2006). Meanwhile, much of the postcommunist transition literature has tended to emphasize other aspects, such as initial elections and power balance (Fish 1998a, 1998b; McFaul 2002) or international factors (Whitehead 1996; Kopstein and Reilly 2000; Vachudova 2005), while largely treating socioeconomic development as control variables or rival hypotheses. Even in studies that focused more directly on developmental legacies to explain either the collapse of communism (Hosking 1991, Lewin 1991; Hough 1997) or postcommunist regime transformations (Vassilev 1999; Kurtz and Barnes 2002; Darden and Grzymala-Busse 2006; Pop-Eleches 2007), the focus has been on explaining regime trajectories within the former Soviet bloc rather than on placing the communist and postcommunist experience in broader international perspective (Kopstein 2003).

By engaging in a systematic comparison of the link between developmental patterns and regime trajectories in both ex-communist and noncommunist countries, this analysis raises two important challenges to the implicit assumption of earlier studies of a uniform link between socioeconomic modernization and democracy: first, the democratic deficit of ex-communist countries is at odds with their fairly high levels of socioeconomic development in 1989; and second, the relationship between traditional development indicators and democracy differs substantially between ex-communist and noncommunist countries.[2] At the most basic level, these two puzzles suggest that to understand the development-democracy link, we need to account not only for the extent, but also for the nature of socioeconomic development. To do so, however, we need to pay closer attention to the causal mechanisms linking socioeconomic development and democratization, and this chapter takes at least a first step in this direction by focusing on the cultural schemata and parameter-setting legacies that resulted from the particularities of the communist development project.

This chapter is organized as follows: the next section provides a brief overview of the peculiarities of communist socioeconomic development and places its achievements and limitations in comparative perspective. Next I present the findings of cross-national statistical tests of the drivers of democracy in the post–Cold War era to establish the magnitude of the postcommunist democracy deficit and the extent to which communist-era developmental legacies can explain this deficit. In the final section, I briefly discuss a few potential mechanisms linking the communist modernization policies to the political values and behavior patterns of (post-)communist citizens and ultimately to the dynamics of postcommunist regime change.

Communist Modernization – Achievements and Limitations

Prior to the arrival of communism, most Eurasian countries were hardly promising democratization candidates from a modernization standpoint: during the interwar period, most of the region was poor and overwhelmingly rural (more than 80%), on average half its population was illiterate, and most Eastern Europeans benefited from only the most rudimentary health and welfare benefits. Moreover, economic development was highly uneven within the region, and these differences largely followed the familiar West-East/South gradient – from the fairly affluent, urbanized, and highly educated Czech lands to the much poorer, illiterate, and overwhelmingly rural Central Asia and Southern Balkans.

Even the harshest anticommunist critics would have a hard time denying that under communist rule most of the Soviet bloc – particularly the initially underprivileged countries and regions – experienced rapid economic growth and modernization, especially during the first quarter century after World War II (Janos 2000). Even though the actual industrialization and modernization process entailed substantial short-term disruption and human suffering, it left behind a much more developed group of countries, which according

Development and the Democratic Deficit

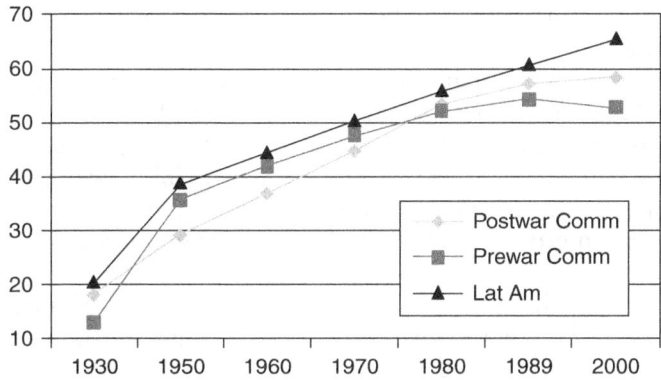

FIGURE 2.1. Comparative urbanization patterns (1930–2000).

to modernization theory should imply significantly improved postcommunist democratization prospects compared to the prewar period. Thus, by 1989, on average in the communist countries, 56 percent of the population lived in urban settings, welfare benefits had been extended to large parts of the population, and poverty had been significantly reduced, largely because of the region's low inequality levels. Educational achievements were even more impressive: by the late 1980s, the communists had virtually eradicated illiteracy throughout the former Soviet bloc, and secondary education enrollments were significantly higher than in other developing countries. Therefore, from a straightforward modernization theory perspective, communist planners may have unwittingly paved the way for the collapse of communism and subsequent democratization (Lewin 1991; Vassilev 1999).

On the other hand, even abstracting for now from the social and psychological implications of communist-style coerced modernization, the developmental record of the Soviet bloc was far from ideal. Thus, the impressive economic growth rates of the 1950s and 1960s were followed by slowdown in the 1970s and stagnation in the 1980s, which was marked by increasing shortages and economic bottlenecks (Kornai 1992). The exhaustion of communist developmental efforts is also illustrated by Figure 2.1, which compares over time the evolution of urbanization in prewar communist countries (the original Soviet republics and Mongolia), the postwar communist countries of Eastern Europe, and the Latin American countries.

The graph confirms that, during the initial communist developmental push, characterized by massive collectivization and industrialization campaigns, communist countries experienced significant urbanization increases in both absolute and relative terms: thus, urbanization rates in the prewar communist countries almost tripled between 1930–50, and in the process surpassed the urbanization levels of their Eastern European neighbors and almost caught up with the Latin American average. Similarly, Eastern European urbanization took off during the first three decades of communism, and by 1980, the newly communist countries had virtually closed the urbanization gap that had separated them from Latin America after the devastation of World War II. However, the pace of urbanization slowed down starting in the 1970s in the interwar Soviet republics (which had belonged to the Soviet Union pre-1939) and in the 1980s in Eastern Europe, and as a result the two regions fell behind Latin America, where urban growth continued steadily throughout the 1980s and 1990s.

Beyond the question about the *extent* of socioeconomic progress, which will be analyzed in greater detail later in this chapter, we need to consider the possibility that the coercive, centrally planned communist approach to development produced a different *type* of modernity, whose implications for democracy may differ substantially not only from early developers, but also from noncommunist late development in other parts of the developing world. Thus, the heavy emphasis on ideological indoctrination and technical subjects in communist education arguably affected its democratizing impact, while the coercive dual process of collectivization and industrialization created towns and cities whose inhabitants arguably had a different urban experience than their noncommunist counterparts. Unfortunately, such qualitative developmental differences are difficult to capture statistically, and will be analyzed indirectly through their impact on individual attitudes and behavior in the final section of the chapter.

The one clear exception in this respect is the nature of communist economic development, whose most distinctive feature was the Stalinist emphasis on heavy industry as the economic backbone for Soviet geopolitical ambitions. Combined with the heavily subsidized supply of Russian energy and raw materials, and an inherent bias of central planning toward quantity over quality (because the former was easier to assess), this developmental strategy resulted in the proliferation of energy-intensive, low-productivity industrial enterprises. This economic profile, which created significant economic and political problems after the collapse of communism, is reflected in the notoriously weak performance of communist countries with respect to the amount of commercial energy use required per dollar of GDP.

Because the rest of the world also developed during the second half of the twentieth century, a proper assessment of the communist developmental record requires a comparative benchmark, which raises the question about the relevant counterfactuals. Eastern Europeans tended to look at West Germany, Austria, Spain, and Greece as possible examples of noncommunist development, but one may of course ask whether Turkey or Latin America are not the more appropriate comparisons. For the purpose of this analysis, I use a simple cross-sectional regression approach, which tests the impact of communist bloc membership on several key developmental indicators at the outset of the transition (around 1990). An overview of country-level indicators used can be

TABLE 2.1. *Variable Overview – Country-Level Indicators*

Variable Name	Coding/Measurement	Source(s)
% Urban 1920	population in towns over 50 K/ total population (in %)	Author using data from Lahmeyer (1999)
% Urban 1990	Urban population in %	World Development Indicators (WDI)
Literacy 1920s	Literate population as % of total population (five categories in 20% increments)	UNESCO (1953)
Literacy 1990	Literate population as % of total population	UNESCO (2013)
Energy intensity	GDP per unit of energy use	WDI
Interwar Soviet Republic	1 = Country belonged to SU pre-1940 0 = otherwise	Author
Income inequality	Income share of top 20%	Finkel et al. (2008)
Ethnic fragmentation	0 (min) – 1 (max)	Finkel et al. (2008)
Population size (log)	Log total population	WDI
FH Democracy	0 (least free) to 12 (most free)[a]	Freedom House (2005)
Income inequality	Ratio between income shares of top and bottom quintile	WDI and UNU-WIDER (2008)
GDP/capita	GDP/capita in const. $ (logged)	WDI
Inflation	Log of inflation in previous year	WDI
GDP change	Cumulative change in past two years (%)	WDI

[a] Obtained by adding the scores for political and civil liberties and then subtracting the sum from 14.

found in Table 2.1. In addition to the dummy variable indicating communist bloc membership, the regressions in Table 2.2 include two indicators of interwar development, which control for precommunist differences and provide a baseline for assessing communist-era performance. Because GDP/capita statistics for the prewar era are notoriously difficult to compare cross-nationally, I collected data on urbanization[3] and literacy[4] in the mid-1920s.[5] In addition, the regressions included a series of regional dummies.

The results of the (admittedly reduced form) regressions in Table 2.2 paint a highly uneven picture of communist modernization achievements. On one hand, the substantively large and statistically significant positive effects in models 1 and 2 confirm the significant comparative advantage of communist states in educating their citizens, who were more likely to be literate and have access to secondary education. Moreover, model 6 confirms another crucial developmental achievement of communism, namely its much more egalitarian income distribution, especially compared to Latin America. On the other hand,

TABLE 2.2. *Communist Modernization and Its Limitations*

	(1) Secondary education enrollment 1990	(2) Literacy 1990	(3) %Urban 1990	(4) GDP/ capita 1990	(5) GDP/unit of energy use 1995	(6) Income inequality 1990
Communist (Eurasia)	19.489** (4.732)	13.355** (2.655)	−5.783# (3.180)	−8.115** (1.675)	−2.272** (.324)	−11.704** (1.552)
Urbanization 1920s	.103 (.178)	−.076 (.102)	.052 (.122)	−.064 (.064)	−.006 (.012)	.003 (.059)
Literacy 1920s	1.240** (1.422)	6.851** (.837)	7.383** (.972)	4.924** (.511)	.686** (.101)	−2.282** (.483)
Constant	35.309** (4.760)	64.524** (2.876)	39.282** (3.264)	−3.093# (1.714)	1.338** (.354)	53.262** (1.632)
Observations	85	82	88	89	79	85
R-squared	.50	.55	.46	.58	.57	.51

Note: OLS regression coefficients with standard errors in parentheses. # significant at 10%; * significant at 5%; ** significant at 1%.

the marginally significant negative effect of Soviet bloc membership in model 3 confirms the modest urbanization progress of communist regimes despite (or perhaps because of) their activist and at times coercive approach to modernization. The communist record is even worse for economic development: while the large deficit with respect to overall output levels (model 4) is at least partially due to the region's lower precommunist economic starting points (which are only imperfectly captured by the urbanization and literacy controls), the much greater energy intensity of Soviet-style economies (model 5) cannot be blamed as readily on precommunist legacies.

Overall, the analysis in this section has presented a mixed and highly uneven picture of communist modernization performance: the countries of the former Soviet bloc entered the post–Cold War era with a significant advantage in terms of education and economic equality, which from a modernization theory standpoint should facilitate democratization through greater civil society involvement and political participation. At the same time, however, communism did not help these countries overcome their deficit in terms of urbanization and wealth, which weakened their democratic prospects from a modernization theory perspective.

Beyond the standard question about *how much* development occurred under communism (or any other system), I argue that we need to understand better *what kind* of development it was. Therefore, the question to be addressed in the following section is not just whether the regime trajectories of ex-communist countries differed because they were more or less developed than other countries at the outset of the transition, but also whether the link between development and regime type differed for the ex-communist countries, given the particularities of their modernization paths and methods over five or more decades.

Nondemocratizing Development: Assessing the Regime Legacies of Communism

Even though the ex-communist countries faced significant challenges at the outset of their simultaneous economic and political transitions, they nevertheless benefited from several favorable conditions, which explains the democratic optimism of the early 1990s. Because Soviet troops had imposed communism for most countries in the region, the removal of the Soviet threat combined with the ideological dominance of Western liberalism produced a widely shared assumption (embodied in the very notion of transition) that the endpoint of the postcommunist transformations would be some form of democratic politics and market-based economics. While not everybody shared this initial optimism (Jowitt 1992), even observers concerned with domestic preconditions had at least some reason to be optimistic, given the significant advantages with respect to education and inequality discussed in the previous section. Indeed, several prominent explanations of the decline and collapse of Soviet communism (Remington 1990; Lewin 1991; Bahry 1993; Hough 1997) interpreted this decline through the lens of modernization theorists' predictions that Soviet totalitarianism would ultimately be undermined by the very socioeconomic transformations it had triggered (Deutsch 1953; Parsons 1967). This argument was extended to postcommunist democratization by Vassilev's (1999) analysis of the Bulgarian experience.

However, the actual regime trajectories of postcommunist countries have not been nearly as democratic or as uniform as these initial accounts predicted. The non-Baltic former Soviet republics have largely experienced either hybrid or fully authoritarian regimes, much of the Balkans had a bumpy and delayed democratization path, and liberal democracy is still far from the only game in town. While the broad democratic parameters of the East-Central European countries have probably been sealed by their accession to the EU, some observers are worried about the possibility of democratic backsliding because of the post-accession weakening of external monitoring and conditionality. Nor is there a clear positive regional trend toward democracy, as the euphoria of the colored revolutions has subsided (Beissinger 2006) and several countries (especially Belarus and Russia) experienced authoritarian backsliding.

What are the implications of these rather mixed postcommunist regime trajectories for our understanding of the link between socioeconomic development and democracy? To address this question, I ran a series of time-series cross-sectional regressions,[6] which analyze the drivers of global democracy patterns from 1990–2004. The dependent variable for the regressions in Table 2.3 is the combined level of civil liberties and political rights according to Freedom House in a given country and year.[7] The main independent variables of interest

TABLE 2.3. *Modernization and the Postcommunist Democracy Deficit*

	(1) FH Democracy	(2) FH Democracy	(3) FH Democracy	(4) FH Democracy	(5) FH Democracy	(6) FH Democracy	(7) FH Democracy
Postcommunist (Eurasia)	-3.159** (.347)		-3.286** (.421)	-8.502** (1.756)			
Prewar Soviet Rep.					-5.500** (.586)		
EE Postcommunism					-2.334** (.441)		
Long-term Communism (30 yrs+)						-3.637** (.310)	
All Communist regimes							-2.141** (.333)
GDP/capita		.056** (.014)	.008 (.016)	.037* (.017)	.018 (.015)	.002 (.015)	.026# (.015)
GDP/capita* Postcommunism				-.036 (.036)			
%Urban		-.012* (.006)	-.013* (.006)	-.031** (.006)	-.019** (.006)	-.013* (.006)	-.013* (.006)
%Urban* Postcommunism				.157** (.025)			

Secondary education enrollment	.024** (.005)	.032** (.005)	.042** (.005)	.040** (.005)	.033** (.005)	.026** (.005)
Secondary education* Postcommunism			-.035* (.017)			
Income inequality	.033* (.015)	-.010 (.017)	-.006 (.017)	-.008 (.017)	-.013 (.016)	.000 (.016)
Ethnic fractionalization	.360 (.516)	.881# (.515)	1.051* (.513)	1.024# (.527)	.994* (.486)	1.335** (.492)
GDP/energy unit	.645** (.071)	.421** (.080)	.428** (.081)	.321** (.079)	.411** (.080)	.536** (.083)
Violent conflict	-.349** (.089)	-.360** (.087)	-.360** (.086)	-.354** (.086)	-.361** (.087)	-.348** (.087)
Raw material dependence	-.024 (.025)	-.023 (.025)	-.020 (.024)	-.022 (.024)	-.023 (.025)	-.022 (.025)
Observations	2,752	2,271	2,267	2,271	2,331	2,331
R-sq	.38	.47	.48	.48	.48	.47

Prais-Winsten regression coefficients with standard errors in parentheses # significant at 10%; * significant at 5%; ** significant at 1%.

Note: Also included but not reported were region dummies, a year variable, population size, and dummies indicating missing values for independent variables.

are a series of dummy indicators capturing different types of ex-communist regimes, and several socioeconomic development indicators, discussed in greater detail later in this chapter. In addition, the regression models include indicators intended to capture several classical explanations of regime patterns, including ethnic fractionalization, natural resource dependence, the presence of violent conflict, as well as a series of standard controls such as population size, regional dummies, and a year variable intended to capture temporal democracy trends.[8]

The first two models in Table 2.3 represent baseline regressions against which subsequent models can be compared: model 1 only includes regional dummies and the year variable, and identifies a substantively large and statistically significant democracy deficit among the twenty-eight Eurasian transition countries if we ignore any alternative drivers of democracy except for regional effects. By contrast, model 2 presents a more completely specified model of regime outcomes, but in line with the standard approach used in cross-national regression analyses of democratization, it does not include an indicator for whether a country was ex-communist. Overall, the regression provides solid support for the main modernization theory predictions, given that richer, more urbanized countries with more educated populations were significantly more likely to be democratic in the post–Cold War period. The results also confirm the negative effects of ethnic fractionalization and violent conflict, which emerged as statistically significant negative predictors of democracy. The only unexpected result was the statistically significant positive effect of income inequality.

Model 3 simply adds the Eurasian transition country dummy from model 1 to the battery of traditional democracy correlates from model 2. While the overall explanatory power of the model does not increase dramatically, the results in model 3 confirm the large and statistically significant democracy handicap of ex-communist countries even after the collapse of communism: thus, once we control for developmental differences, transition countries had a 3.3 point deficit on the twelve-point FH democracy scale compared to their noncommunist counterparts, and this effect was actually somewhat larger than in model 1.[9] Even more important, the inclusion of the postcommunism dummy significantly affected the size, significance, and even the direction of several developmental and structural variables, which suggests that its omission in most democratization studies arguably leads to biased estimates. For example, compared to the baseline in model 2, the magnitude of the GDP/capita effect was reduced by almost 80 percent (and was no longer statistically significant), the impact of secondary education enrollment increased by a third, the income inequality effect was reversed and now pointed in the expected direction, whereas ethnic fractionalization was a substantively larger and marginally statistically significant impediment to democracy.[10]

The causal heterogeneity suggested by the difference between models 2 and 3 is explored in greater detail in model 4, which adds interaction terms between the postcommunism dummy and several developmental indicators. This approach allows us to test not only whether ex-communist countries underperformed relative to their developmental legacies, but also whether the impact of different aspects of modernization varies between ex-communist and noncommunist countries. The interaction effects in model 4 provide strong evidence that this is indeed the case: thus, GDP per capita had a large and significant positive effect on noncommunist countries, but the effect was completely erased among the transition countries, perhaps because of the problematic nature of communist output statistics (Aslund 2001). On the other hand, urbanization had a strong positive effect on postcommunist democracy but was weakly negative elsewhere, a somewhat surprising finding, given the problematic nature of communist urbanization.[11] With respect to the greatest developmental achievement of communism – the widespread educational progress – the results in model 4 suggest that more widespread secondary education enrollment was associated with greater democracy only among noncommunist countries. In other words, it appears that despite its quantitative achievements, something about the nature of communist education prevented citizens from using this empowerment for democratic purposes after the collapse of communism.

While the analysis so far has focused on the twenty-eight ex-communist countries of Eastern Europe and Eurasia,[12] which started their political transition in 1989–91 and are typically grouped together by analyses of postcommunism, such a classification ignores significant differences within this group. Therefore, in model 5 I differentiate between countries that belonged to the pre–WWII Soviet Union and Eastern European countries that came under communist control after World War II, and were therefore spared the harrowing experience of the first two decades of Stalinism. The results in model 5 confirm the analytical utility of this distinction, given that the democracy deficit of the original Soviet republics was much larger in both substantive and statistical terms. Thus, in line with theoretical expectations, it appears that the countries with the longest and most intense communist exposure suffered the greatest postcommunist democratization obstacles (though of course it is impossible to tell whether the problem was the nature of modernization or the intensity of the repression accompanying it). On the other hand, it is worthwhile noting that even their more fortunate Eastern European neighbors underperformed in democratic terms after the collapse of communism, which suggests that the developmental legacies of communism were not immediately overcome by the hopes of returning to Europe.

Because the universe of (ex)communist regimes obviously extends beyond Eastern Europe and the former Soviet Union, the next two models test the regime impact of communism beyond the Eurasian core countries. Thus, the communist regime indicator in model 6 also includes other countries ruled by communist regimes for at least thirty years, and therefore includes Cuba, China, and a number of other Asian countries. Not surprising, the inclusion of these long-term communist regimes produces results that are broadly comparable to model 3, arguably because the limited democratic progress in these countries was partially balanced by their greater relative socioeconomic backwardness. Finally, in line with recent discussions about the need to expand the universe of ex-communist countries (Chen and Sil 2007), model 7 uses an even broader definition by including other developing countries (such as Tanzania, Angola, and Afghanistan) that were ruled by Marxist one-party regimes at some point before 1990. While still substantively important and statistically significant, the democracy deficit for this maximalist definition of communist regimes is somewhat smaller than for longer-term communist dictatorships, arguably reflecting the weaker intensity and shorter duration of communist modernization efforts in these countries.

Because any assessment of historical legacies requires a closer focus on the temporal evolution of postcommunist regime trajectories, in Table 2.4, I present a brief look at how ex-communist countries measured up to their noncommunist counterparts in three equally sized time periods (1990–94, 1995–99, and 2000–04), which can be roughly interpreted as the early, middle, and late transition periods.[13] The model specifications are the same as in model 3 of Table 2.3 (whose results are reproduced in model 1 of Table 2.4) and includes the postcommunism dummy variable plus the battery of developmental indicators discussed previously. The only difference is that the regressions in models 2–4 are run on samples restricted to the three different five-year time periods.

Judging by the size of the regression coefficient for the postcommunism variable in models 2–4, there is little evidence that the democracy deficit of postcommunist countries is simply a function of temporary difficulties in the early transition. Thus, the negative effect is comparatively sized and statistically significant in all three models, and while there was a modest deficit decline between the early and the late 1990s, the magnitude of the negative effect was actually greatest in the most recent period (after 2000). Furthermore, the impact of energy intensiveness, which according to model 5 in Table 2.2 was one of the main economic liabilities of communism, was twice as large after 2000 as in the early 1990s and thus reinforces the idea that the economic and political legacies of communism may have produced vicious cycles that are potentially quite durable fixtures of the post-Soviet period.

Explaining the Unusual Communist Development-Democracy Link
How can we explain the unusual link between communist development and postcommunist democracy that the analysis so far has identified? While an exhaustive answer to this question would arguably require a book-length treatment, and would include more detailed discussions of the institutional legacies that are at least partly responsible for the postcommunist democratic deficit, in the remainder of this chapter I will sketch out a few potential mechanisms that broadly fit into the category of cultural schemata and parameter-setting legacies and largely focus on the individual level. In particular, I will try to explain why higher educational achievements have a much weaker democratizing impact in ex-communist countries, and why another key developmental

TABLE 2.4. *Moving Time Windows Analysis of Postcommunist Democracy Deficit*

	(1) FH Democracy	(2) FH Democracy	(3) FH Democracy	(4) FH Democracy
Time period	1990–2004	1990–94	1995–99	2000–04
Ex-communist (Eurasia)	−3.286** (.421)	−2.941** (.651)	−2.544** (.529)	−3.173** (.539)
GDP/capita	.008 (.016)	.025 (.026)	.034# (.020)	−.013 (.026)
%Urban	−.013* (.006)	−.012 (.009)	−.016* (.007)	−.009 (.008)
Secondary education enrollment	.032** (.005)	.028** (.009)	.023** (.007)	.027** (.006)
Income inequality	−.010 (.017)	−.012 (.026)	.006 (.020)	−.008 (.020)
Ethnic fractionalization	.881# (.515)	.513 (.759)	1.435** (.554)	2.060** (.614)
GDP/energy unit	.421** (.080)	.270* (.116)	.319** (.098)	.540** (.115)
Violent conflict	−.360** (.087)	−.577** (.155)	−.537** (.188)	−.170 (.184)
Raw material dependence	−.023 (.025)	−.146 (.092)	−.086* (.039)	−.073 (.045)
Population size (log)	−.643** (.066)	−.459** (.102)	−.456** (.080)	−.675** (.088)
Observations	2,271	741	765	765
Number of countries	157	157	153	153
R-sq	.47	.61	.70	.70

Prais-Winsten regression coefficients with standard errors in parentheses # significant at 10%; * significant at 5%; ** significant at 1%.

Note: Also included but not reported were region dummies, a year variable, and dummies indicating missing values for independent variables.

aspect – urbanization – actually appears to have a greater democratizing effect in the countries of the former Soviet bloc.

Nondemocratizing Education

Given that a number of observers have pointed to high education levels as one of the greatest potential assets of ex-communist countries in the regime transitions after 1990 (see, e.g., Roberts 2010), the weak relationship between education and postcommunist regime trajectories is puzzling and requires further explanation. To do so, I will first discuss two characteristics of the communist approach to education that differ from educational systems elsewhere and may help explain the uneven education effects. As a second step, I will identify a couple of possible mechanisms that link differences in the nature of education to different regime patterns.

One of the clear distinguishing features of communist education systems was their greater emphasis on technical and vocational training. While systematic cross-country data is only available starting in the late 1990s, Malamud and Pop-Eleches (2010) report that vocational enrollment as a percentage of total secondary enrollment in 1985 was significantly higher in the two communist countries for which data was available (Poland and Hungary) than for the noncommunist countries in their sample. This trend is confirmed by educational data from the World Values Survey, which reveals that, whereas ex-communist countries lagged slightly behind their noncommunist counterparts as far as university-preparatory secondary education is concerned (24% vs. 27%), in terms of technical and vocational training, ex-communist countries had a clear edge (32% vs. 21%).[14] Even within the university-preparatory secondary schools, communist education systems tended to place greater emphasis on math, science, and technical subjects, usually at the expense of social sciences and humanities. Both of these aspects were in line with the broader communist drive to promote industrial development in previously largely agrarian societies, and this push required the "mass production" of skilled industrial workers and engineers.

A second feature that set communist education systems apart from most noncommunist countries was the heavy use of ideological indoctrination and political mobilization through the school system. Despite significant variations across space and time, there were at least three mutually reinforcing ways communist states attempted to inculcate socialist values into their youngest citizens. First, starting as early as kindergarten, and going through successive steps that roughly coincided with the different stages of the educational system (e.g., pioneers in primary school, youth communist leagues in high schools, etc.), students were subjected to a mandatory political socialization process into the structures of the Communist Party. While Party membership itself was not mandatory, it was nevertheless a crucial precondition for many professional careers and was therefore much more frequent among university graduates. While many of the activities associated with these different communist organizations were either nonpolitical (e.g., the Pioneers' Houses in Romania hosted a range of activities such as pottery or drawing classes) or had only a very superficial and formulaic ideological veneer, they may have nonetheless succeeded at least partially in promoting the Party's ideological agenda. A second component, which was incorporated into the official curriculum of most schools (as early as elementary school) were various political awareness campaigns, which essentially required teachers to discuss the main news events (i.e., the latest achievements of the country's communist transformation) with the students. Last, but not least, many of the regular subjects taught in the schools – such as history, social sciences, and even literature – were based on textbooks that were heavily tilted in ideological terms to emphasize the inequities of capitalist systems and the superiority of communist ones.[15]

The obvious next question is through what mechanisms these peculiarities of the educational system may have undermined the democratizing potential of education in the postcommunist period. With respect to the heavy emphasis on technical and vocational training, one possible answer is suggested by Hillygus's (2005) finding that in the United States verbal (but not math) SAT scores and a social science curriculum are related to future political engagement. While the precise psychological mechanisms underlying this link between hard versus social science curricula and aptitude need to be explored in greater detail in future research, for the question at hand it suggests that the weaker democratizing effect of communist education could be due to the lower political participation among educated citizens. This participatory deficit may be further exacerbated to the extent that more educated postcommunist citizens reacted to the forced political participation required by the communist education systems by withdrawing from public life into the private sphere (Jowitt 1992).

Using cross-national survey evidence from the WVS, Pop-Eleches (2009) finds at least some empirical evidence for this "demobilizing education" hypothesis: first, it appears that even after controlling for a range of country-level differences and individual demographic factors, individuals with technical/vocational secondary education are less likely to participate in a range of political activities[16] than their counterparts who attended university-preparatory secondary schools (but without actually attending university). These differences are temporally resilient and substantively large: thus, according to a 2012 survey in Romania (Romanian Electoral Study 2012), respondents who attended vocational schools before 1989 were less than half as likely to report participating in legal protest actions as university-preparatory school graduates, who in turn were only half as likely to protest as college graduates. Therefore, the higher share of vocational school training in ex-communist countries is likely to help explain the postcommunist political participation deficit identified by earlier studies (Bernhard and Karakoc 2007; Pop-Eleches 2009). Second, the participatory boost among university-preparatory secondary school graduates was considerably lower in ex-communist countries than in noncommunist countries, which is consistent with the more technical nature of their curriculum and with their greater emphasis on forced political participation. Finally, even though respondents with higher education were more likely to be politically active in all types of countries, the magnitude of the effect was roughly 40 percent lower in postcommunist countries (Pop-Eleches 2009), which suggests that the demobilizing effect was not limited to secondary education.

A distinctive but related mechanism linking education to democratic outcomes is the type of participation promoted by different educational systems.

More concretely, given that as part of the broader communist political system schools provided participation opportunities that were more attractive – and in some cases were only available – to supporters of the regime, they may have shaped the value mix among active participants in the political sphere in ways that were less conducive for democracy. In other words, if the educational system – especially at the postsecondary stage – promoted the participation of enthusiastic communists (or at least opportunists) while suppressing the activities of anticommunists, then greater degrees of education would not necessarily produce the type of assertive, prodemocracy middle class that according to modernization theorists is the crucial link between development and democracy. This channel receives at least partial support from postcommunist survey data: thus, Pop-Eleches (2009) finds that even though higher education is associated with greater support for democratic values in ex-communist countries (thereby suggesting that ideological indoctrination through the educational system was not particularly effective), the political participation deficit is highest among the most educated and the most prodemocratic postcommunist citizens. This means that the mix of democrats and nondemocrats is less favorable in postcommunist countries than elsewhere, which may help explain the slower than expected democratic process in these highly educated societies.

Of course, the unfavorable relative mix of democratic values and political activism is not the only – and possibly not even the most important – driver for the disappointing democratic progress in many former communist countries. After all, authoritarian regimes may collapse even in the absence of civil society and widespread activism (Kotkin 2009), whereas in other situations even significant prodemocracy activism may be unable to topple determined authoritarian leaders willing the pay the costs of widespread repression. Nonetheless, I would argue that the extent and the nature of political mobilization patterns represent one of the key mechanisms explaining the disappointing democracy yield of the significant educational advances of communism.

The Secret Charm of Communist Cities?

The second theoretical task is to explain the strong association at the aggregate level between communist urbanization and postcommunist democratization. This link is particularly surprising given that communist urbanization was to a large extent a by-product of the coercive twin processes of collectivization and industrialization, and thus differed significantly from the more gradual growth of urban centers in Western Europe (and in precommunist Eastern Europe). Even though the outcome was rarely architecturally appealing, communist cities compare favorably to the sprawling metropolitan areas of many developing countries in a number of areas. Perhaps most important, the centrally planned nature of communist urbanization meant that urban residents had significantly better access to public services (including education, health care, and sanitation) than city dwellers in other developing countries. From this perspective, the postcommunist democratization patterns may actually confirm one of the early findings of modernization theorists whereby urbanization promoted democratization only to the extent to which it was accompanied by comparable progress in education (Lerner 1958; Lipset 1959). Thus, Eastern Europe managed to avoid the predicament of countries like Egypt, which according to Lerner had cities filled with "homeless illiterates" (Lerner 1958).

Less clear, however, is the mechanism through which the more balanced nature of communist urban development contributed to greater democratization. Given the previous discussion about the weak democracy dividends of education, the straightforward modernization theory mechanism about the rise of an educated urban middle class with both the desire and the social capital needed to pursue democracy (see, e.g., Lewin 1991) does not seem particularly persuasive. In fact, judging by recent survey evidence (Pop-Eleches 2009), even though residents of postcommunist cities displayed comparable levels of political participation as urban residents elsewhere, they actually expressed significantly weaker democratic commitments (in terms of both democratic salience and support). However, it is possible that it is precisely because of the relatively low yield of politically mobilized democrats that communist societies are more dependent on large cities to produce the critical mass of opposition activists necessary to challenge authoritarian regimes.

An alternative explanation would be to focus on patterns of electoral support among urban versus rural residents. Thus, to the extent that urban voters were more supportive of anticommunist challengers than their rural counterparts, we would expect stronger electoral showings of noncommunist parties in more urbanized postcommunist countries. Given arguments about the crucial role of initial election outcomes in shaping subsequent economic and political trajectories (Fish 1998b; McFaul 2002), it is possible that the correlation between urbanization and democracy could be due to the democratic dividends of anticommunist victories in founding elections in countries with higher shares of urban voters. This hypothesis is empirically supported by the stronger electoral backing for communist successor parties among rural voters in a number of ex-communist countries (Hough 1994; White, Rose, and McAllister 1997; Tucker 2006). However, a convincing account along these lines would also have to explain why urban residents, who were subjected to much greater ideological indoctrination than their rural counterparts (Jowitt 1992), were more likely to vote against the communists in the founding elections and subsequently. Was this a question of the developmental legacies of communism or simply the greater availability of opposition-friendly media in cities? Furthermore, it is important to remember – as the cases of Croatia, Georgia, Bulgaria, and Romania illustrate – that ousting the communists in the founding elections was neither sufficient nor necessary for subsequent democracy. Therefore, such an initial election-based account has to be complemented by explanations emphasizing the links between urbanization and civic and political mobilization.

Conclusion and Implications

This chapter has started from the empirical puzzle and theoretical challenge posed by the disappointing postcommunist regime trajectories of the countries of the former Soviet bloc. From a modernization theory perspective, this surprisingly weak performance is at odds with the widespread (and at least partially justified) perception that despite their problematic "methods," communists were actually quite effective in modernizing the societies over which they ruled. The comparative evaluation of communist developmental achievements in the first part of this chapter revealed a highly uneven track record, whereby strong achievements in education and income equality were balanced by more modest progress in economic development and considerably higher economic distortions.

The analysis of cross-national regime patterns in the second part of the chapter suggests that ex-communist countries stood out not only with respect to their peculiar mix of developmental strengths and weaknesses, but also in the nature of the link between various development aspects and democracy. In particular, the much weaker democratizing effects of education in ex-communist countries question the implicit assumption of causal homogeneity of many earlier studies of the development-democracy link and emphasize the need to pay closer attention to the nature of development and not only to the "amount of development."

Finally, this chapter has focused on individual-level democratic attitudes and political participation to propose a causal mechanism that accounts for the surprisingly weak democratic performance of the fairly developed ex-communist countries. Survey evidence suggests that communist development – particularly education – yielded weaker dividends in terms of both political participation and the salience of democratic concerns, and therefore postcommunist countries ended up with lower than expected concentrations of active democrats than other countries at similar levels of socioeconomic development. Because politically mobilized democrats are important both for challenging authoritarian regimes and for defending unconsolidated democracies, this lack of a democratic participatory culture at the level of individual citizens translated into a widespread weakness of democratic constituencies at the societal level. This developmentally rooted weakness helps us explain the slow and uneven democratic progress of the countries of the former Soviet bloc. But it needs to be complemented by other explanations to account for the wide variety of authoritarian and semi-authoritarian regimes – ranging from Niyazov's bizarre brand of sultanism in Turkmenistan to the ethnocracy of Milosevic's Serbia – that have emerged in the region since the fall of communism.

Notes

1. After years of relative neglect, in which much of the debate focused on the role of more proximate factors in explaining the Third Wave of democratization (O'Donnell et al. 1986; Di Palma 1990; Karl and Schmitter 1991; Przeworski 1991), several statistically sophisticated approaches (e.g., Przeworski and Limongi 1997; Barro 1999;

Boix and Stokes 2003; Epstein et al. 2006) have assessed the impact of socioeconomic development on the initiation and survival of democracy.

2. Interesting, earlier analysts noted the surprising coexistence of high economic development and nondemocracy among the communist countries, but they generally expected that the communist regimes' ability to resist political liberalization pressures through violent repression would decline in the long run and therefore make them vulnerable to political liberalization pressures (see, e.g., Dallin and Breslauer 1970; Eckstein 1970; Dahl 1971).

3. The data is based on the temporally closest census for the given country. I measure urbanization as the proportion of a country's population living in towns with at least fifty thousand inhabitants, which allows me to get around some of the problems connected to cross-national differences in urbanization definitions. I obtained very similar results using different town size cutoffs (e.g., 20,000 or 100,000).

4. Because many of the estimates were imprecise, I used a five-point scale to measure literacy (see Table 2.1).

5. The timing of these statistical snapshots is justified by the fact that prior to World War I very little data is available for Eastern Europe (most countries were not yet independent), but at the same time it largely precedes the first significant Soviet modernization push and therefore captures most of the developmental effects of communism.

6. I used Prais-Winsten regressions with panel-corrected standard errors and corrections for serial autocorrelation and heteroskedasticity.

7. The scores were reversed to yield a zero to twelve scale whereby higher scores indicate greater democracy. I obtained similar results using Polity regime scores and Vanhanen's polyarchy indicator, but the results are omitted here because of space considerations.

8. For a more detailed description of the variables used in the regressions, see Table 2.1.

9. To test whether these estimates are affected by the choice of time period and whether the postcommunist democracy deficit declines over time as the communist legacy fades into the past, I reran the analysis in model 3 on three different subperiods (1990–94, 1995–99, and 2000–04). However, the postcommunist deficit was highly significant for all periods, while its magnitude declined slightly in the mid-1990s but then increased again after 2000 and in fact surpassed the deficit from the early 1990s (see Table 2.4).

10. Note that similar changes did not occur if I introduced dummy indicators for other geographic regions, which further confirms the developmental exceptionalism of communism (results available from the author).

11. One possible explanation is that communist cities may have integrated their inhabitants to a greater extent in urban life than the large slums of many developing country metropolitan areas – however, this is merely conjecture and deserves greater attention in future research.

12. This group includes twelve Eastern European countries (but not newly independent Montenegro, for which little data is available), the fifteen former Soviet republics, and Mongolia.

13. One may of course argue about whether the transition really ended in 2004, but because that was the year when a third of the countries in my sample joined the EU, it provided a logical endpoint for my statistical analysis.

14 Because these surveys were done after 1990, some of the data is arguably "contaminated" by postcommunist educational reforms, but if anything this is likely to understate the magnitude of the difference (and indeed the differences are larger if we restrict the analysis to the pre-1999 period).
15 As the author can attest, in extreme cases such as Ceausescu's Romania, modern history was almost exclusively a history of the rise and triumph of communism in a given country.
16 The dependent variable for this analysis was an index based on four WVS questions that asked respondents whether they had signed a petition, joined a boycott, participated in a political demonstration or illegal strike, or occupied a building. See Pop-Eleches (2009) for additional details.

References

Aslund, Anders. 2001. "The Myth of Output Collapse after Communism." *Working Paper* vol. 18, Washington, DC: Carnegie Endowment for International Peace.
Bahry, Donna. 1993. "Society Transformed? Rethinking the Social Roots of Perestroika." *Slavic Review* 52(3): 512–54.
Barro, Robert. 1999. "Determinants of Democracy." *The Journal of Political Economy* 107(6): 158–86.
Beissinger, Mark. 2002. *Nationalist Mobilization and the Collapse of the Soviet State*. New York: Cambridge University Press.
Beissinger, Mark 2006. "Promoting Democracy: Is Exporting Revolution a Constructive Strategy?" *Dissent* 53(1): 18–24.
Bernhard, Michael and Ekrem Karakoç. 2007. "Civil Society and the Legacies of Dictatorship." *World Politics* 59(4): 539–67.
Boix, Carles and Susan Stokes. 2003. "Endogenous Democratization." *World Politics* 55(4): 517–49.
Bunce, Valerie. 1998. "Regional Differences in Democratization: The East Versus the South." *Post-Soviet Affairs*, July–Sept., 187.
Chen, Cheng and Rudra Sil. 2007. "Stretching Postcommunism: Diversity, Context, and Comparative Historical Analysis." *Post-Soviet Affairs* 23(4): 275–301.
Crawford, Beverly and Arend Lijphart, eds. 1997. *Liberalization and Leninist Legacies: Comparative Perspectives on Democratic Transitions*. Berkeley, CA: International and Area Studies.
Dahl, Robert A. 1971. *Polyarchy: Participation and Opposition*. New Haven, CT: Yale University Press.
Dallin, Alexander and George Breslauer. 1970. *Political Terror in Communist Systems*. Stanford, CA: Stanford University Press.
Darden, Keith and Anna Grzymala-Busse. 2006. "The Great Divide: Precommunist Schooling and Postcommunist Trajectories." *World Politics* 59(1): 83–115.
Deutsch, Karl W. 1953. "The Growth of Nations: Some Recurrent Patterns of Political and Social Integration." *World Politics* 5(2): 168–95.
Di Palma, Giuseppe. 1990. *To Craft Democracies: An Essay on Democratic Transitions*. Berkeley: University of California Press.
Diamond, Larry Jay and Marc F. Plattner. 1996. *The Global Resurgence of Democracy*. 2nd ed. Baltimore, MD: Johns Hopkins University Press.

EBRD (2001). *Transition Report 2001: Energy in Transition*. London: European Bank for Reconstruction and Development.
Eckstein, Alexander. 1970. "Economic Development and Political Change in Communist Systems." *World Politics* 22: 475–95.
Epstein, David L., Robert Bates, Jack Goldstone, Ida Kristensen, and Sharyn O'Halloran. 2006. "Democratic Transitions." *American Journal of Political Science* 50(3): 551.
Finkel, Steven E., Andrew Green, Aníbal Pérez-Liñán, Mitchell Seligson, and C. Neal Tate. "Cross-National Research on USAID's Democracy and Governance Programs-Codebook (Phase II)." Accessed December 7, 2008) from http://www.pitt.edu/~politics/democracy/downloads/Codebook_Phase_2.pdf.
Fish, M. Steven. 1998a. "Democratization's Requisites: The Postcommunist Experience." *Post-Soviet Affairs*, July–Sept., 212.
  1998b. "The Determinants of Economic Reform in the Post-Communist World." *East European Politics and Societies* 12(1): 31.
Freedom House. 2005. *Freedom in the World 2005: Civic Power and Electoral Politics*. New York: Freedom House.
Green, Andrew T. 2002. "Comparative Development of Post-communist Civil Societies." *Europe-Asia Studies* 54(3): 455–71.
Grzymala-Busse, Anna. 2002. *Redeeming the Communist Past: The Regeneration of Communist Parties in East Central Europe*. Cambridge: Cambridge University Press.
Hanson, Stephen and Jeffrey S. Kopstein. 1997. "The Weimar/Russia Comparison," *Post-Soviet Affairs* 13(3): 252–83.
Hillygus, D. Sunshine. 2005. "The Missing Link: Exploring the Relationship between Higher Education and Political Engagement." *Political Behavior* 27: 25–47.
Horowitz, Shale. 2003. "Sources of Post-communist Democratization: Economic Structure, Political Culture, War, and Political Institutions." *Nationalities Papers* 31 (2003): 119–37.
Hosking, Geoffrey A. 1991. *The Awakening of the Soviet Union*. Cambridge, MA: Harvard University Press.
Hough, Jerry F. 1994. "The Russian Election of 1993: Public Attitudes toward Economic Reform and Democratization," *Post-Soviet Affairs* 10(1): 1–37.
Hough, Jerry F. 1997. *Democratization and Revolution in the USSR, 1985–1991*. Washington, DC: Brookings Institution Press.
Howard, Marc Morje. 2002. "The Weakness of Postcommunist Civil Society." *Journal of Democracy* 13(1): 157–69.
  2003. *The Weakness of Civil Society in Post-Communist Europe*. New York: Cambridge University Press.
Janos, Andrew C. 2000. *East Central Europe in the Modern World: The Politics of the Borderlands from Pre- to Postcommunism*. Stanford, CA: Stanford University Press.
Jowitt, Ken. 1992. *New World Disorder: The Leninist Extinction*. Berkeley, CA: University of California Press.
Karatnycky, Adrian, Alexander J. Motyl, Amanda Schnetzer, and Freedom House (U.S.). 2001. *Nations in Transit, 2001: Civil Society, Democracy, and Markets in East Central Europe and the Newly Independent states*. New Brunswick, NJ: Transaction Publishers.

Karl, Terry L. and Philippe C. Schmitter. 1991. "Modes of Transition in Latin America, Southern and Eastern Europe." *International Social Science Journal* (May 1991): 269–84.

Kopstein, Jeffrey. 2003. "Postcommunist Democracy – Legacies and Outcomes." *Comparative Politics* 35(2): 231–+.

Kopstein, Jeffrey and David Reilly. 2000. "Geographic Diffusion and the Transformation of the Postcommunist World." *World Politics* 53(1): 1–37.

Kornai, János. 1992. *The Socialist System: The Political Economy of Communism.* Princeton, NJ: Princeton University Press.

Kotkin, Stephen. 2009. *Uncivil Society: 1989 and the Implosion of the Communist Establishment.* New York: Random House.

Kurtz, Marcus J. and Andrew Barnes. 2002. "The Political Foundations of Postcommunist Regimes – Marketization, Agrarian Legacies, or International Influences." *Comparative Political Studies* 35(5): 524–53.

Lahmeyer, Jan. 1999. Populstat Web site: http://www.library.uu.nl/wesp/populstat/populhome.html Lerner.

Lerner, Daniel. 1958. *The Passing of Traditional Society.* Glencoe: The Free Press.

Lewin, Moshe. 1991. *The Gorbachev Phenomenon.* Berkeley, CA: University of California Press.

Lipset, Seymour Martin. 1959 "Some Social Requisites of Democracy." *American Political Science Review* 53(1): 69–105.

Malamud, Ofer and Cristian Pop-Eleches. 2010. "General Education versus Vocational Training: Evidence from an Economy in Transition." *Review of Economics and Statistics* 92(1): 43–60.

McFaul, Michael. 2002. "The Fourth Wave of Democracy and Dictatorship – Noncooperative Transitions in the Postcommunist World." *World Politics* 54(2): 212–+.

Mishler, William and Richard Rose. 1996. "Trajectories of Fear and Hope: Support for Democracy in Post-communist Europe." *Comparative Political Studies* 28(4): 553–81.

O'Donnell, Guillermo A., Philippe C. Schmitter, and Laurence Whitehead. 1986. *Transitions from Authoritarian Rule.* Baltimore, MD: Johns Hopkins University Press.

Parsons, Talcott. 1967. *Sociological Theory and Modern Society.* New York: Free Press.

Pop-Eleches, Grigore. 1999. "Separated at Birth or Separated by Birth? The Communist Successor Parties in Romania and Hungary." *East European Politics and Societies* 13(1): 117–47.

Pop-Eleches, Grigore. 2007. "Historical Legacies and Post-Communist Regime Change." *The Journal of Politics,* 69: 908–26.

 2009. "The Post-Communist Democratic Deficit: Roots and Mechanisms." *Annual Meeting of the American Association for the Advancement of Slavic Studies,* Nov. 12–15, Boston, MA.

Pop-Eleches, Grigore and Joshua A. Tucker. 2013a. "Associated with the Past? Communist Legacies and Civic Participation in Post-Communist Countries." *East European Politics & Societies* 27(1): 45–68.

 2013b. "Communist Socialization and Post-Communist Economic and Political Attitudes." *Electoral Studies* 33(1): 77–89.

Przeworski, Adam. 1991. *Democracy and the Market*. Cambridge: Cambridge University Press.
Przeworski, Adam and Fernando Limongi. 1997. "Modernization: Theories and Facts." *World Politics* 49(2): 155–83.
Remington, Thomas F. 1990. "Regime Transition in Communist Systems: The Soviet Case." *Soviet Economy* 6(2): 160–90.
Roberts, Andrew. *The Quality of Democracy in Eastern Europe: Public Preferences and Policy Reforms*. Cambridge University Press, 2010.
Rohrschneider, Robert. 1999. *Learning Democracy: Democratic and Economic Values in Unified Germany*. Oxford: Oxford University Press.
Romanian Electoral Study 2012. *Change and Stability in Romanian Electoral Behaviour, 2009–2014*. http://resproject.wordpress.com/.
Tucker, Joshua A. 2006. *Regional Economic Voting: Russia, Poland, Hungary, Slovakia, and the Czech Republic, 1990–99*. New York: Cambridge University Press.
UNESCO. 1953. *Progress of literacy in various countries: A preliminary statistical study of available census data since 1900*. Paris: United Nations Educational Scientific, and Cultural Organization.
UNESCO. 2013. *Adult and youth literacy: National, regional and global trends, 1985–2015*. Montreal: United Nations Educational Scientific, and Cultural Organization.
UNU-WIDER. 2008. *World Income Inequality Database*, Version 2.0c, May 2008. Available at http://www.wider.unu.edu/research/Database/en_GB/database/.
Vachudova, Milada Anna. 2005. *Europe Undivided: Democracy, Leverage, and Integration after Communism*, Oxford: Oxford University Press.
Varshney, Ashutosh. 2001. "Ethnic Conflict and Civil Society: India and Beyond." *World Politics* 53: 362–98.
Vassilev, Rossen. 1999. "Modernization Theory Revisited: The Case of Bulgaria." *East European Politics and Societies* 13(3): 566–99.
White, Stephen, Richard Rose, and Ian McAllister. 1997. *How Russia Votes*. Chatham, NJ: Chatham House Publishers.
Whitehead, Laurence. 1996. "Democracy and Decolonization: East-Central Europe." In L. Whitehead, ed., *The International Dimensions of Democratization: Europe and the Americas*. Oxford; New York: Oxford University Press: 356–89.
World Development Indicators. 2012. Washington, DC: The World Bank.

3

Room for Error: The Economic Legacy of Soviet Spatial Misallocation

Clifford G. Gaddy

In 1989, Thane Gustafson argued that the most important legacy of the Soviet economic system would not be its institutional features – its flawed systems of information, incentives, and decision making – but rather the accumulated physical effects of that malfunctioning system.

> Western writers sometimes seem to liken the Soviet system to a sailboat straining against an unfavorable wind. Change the wind, we seem to say, and the boat will quickly right itself. But a more appropriate metaphor for the Soviet economy is that of a gnarled tree that has grown up leaning against the north wind of force-draft industrialization. Its past is written into the composition and location of its capital stock, the patterns of its roads and railroads, the size and type of its plants, the distribution of its manpower, the kinds of fuel it burns and ore it uses. Even a perfect leader and a perfect reform, whatever those might be, could not right in a generation what has taken two generations to form.[1]

More than twenty years later, Gustafson's words seem prophetic. The "structure of capital and economic activity"[2] bequeathed to Russia by the Soviet Union has indeed been a major obstacle to changing the entire system. Yet there is something of an irony here. After all, the issue of dealing with the physical assets of past periods is at the very heart of the market economy system. The classic textbook definition of economics is the allocation of scarce resources to the best ends. But this is a *static* problem. There is also a more essential *dynamic* problem. The dynamic economics problem is *re*-allocation of resources to highest-value ends as relative values change. The reallocation problem arises because existing assets (those passed forward from the previous period) are subject to continuous shocks. Their value, or the value of the configurations of which they are a part, changes as tastes and technologies change and as the scope and quality of information change. Economic decision makers (and this includes not just government officials or corporate CEOs, but households and individuals) thus constantly face the challenge of finding new allocations so as to give maximum value to the assets they have from the past period.

Indeed, the fundamentals of a market economy boil down to the institutions that best ensure that impediments to reallocation are removed. Protection of property rights is necessary to guarantee that the owner has both the right to freely dispose of assets (to make them as productive as possible) and the right to profit from a better use of the assets (so as to have an incentive to question the status quo and to look for alternatives). Transparency promotes the completeness and accuracy of information about the value of assets in different configurations, existing and hypothetical. Competition is needed to ensure that as many of the known configurations as possible are tested and new and better ones are invented or discovered.

Whether to reallocate to the known optimal configuration or reallocate to test a hitherto unknown one, the agent's assets must be mobile and liquid. They must be free of binding commitments. The models of neoclassical economics assumed perfect competition, complete information, and thoroughly unfettered mobility of assets. With Ronald Coase's work, the role of transaction costs was introduced. The presence of transition costs imposes constraints on reallocation. It is here that economic legacies cease to be neutral and the "legacy problem" arises.

The legacy problem emerges when the amount, the nature, or the disposition of the inherited assets constrains future reallocation.[3] Assets are rendered immobile or illiquid and are thus not freely re-allocable. Such constraints force the owners of assets, or those who decide on their allocation, to make suboptimal choices. The key question is: What is the (opportunity) cost of not being able to make the optimum allocation? And how difficult is it to remove the constraints? That is, how difficult is it to overcome the legacy?

The Legacy of Spatial Misallocation

There are many dimensions to the negative legacy of accumulated physical allocation decisions that the Soviet Union passed on to post-Soviet Russia. This chapter addresses only one: the spatial dimension. Seen from the vantage point of the market economy that succeeded it, the Soviet economic system produced the "wrong things" in the "wrong way."[4] It also produced them in the "wrong places," to an extreme degree. Part of the reason is a fact of nature and history. Russia has far more territory and more *cold* territory than any other country in the world. Because distance (remoteness) and cold both impede economic activity and interaction, Russia has greater objective potential for incurring added costs of space.

The key word is "potential," for the primary issue is not Russia's size or the cold territories per se. It is the location of people and economic activity within that space. No matter how vast and how cold Russia is by nature, it can be made relatively better or worse off by policies of economic location. It is precisely with respect to location policy that Russia represents a contrast to other countries endowed with cold territories. Canadians live predominantly in the warmest (southernmost) part of the country. The same pattern is true in the Scandinavian countries. Their populations are concentrated along the coasts and in the south, where temperatures are not significantly different from the rest of Europe.

Russia, by contrast, has a much greater proportion of its population (especially its urban population) in the colder and more remote regions. With respect to cold alone, a comparison between Russia, on the one hand, and Canada and the United States, on the other, is instructive. A list of the 100 coldest Russian and North American cities with populations of more than one hundred thousand would have eighty-five Russian, ten Canadian, and five U.S. cities. The coldest Canadian city on the list (Winnipeg) would be in twenty-second place. The coldest U.S. city (Fargo, North Dakota) would rank fifty-eighth. Many Americans are accustomed to thinking of Alaska as the ultimate cold region. But Anchorage, Alaska, would not appear on the list until position number one hundred thirty-five, outranked by no fewer than one hundred twelve Russian cities.[5] For really large cities, the contrast is even starker. The United States has only one metro area with more half a million people (Minneapolis-St. Paul) that has a mean January temperature colder than -8° Celsius. Russia has thirty cities that big and that cold.

The important point is that Russia has not always been like this. At the time of the Bolshevik Revolution in 1917, the coldest of the ten largest cities in the territory of what is today's Russian Federation was Kazan', which had an average January temperature of -13.2°C. By 1970, there were five cities in the top ten that were colder than Kazan'. The new members of the list all lay to the east of Kazan', three in the Urals region and two in Siberia. They each had a population of more than a million. The growth of large, cold, distant cities reflected how much the Soviet Union had pushed its urban population eastward.

The argument of this chapter is that the population was pushed too far eastward. From the standpoint of efficiency in a market economy, Siberia, the Russian Far East, and other remote and eastern locations in Russia are overpopulated, and this is a result of Soviet policies. The geographic location of industry in the Soviet economy was not guided by economic principles. It was done under a system that could not recognize the costs. Factories were built in locations that market-oriented entrepreneurs would not have chosen. Millions of people live in places where they would not be living if they (or their parents or grandparents) had been free to choose. The resulting population distribution is anomalous. It is one of the costliest legacies of the Soviet system. The overdevelopment of large cities in cold and remote places is not likely to be corrected for decades to come, if ever. But as long as it lasts, it is not only costly in terms of the current performance of the economy, but it also constrains policy for the future.

Origin of the Legacy: How Did It Happen?

The following sections will examine the origins of the distorted population distribution, the scale of the distortion, its costs, and, finally, the extent to which the country has been able to correct it.

Running like a red thread through the history of the spatial allocation of economic activity in the USSR is an obsession with national security. It began with the imperative for development of a domestic natural resource base. Stalin wanted the USSR to eliminate the country's economic dependence on the hostile imperialist world. The USSR had all the required resources. Developing them was an absolute imperative.

The geographical dimension was central. The resources themselves were in remote and thoroughly undeveloped regions, predominantly in Siberia. At the end of the tsarist period, the interior of Siberia was barely charted, let alone settled. Large-scale settlement and urbanization of Siberia were not possible under the tsars. The costs were too onerous for their market-oriented economy. Only the Soviet Union – a totalitarian state with coercion at its core, with its highly centralized control of production and redistribution of resources, and with absolutely no sense of cost – could conquer Siberia. The instrument for doing so was the Gulag.

Stalin's 1929 decree establishing the Gulag was explicit on this point. It ordered the OGPU (the name for the security police agency at the time) to set up a network of labor camps "to colonize the least accessible and most difficult to develop" regions of the country, that is, "Siberia, the North, the Far East, and Central Asia."

The Gulag, aptly described by Valery Lazarev (2003, 190) as "a system of coerced labor disguised as a penitentiary institution," had to be massively expanded to manage the task. At the time of the original 1929 order, the handful of prison camps that existed in the USSR had a population of about twenty-three thousand inmates. By 1934, half a million Soviet citizens were in the Gulag. Stalin's great purges of the late 1930s brought the total camp population to more than 2 million. In all, an estimated 18–20 million Gulag inmates over the span of slightly more than two decades did more than exploit timber and mineral resources. They also laid railroads, constructed roads and dams, dug canals, developed oil fields, and built factories and farms in unpopulated remote areas. They thereby created the enduring legacy of spatial allocation that was bequeathed to today's Russia, one that would have been impossible with free labor.[6]

The Gulag was largely dismantled after Stalin's death, but the imperative of developing Siberia had taken on a life of its own. Many motives converged in the postwar development of Siberia. Communist economic planners continued to insist on the importance of Siberia's natural resources as a way to make the Soviet Union self-sufficient in strategic raw materials. During the war, military planners had begun to reconceptualize western Siberia as a strategic redoubt – a defensible core deep in the interior – they wanted to ensure that the entire region was settled and secured. Not least, the development of Siberia was viewed as an ideological imperative: communism had to prove it could do what capitalism could not. Notions of rationality and efficiency were thereby turned on their head. Nowhere is this expressed more clearly than in a 1957 work by Andrei N. Lagovskii, the "first military economist" in the Soviet Union. General Lagovskii was the founder and first chairman of the Department of Military Economics of the Soviet General Staff Academy. In a section on "the geographical location of productive forces," his textbook emphasized that the very idea of allowing cost-benefit thinking to dictate something deemed so fundamental to planning as industrial location and city development made a mockery of the communist ideal. Socialist countries, he wrote, do not suffer from the "uneven and irrational" location of productive forces that characterizes the capitalist countries. The problem with capitalism is that "industry spontaneously develops in those regions where it brings the quickest and greatest profits.... Meanwhile, vast territories of the borderlands of the country and the colonies remain totally undeveloped in terms of industry." In this sense, Lagovskii asserted, "Tsarist Russia was a prime example of inefficient location of industry from the point of view of the overall state interests." But: "The Great October Socialist Revolution ... put an end to irrational location of new construction of industrial enterprises. In the process of construction of socialism, the ugly legacy of capitalist location of productive forces was gradually liquidated, although it has not yet been completely overcome."[7]

Extent of the Distortion

Fortunately, even another three decades of communist planning after Lagovskii was not enough to completely overcome "the ugly legacy of capitalist location of productive forces." But enough nonmarket location decisions were made to leave a legacy that was very different from the one capitalism would have produced. The extent of the difference can only be measured against a benchmark. We need to estimate the counterfactual population of cities and regions as they might have developed in a market economy and then ask how that compares to the actual population. In this and the next section we will cite findings from a project entitled "The Cost of the Cold" to estimate the economic cost of the distortion.[8] That work used three approaches to calculate "market-natural" populations. First, case studies were made for individual Russian cities, and their evolution during the Soviet period was compared to that of similar cities in market economies. Second, a larger set of Russia's cities was examined, and in light of their own pre-Soviet histories and on the basis of certain regularities of city-size distributions in the rest of the world, an assumed trajectory of those cities' sizes was projected forward from the beginning of the Soviet period until the end. Third, a counterfactual evolution of population distribution in

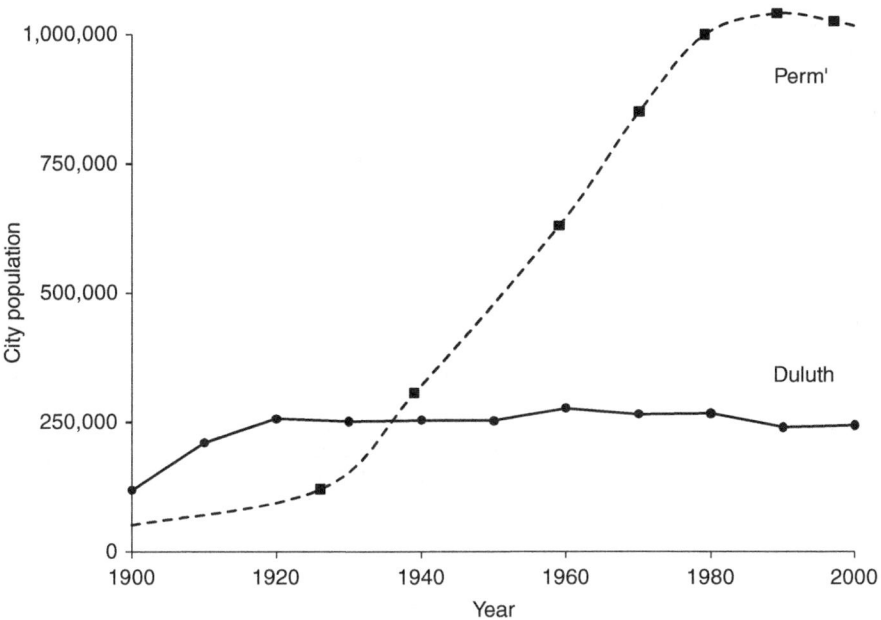

FIGURE 3.1. Duluth and Perm: twentieth-century population growth.

the entire country was modeled using the historical dynamics of the Canadian economy as a benchmark.

Figure 3.1 is from a case study of two cities – Duluth, Minnesota, and Perm, Russia.[9] These two cities are similar in terms of climate and location (distance from markets). They began the twentieth century roughly the same size, and in succeeding decades both would aspire to become major manufacturing centers. Between 1900 and 1910, Duluth was one of America's fastest-growing cities, as its population rose from one hundred nineteen thousand to two hundred eleven thousand. When the United States Steel Corporation announced it would build a huge steel plant there, there were predictions that Duluth would become a new Pittsburgh, Detroit, or even Chicago. However, U.S. Steel's huge investments proved to be a mistake. Duluth's extremely cold climate and its distance from major iron and steel markets squelched the dreams of greatness. It stopped growing. The result is that today fewer than two hundred fifty thousand people live in metropolitan Duluth-Superior – about the same number as in 1920. The case of Duluth was described in the classic 1937 article by economic geographers Langdon White and George Primmer, subtitled "A Study in Locational Maladjustment."

A few decades later, the Urals city of Perm underwent similar explosive growth. From a population of sixty-seven thousand in 1923, Russia's thirty-first largest city, it tripled in size by 1939 to become Russia's thirteenth largest. Virtually all the growth came from defense industry, as a dozen plants, each of which would eventually have more than ten thousand workers, located in

TABLE 3.1. *Actual and Counterfactual Market Economy Populations of Selected Russian Cities*

City	Population in Thousands (1997)	
	Actual	Counterfactual "Market"
Novosibirsk	1,367	?*
Yekaterinburg	1,275	406
Omsk	1,158	351
Chelyabinsk	1,084	< 250
Ufa	1,082	520
Perm	1,025	433
Krasnoyarsk	874	271

* Because Novosibirsk, in contrast to the other cities in the table, had not yet emerged as a city prior to the Russian Revolution, it had no historical trajectory on which to base an estimate of the counterfactual market-economy population.

Perm. Objectively, Perm faced even greater competitive disadvantages of cold and remoteness than Duluth. But Perm continued to grow far longer than Duluth had. The difference was that Perm's growth was decided by communist central planners, while Duluth's was ultimately constrained by the market. As Figure 3.1 shows, Perm's population did eventually slow down and plateau, but not until the 1980s. This did not reflect so much a change in the planners' policy as a sheer lack of physical resources (including people) that could be moved there. Since the late 1980s, Perm's population has even declined slightly. But it remains larger than Duluth (in fact, larger than the entire Duluth-Superior, Wisconsin, metropolitan area) by a factor of four.

Individual studies of other Russian cities showed that some followed the pattern of Perm, growing larger than one would have expected in a market economy, while others grew less. A further step was to determine a more complete counterfactual Russian population distribution by imagining what the sizes of Russia's largest cities would have been if the urban population had been distributed relatively as it was prior to the Bolshevik Revolution of 1917, when it was concentrated in the European part of the country. In the simulation of a counterfactual "virtual" history, the Siberian and Urals cities were not prohibited from growing. It was merely assumed that they would continue to grow at the same pace as they had before the advent of communist planning.[10] Table 3.1 shows the results for a few large cities. According to this calculation, these cities' current populations are two to four times larger than what would have been expected in the absence of Soviet policies. The difference between the actual and the counterfactual populations – the "excess" population – is the Soviet legacy.

To simulate a desired benchmark population distribution for the country as a whole, the Cost of the Cold Project used a comparison with Canada, a country also big in territory and endowed with natural resources (Mikhailova 2004). The idea was to take Canada as a proxy for a market economy, control for Russia's distribution of natural resources, distance to markets, transportation routes and costs, and climate, as well as Russia's initial (1910) conditions, and then apply the Canadian dynamics of investment and population movement. In other words, the exercise asked, what would have happened if Russians had behaved like Canadians? The simulation showed that Siberia (western and eastern) and the Far Eastern regions of Russia ended up with excess populations of between 10 million and 15 million people.[11]

The idea that Siberia is overpopulated of course flies in the face of much conventional wisdom, particularly in the internal Russian debate. But Siberia and the Russian Far East are not underpopulated in an international comparison. Compare Eastern Siberia and the Russian Far East with Alaska in terms of their relative shares of population and territory for Russia and the United States. If Alaska had been populated according to the Soviet model, it would have today not seven hundred ten thousand residents, but 13 million. Similarly, a "Soviet" Canada would have put 1.5 million people in its Northwest Territory and Yukon Territory instead of the seventy-nine thousand who actually reside there now. Conversely, if Eastern Siberia and the Russian Far East had followed the American and Canadian patterns, they would in total have barely one million residents instead of their current 15 million.

The Cost of the Distortion

The Cost of the Cold Project, as the name implies, focused only on one dimension of the cost of the geographical location of economic activity. The discussion later in this chapter will follow that approach. But it is important to recognize that there is more to the legacy of location than simply temperature. Cold is only one part of climate more generally. The nature of the terrain is important, that is, whether the land is mountainous or otherwise not suitable for construction and transport. Proximity to cheaper transportation routes, especially river and sea-based transportation as opposed to overland transportation, is important. Finally, there is the pure effect of distance. Distance is the most basic obstacle to all economic interaction in market economies. This is typically thought of in terms of transportation costs. But it is more. When potential exchange partners are separated from one another physically, they are less likely to know about each other or to know what goods and services that they have to offer or that they demand. They are less likely to know the other's reputation. They are less likely to share the same social networks. Trust is lower. Consequently, trade, investment, and migration diminish with increasing distance, whether across borders or within countries.[12] The result is a loss of efficiency.

The costs of cold are twofold. The first are the direct costs, owing to the fact that cold reduces the work efficiency of both humans and machines and causes damage to buildings, equipment, infrastructure, agriculture, fishing, and

TABLE 3.2. *TPCs of the United States and Three Northern Countries, Around 1930*

Country and Year	TPC (°C)
United States 1930	1.1
Sweden 1930	−3.9
Canada 1931	−9.9
Russia 1926	−11.6

to human beings (including deaths). The second type of costs are adaptation costs. These include expenditures of energy for heating and extra materials (including special materials) that are used in the construction of buildings and infrastructure – in general, all the money and effort that goes into protecting or at least buffering society from the cold.

To sum up the total cost of misallocation in "temperature space," the Cost of the Cold Project began with a simple analytical concept – "temperature per capita" (TPC). TPC is a population-weighted index of the average January temperature of a region or country.[13] Climate scientists typically report country temperatures as an "average national temperature," which is the mean of recorded temperatures spaced as evenly as possible across the territory of the country. For economic studies, however, this is inadequate. To discuss the role of temperature across countries in an economically meaningful way, we need to account for the fact that climate varies within a country and economic activity (population) is not uniformly distributed across territories. In other words, what is important is the temperature of places where people actually live and work.

TPC is a single index that sums up all the issues of population distribution seen in the city examples cited earlier. It allows comparison of the temperature of one country with that of another in an economically meaningful way, addressing, for instance, the issue of whether Russia is economically colder than Canada or other northern countries, and by how much. As the data in Table 3.2 illustrate, around 1930, as Russia entered the period of central economic planning, it was already "economically colder" than not only the United States, but also Sweden and Canada. It was more than a degree and a half colder than Canada and well more than seven degrees colder than Sweden.

But what is particularly noteworthy is the contrast between what happened in Russia and in the other countries in the subsequent period. Measured by its TPC, a country can become warmer or colder not (only) because of global warming or cooling, but because of population movement. If a country's territory offers a range of temperature zones, its TPC could theoretically rise or fall if people moved to warmer or colder regions. It is thus meaningful to ask, for instance, whether Russia today is economically colder than it was in 1917. Figures 3.2a and 3.2b show that it is. Russia's TPC declined steadily

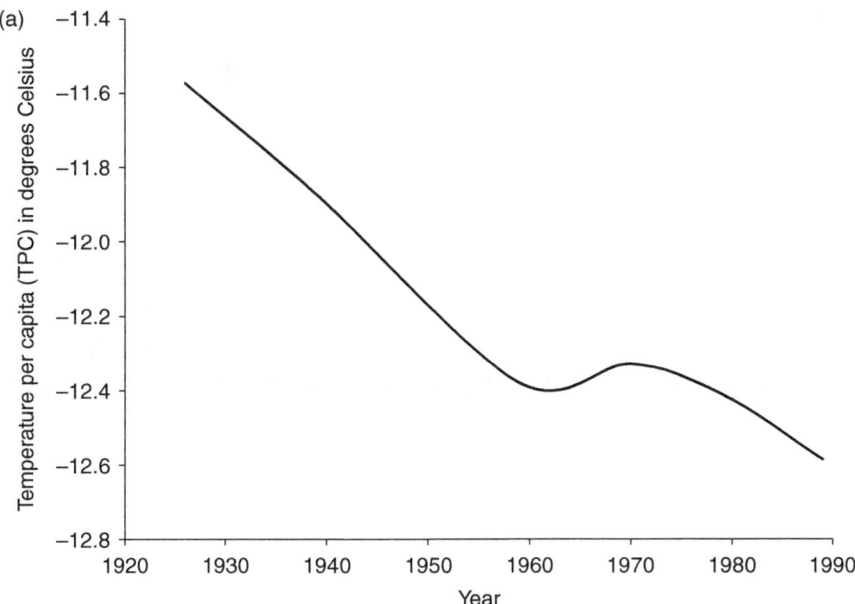

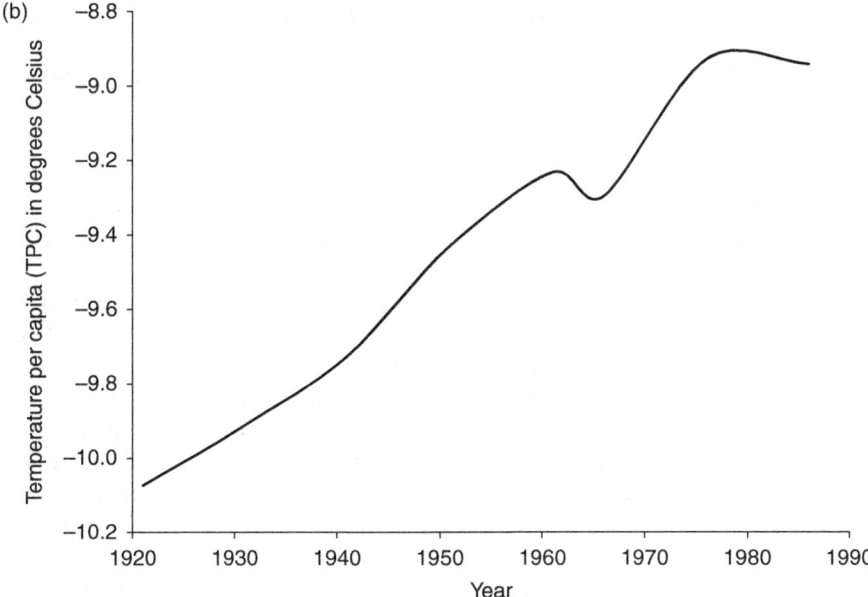

FIGURE 3.2. (a) Russia's TPC, 1920s–1990 (b) Canada's TPC, 1920s–1990.

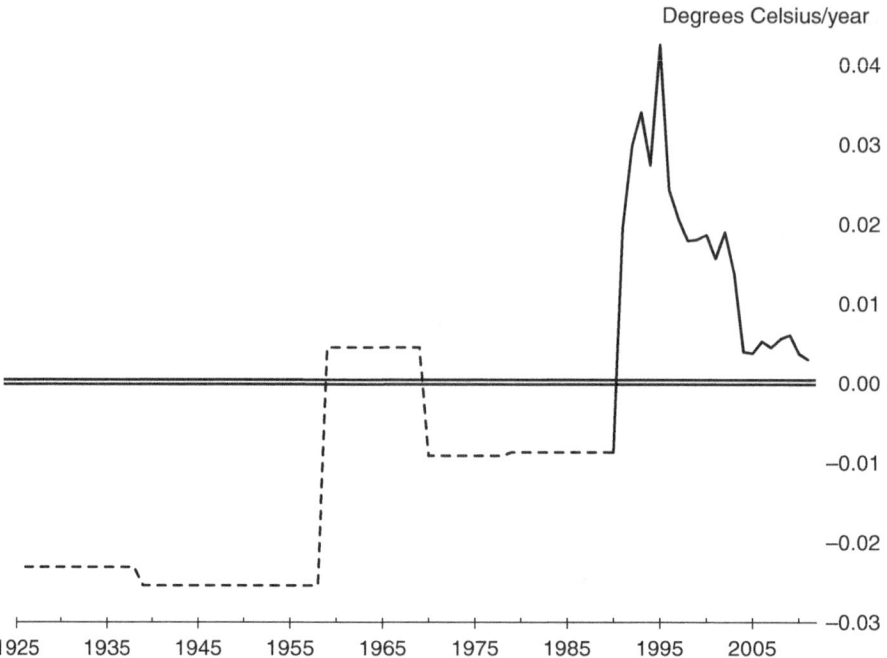

FIGURE 3.3. Russia's economic cooling/warming rate, 1926–2011 (annual rate of change in TPC).
Note: Values shown for the intervals 1930–38, 1939–58, 1959–70, 1971–79, and 1980–90 are averages for each period.

during the Soviet era, ending up a full degree colder by 1989 (Figure 3.2a), while Canada's TPC rose by more than one degree during the same period (Figure 3.2b).

The next step in using the TPC for analysis is to translate the findings regarding the difference between the actual and hypothetical ("market") population distributions of Russia from population numbers and locations into degrees of TPC. It turns out that Mikhailova's counterfactual, Canada-like Russia of 1990 would have been as much as 1.5 degrees warmer than Russia actually was by the end of the Soviet period. (That is, without Soviet policies, the TPC would have risen by 0.5 degrees; with them it fell by 1.0 degree.) The final step in the Cost of the Cold Project was to estimate the extent to which this 1.5 degree lowering of Russia's TPC during the Soviet period burdened the national economy. Mikhailova calculated that the annual costs, compounded over the last thirty years of the Soviet era, resulted in a huge GDP loss. "Every person in Russia gave up at least one-fourth (perhaps as much as one-half) of his or her income for the sake of Siberian development."

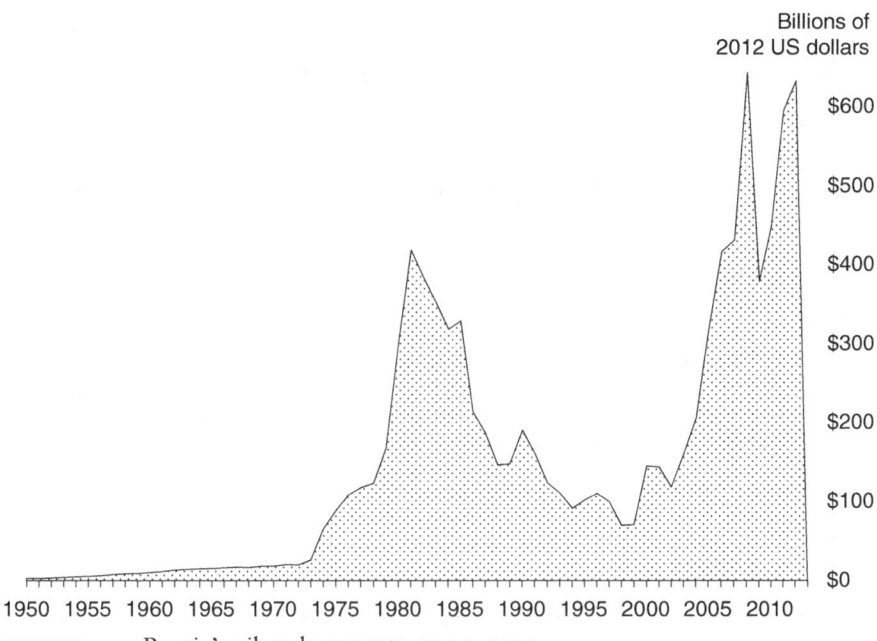

FIGURE 3.4. Russia's oil and gas rents, 1950–2012.

Is the Legacy Being Overcome?

What has happened in the post-Soviet period? Is the legacy of spatial misallocation being corrected? There is an American saying: "If you find yourself in a deep hole, Rule No. 1 is: 'Stop digging!'" In other words, don't make things worse. Russia was in a very deep hole in the 1980s, and in the 1990s it did stop digging (in large part because it couldn't afford to keep digging) and instead began climbing out of the hole, slowly. That is, it began to reallocate resources and people away from Siberia to the rest of the country. But in the new millennium the trend has shifted back.

Figure 3.3 compares the rate of Russia's overall change in TPC from 1930 to the present. A dramatic shift from cooling to warming took place in the 1990s, to an extent never seen during the Soviet period. Since 2004, the change in TPC, although still in the positive (warming) direction, has been minimal. On an annual basis, migration from 2004–10 has been warming the country at a rate of less than 5/1000 of a degree per year. At this rate, it would take two centuries for Russia to undo the spatial allocation the Soviets began in the 1930s!

Other indicators (for instance, for investment in housing, roads, and fixed capital in production) reflect the same trends. Relatively more is being spent in the colder regions than was the case in the 1990s. What has changed since 1999? The most important factor is the dramatic rise in oil and gas prices and the greatly increased flow of so-called resource rents into Russia. As Figure 3.4

FIGURE 3.5. Russia's working-age population, 1959–2030.
Note: Working age defined as per current Russian legislation, 16–59 for men and 16–54 for women.

shows, 2000–08 saw the fastest growth in oil and gas rents in Russia's history. Even today they remain historically high. In other words, Russia again has the physical and financial resources to misallocate.

What Russia does not have in abundance as it did in the 1970s and 1980s is human capital. Russia's working-aged population is shrinking and will continue to do so (see Figure 3.5). This means that it is more important than ever that human capital – people – be employed in the geographical regions where it can be most productive. Moving more people to the east is wasteful. Contrary to stated Russian government programs to "repopulate the East," the goal ought to be to use as few people as possible to develop the resources of Siberia in an economically sensible manner. Put starkly, this should mean to create as few jobs as feasibly possible in zones where the climate and geography lead to increased production and marketing costs.

Conclusion: Dealing with the "Gnarled Tree Economy"

Among the negative legacies communism left to market-economy Russia is a distorted economic geography. The economist measures the negative legacy by its welfare cost. The effects of the old system involve costs incurred during the life of the old system, costs at the starting point of the new regime, and costs that persist over time. A main point in this chapter is that Soviet-era policies of spatial misallocation lowered Russians' welfare throughout the period. To the extent that the structural legacy remains, it will continue to lower welfare. This puts Russia in a trap. The extra costs required to make mislocated cities livable and their economies viable are a tax on the country's growth. Yet the costs, financially, politically, and in human terms, of dismantling the old structure and relocating millions of people are prohibitive, at least in a democratic society. This suggests that the Soviet legacy discussed in this chapter may have permanently damaged Russia's economy. In that case, it would be wise, though painful, to acknowledge that handicap publicly and then be very careful not to make things worse. We cannot straighten the trunk and branches of a gnarled tree. But we should not pretend that it is not gnarled or ignore the forces that made it that way. The value of rigorous study of the origins and costs of the misallocation legacy is to make clear one thing: continuing the policies that made the tree gnarled in the first place only reinforces and reproduces the problem.

Notes

1. Gustafson noted that the earliest reference to the Soviet economic "legacy problem" may have dated back a full twenty years before then (Gustafston 1989, 11). In 1968, Egon Neuberger wrote an article entitled "Central Planning and Its Legacies: Implications for Foreign Trade," in which he made the prescient observation: "In the voluminous literature on the relative merits of the Soviet-type system of central planning, one key aspect has been relatively neglected – the legacies this system bequeaths to the system or systems that follow it. Marx, Schumpeter, and others have discussed the transition problem from capitalism to socialism and the legacies that socialism inherits from capitalism. I suggest that now is the time to begin a similar discussion of the transition from Soviet-type socialism to a new system, and of the desirable and undesirable legacies that this system will inherit. This paper is an exploratory attempt to initiate a discussion of the 'legacy problem'"(Neuberger 1968, 349, note 1).
2. This is from the oft-cited statement by Ericson (1999) that the Soviet Union had a "structure of capital and economic activity that is fundamentally nonviable in an environment determined by market valuation."
3. In a perfect market (competitive, no transaction costs), there would be no legacies, only endowments. All new allocation would be unconditional, from scratch.
4. These relate to, respectively, technical efficiency and allocative efficiency.
5. The explanation for this result is not that Alaska isn't cold. It is. It's just that Americans don't build large cities there. In fact, Anchorage is the only city in Alaska with a population of more than one hundred thousand.
6. The Gulag's share of total construction investment and construction employment in the USSR in the late 1940s and early 1950s was about 20 percent (Gregory 2003, 19, 21).
7. Lagovskii (1957, 107).

8 The Cost of the Cold was a joint project at the Brookings Institution and the Pennsylvania State University Economics Department. Initial research was conducted by the author and Barry W. Ickes, joined later by Pennsylvania State PhD student Tatiana Mikhailova. Gaddy and Ickes (2013) is based partly on the project's work. Results of the research, placed in a historical and political context, were presented in Hill and Gaddy (2003).
9 The story of Duluth and Perm is adapted from the more detailed presentation in Hill and Gaddy (2003, 53–56).
10 In estimating the counterfactual city evolution, a further adjustment was to make the Russian city-size distribution better conform to the power-law size distribution (the so-called Zipf distribution) observed in most countries. See Hill and Gaddy (2003).
11 The lower number takes the relocations associated with World War II as given.
12 Helliwell (1998, 2000). Studies cited by Helliwell point out that transportation costs account for only about 3 percent of the total costs of distance.
13 Formally, the TPC of country k is defined as $TPC_k = \Sigma_j\, n_j\, t_j$, where n_j is the share of the country's total population that resides in region j, and t_j is the average mean temperature in region j. Here, temperatures are for the month of January and the regions are oblasts (krays, republics).

References

Ericson, Richard E. 1999. "The Structural Barrier to Transition Hidden in Input-Output Tables of Centrally Planned Economies." *Economic Systems* 23(3): 199–244.

Gaddy, Clifford G. 2006. Comment on the paper, "Boom Towns and Ghost Countries: Geography, Agglomeration, and Population Mobility," by Lant Pritchett. In *Global Labor Markets?* ed. Susan M. Collins and Carol Graham, 43–49. Brookings Trade Forum. Washington, DC: Brookings Press.

Gaddy, Clifford G. and Barry W. Ickes. 2013. *Bear Traps on Russia's Road to Modernization*. New York: Routledge.

Gregory, Paul R. 2003. "An Introduction to the Economics of the Gulag." In *The Economics of Forced Labor: The Soviet Gulag*, ed. Paul R. Gregory and Valery Lazarev, 1–21. Stanford, CA: Hoover Institution Press.

Gustafson, Thane. 1989. *Crisis amid Plenty: The Politics of Soviet Energy under Brezhnev and Gorbachev*. Princeton, NJ: Princeton University Press.

Helliwell, John F. 1998. *How Much Do National Borders Matter?* Washington, DC: Brookings Press.

   2000. "Globalization: Myths, Facts, and Consequences." Toronto: Benefactors Lecture, C. D. Howe Institute.

Hill, Fiona and Clifford G. Gaddy. 2003. *The Siberian Curse. How Communist Planners Left Russia Out in the Cold*. Washington, DC: Brookings Press.

Lagovskii, Andrei N. 1957. *Strategiia i ekonomika. Kratkii ocherk ikh vzaimnoi svyazi i vzaimnogo vliianiia* [*Strategy and Economics: Brief Outline of Their Mutual Ties and Mutual Influence*], 1st edition. Moscow: Voennoe izdatel'stvo Ministersta oboronoi Soviuza SSR.

Lazarev, Valery. 2003. "Conclusions." In *The Economics of Forced Labor: The Soviet Gulag*, ed. Paul R. Gregory and Valery Lazarev, 189–98. Stanford, CA: Hoover Institution Press.

Lynch, Alan C. 2002. "Roots of Russia's Economic Dilemmas: Liberal Economics and Illiberal Geography." *Europe-Asia Studies* 54(1): 31–49.
Mikhailova, Tatiana. 2004. "Essays on Russian Economic Geography: Measuring Spatial Inefficiency." PhD dissertation, Pennsylvania State University.
Neuberger, Egon. 1968. "Central Planning and Its Legacies: Implications for Foreign Trade." In *International Trade and Central Planning*, ed. Alan A. Brown and Egon Neuberger, 349–77. Berkeley: University of California Press.
Tikhonov, Aleksei. 2003. "The End of the Gulag." In *The Economics of Forced Labor: The Soviet Gulag*, ed. Paul R. Gregory and Valery Lazarev, 67–73. Stanford, CA: Hoover Institution Press.
White, Langdon and George Primmer. 1937. "The Iron and Steel Industry of Duluth: A Study in Locational Maladjustment." *Geographical Review* 27(1): 82–91.

4

Legacies of Industrialization and Paths of Transnational Integration after Socialism

Béla Greskovits

Recent comparative research has established that once the socialist system fell apart, its pieces began to move on different trajectories that led to a variety of capitalist regimes. These regimes were characterized, among other features, by a patterned rather than random diversity of new industrial production and export profiles. Some postsocialist economies started to export what the West usually exports to the rest of the world: chemicals and machinery turned out by technologically advanced capital-intensive plants. Others set up a multitude of low-skill and low-wage sweatshops and specialized in exports of textiles, footwear, food, wood, and simple electronics assembly. A third group of countries integrated into the global economy via markets of natural resources: oil, gas, metals, or cotton (Bohle and Greskovits 2007).

When tracing the links between the postsocialist varieties of capitalism and past industrialization, we are faced with puzzling questions. This diversity is surprising against the background that the new capitalisms' point of departure – socialism – is widely seen as a system that had been remarkably successful in forcing uniform institutions and practices on the republics and satellite states of the Soviet Empire. How could so variegated an industrial architecture have been built on the "ruins" of alleged uniform patterns of socialist industrialization?

The diversity remains puzzling even if the assumption of uniform legacy is relaxed and the existence of varied industrial profiles under socialism is acknowledged (Stark and Bruszt 1998). After all, the inherited economies moved "from the frying pan to the fire" when they entered a global economy perceived by many as no less powerful a homogenizing agent than Soviet domination had been. The question, then, is: If global competitive pressures generally narrowed the range of options open to latecomers, why have they allowed a group of postsocialist economies to capture market segments and niches in complex industries that are seen (because of their reliance on physical and human capital) as key sources of the competitive advantages of advanced economies?

To find answers, relying on the conceptual framework of Bohle and Greskovits (2012), I shall combine a positivist with a constructivist argument. First, I shall provide and analyze empirical evidence on Eastern European industrial structures and performance of the early and mid-1990s and the mid-2000s. While the former directly bear the mark of varied specializations in socialism, the latter also reflect the impact of new factors that have shaped the paths of industrial restructuring after the system's demise. The data allow one to identify instances in which sizeable complex industries were part of the socialist inheritance. At the same time, comparison of both patterns helps to single out cases in which there are empirical grounds for assuming a lasting impact of the inherited sector.

Focusing on East-Central Europe, which for the purposes of this chapter includes all the EU's former socialist member states, I shall explore the resilience of complex manufacturing industries in the Czech and Slovak Republics, Hungary, Poland, and Slovenia and contrast it with the situation of Estonia, Latvia, Lithuania, Bulgaria, and Romania, where these industries' influence has been much weaker or even faded away. I shall analyze how this sectoral legacy, in interplay with policy choices, conspired for foreign-led reindustrialization and skills upgrading in the former and for deindustrialization and deskilling in the latter.

Yet I contend that a compelling account of continuity versus discontinuity must go beyond the analysis of objective facts. To link outcomes with inherited structures in a convincing way, influential actors' interpretations of legacies and the way these informed their decisions ought to be factored in. Taking these interpretations seriously, I argue, is especially important in the context of the radical uncertainty characteristic of the early 1990s, when neither domestic policy makers nor external agents could be sure about the true opportunities and risks the socialist legacy entailed. In the given circumstances, perceptions of the legacy as an asset or a liability from the viewpoint of economic development or national sovereignty played a crucial role in reducing uncertainty and guiding transformative policies.

Inherited Socialist and Emerging Capitalist Industries: Continuity and Change

Two decades after the collapse of socialism, capturing what its legacy actually entails remains a daunting task. The empirical dimensions of socialist industrialization remain elusive because of the system's well-known secretiveness, intentional doctoring of official figures for propaganda purposes, and lack of documentation for many key features and processes. Furthermore, "[t]he continuity of the time series is broken by constant reorganizations" by which statisticians tried to make the data produced in the fundamentally different systems of socialist and postsocialist national accounting comparable (Kornai 1992, 14). Last but not least, the analysis is further complicated by the fact that the transformation led to the emergence of many new nation-states, forcing statisticians to reconstruct (and allowing politicians and their foreign and domestic advisers to reinvent) many facts of their history, including those of industrial development.

Bearing all of this in mind, I use simple but broadly comparable and reliable data to characterize the complex manufacturing industries during socialism and postsocialist capitalism. I proxy the competitive strength of the inherited complex manufacturing sector by the earliest available figures for 1990 on the export share of chemicals and machinery and equipment within total goods exports. Correspondingly, the competitive strength of the new capitalist manufacturing sector is captured by the export shares of the same categories in 2002 and 2006. These ensembles of industries are termed *complex manufacturing* because they rely heavily on technologically sophisticated physical and/or human capital embodied in workers', professionals', and managers' skills.

In Table 4.1, countries in which the share of exports of complex manufactured goods exceeded a pragmatically set 25 percent threshold in the early to mid-1990s represent instances of relatively encompassing complex industrialization in socialist times. All other countries are assumed to lack such an inheritance. In turn, economies with complex manufacturing export shares say at or above 40 percent during the 2000s are considered to be cases for successful complex manufacturing reindustrialization during postsocialist capitalism. In other countries, such efforts, if they existed, failed to produce complex manufacturing specializations. Finally, it is only in those cases distinguished by the strong presence of complex manufacturing export industries *over the whole period* that a robust legacy effect of earlier complex specialization appears to have some basis in fact.

While some data are available for most of the former socialist countries, the rigor of analysis is undermined by the fact that in a number of cases the earliest figures are those of 1991–94, while in others the earliest are for 1996–97. Nevertheless, other evidence on export structures in the 1980s covering Czechoslovakia instead of the Czech and Slovak republics, or the USSR rather than Russia give the same impression: the relatively pronounced existence of socialist complex manufacturing activities had set apart the later East-Central European states from most other countries of the Second World (Lavigne 1991, 390–91). However, only in about half of the former cases – including the Visegrád states and Slovenia – can we reasonably assume these industries' strong and enduring effects, in the terms of Kotkin and Beissinger in the introduction to this volume, "long beyond the life of the regimes, institutions, and policies that gave birth to them." The remarkable revival of the complex sector in these countries and its weaker performance or even atrophy in the Baltic states or Bulgaria and Romania is also confirmed by a more detailed comparison of inherited socialist and restructured capitalist industries in Table 4.2.

TABLE 4.1. *Complex Manufacturing Exports in the Early to Mid-1990s, 2002, and 2006 in the Post-Soviet World (% of Total Goods Exports)*

	Early to Mid-1990s	2002	2006
Albania	3.1 ('96)	3.3	5.0
Armenia	13.4 ('96)	4.0	3.0
Azerbaijan	14.6 ('96)	3.4	7.0
Belarus	**34.5 ('96)**	**35.1**	**30.0**
Bulgaria	**30.2 ('92)**	20.3	22.0
Croatia	**31.1 ('92)**	38.8	40.0
Czech Republic	**35.2 ('93)**	57.7	61.0
Estonia	**29.6 ('96)**	33.1	38.0
Georgia	16.6 ('96)	18.8	30.0
Hungary	**31.6 ('92)**	64.8	79.0
Kazakhstan	16.3 ('92)	5.0	6.0
Kyrgyzstan	22.7 ('96)	12.2	13.0
Latvia	**26.9 ('94)**	14.2	26.0
Lithuania	**28.2 ('94)**	33.3	35.0
Macedonia	20.7 ('93)	12.5	10.0
Moldova	13.6 ('94)	5.6	11.0
Poland	27.7 ('92)	44.1	50.0
Romania	**35.4 ('91)**	25.3	37.0
Russia	12.9 ('96)	10.2	8.0
Slovak Republic	**31.4 ('93)**	46.5	57.0
Slovenia	**38.2 ('92)**	49.4	56.0
Tajikistan	1.0 ('95)	n.a.	3.0
Turkmenistan	0.1 ('95)	n.a.	7.0
Ukraine	23.2 ('97)	21.6	24.0
Uzbekistan	4.6 ('95)	n.a.	20.0

Author's calculation based on *UN Tradecom Database*. Complex manufacturing exports are defined as exports of chemicals and machinery and equipment, coded 5 and 7 in one digit Standard International Trade Code (SITC). The 2006 data are from László Bruszt and Béla Greskovits, "Transnationalization, Social Integration, and Capitalist Diversity in the East and South." *Studies in Comparative International Development*, 44(4) (Winter 2009): 411–34. The first year with available data is in parentheses. Bold figures indicate the persistence of complex manufacturing legacies.

These findings have two implications. On the one hand, there is no case in which a First World type of pronounced complex manufacturing specialization could emerge *without having some origins* in the past industrial structures of the Second World. Put differently, the absence of a relatively strong complex manufacturing sector before the fall of socialism appears to have "sentenced" countries to an inability to establish one in the system's aftermath. On the other hand, not all economies that had a complex manufacturing sector under socialism have continued with this variant of international economic integration after socialism's demise. Furthermore, consistent with

TABLE 4.2. *Complex Manufacturing Output and Employment in the Early 1990s and 2004 in East-Central Europe*

	Complex Manufacturing Production (% of Manufacturing Production)		Complex Manufacturing Employment (% of Manufacturing Employment)		Complex Manufacturing Employment (Persons in 1,000s)	
	Early '90s	2004	Early '90s	2004	Early '90s	2004
Estonia	29.6	23.0	23.6	19.2	33.1	24.6
Latvia	40.8	12.6	37.0	13.9	71.7	23.3
Lithuania	18.1	18.2	34.1	17.7	126.2	39.0
Bulgaria	23.1	21.4	31.5	21.7	233.6	131.7
Romania	31.4	25.2	39.3	24.9	1,354.0	372.0
Average/sum	28.6	20.1	33.1	19.5	1,818.6	590.6
Czech Republic	36.2	48.2	45.3	41.2	752.2	421.0
Hungary	33.9	60.6	30.3	39.3	259.4	280.7
Poland	29.3	33.6	32.5	26.6	900.6	595.6
Slovak Republic	33.3	38.8	43.8	32.6	263.0	165.3
Slovenia	40.0	46.2	31.1	33.9	124.3	75.9
Average/sum	34.5	45.5	36.3	34.7	2,299.5	1,538.5

Author's calculation based on WIIW *Industrial Database on Central and Eastern Europe*, 2008 (Vienna: Wiener Institut für Internationale Wirtschaftsforschung). Complex industries are chemicals, chemical products and man-made fibers, machinery and equipment, electrical and optical equipment, and transport equipment, respectively coded DG, DK, DL, DM in the NACE-14 system. Earliest available data: Estonia (1992–94), Latvia (1993), Lithuania (1992), Bulgaria (1996), Romania (1990), Czech Republic (1989), Hungary (1992), Poland (1990–92), Slovak Republic (1989–91), Slovenia (1989). Output is calculated at 2002 prices.

the Kotkin and Beissinger definition, in the Visegrád states and Slovenia, the legacy effect entailed "the persisting influence of the past within a broader context of large-scale macrohistorical change" on a host of key dimensions: the main markets, dominant investors, practices of management, employment, and interfirm contacts.

All this indicates that if a causal relationship exists, it is far from trivial and calls for an investigation of the actors and factors involved. Having in mind that, especially for latecomers, capturing sizeable world market shares is no longer possible without integration into the global flows of goods, capital, knowledge, and finance, it is plausible to propose that transnational corporations' decisions have had an immense influence on whether the complex manufacturing inheritance from socialism persisted or atrophied.

In terms of attraction for foreign capital in general, the first impression one gets from some essential facts on the East-Central European economies is that of similarity rather than difference – especially when contrasted with members

TABLE 4.3. *Complex Manufacturing Foreign Direct Investment (FDI) Stock in the Mid-1990s and 2005 in East-Central Europe*

	Complex Manufacturing FDI Stock (% of total stock)		Complex Manufacturing FDI stock (EUR Per Head of Population in 2000)		Total FDI Stock (% of GDP)	
	Mid-90s	2005	Mid-90s	2005	2000	2005
Estonia	9.2	3.1	68.3	210.4	48.4	43.6
Latvia	1.5	1.3	2.5	21.8	27.0	28.7
Lithuania	7.8	8.8	11.9	165.3	20.5	25.1
Bulgaria	n.a.	n.a.	n.a.	n.a.	17.9	34.3
Romania	n.a.	8.5	n.a.	83.6	17.5	24.2
Average	6.2	5.4	27.6	120.3	n.a.	n.a.
Czech Republic	18.1	18.8	146.8	936.9	38.9	48.1
Hungary	20.4	26.9	311.6	1,257.0	49.0	55.9
Poland	14.2	12.7	33.9	250.8	20.5	31.1
Slovak Republic	20.9	15.9	45.2	609.0	18.4	32.8
Slovenia	26.4	26.1	142.8	800.7	15.2	23.7
Average	20.0	20.1	136.1	770.9	n.a.	n.a.

Author's calculation based on *WIIW Foreign Direct Investment Database on Central and Eastern Europe, 2008* (Vienna: Wiener Institut für Internationale Wirtschaftsforschung). Complex industries: DG, DK, DL, DM in NACE-14 codes. Earliest available data: Estonia (1997), Latvia (1995), Lithuania (1996), Bulgaria (-), Romania (-), Czech Republic (1997), Hungary (1998), Poland (1996), Slovak Republic (1996), Slovenia (1994). FDI stock per GDP data are from *World Investment Report*, 2006.

of the Commonwealth of Independent States or the majority of southeastern European countries. Via substantial capital imports, the East-Central European economies' assets have been incorporated into global and European systems of production, commerce, and finance. By the early to mid-2000s, foreign control became the norm in all major export industries and in many services and utilities. The banking sector is one strategic area where foreign penetration has reached levels almost unprecedented in other parts of Europe and the world.

A closer scrutiny of the sectoral distribution of imported capital reveals significant differences among former socialist EU members. Table 4.3 shows similarities between the regional distribution of foreign direct investment stocks in complex industries, and the pattern of complex manufacturing exports, output, and employment (Tables 4.1 and 4.2). In the mid-1990s and mid-2000s, the data for the Visegrád states and Slovenia exceeded the Baltic-Balkan figures fourfold (and by a factor of five to six when measured as a share of total inward stock and in per capita terms).

On what grounds have transnational corporations decided how much to invest, in which countries, and in which sectors? To answer these questions, we have to consider that, crucial as they were for the emerging industrial profiles, the choices of powerful external actors were themselves influenced by opportunities and risks that are only partly captured at the domestic level. Accordingly, a plausible regional explanation of the paths of foreign-led complex reindustrialization and deindustrialization must convincingly link the sectoral pattern of foreign capital inflows to country-specific combinations of inherited assets and with newly designed public policies and institutions for attracting and hosting transnational firms.

Logics of Foreign-led Reindustrialization and Deindustrialization

In the dominant account, foreign direct investment has been endogenous to the region-wide advance of market reforms. As an analysis of the World Bank has put it: "Among advanced reformers ... [p]roduction has shifted from industry to services, trade has been reoriented toward world markets, and foreign direct investment (FDI) inflows have risen sharply." Later studies also confirmed that, besides other factors such as the market size and geographic proximity of the country of origin and the receiving country, "general progress in economic reform and the creation of supporting institutions ... has a positive impact on FDI in the transition countries" (The World Bank 1996, 18).

While progress in market reforms is a good predictor of the distribution of foreign investment stock, it falls short of making sense of the meager complex manufacturing investment that had occurred in the Baltic, Bulgarian, and Romanian economies by the mid-2000s and the related dominance of low-skill export activities and services. Despite impressive results in creating many of the alleged conditions for foreign-led industrial upgrading (radically reformed economies, low taxes, and political stability), these states proved less effective than their Visegrád area neighbors in attracting foreign investment in complex manufacturing.

Even if differences in market size might have had some impact on these outcomes, the fact that the locations preferred by complex investors and those neglected by them include both small and large economies points to the role of other factors. And although geographical distance from Western markets and capital-rich countries might be part of the explanation, it cannot solve the puzzle that Finnish cell phone specialist Nokia and Swedish household appliances producer Electrolux have established their largest production facilities in relatively distant Hungary rather than in neighboring Estonia or Latvia. Finally, if low labor costs are important for investors, then it is even more puzzling that complex manufacturing investors consistently preferred Visegrád and Slovenian locations to Baltic or southeastern European ones, where wages and social benefits have long been lower (Bohle 2008).

In a nutshell, my answer to why complex manufacturing investment occurred in certain countries rather than others is that the corporations' choices responded to the signals stemming from the interplay between inherited and restructured production profiles, inherited and newly built market and compensatory institutions, and special incentive packages. In this respect, the specific legacy relationship at work in Kotkin and Beissinger's classification of legacy relationships is "bricolage," whereby "elements of the past" are "thoroughly intermixed and interpenetrated with the present" to create a new foreign-controlled and foreign-coordinated industrial structure "that only vaguely resembles the old, but still profoundly bears its imprint" (see also Stark and Bruszt 1998).

To account for the foreign firms' possible motivations, I adapt Raymond Vernon's (1971) product cycle theory, and on these grounds argue that export-oriented complex manufacturing investment was likely to flow first to those former socialist economies whose initial production profiles already included complex manufacturing.

Accordingly, the Visegrád countries and Slovenia, which specialized in chemicals and machine building (including automobiles and electronics) during late socialism, could rightly expect larger inflows of industry-specific capital than other (southeastern European or Central Asian) states where these sectors were virtually absent. Yet the primary attractions of the Visegrád and Slovenian economies might not have been industry-specific physical plants, equipment, or infrastructure. These actually needed significant modernization, renewal, and upgrading – tasks foreign investors rapidly undertook. Rather, I propose that these states' advantages in the competition for complex manufacturing investment stemmed above all from inherited *human* capital.

Tracing the role of human factors in the successes of developing countries within the global economy, Alice Amsden has stressed the key role of "manufacturing experience" embodied in the capabilities of blue- and white-collar labor, as well as those of management for production, project execution, and innovation. "Past manufacturing experience creates relatively high expectations on the part of potential investors that future manufacturing activity will succeed, which ... provides an incentive to use resources to expand manufacturing capacity rather than to achieve immediate self-enrichment. Manufacturing experience also creates the qualified managers and engineers necessary to implement investment plans" (Amsden 2001, 15). On these grounds, inherited "manufacturing experience emerges as the necessary condition for post-war industrial expansion given that no successful latecomer country managed to industrialize without it" (ibid., 121).

The statistical data cited earlier indicate that the legacy of manufacturing experience is likely a necessary condition for complex manufacturing export specialization of postsocialist economies as well. The findings of case studies also support this assertion. For example, as a study on the restructuring of the region's electronics industries observed, regional "patterns at the high-end (microfabrication and software) and low-end (final assembly) ... suggest that the national capabilities make a difference in the ability to attract certain investments." Accordingly, while "investments in assembly are spread roughly evenly across the three countries [the Czech Republic, Hungary, and Poland], more advanced technologies have initially concentrated where there is already an established capability" (Linden 1998, 7). Similarly, in the car industry, "[m]ost of the initial FDI in the region was in take-overs rather than in the establishment of greenfield sites. Anno 1998, almost all of the existing car production capacity has been taken over, or is controlled, by Western car makers ... Central and Eastern European countries, situated close to the EU, can be an obvious source of cheap but skilled labour" (Van Tulder and Ruigrok 1998, 2).

However, while the legacy of manufacturing experience could well have been a necessary condition, it falls short of a sufficient explanation for complex manufacturing expansion after socialism: recall the modest results or even atrophy of the Baltic and southeastern European complex sectors despite their previous roles under socialism in trading human capital-intensive goods for natural resources from other parts of the Soviet Empire or the Third World (Csaba 1990). Given that on the basis of their relatively robust prior complex manufacturing experiences *all* of the East-Central European countries initially seem to have had comparable advantages as new locations for transnational export production, product cycle theory alone cannot account for the diverging paths. How then did foreign investors choose among them?

For an answer that relies on Brown, Greskovits, and Kulcsár (2007), we have to consider that similar production profiles might fail to raise investors' interest if institutional and policy barriers hampered access to the demanded local factors of production. It follows, then, that countries that advanced furthest in removing entry barriers and rebuilding their institutions and policy regimes by the time investors were ready and able to cross the former Cold War borders were better able to attract foreign investment. With respect to liberalization, privatization, and the existence of market-supporting institutions and legal frameworks, the Visegrád states and Slovenia outcompeted the region's other states in the first half of the 1990s.

This is partly explained by another aspect of legacy. Thanks to their long experimentation with market reforms under socialism, Hungary, Poland, and Slovenia (unlike Czechoslovakia) already had relatively liberalized economies in 1989 and could capitalize on their inheritance of market-oriented institutions and practices. By contrast, the Baltic states, Bulgaria, and Romania were disadvantaged in this respect, as they started building markets largely from scratch. Furthermore, Estonia, Latvia, and Lithuania completed their struggle for independence only after August 1991, and their comprehensive market reforms could start at full speed only two years later than in other countries.

In the first phase of the transformation, then, in the context of inherited similar production and skill profiles, temporary institutional advantages tilted the balance of investors' preferences in favor of the Visegrád countries. Complex foreign capital inflows had been endogenous to the levels of marketization inherited and achieved by the early to mid-1990s.

After the mid-1990s, the interplay of structural and institutional factors seems to have fully reversed, and the relationship between complex manufacturing foreign direct investment and marketization no longer mattered. The Baltic states and later Bulgaria and Romania gradually worked off their initial disadvantage in marketization and by the mid-2000s arrived at a high degree of institutional congruence in this respect with their regional rivals and the West. However, transnational complex manufacturing investors do not seem to have appreciated this institutional convergence. What seems to explain these states' inability to attract the relevant investment after the mid-1990s is that their institutional convergence (the pace of which was dramatic in the Baltic cases) was achieved at the expense of increasing divergence in production and skill profiles.

Since the late 1990s, in a context of increasing institutional congruence, transnational corporations continued to prefer the same Visegrád and Slovenian locations mainly because of their enhanced structural congruence with the West, whereas the Baltic and southeastern European countries lost out because of the increasing divergence of their industrial profile. What explains this divergence?

Initial investor preferences, motivated by a combination of structural and institutional factors, seem to have launched both virtuous and vicious circles of capital accumulation. Their driving forces included: the contrasting trends of industry upgrading versus deindustrialization; the tendency for many foreign firms to "follow the leaders," their rivals, suppliers, and buyers to originally preferred locations; the concomitant clustering of complex manufacturing industries; and last, the generous subsidy packages offered to complex manufacturing investors.

Concretely, through foreign investment, the complex manufacturing industries of the Visegrád states and Slovenia gained access to much needed tangible and intangible factors of production, upgraded their activities and knowledge, and in this way developed competitive strengths in the demanding European and global markets. By contrast, permanently deprived of such means, these same industrial sectors of the Baltic and southeastern European states could not survive the intense global competition, and all but lost their markets, factors of production, and policy influence.

In addition to liberalizing their economies and building market institutions, governments in the Visegrád states and Slovenia tried to ease adjustment through varied combinations of gradualism in phasing out subsidies, partially and selectively maintained protective tariffs, new credits for survival and/or restructuring, and labor market and social policy measures that helped owners of industry-specific human capital weather the hardest times. Although the original focus of protective industrial and social policies had been domestic firms and labor, some states had simultaneously laid the groundwork for incentive packages, export-processing zones, and promotion agencies to attract foreign firms. While Hungary had been a pioneer in nurturing transnational "infant industries" through generous compensation for the costs of investment in its high-risk transitory setting, from the late 1990s other Visegrád countries (and to a lesser extent Slovenia) followed suit (Drahokoupil 2009).

The Baltic approach to compensation diverged from this pattern. Estonia, Latvia, and Lithuania virtually eliminated tariffs and subsidies in the first half of the 1990s, and were reluctant to shelter enterprises and their workers through protective industrial and social policies. Moreover, strict monetary policies sentenced the Baltic firms to a virtual credit crunch throughout the decade. The Baltic states' industrial policy vis-à-vis transnational corporations was similarly minimalist – at least initially. Foreign investors were offered limited incentives with a focus on low tax rates. Investment promotion agencies were established with a delay, and their scope of activity and budgets remained relatively modest. Although in the 2000s the incentives and services granted to foreign firms started to be more generous, the Baltic region continued to lag behind the Visegrád area in the terms offered (Cass 2007).

To make things worse, the radical course of liberalization without compensation for costs in the Baltic, rather than breaking the vicious circle, hampered the emergence or accelerated the atrophy of complex manufacturing activities and the embodied manufacturing experience. Instead, in Estonia and the other Baltic states (as well as Bulgaria and Romania), an entirely new production profile emerged in a relatively short time, with foreign-controlled traditional light and resource-based industries and services and the required typically modest skills at its core.

Finally, we have to consider that transnational corporations usually follow their competitors and clients to new production locations, while first investors try to fend off rival followers, not least by enlarging their already existing facilities (Vernon 1971). This strategy, observed in all Visegrád countries, further contributed to the virtuous circles of accumulating complex manufacturing investment stocks. By contrast, the Baltic and southeastern European states, because of the increasing divergence of their production profiles and skills, could neither establish dense linkages to the Visegrád cluster nor attract adequate foreign capital to build their own complex manufacturing growth pole. The competition for complex manufacturing investors through generous incentive packages, which intensified within the Visegrád group from the first half of the 2000s, made it even more difficult for outsiders to acquire new investments in these industries. The resulting "bidding war" in incentives magnified the overall cost of complex manufacturing capital inflows and exacerbated the competitive disadvantages of countries outside the cluster, especially if they were also structurally handicapped.

While this positivist logic advances our understanding of the emergence of East-Central European capitalism and the role of legacies in its diversity, it still falls short of capturing all the factors that contributed to persistent versus weak or fading effects of the past. *Why* had the Visegrád states and Slovenia settled on policies to preserve inherited manufacturing experiences until foreign firms were ready and willing to incorporate these assets into their own competitive strategies? Conversely, why did the Baltic and southeastern European policy makers adopt a different stance implying a neglect of initially existing pockets of complex manufacturing knowledge?

Differently put: On what grounds did the East-Central European states decide whether socialist industrialization left behind valuable assets worth protecting and nurturing, or viewed them as merely liabilities (or even threats) that had to be transcended as fast as possible? Indeed, a similar question can be asked about the motifs and perceptions of investing transnational corporations; just like their new host authorities, they had to judge the opportunities and risks inherent to their first projects in the context of systemic chaos and disintegration, which made any sort of strategic vision difficult.

Perceptions and Choices in Uncertain Conditions

As Amsden stated, "manufacturing experience is not simply a stock of knowledge. It is a stock of knowledge that passes through a specific historical and institutional filter." Thus, the distinction between "émigré" versus "colonial" experiences "may be hypothesized to differentiate a wide range of practices among latecomers" (Amsden 2001, 15–16). After World War II:

> countries with colonial manufacturing experience were able to nationalize, expropriate, or acquire foreign-owned business enterprises.... Countries with North-Atlantic émigré experience, by contrast, had no comparable discontinuity [and] also tended to have a larger stock of foreign investment because their prewar manufacturing experience had gone furthest and hence their domestic markets had become relatively large and an attraction to foreign investors.... Thus, the *depth* of prewar manufacturing experience distinguished the "rest" and "the remainder." The *type* of prewar manufacturing experience distinguished countries *within* "the rest." (ibid.)

The manufacturing industries of East-Central European countries also passed through specific historical and institutional filters. First, I demonstrate that when adapted to the region's peculiar conditions, Amsden's categories, namely the home-grown artisanal, émigré, and colonial types, offer fruitful analogies and contrasts for our understanding of (dis)continuity after socialism. Second, I develop Amsden's concept a step further by considering that, because inherited "structures do not come with an instruction sheet" (Blyth 2002, 7), varied *visions* of the industrial past are likely to interfere and combine with its objective aspects in bringing about legacy effects. Third, I argue that such intellectual "bridges" between the past and present have been constructed in *politically conditioned and politically consequential* processes. When skillfully deployed, the contested visions of the industrial legacy helped the new democratic politicians to mobilize consent for crucial policy choices and to achieve legitimacy.

Economic historians long ago established that the region's complex manufacturing experience had not been produced by a single encompassing and sustained modernization effort, but was pieced together from partial and reversible learning processes during *unfinished and dependent* episodes. This raised puzzling questions about *which* period of the past would cast the longest shadow. According to received wisdom, the main driving forces of the region's first modernization thrust – namely foreign capital and immigrant (mainly German and Jewish) entrepreneurs and workers – fell into the émigré category. From the last decades of the nineteenth century to the first half of the twentieth century, "it is ... the import of capital, promoted and motivated by state activity, which may be regarded as the feature distinguishing Eastern Europe from the rest of the Continent in the modern transformation of the economy" (Berend and Ránki 1974, 92).

While these beginnings were certainly important, a substantial part of manufacturing experience originated from socialist industrialization. Yet there had been important variation in the relative strength and quality of domestic versus external sources and forces of development under socialism. Take the intensity of Soviet influence: although the impact of the empire and its quasi-markets had been deep all over the region, its extent and forms had varied.

In a number of countries, postwar socialist industrialization drew on prewar industrial legacies and relied on domestic managerial and labor forces and national communist authorities for production and coordination respectively. In these aspects, the manufacturing experience of the Visegrád countries, Slovenia, Bulgaria, and Romania can be viewed as partly homegrown. This is in striking contrast with the Baltic states and other Soviet republics, where industrialization had been directly forced and driven by immigrant masses of Russian-speaking workers and management, tight incorporation into the Soviet military-industrial complex, and subordination to all-union enterprises and quasi-federal public authorities.

At the same time, the more frequent and multifaceted economic contacts with the West (which can be viewed as sources of the émigré type of manufacturing experience) had also set the satellite countries apart from the Soviet republics. At this point, it is useful to recall that by the 1980s, the USSR forced these states to pay for its natural resources with "hard" goods, the production of which increasingly depended on the legal and illegal inflow of Western technology in the form of licenses, know-how, and equipment. As a consequence, especially in the reform-socialist countries, where market-oriented experiments and skyrocketing foreign debt also conspired for economic opening to the West, the industrial experience included not merely the features of Sovietization, but certain aspects of Westernization too (Bandelj 2008).

To be sure, none of these modernization efforts was evaluated by contemporaries in unambiguous terms. Precisely because the region's past was replete with *incomplete* modernization projects, the repeated frustration over failures and less frequent euphoria over partial successes led to ambiguous assessments. This ambivalence concerning the actual value of accomplishments itself became a legacy – that is, a resilient part of the *longue durée* of modern industrialization. Simply put, this "glass" could be permanently viewed as it were half full as well as half empty.

For example, at the beginning of the twentieth century, and after four decades of the "Golden Age" of rapid foreign-led modernization, Hungarian sociologist Lajos Leopold coined the term "simulated capitalism" to describe a situation in which imported Westernization failed to sink deep enough roots in Eastern European soil, simultaneously keeping these countries in the position of dependants and epigones.

[T]he capitalist economic order functions as division of labor between two states: one endowed with capital's historical-legal postulates and the other with appropriate economic conditions. To please Western markets and creditors, the East European mimicry-societies – albeit with great difficulty – put together a capitalist legal order, maintain oversize bureaucracies, burdensome military preparations, and a Quixotic diplomacy; copy Western legal codes, dress in Western uniforms, import the masterpieces of Schneider and Krupp, and grind language and habits – just to simulate capitalism more credibly.(Leopold 1917)

Conversely, critics of the later socialist attempt at modernization complained about its isolated homegrown character and lack of embeddedness in worldwide processes of economic structural change. At the end of the 1960s (right after the beginning of Hungary's reform-socialist period, which entailed various forms of opening to the West), economist Ferenc Jánossy was among the first to recognize a remarkable but superficial similarity between the industrial structure of the East-Central European countries and that of advanced capitalist economies.

According to his data, in the late 1960s, Hungary occupied third place in the world in terms of the share of machinery and equipment within total industrial output, and Czechoslovakia did not lag far behind. This indicated the presence of considerable manufacturing experience. However, for Jánossy, it was "one of the most characteristic symptoms of a 'quasi-developed' economic structure" hiding a host of shortcomings in the efficiency of labor force, investment, and product quality. Unless remedied by deeper integration into the world economy, quasi-development, he argued, would remain a "characteristic deformation of our economic life that manifests itself in the fact that in our country everything is only *almost* functioning, only almost proper, knowledge is only almost acquired, and the needed experience only almost available" (Jánossy 2001 [1969], 136).

Irony of ironies, two decades later, when the satellite states of the Soviet Empire tried to accelerate industrial modernization via massive imports of Western licenses and know-how, the obstacles were partly the same as at the beginning of the century, namely these economies' limited capacity to absorb and utilize borrowed innovation and technology, or develop competitive indigenous substitutes.

The recession and disintegration of the early 1990s instigated new political leaders to formulate transformative visions and implement policies despite the dearth of trusted data. It should not take us by surprise that the controversy about the economic inheritance became especially heated and replete with bold statements on its true virtues and vices. Let me illustrate with a few examples of the conflicting views on the performance of socialist economies and industries and the skills and social status of their employees.

The *economic output* of the socialist system – whether captured by its aggregate measure GDP or the actual contribution of manufacturing industries – was perceived differently by politicians in various countries. Because over the 1990s there was no expert consensus on this matter, the confusion about the "true" figures allowed wildly diverging interpretations. At the onset of transformation, Czech reformers, for instance, seem to have believed that their country's per capita GDP had been close to EU levels (Drahokoupil 2009, 71). Estonian politicians had different perceptions. Assessing the economic legacy, Premier Mart Laar assumed that part of production could be maintained only in a socialist economy, while under "normal" capitalist conditions such production was "unwanted," not demanded by anyone (Laar 2002, 24–25).

Divergent views on the actual contribution of the socialist economy and its industries to development went hand in hand with no less contradictory perceptions of the *skills and social standing* of employees. For example, Czech leaders credited workers with the capacity for meeting the high standards of sophisticated production after socialism (Drahokoupil 2009, 70). In contrast, criticizing employees in the public sector, Estonian Premier Laar commented that, "[it] is not possible to teach an old dog new tricks. People who worked in the Soviet system and made careers for themselves find it hard to adapt to the requirements set by society. If you have based your entire career not on honest work but on lies and deceit, then it is unrealistic to expect that you will now start to change" (Laar 2002, 168).

Similar to the negative assessments of the value created by socialist industries, critical accounts of the work habits and skills of workers were frequent in Eastern Europeanist scholarship. For example, comparing the situation of Polish workers under Bolshevik rule with that of English laborers under the ill-conceived Speenhamland welfare regime of 1795 analyzed by Karl Polanyi, Maurice Glassman concluded that, in both cases, "The effects of paternalism on the 'substance' of the common culture were so devastating that anything seemed better in comparison" (Glassman 1994, 198).

The political significance of these perceptions cannot be fully grasped unless we trace them to widespread popular sentiments about individual social status acquired during socialism, or national identity. It was above all through their relationship with the varied purposes of transformation – namely building markets while protecting the populations' welfare or (re)building independent nation states – that the contradictory assessments of the socialist industrial legacy could become politically consequential and interfere with actual policy strategies. To paraphrase Peter Katzenstein, "[w]hat really mattered politically was the perception of vulnerability, economic or otherwise" to the negative effects of the socialist past (Katzenstein 2003, 11). Different perceptions of vulnerability could become (in Blyth's phrase) "instruction sheets" – reducing uncertainty and offering guidelines for transformative policies – as they allowed elites to relate their societies' future and past in varied form, emphasizing either continuity or discontinuity.

To make new institutions accepted and worthy of effort and sacrifice, politicians could advocate them as heralds of a "golden future" and simultaneously justify them as improved replicas of the institutional assets left behind and "tested" by history, including the socialist period. Most common in the Visegrád states and Slovenia, such interpretations emphasized that while returning to Europe, members of postsocialist societies did not have to leave the East "empty-handed" as there *was* an industrial legacy worthy of protection against destructive market forces and of state assistance for gradual restructuring. Because Czechoslovak leaders were convinced that their economy was relatively well endowed with inherited assets, and actors needed a grace period to adapt, they were "looking for a non-crisis scenario" (Klaus and Jezek 1991, 39). Similarly, Slovenian gradualists who, in Deputy Prime Minister Joze Mencinger's words, "considered the legacy of the past an exploitable advantage," settled on a "pragmatic economic policy and a floating exchange rate system for the new currency ... that ... would result in smaller output losses and lower unemployment by allowing some inflation" (Mencinger 2004, 76–78).

By the same token, in these countries, which prior to and/or during socialism had built substantial complex manufacturing industries, the possibility of an overwhelming new inflow of manufacturing experience via Western foreign investments raised concerns about the survival of inherited assets (Klaus 1997). The Czech premier's discomfort with the possibility of an overly fast takeover of the Czech economy by German capital might also have had much to do with historically engrained fears of the neighboring power – just like the public worries about the expansion of German and Italian capital in Poland and Slovenia respectively.

Despite similarities in the objective and perceived positive aspects of its inherited complex manufacturing sector, Hungary opted for foreign-led capitalism early on. This, in addition to stronger reliance on foreign investment in the last decade of socialism, can be explained by the country's record-level debt, reformers' decision to refrain from debt rescheduling and relief, and the implied strategy of privatization to strategic investors for hard currency cash receipts crucial for debt service.

In turn, politicians in the Baltic states saw the main advantages of the new capitalist institutions in their *sharp contrast* with the remnants of Soviet past. They stressed the need for leaving the East as fast as possible, emphasized the merits of radical parting with socialism's worthless or outright dangerous legacies, belittled the economic and social losses caused by purely market-driven restructuring, and interpreted leaving socialism and European integration as a *return* to "normality." This is what Estonia's Premier Laar might have meant by his paradoxical claim that transition was "some kind of return to the future," but it required first a detour to the presocialist past (Laar 2002, 22). If forced Sovietization meant a break with normality, then rooting out its legacies could rightly be termed normalization.

In the economy, the process of normalization was accelerated by the region's most radical marketization strategy. In the eyes of reformers, this could not be destructive, as ceasing unwanted production did not imply real but merely virtual losses. The resulting social costs fell disproportionately on Estonia and Latvia's mostly Russian-speaking manufacturing labor force. While their high occupational status under Soviet rule had manifested itself in privileged access to firm-based social provisions, with the collapse of inherited industries not only had they lost their job-related benefits, but they suffered more frequent and longer periods of unemployment (or losses of employment quality) due to wage arrears or compulsory unpaid holidays than members of the titular majority (Rose et al. 2002, 6–10).

Protective industrial policies were not adopted to slow down the process of dislocation, nor were adequately funded unemployment benefit and retraining programs offered to ease the implied social stress and save inherited manufacturing experiences. Although the refusal of state assistance (in the form of subsidies and grace periods for restructuring) to troubled industrial firms had been justified by the requirements of fiscal discipline and monetary stability, identity politics helped to cement the hegemony of the stability-oriented agenda. Denial of industry protection, even if it led to deindustrialization, could be more easily justified on grounds of perceived vulnerability of the national economy to postcolonial influences (Laar 2002, 37).

Is it not reasonable to assume that transnational corporations – when judging the value of socialist industries for their own plans to expand – were more capable of strategic developmental thinking than host governments, whose foresight was blurred by the lack of trusted inventories of assets and liabilities, and whose considerations were guided by a mixture of conflicting economic and political logics rather than pure economic rationality? After all, the forecasting, planning, global sourcing, and marketing capabilities of transnational giants exceeded those of the small latecomer states by several factors. Is it not the case, then, that the survival of complex manufacturing industries in the aftermath of socialism ought to be traced much more to the long-term strategic intentions of global corporate headquarters than to any decision taken in domestic political arenas?

I do not think so. The reason is that the transformation had confronted foreign investors with the same bewildering task of assessing an elusive and ambiguous inheritance, which the heirs of the past system had been facing. Indeed, evidence suggests that the implementation of foreign investors' initial master plans had been hampered by the radical uncertainty of the early transformation years.

Legacies of Industrialization

Take the example of foreign investors' actual initial motivations: most of them did *not* cross the former iron curtain with the original intention to exploit the inherited pool of human capital. Indeed, according to opinion polls conducted in 1990–94 among transnational firms, the inherited complex manufacturing experience did not feature prominently among the key factors of initial location choices at all – partly because foreign perceptions of the quality of socialist labor were as ambivalent as those of national policy makers. The skepticism about the available skills was widespread (EBRD 1994, 132).

Instead, the majority of surveys confirmed the initial dominance of *market-seeking* over asset-seeking motifs: "Most striking perhaps is the predominance of market access among factors of importance for investors.... While the domestic market of the host economy appears to be the main target, some studies also indicate that the possibility of subsequent expansion into regional (transition economy) market is of importance to investors. Factor cost advantages are clearly rated as less important than market access in all surveys" (ibid). Such perceptions were especially prevalent in the car industry, where "[m]ost observers – in particular directly after the turnaround in 1989 – have expressed the idea that Central and Eastern European countries are promising future markets for cars" (Van Tulder and Ruigrok 1998, 2).

However, the initial "expectation has proven to be overly optimistic. Sales in most CEEC countries declined after the break-up of COMECON. In Poland – by far the biggest market after Russia – new car sales halved" (ibid). Generally, uncertainty hampered accurate forecasting of purchasing power and its dynamics. It is hard to see how it could be otherwise, because (as shown in Table 4.4), over the 1990s even professional data producers (such as the World Bank) circulated widely diverging retrospective estimates of the socialist countries' GDP and the purchasing power of wages and salaries before the breakdown (Greskovits 2001). The transforming region's economic dynamics proved no less unexpected: neither the fact nor the depth and length of the recession of the early 1990s was predicted – let alone its sectoral variation or effect on volumes and patterns of consumption.

In turn, pervasive uncertainty made a deep impact on foreign firms' strategies. Most investors decided to wait and see and to postpone larger investment projects. Risk takers, whose pioneering investments had been driven by the initial optimistic perceptions of market opportunities, discontinued their operations, or, if trapped by the initial high costs of their investments, put their faith in recovery and/or modified their original strategy. One of the foreign investor surveys found that, "[o]bstacles led to change of strategy for 40%, cancellation or postponement of 18% of projects" (EBRD 1994, 131). One possible modification entailed export activities utilizing the existing labor force, which, according to surveys, led to markedly improved perceptions of local skills and experience. For instance, heavily investing in Poland, automaker Fiat confirmed that, "the level of technical education of workers ... is considered ...

TABLE 4.4. *Varied Estimates of the East-Central European Former Socialist Countries' GNP for the Same Year of 1987 Published by The World Bank in 1993–97*

Country	Per capita GNP at Purchasing Power Parity in 1987 (% of the U.S. figure)				
	1993	1994	1995	1996	1997
Bulgaria	31.1[a]	29.0[a]	28.5[a]	23.5[e]	23.4
Czech Republic	–	40.5[d]	39.2[d]	44.1	44.9
Estonia	45.8	43.0	45.0	29.9[e]	25.5
Hungary	31.9[b]	30.4[b]	28.5[b]	28.9	28.9
Latvia	37.2	36.2	35.7	24.1[e]	24.5
Lithuania	29.4	28.1	27.9	33.8[e]	25.2
Poland	24.8[b]	25.8[b]	23.0[b]	21.4[e]	21.5
Romania	42.3[c]	19.1[c]	18.4[c]	22.7[e]	22.2
Slovak Republic	–	32.4[a]	35.0[d]	–	17.6
Slovenia	–	–	–	33.3[c]	–

[1] PPC estimates of GDP per capita in 1993, and PPP estimates of GNP per capita in 1994, 1995, 1996, and 1997. According to the Bank's repeated warning: values for the "economies of the former Soviet Union are subject to more than the usual margin of error" (e.g., *World Development Report* 1995, 221). In later formulation: "Estimates for economies of the former Soviet Union are preliminary; their classification will be kept under review" (*World Development Report* 1996, 189, *World Development Report* 1997, 215).
[a] Obtained from the regression estimates.
[b] Extrapolated from 1985 ICP estimates.
[c] Extrapolated from 1975 ICP estimates and scaled up by the corresponding U.S. deflator.
[d] Extrapolated from 1990 ICP estimates.
[e] Extrapolated from 1993 ICP estimates.

Source: Author's compilation. Column 1: *World Development Report 1993* (Washington, DC: The World Bank), 296–97; column 2: *World Development Report 1994*, 220–21; column 3: *World Development Report 1995* 220–21; column 4: *World Development Report 1996*, 188–89; column 5: *World Development Report 1997*, 214–15.

superior to the level of corresponding workers in Northern Italy" (Balcet and Enrietti 1997, 11).

There was, then, a long way to go from the initial plans of capturing a seemingly large and lucrative East-Central European market and building a postsocialist consumer society to transforming these economies into what they ultimately became: complex manufacturing export-oriented platforms, in which most workers could not afford to buy the cars, clothing, or shoes that they made. This was a bumpy road even for foreign investors because of their initial misperceptions, the trial and error of attempted but failed or modified investment projects, and much experimentation with the strategy that would match the postsocialist context.

Conclusions

Hence, my brief conclusions are the following. The bridges between the socialist industrial legacy and capitalist specialization in the world economy have not been merely built by purposive action rooted in the preexisting master plans, pure economic rationality, and strategic foresight of national technocrats and transnational corporations.

Rather, the continuities within discontinuity have resulted from an intricate and dynamic interplay among objective assets and liabilities, historically formed and politically conditioned perceptions, and experimentation with policy and strategy choices in domestic and transnational arenas. In this way, it was in part human sentiment, vision, and often incoherent derived action that determined whether the past did (or alternatively failed to) cast a long shadow in the aftermath of socialism. It is in this sense that we may say that the industrial legacy of socialism is partly what political and economic actors *made* of it.

The complexity of encompassing change, uncertainty about its true risks and opportunities, and the high political stakes involved can account for the fact that the new industrial structures (which preserved or transcended the communist inheritance) emerged, to paraphrase Stephan Haggard, "by default, trial-and-error, and compromise" and took many "years to crystallize" (Haggard 1990, 23).

Finally, historically oriented analysts have had to put up with the existence of large gaps between the data of the past and present. "Even so," János Kornai suggested in the early 1990s, "the first draft of theories cannot be postponed until all the required observations and data have been gathered and subjected to statistical analysis in a conscientious and objective way. After all, it is often theoretical analysis itself that prompts the making of some observation, measurement, or empirical examination" (Kornai 1992, 14–15). While we certainly do not lack theories today, the "empirical wasteland" (Bernhard 2000) left behind by the system all too often sentences us to working with "factoids" rather than reliable facts. In the end, then, there is perhaps little that we can be certain about and rigorously prove about the socialist legacy.

References

Amsden, Alice. 2001. *The Rise of "the Rest." Challenges to the West from Late-Industrializing Economies*. Oxford: Oxford University Press.

Balcet, Giovanni and Aldo Enrietti. 1997. "Regionalisation and Globalisation in Europe: The Case of Fiat Auto Poland and Its Suppliers." *Actes de Gerpisa* 20: 1–19.

Bandelj, Nina. 2008. *From Communists to Foreign Capitalists: The Social Foundations of Foreign Direct Investment*. Princeton, NJ and Oxford: Princeton University Press.

Berend, Iván T. and György Ránki. 1974. *Economic Development in East-Central Europe in the 19th and 20th Centuries*. New York and London: Columbia University Press.

Bernhard, Michael. 2000. "Institutional Choice after Communism: A Critique of Theory-building in an Empirical Wasteland." *East European Politics and Societies* 14(2): 316–47.
Blyth, Mark. 2002. *Great Transformations: Economic Ideas and Institutional Change in the Twentieth Century*. Cambridge: Cambridge University Press.
Bohle, Dorothee. 2008. "Race to the Bottom? Transnational Companies and Reinforced Competition in the Enlarged European Union." In *Neoliberal European Governance and Beyond: The Contradictions and Limits of a Political Project*, ed. Bastiaan van Apeldoorn, Jan Drahokoupil, and Laura Horn, 163–83. Houndsmills: Palgrave MacMillan.
Bohle, Dorothee and Béla Greskovits. 2007. "Neoliberalism, Embedded Neoliberalism, and Neocorporatism: Towards Transnational Capitalism in Central-Eastern Europe." *West European Politics* 30(3) (May): 443–66.
Bohle, Dorothee and Béla Greskovits. 2012. *Capitalist Diversity on Europe's Periphery*. Ithaca, NY: Cornell University Press.
Brown, David, Béla Greskovits, and László Kulcsár. 2007. "Leading Sectors and Leading Regions: Economic Restructuring and Regional Inequality in Hungary since 1990." *International Journal of Urban and Regional Research* 31(3) (September): 522–42.
Cass, Fergus. 2007. "Attracting FDI to Transition Countries: The Use of Incentives and Promotion Agencies." *Transnational Corporations* 16(2) (August): 77–122.
Csaba, László. 1990. *Eastern Europe in the World Economy*. Cambridge and Budapest: Cambridge University Press and Akadémiai Kiadó.
Drahokoupil, Jan. 2009. *Globalization and the State in Central and Eastern Europe: The Politics of Foreign Direct Investment*. London: Routledge.
EBRD Transition Report 1994. London: European Bank for Reconstruction and Development.
Glassman, Maurice. 1994. "The Great Deformation: Polanyi, Poland and the Terrors of Planned Spontaneity." In *The New Great Transformation? Change and Continuity in East-Central Europe*, ed. Chris Bryant and Edmund Mokrzycki, 191–218. London and New York: Routledge.
Greskovits, Béla. 2001. "The Search for the 'True' Socialist GNP: Contrasting Perceptions of the Economic Potential of the Socialist System before and after its Collapse." Unpublished Manuscript. Budapest: Central European University.
Greskovits, Béla. 2003. "Beyond Transition: The Variety of Post-Socialist Development." In *From Liberal Values to Democratic Transition: Essays in Honor of János Kis*, ed. Ronald Dworkin et al. 201–25. Budapest: Central European University Press.
Haggard, Stephan. 1990. *Pathways from the Periphery. The Politics of Growth in the Newly Industrializing Countries*. Ithaca, NY: Cornell University Press.
Jánossy, Ferenc. 2001/1969. "*Gazdaságunk mai ellentmondásainak eredete és felszámolásuk útja* [The Origin of the Current Contradictions of Our Economy, and the Road to Their Elimination]." In Ferenc Jánossy, *Mérés, Trend, Evolúció. Válogatott Írások* [*Measurement, Trend, Evolution. Selected Writings*], ed. Zsuzsa Bekker, 114–36. Budapest: Aula, 2001[1969]). Translation by B. G.
Katzenstein, Peter. 2003. "*Small States* and Small States Revisited." *New Political Economy* 8(1): 9–30.

Klaus, Václav. 1997. "The Ten Commandments of Systemic Reform." In *Renaissance: The Rebirth of Liberty in the Heart of Europe*, 43–49. Washington, DC: Cato Institute.

Klaus, Václav and Tomás Jezek. 1991. "Social Criticism, False Liberalism, and Recent Changes in Czechoslovakia." *East European Politics and Societies* 5(1) (Winter): 26–40.

Kornai, János. 1992. *The Socialist System: The Political Economy of Communism*. Princeton, NJ: Princeton University Press.

Laar, Mart. 2002. *Estonia: Little Country that Could*. Bury St. Edmunds: St Edmundsbury Press.

Lavigne, Marie. 1991. *International Political Economy and Socialism*. Cambridge: Cambridge University Press.

Leopold, Lajos Jr. 1917. "Színlelt kapitálizmus [Simulated Capitalism]." In *Elmélet nélkül [Without Theory]*, 91–133. Budapest. Translation by B. G.

Linden, Greg. 1998. *Building Production Networks in Central Europe: The Case of the Electronics Industry*. Working Paper 126. Berkeley, CA: The Berkeley Roundtable on the International Economy.

Mencinger, Joze. 2004. "Transition to a National and a Market Economy." In *Slovenia: From Yugoslavia to the European Union*, ed. Mojmir Mrak, Matija Rojec, and Carlos Silva-Jáuregui, 67–82. Washington, DC: The World Bank.

Rose, Richard, William Maley, Vilmoris Lasopec, and EMOR. 2002. "Nationalities in the Baltic States. A Survey Study." *Studies in Public Policy* 222. Glasgow: University of Strathclyde Center for the Study of Public Policy.

Stark, David and László Bruszt. 1998. *Post-Socialist Pathways: Transforming Politics and Property in East Central Europe*. Cambridge and New York: Cambridge University Press.

The World Bank. 1996. *From Plan to Market: World Development Report 1996*. Washington, DC, 18.

Van Tulder, Rob and Winfried Ruigrok. 1998. *European Cross-National Production Networks in the Auto Industry: Eastern Europe as the Low End of the European Car Complex*. Working Paper 121. Berkeley, CA: The Berkeley Roundtable on the International Economy.

Vernon, Raymond. 1971. *Sovereignty at Bay: The Multinational Spread of U.S. Enterprises*. New York: Basic Books.

5

The Limits of Legacies: Property Rights in Russian Energy

Timothy Frye

In recent years, scholars have identified the impact of institutional legacies on a host of outcomes, from economic development to civil wars (Acemoglu, Johnson, and Robinson 2001; Engerman and Sokoloff 2002). Scholars of postcommunism have played an important role in this debate by pointing to the myriad ways that precommunist and communist legacies have shaped outcomes after 1989 (Kitschelt 2003; Darden and Grzymala-Busse 2006; Grosfeld, Rodnyansky, and Zhuravskaya 2011). Despite the increasing sophistication of this body of work, considerable conceptual confusion remains regarding the logic of legacy arguments, the impact of legacy arguments over time, and the proper scope conditions for these types of explanations.

This chapter explores the nature of legacy explanations by examining the impact of the command economy on three aspects of property rights in the energy sector in Russia. In some respects, the energy sector can be seen as a "most likely" case for demonstrating the impact of institutional legacies on property rights. It was critical to the Soviet economy and experienced much greater continuity of personnel and ownership structure than other sectors in the Russian economy (more so in gas than in oil). Moreover, references to the "soviet" style of operations at Gazprom and other energy companies in the post-Soviet era are easy to come by (Victor 2007, 62; Goldman 2008; Aslund 2010).

Yet the impact of the institutional legacy of the command economy on three areas of property rights in the energy sector in post-Soviet Russia is difficult to discern.[1] This chapter begins with an analysis of the impact of the legacy of the command economy on the privatization of oil and gas enterprises in Russia in the 1990s. Why did these two sectors experience such different paths of privatization? Why was the oil ministry broken into competing firms, while the gas ministry was kept whole? Despite the common institutional legacy inherited in the oil and gas sectors, the Russian government pursued very different privatization strategies. In accounting for variation in the strategies for privatizing oil and gas enterprises in Russia, contingency rather than legacy seems to get the upper hand. More generally, this section illustrates the importance of theorizing forward from specific legacies to specific outcomes rather than from outcomes back to legacies. The latter strategy risks survivor bias by neglecting potential legacies that do not survive.

It then assesses the legacy of the command economy on the renationalizations of largely privately owned oil companies in the mid-2000s. Why did the Russian government take back that which it had given away in the previous decade? What role did the legacy of the command economy play in this process? The renationalizations that swept the oil sector after 2003 can be seen as part of a broader trend of renationalizations in resource-rich and institution-poor countries rather than as a direct impact of the legacy of the command economy. More generally, the findings suggest that legacy explanations have difficulty capturing the timing of changes in outcomes. Indeed, if we treat legacies as a constant, then it is difficult for legacy explanations to account for change in outcomes over time once an institutional legacy has taken hold.[2]

It concludes by examining various aspects of corporate governance in comparative perspective. Are oil and gas sector firms in Russia more poorly governed than their counterparts in countries that did not experience the command economy? Evidence on the impact of the legacy of the command economy on corporate governance is mixed. In certain respects, corporate governance in the energy sector in Russia has been better than in other resource-rich countries; but in other respects, it appears to have been worse. On a methodological note, this section illustrates the importance of comparisons across legacies to identify scope conditions. That is, cross-legacy comparisons can help identify whether the outcome is generated by processes independent of the legacy itself.

The empirical results point to the limits of the institutional legacy of the command economy on property rights in the energy sector, at least in the three areas under study. In other areas, the legacy of the command economy has been far more pronounced. For example, Russia's energy intensity is extraordinarily high, and this is likely due to the legacy of central planning (McKinsey 2009). Collier (2009) finds that efforts to improve energy efficiency in home and industrial heating in postcommunist Russia have been plagued by the physical infrastructure it inherited from the Soviet economy. The lack of meters for individual end users and the decision to monitor energy usage in "blocks" of users dramatically raised the costs of reforming the market for energy consumption. Thus, generalizations about the impact of the legacy of the planned economy beyond the cases at hand are unwarranted.

In addition to exploring how the legacy of the planned economy shaped property rights, this chapter has a methodological aim. By employing a number of different strategies including within-case analysis, over time comparisons, and cross-national analyses, this chapter offers a chance to evaluate the merits of different research designs. Each section concludes with a discussion of the potential drawbacks and advantages of different research designs for testing legacy-based arguments.

Common Legacy, Different Outcomes: The Privatization of Oil and Gas

One way to test legacy arguments is to examine variation within a single case in units that were exposed to a common legacy. Here I focus on privatization in the oil and gas sectors; two sectors that were central to the Soviet and post-Soviet economies and that share similar institutional legacies but experienced vastly different privatization outcomes in the 1990s.

Soviet economic development, particularly after World War II, relied heavily on oil and gas (Campbell 1968). During the 1960s and 1970s, the Soviet economy grew increasingly dependent on the export of oil and gas to keep the planned economy running (Wright 1983; Kotkin 2001, 15–19). Indeed, some have traced the end of Soviet power in part to the revenue collapse associated with declining world energy prices in the 1980s (Gaidar 2006, 100–12).

The oil and gas sectors in Russia faced similar constraints and exhibited many of the well-known problems associated with a planned economy. The Ministry of the Oil Industry governed the oil sector and was in charge of oil production. Together with Gosplan, the Oil Industry Ministry set production targets, made delivery plans, and created targets for investment. The Ministry oversaw a host of regional production associations and agencies whose primary goals were to meet targets established by the Ministry. Different departments within the Ministry were responsible for production, transport, and sales. For example, the oil pipeline company Transneft' was in charge of oil transportation via pipelines. Managing this sprawling mix of production associations and departments presented great challenges for the Ministry. At its peak level of production in 1988, the Soviet Union was the world's largest oil producer at almost 12 million barrels per day. However, the 1980s also witnessed growing problems in the sector, including declining investment, falling rates of growth, and unfavorable prices that led to concerns about whether the oil sector could continue to serve as the milk cow for the rest of the economy.

The Ministry of the Gas Industry was founded in 1965 and was responsible for the exploration, development, and distribution of gas. Relying on large natural gas reserves discovered in Siberia, the Urals, and the Volga regions during the 1970s and 1980s, the Soviet Union became a major gas producer and exporter. By 1988, the Soviet Union produced almost 50 percent more gas than the next largest producer, the United States. Like the oil sector, the Ministry of the Gas Industry governed a wide range of regionally based associations that were responsible for production, transport, and sales. It too suffered from considerable shortages in investment in the 1980s, as this sector was heavily "taxed" to support other sectors of the economy.

The oil and gas ministries and their related enterprises operated in a similar economic environment of extreme centralization, controlled prices, and almost insatiable demand for their product by domestic industry and households. Indeed, both the oil and gas sectors were privileged in their access to resources relative to other possible sources of energy such as nuclear and hydropower. Both sectors were characterized by drastic shifts in policy, neglect of essential infrastructure, and failures "to make coherent use of the world economy" (Gustafson 1989, 59, 141).[3] In addition, both sectors responded to policy failures by throwing massive resources at short-term problems while neglecting longer-term goals. In comparing the oil and gas campaigns of the 1980s, Gustafson notes: "At bottom, the strategy used by the gas industry has been as unbalanced as that of the oil industry farther south. Housing, roads, and power lines have been neglected along with infrastructure of all sorts. To observers in the Soviet press the most striking feature of the gas campaign to date is its close resemblance to the earlier history of Soviet oil. In short the Soviet gas campaign is another case of an 'extensive' response to crisis and mirrors in its essential features the rest of Soviet energy policy" (1989, 141).

Similarly, Drayton observes that, beginning in the 1970s, the management of the oil and gas sectors became increasingly interrelated. He notes that "policy for the fuel-producing sector is elaborated by a special committee of the Council Ministers headed by Gosplan Chairman Nikolai Baibakov, a former minister of the oil industry. The committee consists of the ministers of all the 14 ministries involved in various aspects of the fuel industries as well as political leaders from fuel producing regions" (1982, 2).

Both ministries exhibited the well-known pathologies common to central planning, such as measuring success by outcomes that were easy to count but trivial, while paying less attention to those that were important but hard to count. The Gas Ministry and the Oil Ministry both relied on the Ministry of Geology for exploration of energy sources, but the Gas and Oil Ministries alone were responsible for determining the size of the find. Thus, both the Oil and the Gas Ministries had to retain significant drilling and exploration capacity even as this was the main province of the Ministry of Geology (Goldman 2008, 42). Based only on the institutional legacies bequeathed by the command economy, one might have expected that these two sectors were unlikely to experience significant changes in their property rights given their deep roots in the command economy. In addition, one might have expected that ownership structures in the two sectors would be relatively similar. Each sector had a similar role in the command economy and similar (at times common) governance structures. Both had considerable weight in Soviet economic planning, and exhibited similar pathologies. Moreover, each sector promised the possibility of great wealth for those who would control these assets. Because oil and gas prices have historically been tightly linked, the market prospects of each were roughly similar.

Despite this common legacy, we find very different patterns of ownership in the post-Soviet period. Beginning in the early 1990s, the government created a number of vertically integrated oil companies that were later privatized using a range of different methods, including voucher auctions and direct sales (Boycko, Shleifer, and Vishny 1995; Blasi, Kroumova, and Kruse 1997; Black and Tarasova 2000; Adachi 2010). In 1991, the Russian Ministry of Fuel and Energy created the first stand-alone oil company, Lukoil, which combined three oil fields under the command of First Deputy Minister of USSR Oil and Gas Ministry Vagit Alekperov. Lukoil remained a state enterprise, but had been corporatized as an entity distinct from the Oil and Gas Ministry. In 1992, the government followed up this measure by creating Surgutneftegaz and YUKOS, and in November of that year, a presidential decree allowed these three companies to issue shares to private investors for up to 49 percent of their respective companies (*Kommersant Daily* 2011; Oil Industry Report). In 1993 and 1994, the Russian government recognized Lukoil, YUKOS, and Surgutneftegaz as private entities and placed the remaining oil production units in a holding company called Rosneft (Alekperov 2011, 325–26). In 1995, a presidential decree created Sibneft by uniting the Noyabrskneftegaz and the Omsk refineries. About a half dozen smaller oil firms were created in a roughly similar fashion: first corporatization of a Soviet-era production unit, then privatization to a concentrated group of domestic shareholders with a small free float of shares to the public.

The Russian government included some of these vertically integrated companies in the voucher privatization that began in 1993. More dramatically, in the mid-1990s the government privatized large portions of YUKOS, Surgutneftegaz, Sibneft, Sidanco, and Lukoil in the "loans for shares" auctions that concentrated ownership in each of these firms in relatively few hands. By 2000, the Russian oil sector had about a dozen firms, and most of these were majority held by private owners (Gustafson 2012: 98–145).[4]

In contrast, the Yeltsin administration largely preserved the state monopoly in the gas sector by carving out a single dominant entity from the Ministry of the Gas Industry. In 1989, insiders within the Ministry of the Gas Industry created Gazprom Kontsern, which in 1992 became the closed shareholder company RAO Gazprom – and eventually in February 1993, an open shareholder company, Gazprom OAO. The ownership structure of Gazprom for much of the period under study was relatively stable. About one-third of shares in Gazprom were put up for sale in the voucher auctions of 1993 and were largely held by the public, although Gazprom insiders reportedly made large purchasers of these shares. In addition, the government allowed insiders within Gazprom to "manage" its portion of shares. In sum, throughout this period, the federal government officially held 35–40 percent of shares, while Gazprom insiders, many of whom were state officials, likely held an equal amount. Private citizens held the rest. Despite many attempts by reformist elements within the Russian government to break its hold on the production, transportation, and sale of gas in Russia, Gazprom has remained a single corporate entity operating as a largely unchallenged monopolist in each of these markets in Russia, and state ownership remains just more than 50 percent of shares. As one observer noted: "From 1993–2004, the ownership structure of the company changed little" (Stern 2005, 170). More colorfully, Aslund notes: "the very symbol of a post-Soviet monopoly was Gazprom, the Russian natural gas monopoly company, which was the only Soviet ministry to be corporatized lock, stock, and barrel" (2002, 183).

Although its monopoly on gas has been chipped away somewhat in recent years, Gazprom remains a behemoth. The dominant purveyor of gas in Russia, it provides about 8 percent of Russia's GDP and employs more than three hundred fifty thousand workers. Even the rise of independent gas producers (such as Novatek and Itera) in recent years is a less important event than it seems because the shareholders of these independents have close ties to Gazprom (*Vedemosti*, December 29, 2010).

In accounting for variation in the nature of property rights in these two sectors, contingency rather than legacy seems to provide a better explanation. Although accounts are of course murky, observers point to the importance of Viktor Chernomyrdin, the head of the Ministry of Gas Industry during the Soviet period, who became head of the Ministry of Oil and Gas and subsequently the prime minister of Russia from 1992 to 1998. As the key protector of the interests of Gazprom within the Russian state, Chernomyrdin stepped in to block attempts to shift control of ownership of Gazprom at several points in the 1990s. Rosner observes that "Chernomyrdin fought diligently to prohibit Gazprom's unbundling in such a way that it would lead to a dilution of ownership and control." He adds that "Gazprom's experience with privatization was nominal at best. This was in no small part due to Chernomyrdin's success in preserving the company's monopoly over upstream gas development" (2006, 13). Similarly, Aslund notes that, even as economic liberalization was under way in 1992 and 1993, "Chernomyrdin sponsored a decree that guaranteed Gazprom a complete monopoly on the production, sale, transport, and export of natural gas" (2008, 140). Moreover, he later helped to craft the legislation that barred the trading of Gazprom stocks without permission from the Gazprom board. Victor adds that "Gazprom didn't go through the shares-for-loans stage ... because Chernomyrdin and company didn't want to lose control over the gas sector or introduce new competition that might weaken government control" (2007, 47).

The appointment of Chernomyrdin – likely made for reasons exogenous to the decision to privatize oil but not gas – points to the importance of contingency rather than legacy in determining the structure of the energy sector. That Yeltsin chose Chernomyrdin as prime minister in December 1992 (his second choice after allowing Yegor Gaidar to retain the post) appears to have been more critical to the paths of privatization of oil and gas than was the legacy of the command economy in any direct sense.

Another potential explanation suggests that the difference in the market structure of oil and gas can account for the different privatization experiences. Gas is used more heavily than oil for generating electricity in Russia, and thus the politics of risking disruption in the electricity market may have made politicians more reluctant to push privatization in this sector. Of course, this is also an argument for why a politician might be especially interested in privatizing this sector to a capable and competent company. In addition, it is easier to tax gas than oil given the nature of distribution and transportation, which may have lowered the government's enthusiasm for privatizing this sector. On the other hand, this approach is not helpful in accounting for why the oil sector was privatized in the 1990s given that national oil companies are the norm in other countries. Most important, if technical features of the market, such as the taxability of gas or the means of delivery, rather than institutional legacies of the command economy can account for variation in privatization outcomes across sectors, this finding also points to the weakness of legacy arguments, as these technical features are hardly unique to the command economy.

One mechanism by which the legacy of the command economy could exert its influence is through the socialization of personnel. For example, the difference in privatization outcomes between the oil and gas sectors might be due to differences in the backgrounds of high officials in these sectors. However, holdovers from the Soviet period were very well represented at the highest levels of management in both the oil and gas sectors. Viktor Chernomyrdin at Gazprom, Vagit Alekperov at Lukoil, and Vladimir Bogdanov at Surgutneftegaz all had deep roots in the command economy.

One could try to resurrect a legacy argument in this case by claiming that the changes in property rights in the oil and gas sectors in Russia in the 1990s were only formal. That is, the ownership structures changed in oil and gas, but the underlying behavior of the firm and the workers it employed were largely unchanged. In this view, the common legacy eventually led firms in both sectors to adopt similar practices despite the outward appearance of different outcomes. Yet we do see some differences in the behavior of private and state-owned oil companies and between the oil sector and the gas sector. Both largely state-owned and largely private oil companies were much quicker to list their firms on stock exchanges in Russia in the 1990s than was Gazprom (Frye 2000). In addition, in the period 2000–03, when private ownership in the oil sector reached its apex, we see that private oil companies were much more productive than their state-owned counterparts (Desai, Dyck, and Zingales 2007; Jones-Luong and Weinthal 2010, 172–73).

Another possibility is to find some way the oil and gas sectors differed in the Soviet period that could then be offered to account for variation in the privatization outcomes across these two sectors during the post-Soviet period. Here the argument would emphasize that the ways the oil sector and the gas sector differed during the Soviet period were critical to their privatization paths after 1991. Perhaps the somewhat greater decentralization of oil production during

The Limits of Legacies

the Soviet period made privatization into smaller units during the post-Soviet period more likely. Or perhaps the better performance of the gas sector in the 1980s relative to oil made it more attractive to keep in state hands. This strategy, however, runs the risk that one can rummage around in the institutional legacy and find some features of the past that "fit" the data. To the extent that one can find equally plausible ways the sectors were similar in the past, it becomes difficult to add up these similarities and differences in a nonarbitrary way that would allow for a clear prediction about future outcomes. The key is to discipline the search by grounding it in theory and to have some decision rule of adding up the ways sectors were similar and different that is logically independent from the observed outcomes. More generally, this research strategy exacerbates the possibility of selection bias by only examining outcomes that persist and by neglecting legacies that did not. If we begin with outcomes and then reason back into the legacy, we fail to consider all the features of the command economy that did not leave an imprint on the postcommunist polity or economy.[5] Thus, this case emphasizes the importance of reasoning from a legacy to an outcome rather than vice versa.

A critic might rightfully point out that the test of similarity in privatization outcomes in sectors with similar legacies is a high bar.[6] It may be that institutional legacies interact in complex ways with other variables but still drive the results. Certainly one should not draw deeper conclusions on the bases of two cases, but the evidence suggests at best a limited role for legacies in the privatization experiences of the oil and gas sectors in Russia despite their status as "most likely" cases to avoid privatization.

One Legacy, Different Outcomes over Time: Expropriation in the Oil Sector

It is hardly unusual for scholars to point to "turning points," "crossroads," or watersheds in postcommunist Russia. Over the past twenty years, it sometimes seems that rarely a month passed without a new one: the rise of Zhirinovsky in 1993, the appointment of Sergei Kirienko as prime minister in 1998, the sinking of the *Kursk* in 2000, President Medvedev's anti-Stalin speech in 2009. Each made headlines at the time, but are much less important in retrospect. Yet a case can be made that renationalization of the energy sector beginning in 2003 fundamentally changed Russia's economic direction. If in 2000, state-owned oil companies produced only about 10 percent of total output in the oil sector, this figure had risen to 50 percent by 2007. More generally, the share of state ownership among listed companies on the main stock exchange increased from 20 percent in 2003 to 30 percent in 2007.

Beginning in 2004, the government effectively took control of the main production unit of YUKOS, known as Yuganskneftegaz, via a forced sale to Baikalfinansgroup, a previously unknown firm that immediately sold the firm to state-owned oil company Rosneft (Adachi 2010, 42–62). In 2005, this was followed by the sale of 73 percent of Sibneft' to Gazprom at the announced price of $13 billion, although many observers were skeptical that the owners of Sibneft received the full amount (*Financial Times*, September 28, 2005). In addition, the Russian government reestablished its majority position in Gazprom by increasing its shares from 38 percent to 50.1 percent. Shortly thereafter, the Sakhalin Energy consortium sold a majority stake of its gas operations in Sakhalin II to Gazprom under great legal and political pressures. Royal Dutch Shell, which previously owned a majority stake in the project, complained bitterly of having to sell the shares to Gazprom, and the European Bank for Reconstruction and Development withdrew its support for the project in large part because of the way Royal Dutch Shell was pressured (European Bank for Reconstruction and Development, January 11, 2007).

The resurgence of state ownership went beyond the energy sector as firms in the helicopter and aircraft (c.f. Tupolev, Sukhoi Aviation), trucking and automobiles (c.f. Kamaz and Avtovaz), and communications (Svyazinvest' and Rostelecom) industries also fell under state control in the years 2004–06. In her sample of one hundred fifty-three of the largest listed and unlisted companies in Russia, Chernykh (2011) identifies twenty-six formerly privately held firms that were taken over in one form or another and became majority owned by the state.

Few events are more frequently debated than the causes of the renationalization of the energy sector in the mid-2000s (Gustafson 2012: 272–319). The renationalization of YUKOS has been linked to general political concerns (Khodorkovsky funded opposition parties and was positioning to run for president), to foreign policy interests (YUKOS was planning to sell a majority stake to a foreign company), to simple greed (the security forces failed to get rich in the 1990s and saw YUKOS as the easiest path to wealth), to a personal conflict (Khodorkovsky did not wear a tie when he met Putin), and to positioning prior to elections in 2003 and 2004 (Frye 2010, 189).

Observers have linked this wave of renationalization in part to the legacy of Soviet rule, "resovietization," or a reassertion of the power of the old *nomenklatura* (Economides and D'Aleo 2011). Goldman supports most strongly the view that the motivation behind the YUKOS privatization was the "revenge of former apparatchiks of the Soviet era for these arriviste new owners of Russia's oil and gas" (2008, 114).

If the legacy argument is correct, then we are not likely to find similar patterns of renationalization in countries that did not experience the legacy of the command economy. Yet, in looking across countries that were and were not exposed to the Soviet legacy, we find significant expansions of state ownership in critical natural resource sectors in recent years. In 2006 alone, forced nationalizations of oil companies occurred in Algeria, Bolivia, Chad, Dubai, Ecuador, Senegal, and Venezuela (Samiento 2009; Boyarchenko 2011).[7] As in Russia in 2006, the state in each of these cases used a variety of means to compel private owners to sell majority stakes in their firms at below market prices. These forced nationalizations are significant given that in most countries oil and gas companies are state owned, and there were relatively few large, private oil and gas companies that could be targets of such a takeover in the first place.

Similarly, Guriev, Kotolin, and Sonin (2011) analyzed data from one hundred sixty-one countries from 1960 to 2006 and identified ninety-two cases of forced nationalizations of oil companies that can be placed into four categories: (i) formal nationalization, (ii) intervention, (iii) forced sale, and (iv) contract renegotiation. They find that forced nationalizations of oil firms are significantly more likely to occur when the price of oil increases rapidly and in countries in which there are fewer constraints on executive power – two factors that seem especially relevant to the Russian case.[8]

In sum, the timing of renationalizations appears to be more tightly linked to fluctuations in oil prices than to the institutional legacy of the command economy.[9] Thinking more generally, it is better to view the resumption of state control of the energy sector in Russia as part of a broader trend of renationalization across countries during a period of high commodity prices than as a direct consequence of the legacy of the command economy.

On a methodological note, legacy arguments tend to offer rather imprecise predictions about the timing of events. In the Russia case, the revanche of the *nomenklatura* occurs in 2004–06, but it is difficult to know whether this supports or refutes a legacy argument. Where explanation is aided by a precise prediction of when an event is more likely to occur, legacy arguments may provide less analytical leverage. Legacy arguments may be better suited for arguments that make predictions about the relative timing of events. They may permit claims that in countries with a certain institutional legacy, some outcome will likely occur later than in countries without that legacy. For example, one might argue countries with a longer exposure to the Soviet legacy might privatize later than countries with less exposure to the Soviet legacy.

In addition, legacy accounts may have difficulty explaining outcomes that vary over time once the institutions that accounted for the legacy's origins have receded from view. Institutional legacies are often seen as constants, so that if a country privatizes and then renationalizes, it is hard to see how an argument rooted in institutional legacies alone can account for both outcomes. Perhaps a prediction could be made that certain institutional legacies make it more likely that an outcome will oscillate back and forth, but it is difficult to see how they can systematically account for the direction of change in outcomes over time. For example, countries with greater exposure to the command economy may be more susceptible to cycles of privatization and nationalization than other countries, but in such circumstances it would be hard for a legacy argument to make predictions about the conditions under which privatization and nationalization are likely to occur. This may limit the power of legacy arguments to account for outcomes that change over time.

One area of future research is in whether the impact of legacies is increasing or decreasing over time. For example, Pop-Eleches (2007) finds that the institutional legacies of communist rule had an increasing impact on the democracy scores of postcommunist countries as the transition advanced. Countries tended to revert to the predictions made by their institutional legacies. Frye (2010) finds that the impact of a composite measure of initial conditions has a significant and negative impact on rates of economic growth. That is, poor institutional legacies of a command economy had a sharp effect on economic growth rates during the first years of transition, but this impact receded over time. The conditions under which institutional legacies have an increasing or decreasing effect on outcomes is a topic worthy of future exploration. Thus, even where we find correlations between legacies and outcomes, we also need a theory as to why we would expect the impact of a legacy to be decreasing, increasing or constant over time, but these arguments are rarely explored.

Different Legacies, Similar Outcomes?

Finally, it is often helpful to test claims about the impact of institutional legacies on outcomes in countries that did not experience the legacy. For example, to what extent does the corporate governance of national energy firms in countries that experienced the command economy differ from those that did not? More specifically, does the behavior of Gazprom differ in significant ways from other national energy champions because of its exposure to the Soviet legacy? Gazprom is in certain respects an easy case for a legacy argument. Observers have frequently noted the "Soviet" features of Gazprom operations. Aslund observes that Gazprom "retains many features of a Soviet ministry" (2010, 151). Victor notes that Gazprom is "managed essentially [as] a soviet enterprise" (2007, 62). By most accounts, it continues to exhibit many of the pathologies for which the command economy was renowned, including, among others, opacity, short-termism, underinvestment, and overstaffing (Granick 1954; Berliner 1957). To the extent that these features are especially pronounced at Gazprom relative to other national energy champions, one can begin to make a case that the institutional legacy of the command economy has had a lasting impact on Gazprom.

Measuring levels of opacity, short-termism, underinvestment, and overstaffing is decidedly difficult, particularly given that most national energy companies are very reluctant to provide information on their internal decision-making practices. National energy companies are notorious for overstating their reserves to attract investors while understating them to repel tax collectors (Yergin 1991). Because most national oil companies are not publicly traded and work in close cooperation with autocratic governments, gaining reliable information that permits clear cross-national comparisons is especially challenging. In reading the literature on national energy champions, the cliché de jour seems to be that national oil and gas companies are a "state within a state."[10]

The Limits of Legacies

One first cut is to examine the level of transparency of reporting of information on the policies and practices of countries rich in natural resources. Gazprom's decision-making structure is opaque and rather informal (Victor and Sayfer 2012). Gazprom holds regular board and stockholder meetings, but the real decisions are made within an informal circle around the Russian president and are communicated through the deputy prime ministers and the chairman of Gazprom.[11] Victor notes that its opacity "reflects Gazprom's insular history as a Soviet ministry" (2007, 6). Noted Gazprom critics Milov and Nemtsov (2008) observe that Gazprom has repeatedly left shareholders in the dark about sales and purchases of assets worth tens of millions of dollars.

Gazprom has, however, provided standard financial information about its economic activities, undergone annual audits by foreign accounting firms, and meets regularly with minority shareholders. It has satisfied the listing requirements to issue depository receipts, and Gazprom shares are traded over the counter in the United States. Gazprom has met the requirements for listing shares in London as well. One can criticize the quality of data provided by Gazprom, but in many respects Gazprom's reporting during the Putin years appears to be better than that of state-owned national oil companies in other countries (Stern 2005; Revenue Watch Index 2011). This is a rather low bar given the great opacity of most national energy champions.

Data from the nongovernmental organization Revenue Watch Institute (RWI) can help put Russia and Gazprom in comparative perspective. RWI collected data on financial reporting in natural resource sectors, including oil, gas, and minerals in forty-one resource-rich countries in 2010.[12] The RWI applied fifty-one indicators in seven different types of activity, including reporting on access to resources, the generation of revenue, the institutional setting governing natural resources, natural resource funds, subnational transfers, and participation in the Extractive Industries Transparency Initiative. The Revenue Watch Index only uses information from 2010 and captures the law on the books rather than the law in practice. Transparency is important, but is just one element of a strong property rights regime. Transparent thievery is not punished in the Index. Yet the Index does provide a relatively clear and consistent measure of the formal rules associated with reporting financial indictors related to natural resource management.

Looking at the three most relevant indicators, access to resources, generation of revenue, and institutional setting, we find that of the forty-one countries under study Russia places seventh, Kazakhstan fourteenth, Azerbaijan twenty-eighth, and Turkmenistan fortieth. The worst performers include Saudi Arabia, Ghana, Kuwait, Tanzania, Algeria, the Democratic Republic of Congo, and Equatorial Guinea. The best performers include Brazil, Norway, Colombia, and the United States, all of which rank higher than Russia. Unreported regression analysis finds that countries that were part of the former Soviet Union are no less transparent than other countries in the sample controlling for a country's level of GDP per capita and whether its wealth lies in oil and gas or minerals. This suggests that the legacy of the command economy does not have a discernible impact on the transparency in reporting in the energy sector, at least as measured by Revenue Watch.

Similarly, the World Bank (2008a, 2008b) rated thirty-three state-owned energy companies on more than thirty indicators related to the quality of corporate governance, including ownership structure, independence of the board of directors, SEC filings, transparency of finances, and disclosure of audit data. Gazprom fares quite well by this measure, as it rates fourth of thirty-three, after Statoil-Hydro of Norway, GDF of France, and PTT of Thailand. Gazprom's relatively strong performance is likely due to the substantial shareholding of private investors as the top rated state-owned energy companies in this study all have substantial private holdings, while the more opaque firms are all 100 percent state owned. Again, firms from former Soviet countries do not score systematically worse or better than other state-owned companies controlling for their level of wealth.

A different way to measure the impact of the Soviet legacy in the energy sector is to examine the efficiency of energy companies in countries with and without exposure to the legacy of the command economy. For example, Victor (2007) finds that relative to other national energy companies and international oil companies in the period 1999–2004, Gazprom appears to be more inefficient; however, the measure she uses to make this comparison is very noisy. More specifically, she compares the ratio of stock market capitalization to reserves of the 100 largest energy companies in the world. The assumption here is that stock market capitalization should largely reflect the size of reserves, that this relationship largely holds for international oil companies and national oil companies, and that differences between the stock price and reserves reflect concerns about the institutional environment or the company itself. She finds that the stock market capitalization of Russian energy firms traded in the stock market as a proportion of their reserves is decidedly lower than for other firms and that Gazprom is far below its expected value. Again, these are crude measures (pardon the pun), but point toward the possibility of a legacy effect.

These broad cross-national comparisons can only provide rough gauges (and with rather noisy data at that). A slightly more nuanced approach is to compare the governance and investment of a national energy champion that is similar to Gazprom in many respects but differs in its institutional legacy. The ways these two companies are similar are unlikely to be accounted for by the Soviet legacy. Finding relevant comparisons for Gazprom is not easy. Gazprom is by far the largest gas company in the world. Moreover, if Gazprom were a country, its combined oil and gas reserves would rank only behind those of Saudi Arabia and Iran. In 2006, Gazprom controlled about 20 percent of the world's natural gas reserves, 70 percent of Russia's gas reserves, and 94 percent of Russia's gas production. It provides about 8–10 percent of Russia's GDP and about 20 percent of its exports.

One potentially useful comparison with Gazprom since 2000 is PEMEX in Mexico in its authoritarian period prior to 1994. Both contemporary Russia and Mexico during the period under study were middle-income countries with autocratic governments in which dominant parties featured prominently. Both exhibited high levels of corruption, weak legal institutions, and highly biased national media. Both relied heavily on national energy champions for state revenue, as the energy sector in each country accounted for more than half of export revenue. And governments in both countries placed great importance on keeping energy prices of the national energy champions low to promote domestic manufacturing and subsidize consumers (Philip 1999, 47). In terms of importance to their relative national economies, PEMEX under the PRI and Gazprom are relatively similar. In addition, both countries experienced booms and busts in prices during these periods. PEMEX and Gazprom are by far the largest companies in their respective countries by employment and output and are central to economic and political life. These comparisons are far from perfect as PEMEX is an oil company and Gazprom is primarily a gas company for the much of the period under study. In addition, the global energy market facing PEMEX in the 1970s and 1980s differs from that facing Gazprom in the 1990s–2000s.

Yet these cases can shed light on legacy arguments in the following respect: PEMEX and Gazprom inherited different institutional legacies, and therefore their institutional legacies are not likely to account for the commonalities in their degree of opacity, governance, and investment patterns. To reframe the question, here we are interested in exploring whether these outcomes are better accounted for by differences in institutional legacies or by the structural position of these firms in their political systems and the global economy.

PEMEX was founded in 1938 following the nationalization of foreign oil companies. It is a fully state-owned company, and the Mexican constitution bars foreigners from owning shares (Wirth 1985; Philip 1999; Stojanovski 2012). As with Gazprom in Russia, there is broad public support for keeping PEMEX in government hands. The 1970s were a time of great optimism in Mexico thanks to new discoveries in the Cantarell oil field. Millor referred to Mexico as "the new Saudi Arabia" (1982: 125), and expectations were high for Mexico as a reliable supplier of oil in comparison to less reliable sources in the Middle East. The 1980s saw cronyism run rampant as successive governments relied heavily on the company to fund patronage networks to secure political support (Stojanovski 2012, 311–12). In 1992, Mexico liberalized its political system, and PEMEX underwent considerable reforms. However, in the past two decades, Mexico has drawn down its main sources of oil and now faces the prospects of more significant declines in output; this peaked at 3.3 million barrels per day in 2004, but is currently only 2.7 million barrels per day. Without substantial new investment in deep water production technologies, PEMEX's future looks somewhat grim, and some expect Mexico to become a net importer of oil in the next decade (*New York Times*, March 9, 2010).

In many respects, governance at the two energy giants has much in common despite the different legacies. Like Gazprom, PEMEX in the PRI period was rather opaque, and information was highly compartmentalized. Philip labels PEMEX during this period "a technically talented, but administratively chaotic institution" (1999, 362), adding that all major departments in PEMEX, exploration, production, petroleum, sales and finance, "behave like feudal fiefdoms." In addition, he notes: "Indeed, one of the consistent themes running through commentary on PEMEX has concerned the difficulty of extracting information, even from within the organization" (1999, 349–50).

PEMEX under PRI also built and/or operated many non-core assets, including hospitals, roads, ports, and railroads (Stojanovski 2012, 286). It conducted many of the engineering tasks that would fall to other companies in the 1990s and 2000s. Similarly, Gazprom's investments range far from its core operations. Gazprom not only owns energy-related firms, it is the largest holder of agricultural land in Russia and owns breweries, hotels, and media outlets (Victor and Sayfer 2012).

Moreover, charges of corruption and embezzlement surround both companies. In Mexico, the PEMEXGATE scandal revealed a $100 million loan to back a presidential candidate in 2000, a crime for which no one was convicted even though the firm paid a large fine. Much corruption also surrounded the awarding of contracts to companies owned in part by PEMEX officials – a strategy for which Gazprom is also well known (Aslund 2010; Stojanovski 2012). While we lack systematic data on corruption levels at PEMEX during the period under study, Grayson wrote: "The need to pay off key company and union officials in return for economic opportunities is as great, if not greater, than at any time in the industry's history" (1981, 59).

Soviet enterprises were well known for emphasizing short-term production targets at the expense of more balanced investment plans. Both PEMEX and Gazprom surely fit this characterization as well. PEMEX underinvested during the 1970s and 1980s, as much oil revenue was used to pay down government debt rather than plowed back into the company. Moreover, the company went on a hiring and spending spree with its newfound wealth in the late 1970s and 1980s rather than seek new sources of production (Bogan 2009). Short-termism reigned at PEMEX, as cash-hungry governments pressured the company to pump liquid into wells to increase output during the 1980s, thereby accelerating future declines (Philip 1999). Even during periods of boom that followed, PEMEX has underinvested in large part to serve PRI political goals and policy preferences (Stojanovski 2012, 31). That PEMEX currently has little technical capacity to tap its deep water oil is in part a reflection of an emphasis on producing results in the short term while forsaking longer-term capital investment.

Gazprom followed a similar pattern of investment when faced with bust and boom. During the 1990s, Gazprom investment plummeted and the government used revenue from the energy sector to shore up its debts (Stern 2005). For example, in 1997, President Boris Yeltsin ordered Gazprom to deliver $2 billion to the government to cover pension arrears (Milov and Nemtsov 2008).

The boom period that followed has also seen Gazprom misdirect its investment for short-term benefit. The gas shortage in Russia in recent years is not the result of limited reserves, but is due in large part to Gazprom's investment strategy. Gazprom has purchased unrelated assets at home and abroad and preferred to invest in building pipelines where it does not have a comparative advantage to exploring and producing gas where it does (Victor 2007; Aslund 2010; Victor and Sayfer 2012). It seems that many of Gazprom's investments were undertaken to serve the Kremlin's internal and foreign agendas or to increase its capitalization. Thus, while underinvestment and politically motivated investment were common features of Soviet enterprises and have been persistent problems at Gazprom, a similarly situated company that was not exposed to the Soviet legacy (PEMEX) also experienced this problem. In both cases, we see cash-starved governments during periods of bust raid the finances of their national energy company, then direct revenue away from investment during periods of boom. Of course, the comparison is far from perfect. One important difference in the corporate governance of the two energy giants is the means by which the state monitors firm officials. The finances of PEMEX have historically been tightly regulated by congressional committees and the Finance Ministry. As Lopez-Velarde notes: "Pemex and its subsidiaries' budget and planning are governed by federal regulators. Each fiscal year the budget of Pemex and its subsidiaries must be prepared by the federal government, approved by the Congress, and published in the official newspaper in order to be legally binding" (1994, 5). Moreover, credit requests are tightly supervised by the Ministry of Finance and Public Credit. Many observers have complained that this tight oversight, particularly the review by Congress, allows powerful political actors to influence PEMEX decision making to serve political rather than economic ends (Stojanovski 2012). This serves in stark contrast to Gazprom, where decision making is largely insulated from formal political institutions, such as the Duma and regulatory agencies, but is still subject to great informal pressure, often via the personal involvement of the president. As Hults notes: "Gazprom has nominal power over investment decisions, but the state frequently uses its informal authority to control decision making" (2012, 100).

This brief comparison suggests that high levels of opacity, corruption, and politically motivated investment at PEMEX and Gazprom appear to have more to do with these companies' positions in the political systems and exposure to global market forces than to particular institutional legacies. As a methodological note, these types of cross-legacy comparisons can help rule out the impact of the institutional legacy when outcomes are similar, and the mechanisms used to produce those outcomes are similar, in units experiencing different legacies. However, to demonstrate the force of a legacy argument requires two additional steps: ruling out alternative explanations and establishing that the legacy itself rather than changes in behavior in the interim period are driving the variation in outcomes.

Conclusion

This chapter is closer to a cautionary tale than an enthusiastic call to integrate legacy-based arguments into our analyses of political and economic outcomes in the post-Soviet era. Evidence from three areas of property rights in the energy sector in Russia revealed ambiguous evidence for legacy arguments. Certainly, legacy-based arguments may have more purchase on other topics, but at least in the three cases examined here the results were mixed at best.

More generally, the results speak to broader conceptual and methodological issues about legacy-based arguments in four ways. First, they highlight the value of building theories rooted in a detailed understanding of legacies and then projecting hypotheses forward rather than beginning with outcomes and retrofitting them to particular legacies. Second, the cases suggest the limits of legacy arguments in accounting for outcomes that vary over time once a legacy has been established. In this way, legacy explanations are one-way arguments that can predict a constant difference between outcomes, but may struggle to account for outcomes that vary over time. For example, it is difficult for the legacy of the command economy to account for both the privatization and subsequent renationalization of the oil sector in Russia. Third, legacy arguments should consider more carefully whether the impact of a particular legacy is increasing, decreasing, or constant over time. Finally, these cases illustrate the value of making comparisons across units experiencing different institutional legacies to generate scope conditions for legacy arguments.

Notes

1. Here I adopt Kotkin and Beissinger's definition of legacy as "a durable causal relationship between past institutions and policies on subsequent practices or beliefs, long beyond the life of the regimes, institutions, and policies that gave birth to them."
2. If we conceive of legacies as socially constructed, then one can permit them to vary over time (c.f. Abdelal 2001).
3. Gustafson notes that, as of the late 1980s, "energy policy has been in a permanent state of emergency since the 1970s."
4. For a good chart depicting the dizzying changes of ownership in the oil sector, see Goldman (2008, 62–63).
5. Tilly (1990) makes a similar point about examining state formation in Europe. If one only looks at the survivor states, then one omits information from all the potential states that fell by the wayside over the past millennium.
6. This is closer to a "straw in the wind" test (Collier 2011).
7. Even in Slovakia in 2008, populist Prime Minister Robert Fico threatened to take control of the partly privatized gas supplier SPP (Nosko 2008). Note that the nationalizations take place prior to the 2008 financial crash, and thus operated from a different logic than the temporary nationalizations of financially strapped firms that occurred in many countries.

8   This result is robust to the inclusion of fixed effects, so there should be no unobserved heterogeneity at the country level that is accounting for this result. Boyarchenko (2011) also finds strong evidence of a price effect in her study of resource-rich countries over a thirty-year period.
9   One might argue that the institutional legacy of the command economy led to weak institutions that made a forced nationalization more likely, but this is not much help in accounting for the timing of renationalization, as weak institutions have been in place for many years.
10 For example, authors in the Victor and colleagues 2012 compendium of case studies on national oil companies use the term to refer to firms in Angola, Algeria, Brazil, Kuwait, Mexico, Russia, and Saudi Arabia.
11 *New York Times*, April 24, 2006.
12 New York-based Revenue Watch Institute and Berlin-based Transparency International are nongovernmental groups tracking corruption. Independent consultants gathered the information to complete each country questionnaire from November 2009 to April 2010. Research concentrated on identifying publicly available information covering the period from January 2006 to December 2009. See http://www.revenuewatch.org/.

References

Abdelal, Rawi. 2001. *National Purpose in the World Economy: Post-Soviet States in Comparative Perspective*. Ithaca, NY: Cornell University Press.
Acemoglu, D., S. Johnson, and J. Robinson. 2001. "The Colonial Origins of Comparative Development: An Empirical Investigation." *American Economic Review* 91: 1369–401.
Adachi, Yuko. 2010. *Building Big Business in Russia: The Impact of Informal Corporate Governance Practices*. New York: Routledge.
Alekperov, Vagit. 2011. *Oil of Russia: Past, Present, and Future*. Minneapolis, MN: Eastview Press.
Aslund, Anders. 2002. *Building Capitalism: The Transformation of the Former Soviet Bloc*. New York: Cambridge University Press.
  2008. *Russia's Capitalist Revolution: Why Market Reforms Succeeded and Democracy Failed*. Washington, DC: Petersen Institute for International Economics.
  2010. "Gazprom: A Challenged Giant in Need of Reform." In *Russia after the Global Economic Crisis*. Ed. Anders Aslund, Sergei Guriev, and Andrew Kuchins. Washington, DC: Petersen Institute and Center for Strategic and International Studies, 151–68.
Berliner, Joseph. 1957. *Factory and Manager in the USSR*. Cambridge, MA: Harvard University Press.
Black, Bernard and Anna Tarasova. 2000. "Russian Privatization: What Went Wrong?" *Stanford Law Review* 1731–1808.
Blasi, Joseph, Maya Kroumova, and Douglas Kruse. 1997. *Kremlin Capitalism: The Privatization of the Russian Economy*. Ithaca, NY: Cornell University Press.
Bogan, Jesse. 2009. "With Easy Oil Gone, Pemex Sobers Up." *Forbes*. May 7.
Boyarchenko, Nina. 2011. "Turning off the Tap: Determinants of Expropriation in the Energy Sector." Ms. Chicago. Chicago, IL: University of Chicago Business School.
Boycko, Maksim, Andrei Shleifer, and Robert Vishny. 1995. *Privatizing Russia*. Cambridge, MA: MIT Press.

Campbell, Robert. 1968. *The Economics of Soviet Oil and Gas*. Baltimore, MD: Johns Hopkins University Press.
Chernykh, Lucy. 2011. "Profit or Politics? Understanding Renationalizations in Russia." *Journal of Corporate Finance* 17, 1237–53.
Collier, David. 2011. "Understanding Process Tracing." *PS. Political Science and Politics* 44(4): 823–30.
Collier, Stephen. 2009. *Post-Soviet Social: Neoliberalism, Social Modernity, and Biopolitics*. Princeton, NJ: Princeton University Press.
Coronel, Gustavo. 2006. "Corruption, Mismanagement, and Abuse of Power in Hugo Chávez's Venezuela." Washington, DC: Cato Institute, November 27, (2): 1–24.
Darden, Keith and Anna Grzymala-Busse. 2006. "The Great Divide: Pre-Communist Schooling and Post-Communist Trajectories." *World Politics* 59(1): 83–115.
Desai, Mihir, Alexander Dyck, and Luigi Zingales. 2007. "Theft and Taxes." *Journal of Finances* 84(3) (June 2007): 591–623.
Drayton, Geoffrey. 1982. *Soviet Oil and Gas to 1990*. Washington, DC: ABT Books.
Dunning, Thad. 2008. *Crude Democracy: Natural Resource Wealth and Political Regimes*. New York: Cambridge University Press.
Economides, Michael J. and Donna Marie D'Aleo. 2011. *From Soviet to Putin and Back: The Dominance of Energy in Today's Russia*. Houston, TX: ET Publishing.
Engerman, S. and K. Sokoloff. 2002. "Factor Endowments, Inequality, and Paths of Development among New World Economies." *Economia* 3(1): 41–88.
Frye, Timothy. 2000. *Brokers and Bureaucrats: Building Market Institutions in Russia*. Ann Arbor: University of Michigan Press.
  2010. *Building States and Markets after Communism: The Perils of Polarized Democracy*. New York: Cambridge University Press.
Gaddy, Clifford and Barry W. Ickes. 2010. "Russia after the Global Financial Crisis." *Eurasian Geography and Economics* 51(3): 281–311.
Gaidar, Yegor. 2006. *Collapse of an Empire: Lessons for Modern Russia*. Washington, DC: Brookings Institution.
Goldman, Marshall. 2008. *Petrostate: Putin, Power and the New Russia*. New York: Oxford University Press.
Granick, David. 1954. *Management of the Industrial Firm in the USSR*. New York: Columbia University Press.
Grayson, George. 1981. *The Politics of Mexican Oil*. Pittsburgh: University of Pittsburgh Press.
Grosfeld, I., A. Rodnyansky, and E. Zhuravskaya. 2011. "Persistent Anti-Market Culture: A Legacy of the Pale of Settlement and the Holocaust." Unpublished manuscript, Department of Economics, Paris School of Economics; Center for Financial and Economic Research (CEFIR), Moscow; New Economics School, Moscow.
Guriev, Sergei, Antol Kotolin, and Konstantin Sonin. 2011. "Determinants of Nationalization in Oil Sector: A Theory and Evidence from Panel Data." *Journal of Law Economics and Organization* 25: 1–29.
Gustafson, Thane. 1989. *Crisis amidst Plenty: The Politics of Energy under Brezhnev and Gorbachev*. Princeton, NJ: Princeton University Press.
  2012. *Wheel of Fortune: The Battle for Oil and Power in Russia*. Cambridge, MA: Harvard University Press.

Hults, David. 2012a. "Hybrid Governance: State Management of National Oil Companies." In *Oil and Governance*. Ed. David Victor, David R. Hults, and Mark Thurber. New York: Cambridge University Press, 62–120.
  2012b. "Venezuela – Petróleos de Venezuela, S. A.: From Independence to Subservience." In *Oil and Governance*. Ed. David Victor, David R. Hults, and Mark Thurber. New York: Cambridge University Press, 418–77.
Jensen, Robert, Theodore Shabad, and Arthur Wright. 1983. *Soviet Natural Resources in the World Economy*. Chicago, IL: University of Chicago Press.
Jones-Luong, Pauline and Erica Weinthal. 2010. *Oil is Not a Curse: Ownership Structure and Institutions in Post-Soviet States*. New York: Cambridge University Press.
Kitschelt, H. 2003. "Accounting for Postcommunist Regime Diversity: What Counts as a Good Cause?" In *Capitalism and Democracy in Central and Eastern Europe*. Ed. G Ekiert and S. E. Hanson, 49–86. Cambridge: Cambridge University Press.
Kommersant', on line. April 13, 2011. "Oil Industry Report."
Kotkin, Stephen. 2001. *Armageddon Averted: The Soviet Collapse, 1970–2000*. New York: Oxford University Press.
Lopez-Velarde, Rogelio. 1994. "Mexico's New Petroleum Law: The Internal Reforms at Pemex and the North American Free Trade Agreement." *International Lawyer* 1: 1–27.
Magaloni, Beatriz. 2006. *Voting for Autocracy: Hegemonic Party Survival and Its Demise in Mexico*. New York: Cambridge University Press.
Mckinsey Consulting. 2009. "Pathways to an Energy and Carbon Efficient Economy: Opportunities to Increase Energy Efficiency and Reduce Greenhouse Gases." ms. Moscow, Russia.
Milov, Vladimir and Boris Nemtsov. 2008. *Putin and Gazprom: An Independent Report*. Moscow.
Millor, Manuel R. 1982. *Mexico's Oil: Catalyst for a New Relationship with the U.S.?* Boulder, CO: Westview Press.
Nosko, Andrej. 2008. "Nationalization of Oil Companies (Slovakia not Venezuela this time)." http://pergceu.blogspot.com/2008/11/nationalization-of-energy-companies.html, Accessed November 30, 2011.
Philip, George. 1999. "The Political Constraints on Economic Policy in Post-1982 Mexico: The Case of Pemex." *Bulletin of Latin American Research* 18(1): 35–50.
Pop-Eleches Grigore. 2007. "Historical Legacies and Post-Communist Regime Change." *Journal of Politics* 69(4): 908–26.
Revenue Watch Index. 2011. http://www.revenuewatch.org/publications/promoting-revenue-transparency-2011-report-oil-and-gas-companies accessed on January 4, 2014.
Rosner, Kevin. 2006. *Gazprom and the Russian State*. London: GMB.
Samiento, Salvador. 2009. September 21. "Oil Nationalism in Latin America." Institute for Policy Studies. http://www.ips-dc.org/articles/oil_nationalism_in_latin_america, accessed January 8, 2014.
Stern, Johnathan. 2005. *The Future of Russian Gas and Gazprom*. Oxford: Oxford University Press.

Stojanovski, Ognan. 2012. "Mexico – Handcuffed: An Assessment of Pemex's Performance and Strategy." In *Oil and Governance*. Ed. David Victor, David R. Hults, and Mark Thurber. New York: Cambridge University Press, 280–333.

Tilly, Charles. 1990. *Coercion, Capital, and European States, AD 990–1992*. Cambridge: Basil Blackwell Press.

Victor, David, David R. Hults, and Mark Thurber, eds. 2012. *Oil and Governance*. New York: Cambridge University Press.

Victor, Nadejda. 2007. "On Measuring the Performance of National Oil Companies." Ms. Stanford.

Victor, Nadejda and Inna Sayfer. 2012. "Russia – Gazprom: The Struggle for Power." In *Oil and Governance*. Ed. David Victor, David R. Hults, and Mark Thurber. New York: Cambridge University Press, 655–700.

Wirth, John D. 1985. "Introduction." In *Latin American Oil Companies and the Politics of Energy*. Lincoln: University of Nebraska Press.

Wright, Arthur W. 1983. "The Role of Raw Materials in Soviet Foreign Trade." In *Soviet Natural Resources in the World Economy*. Ed. Robert G. Jensen, Theodore Shabad, and Arthur W. Wright. Chicago: University of Chicago Press, 617–22.

World Bank, 2008a. *A Citizen's Guide to National Oil Companies. Technical Guide*. Washington, DC: World Bank.

   2008b. *A Citizen's Guide to National Oil Companies. Data Appendix*. Washington, DC: World Bank.

Yergin, Daniel. 1991. *The Prize: The Epic Quest for Oil, Money and Power*. New York: Simon and Schuster.

6

Legacies and Departures in the Russian State Executive

Eugene Huskey

Soviet executive power rested on the peculiar institutional pillars of the party/state, which was an interlocking set of organizations and personnel that shared responsibility for governing the USSR. Designed to mimic the appearance of European democracies, with a dominant party – the Communist Party in this case – ruling through the government, or a council of ministers, the Soviet institutional model merged politics and public administration into a new party/state synthesis. With the disappearance of the Communist Party as a "ruling party" in 1991, the Soviet incarnation of the party/state passed into history. However, many of the legacies of this unusual form of executive power are evident in postcommunist institutions in Russia. This chapter identifies, in Kotkin and Beissinger's words in Chapter 1 of this volume, "eerily familiar" features of the postcommunist Russian executive and argues that, in many cases, Soviet practices and beliefs "found new or renewed meaning ... within [the] different macro-historical context" of postcommunist rule.[1]

Short of tracing the precise causal mechanisms that link tsarist and/or Soviet-era practices and beliefs to their postcommunist incarnations, the best method of advancing a compelling legacy argument is to assess whether a postcommunist pattern of thought and behavior meets one or more tests of endurance or distinctiveness. The more tests passed, the more convincing the legacy explanation. First, and most important, are the practices and beliefs found on both sides of the regime divide present only, or almost exclusively, in postcommunist countries? If so, it is likely that earlier traditions associated with the tsarist and/or Soviet experiences were influential in shaping current practice. In other words, the weight of the past, not present circumstances or future interests, explains the similarities. Second, was a practice or belief inherited from the old regime revived after falling into disuse? Certain institutions, like the Procuracy, passed into the new order relatively unscathed and may be considered a "thin" form of legacy in the sense that they continued across the regime divide simply by force of inertia, without being seriously questioned. However, institutions that satisfy this second test are clearly more than thin legacies, having been, in Kotkin and Beissinger's terms, reproduced, recombined, resurrected, or redeployed in entirely new conditions. Their ability to resurface after having been submerged is a testament to their potency and tenacity – either because they "embody and express deeply rooted habits" (Brubaker 1992, 187) of thought and action, or because they arise in response to similar needs on both sides of the regime divide.[2] A final question asks whether particular practices or beliefs associated with the old regime had endured despite direct attempts from above to reform them or despite direct challenges to their existence by alternative institutions. If forces in the new regime sought unsuccessfully to eliminate portions of the institutional and ideational inheritance, these practices and beliefs would also appear to be robust legacies from the old order.

With this framework of analysis in place, we can begin to interrogate the postcommunist executive institutions that bear a remarkable resemblance to institutions of the Soviet era. These institutions may be grouped into three categories: formal organizations; elite recruitment; and rituals of rule. We argue that each of the institutions discussed in this chapter satisfies one or more of the legacy tests just outlined.

Legacy Patterns in the Organization of the Postcommunist Russian Executive

In the past 100 years, Russia has been governed by three different regimes: tsarist, Soviet, and postcommunist. Despite operating with different ideologies, populations, economic systems, policy challenges, and international environments, the Russian executive has retained a structure that is remarkably similar across the three periods. In each case, a central political figure – tsar, general secretary, or president – has occupied a superordinate position above the workaday branches of government.[3] Building on tsarist and Soviet traditions, Russian constitutional theory today does not view the president as part of the executive branch narrowly understood, which is headed by the prime minister, but as a kind of vibrant monarch who, in the language of the current constitution (art. 80), "establishes the basic directions of domestic and foreign policy." The tsar's chancellery, the Central Committee of the Communist Party, and now the Administration (or bureaucracy) of the Russian President have performed similar functions in guiding the state. In some areas of policy, such as agriculture and communications for the Communist Party or security affairs for the Russian president, the leader of the day has chosen to assume direct management responsibility, but in most fields the leader "rules but does not govern" (to use a favorite phrase of sovietologists, who borrowed it from studies of European monarchical politics) (Hill 1980).[4] This is to say that it is the job of the prime minister and his or her government (*pravitel'stvo*) to carry out the basic policy line established by the president.[5]

One indication of the superordinate status of the Russian president is the institution of personal representatives of the president (*polnomochennye predstaviteli*), who serve as presidential agents in each of the major organs of state. Personal representatives of the president now work in each of the two chambers of the legislature, in each of the three highest courts in the land, and in each of the eight federal districts. At certain times, most notably during the Putin presidency (and especially in the wake of Mikhail Kasianov's removal), the prime minister himself has assumed the role of the president's personal agent in the government. Thus, even though the formal outlines of Russian government fit into a semi-presidential mold, the pattern of authority bears little resemblance to that found in traditional semi-presidentialism of the French variety.

This structure of executive power did not take root in postcommunist Russia without resistance. In the period from late 1991 to late 1993, two different legacy models of government competed for dominance in Russia. The first was a presidential structure, which had been introduced originally at the USSR level by Gorbachev in 1990 as a means of strengthening his personal authority and transferring power from party to state institutions. The institution of the presidency was then replicated in each of the fifteen republics, now with direct presidential elections instead of the indirect election that brought Gorbachev to the USSR presidency (Huskey 1999, 12–20). Challenging this presidential structure was soviet parliamentarism, whose institutional champion was the Congress of People's Deputies, headed by Ruslan Khasbulatov.[6] Soviet parliamentarism had its origins in the romantic governing concepts present at the launch of the Bolshevik state, when some believed that executive and legislative functions could be fused into a single institution. In the fall of 1993, the more recent and deeply embedded of the two models, which gave rise to the president-centered structure, won the day. Thus, the inheritance of a dominating executive endured despite a formidable challenge from an alternative institution.[7]

To make a legacy argument is not to deny that contemporary circumstances and the interests of elites had no role in the shaping of postcommunist Russian institutional design. Clearly, the hyper-presidential structure of government offered numerous advantages to Yeltsin and his team: it reduced legislative constraints on executive power at a moment when major policy changes were still under way; it enhanced presidential authority by granting Yeltsin a magisterial perch above the everyday work of government; and it created a useful scapegoat in a prime minister, who could be berated or jettisoned to deflect criticism from the president (Huskey 1999, chapter 2). These are all powerful reasons for Yeltsin and his allies, at a key juncture in postcommunist development, to have retained the structure of government inherited from tsarist and Soviet Russia. However, the legacy of a superordinate presidency also persisted because it had first-mover advantage at the collapse of the old order, and because it shaped the mental framework of those designing formal institutions. In fact, most of the thirteen major constitutional drafts appearing between

November 1990 and November 1993 in Russia favored a governing diarchy of president and government based on the Communist Party/Council of Ministers model (Ogushi 2011).

Unwilling to rely on patronage powers alone to assure the faithful execution of presidential directives, the postcommunist president has continued the tsarist and Soviet-era traditions of constructing a vast bureaucracy of *kontrol'* to oversee the operation of the state bureaucracy. The tsarist chancellery and Communist Party Central Committee shadowed the Council of Ministers and representatives of regional power; the Administration of the President in the postcommunist era similarly supports a large staff that develops and reviews the implementation of policy at federal and regional levels. It is a form of organizational redundancy that has no equal in dual executive systems outside the postcommunist world. Moreover, the meta-level redundancy apparent in the large, parallel management bureaucracies in the president and government is replicated within certain state organizations. The Russian government itself, for example, maintains sizable departments that oversee the work of individual ministries. This reliance on organizational redundancy as a form of rule reflects in part the continued absence or underdevelopment of reliable alternative mechanisms in Russia for controlling the agents of state, such as the rule of law, a professional civil service, and independent media. Such traditions are also in short supply in other developing societies, yet these societies do not employ checking mechanisms on the scale that one finds in Russia and some other postcommunist countries.

Personnel redundancy reminiscent of Soviet rule is also built into Russia's distinctive ministerial system, whose origins lie in the early nineteenth century. Russia and other postcommunist states, from Kazakhstan to Vietnam, are rare examples of countries that maintain large numbers of deputy prime ministers between the prime minister and individual ministers as well as large numbers of deputy ministers between the ministers and ministerial department heads. This inheritance from the communist era complicates Russian governance by introducing unnecessary veto or choke points into policy making and implementation. Recognizing the deleterious effects of this feature of Russian organizational life, President Putin agreed to streamline the government's management teams, apparently on the recommendation of Dmitrii Medvedev. Whereas ministries prior to Putin's second term tended to have six to twelve first deputy and deputy ministers, an administrative reform of 2004 reduced that number to two to four. However, by 2008, the number of deputy ministers had crept back to seven, eight, and nine in many ministries, and the number of deputy prime ministers was nine in 2011, up from three seven years earlier. In early December 2010, an official in the presidential administration announced that it was planned once again to reduce the number in each ministry to two, but there was no guarantee that this reform would succeed. Thus, the redundancy in personnel inherited from the Soviet era not only departed from world practice, but it also endured despite a serious attempt to eliminate it.

What explains the persistence of this dysfunctional organizational buffer in Russian government? Corruption is one likely explanation for the retention of a system whose roots in the Soviet era appear to lie in a penchant for relying on checking mechanisms to render the state bureaucracy legible and responsive. In the postcommunist era, many deputy ministerial positions are allegedly sold for handsome sums because the occupant can use the post to collect rents from supplicants interested in obtaining licenses, customs or tax waivers, and other benefits. In this case, then, the logic sustaining this executive institution appears to have shifted somewhat from the Soviet to the postcommunist era, yet the practice remains. In the words of Beissinger and Young, "some factors, like corruption, were not mere continuations of the past; they were appropriations and magnifications of the Soviet legacy – a massive inversion in which the implicit became the predominant practice" (2002, 47). Uprooting this legacy, therefore, will take more than a campaign targeting redundancy in personnel; it will require a thoroughgoing reform of administrative culture and what Ken Jowitt called the institutionalization of public virtues (1992, 293).

A further institutional legacy from the Soviet era is the constant renaming, realigning, and reorganizing of ministries, agencies, and state committees. The instability of the country's executive structures appears to reflect attempts to reward or punish officials heading these agencies and/or to improve the monitoring of poorly performing organizations. Although the postcommunist era has elevated the importance of electoral and public politics in comparison with the Soviet era, in both periods the major focus of political activity has been on inter- and intra-bureaucratic conflict. Thus, individuals and political networks seeking to advance their interests benefit from rearranging formal lines of authority through administrative reorganization. One of the most contested administrative reforms surrounded the creation of a criminal investigative committee that was independent of overseers in the Procuracy. Most observers believe that this committee has become a potent political weapon in the hands of Vladimir Putin.[8]

In some instances, the organizational offspring of the Soviet order survived the transition from communism intact, but assumed additional or revised functions in the postcommunist era. One such organization was the Business Office (*Upravliaiushchii delami*) in the Administration of the Presidency, the direct successor to a similarly named body in the Communist Party Central Committee. On both sides of the regime divide, the Business Office was charged with providing goods and services to the country's elite, from dachas and transport to medical care and holidays (Huskey 1999, 51–54). In other words, instead of monetizing payments to the country's ruling class (a policy pursued with regard to many traditional beneficiaries of entitlements in the mid-2000s, such as veterans and pensioners), postcommunist Russia continued to use the Business Office to support a lifestyle for the political elite based in good measure on state perquisites rather than market exchange. This meant that the Business Office, like its party predecessor, was a small business empire – one that had a network of special kindergartens and schools, hospitals and clinics, hotels and resorts, and cars and drivers.[9]

In two respects, life in postcommunist Russia altered the role and impact of the Business Office. First, some members of the postcommunist elite had become sufficiently affluent by the end of the 1990s to survive without the goods and services distributed by the Business Office. However, many officials remained dependent on the largesse of this presidential agency for provisions essential to an elite lifestyle. Thus, this organizational inheritance assured the continuation of the economic, psychological, and political dependency of a portion of the ruling class on an agency controlled by the country's leader. Second, the partial marketization of the Russian economy in the postcommunist era encouraged the Business Office to operate as a business in the private sector as well as a purveyor of state benefits to the upper reaches of officialdom. Instead of denationalizing its surplus assets in sectors ranging from hospitality to transport, the Business Office chose to sell its goods and services to the public on a commercial basis. In Moscow, for example, it currently operates three three-star and two five-star hotels.[10] In 2011, the Kremlin Trading House, owned by the Business Office, began the sale of candies with the Kremlin trademark, which added to its branded lines of vodka, cognac, and champagne (Upravlenie delami prezidenta 2012).[11]

It is common in neo-patrimonial regimes, such as those in the Arab world and Central Asia, to find private business networks dominated by a leader's family or close associates, but the maintenance of a state-owned business empire at the core of presidential power appears to be a unique feature of Russian government and one of the more unusual legacies of Soviet rule. Many other post-Soviet presidencies maintain Business Offices inherited from the USSR, and in some cases the agencies retained unlikely properties once controlled by their Soviet-era predecessors. For example, the Business Office of the President of Kyrgyzstan still owns and manages one of the country's most visited national parks, Ala-Archa, outside the capital of Bishkek. However, the Russian case is distinct because much of the inheritance of the USSR Communist Party's Business Office, which dwarfed that of the individual republican party apparatuses, passed directly to the Business Office in the Russian presidency.

Legacy Patterns in the Recruitment of the Postcommunist Russian Executive

Several features of elite recruitment in the Russian executive mirror patterns found in the Soviet era. The first is the role of the Communist Party Central Committee and the postcommunist Russian presidential bureaucracy as way stations in the careers of promising mid-career cadres. In Western states, institutions such as political parties and a senior executive service help to instill a global perspective in leaders from diverse sectoral or geographical backgrounds. Lacking these traditional integrative mechanisms that can resolve collective action problems, Russia has relied heavily on temporary service in a socializing institution, the contemporary presidency (or before it the Soviet Central Committee), to break down silo mentalities and create a common approach to governance. Although the practice of elite circulation through the presidential bureaucracy is less extensive and institutionalized than the secondment of cadres to the Soviet Central Committee, the Russian presidency is clearly a vital training ground for Russia's ruling class. As one might expect, the higher one's position in the state, the more likely it is that he or she will have served in the presidential bureaucracy. Thus, in Prime Minister Putin's first government, announced in the spring of 2008, where 18 percent of the deputy ministers and 27 percent of the ministers had worked in the Administration of the President, 67 percent of the government's inner circle (the prime minister and deputy prime ministers) had served in the presidential apparatus – figures that are admittedly slightly inflated by the fact that Putin shifted to the government from the presidency in 2008.[12]

The second institution designed to enhance the quality and reliability of executive personnel is the cadres reserve list. Established during the Soviet era as an essential part of the *nomenklatura* system, cadres reserves were revived by Putin after a hiatus of more than a decade, and therefore may be regarded as an example of the "resurrection" of a prominent practice from the old regime that had fallen into disuse. In essence, cadres reserves lists are pools of prospective candidates for leading positions in the Russian state. The most important reserve list is the "Presidential 1000," which is supposed to contain the names of up to one thousand candidates eligible to fill many of the posts within the patronage purview of the president, which in Russia covers not only executive vacancies, but also positions at the commanding heights of the Russian economy (Huskey 2004). The profile of the Presidential 1000 in 2011 revealed that 57 percent were classic mid-career cadres (from 35–44 years of age). In terms of their occupational background, 52 percent occupied posts in state service, while 30 percent worked in business and 18 percent in education or other social or cultural fields (Kadrovyi rezerv 2011). There are also so-called unified cadres reserve lists being formed by heads of administration in each of the more than eighty regions of Russia. Their members will fill leading posts in government and business at the regional level.[13] Finally, since 2008 the United Russia Party has developed its own extensive cadres reserve list. In the fall of 2010, the new mayor of Moscow, Sergei Sobianin, asked United Russia to help him fill three hundred vacancies in the Moscow government with their reservists, who numbered about one hundred ten in the city, mostly males from thirty-one to forty years of age (Vtoroi prizyv 2010).[14]

Although the postcommunist cadres reserve system differs from its Soviet predecessor in its smaller scale and its greater transparency, it follows the Soviet model in creating a structure of incentives that undermines the political neutrality of officialdom. Because those enlisted in the cadres reserve have a stake in maintaining in office superiors who tapped them for future promotion, they will be tempted to prove their loyalty to their political and administrative superiors, which includes employing "administrative resources" on behalf of their patrons. Aligning the career prospects of present and future leaders so closely co-opts potential opposition forces and makes it difficult to ensure that power is wielded only pro tempore by political elites.[15]

Why was the cadres reserve system revived? Several factors appear to be at work, all of which were also present during the Soviet era: a lack of confidence (especially in remote regions) in the ability of a free market in labor to produce the necessary personnel for leading posts in state and society; a general preference for technocratic solutions to problems – in this case the conceit that one can advance state interests by employing a scientific approach to elite recruitment; and the desire of those in power to control who rises to political prominence in the next generation, and thereby assure their own longevity in office. One could say that at least two of these explanations imply a strategic choice by elites and therefore may not fit neatly in a legacy argument. But the point here is that the past has framed the alternatives, and elites with similar interests and even similar values in other parts of the world would be unlikely to introduce cadres reserve lists because the choice would not present itself. Reviving an institution is far easier than constructing one *ab ovo*.

In terms of their career paths and their worldview, Russia's leaders are not so much politicians as *chinovniki* (bureaucrats), a feature they share with their Soviet predecessors. Olga Kryshtanovskaya and Stephen White have written much about Russia as a militocracy, and it is certainly the case that since the late 1990s the *siloviki* have had an outsized influence on policy debates and an impressive presence in leadership circles, much as they did during parts of the tsarist and Soviet eras (Kryshtanovskaya and White 2003). But the larger truth is that Russia, like the Soviet Union, is in large part a technocracy, where specialists from various technical backgrounds rise to power without passing through the kind of crucible of elective politics that might sensitize leaders to the concerns of the public (Huskey 2012).[16] This is most evident in the careers of Putin and Medvedev, who used administrative service rather than elective office as a springboard to the presidency.

Technocratic and/or administrative careers remain the norm throughout Russia's ruling class. If we look at the government Putin appointed when he became prime minister in 2008, only one of the twenty-seven members had served in the national parliament, and only one in five had served in an elective capacity of any kind, even if one includes elections from the late Soviet period. Like their Soviet predecessors, Russian leaders seek to depoliticize and de-ideologize policy decisions by presenting them as an outgrowth of "instrumentally rational techniques" (Centeno 1993, 314).[17] It is instructive that in describing himself to a reporter in 2006, the elected governor of Tver' did not refer to himself as a politician but a *chinovnik* (Prilepina 2006, 22). All authoritarian regimes, of course, lack politicians in the Western sense, but what makes Russia noteworthy is the continuing embrace of discursive and recruitment patterns that represent an odd blend of technocracy and neopatrimonialism.

Just as during the tsarist and Soviet eras, executive power in contemporary Russia rests in part on a complex and opaque network of family circles whose members occupy strategic positions in state institutions and in the commanding heights of the economy.[18] Despite the many changes in Russian life since 1991, the conditions that gave rise to these networks during the tsarist and Soviet eras remain in place. These conditions include the broad patronage powers of bosses, who are little constrained by elections or other institutions, and the need for client protection (*krysha*) in a system where law and transparency are lacking. With reference to tsarist Russia, Marc Raeff noted that officials needed to cultivate a "special personal relationship with the sovereign ... [because] no regularized system of law and judicial hierarchy protected them in the performance of their duties or safeguarded them from the consequences of even routine action" (1979, 405). Similar conditions obtain in Russia today, especially with regard to the most visible members of the country's elite.

The impact of Soviet-era legacies on elite networks and regime legitimacy is perhaps most evident in postcommunist Central Asia, where Moscow's willingness from the 1930s onward to privilege one regional group over others in each republic ensured that intra-elite competition based on regionalism (or in some cases *zhuz*, tribe, or clan) would dominate the postcommunist political game. Politics in Kyrgyzstan, for example, continues to be framed by the north-south rivalry, whose origins lie in the Soviet era, when alternation between northern and southern ruling groups became the norm. The two revolutions in Kyrgyzstan in the past decade were products of this legacy.

Until 2005, it seemed that Russia had rejected one important part of the Soviet inheritance in elite recruitment. This was the geographic rotation of cadres, in which the Soviet leadership, at least prior to the Brezhnev era, tended to select outsiders and not favorite sons or daughters to lead regional party organizations in the Russian republic. Used to fight localism, which has been a scourge for centuries in Russian administration, the geographic rotation of regional leaders had no place in postcommunist Russia from 1994 to 2005 because governors were popularly elected. But Putin's decision after the Beslan massacre to return to the Soviet and early postcommunist practice of appointing regional executives created a new political context. As part of his campaign to create a power vertical, Putin began to revive the practice of cadre rotation in his second presidential term. From 2005 to 2008, 37 percent (22) of all new regional leaders were "outsiders," that is, they had no prior connections to the regions. This trend intensified under President Medvedev, who, in the seven months prior to March 2009, appointed outsiders as new regional leaders in seven of ten cases (Moses 2010, 1437–41). At what percentage and at what moment can we conclude that the practice of geographic rotation of cadres has been institutionalized? And if this practice becomes a permanent part of the landscape, will we view it as a legacy from the Soviet past or as a strategic choice made by a leader who believes that faux federalism is in his and Russia's best interest? In other words, is the geographic rotation of cadres a common functional adaptation to a similar administrative problem or a conscious or unconscious borrowing from the past? If the latter, through what mechanisms did the past make its way into the present? Whatever our answers to these questions, the revival of the geographic rotation of cadres may force us to reconsider whether twenty years, a generation in sociological terms, is long enough to reach firm conclusions about the persistence of practices and beliefs across a regime divide.

Legacy Patterns in the Rituals of the Postcommunist Russian Executive

Like its Soviet predecessor, the Russian executive operates according to a highly ritualized planning process whose centerpiece is the annual state of the union address (P*oslanie Federal'nomu sobraniiu*). Where the set speeches of the general secretaries signaled policy direction during the Soviet era, each presidential state of the union address informs the nation and the state bureaucracy of the broad priorities of the political leadership, with an emphasis on a handful of special initiatives. It serves in many respects as the annual plan for the operation of the Russian state. Traditionally drafted in the presidential bureaucracy with input from all important governing institutions, this address – mandated by the Constitution of 1993 – represents the culmination of months of research and intra-bureaucratic bargaining over national priorities, a process similar to that which preceded the delivery of major speeches to Communist Party plenums and conferences during the Soviet era.[19]

What Russian scholars have called the "political-legal" character of the state of the union address is evident in the binding presidential "assignments" (*porucheniia*) to which it gives birth. Approximately one month after the delivery of the *Poslanie*, the president issues a formal document setting out the specific legislative and policy changes that should follow from the state of the union address (Prezident obnarodal 2008).[20] Based on this document, the government, parliament, and regional governments construct action plans that divide the labor for implementing the assignments among specific organizations and officials. Thus, as former Prime Minister Fradkov noted in 2005 with regard to the distribution of tasks within the government and ministries, "the assignments are clear, with the last names of the implementers [attached]" (Prem'er Rossii 2005). A similar devolution of responsibilities occurs in the regions and republics. In the republic of Karelia, for example, there is a special Council for the Realization of the Main Provisions of the Annual Address of the President that creates a chart with specific assignments and the ministries (and ministers) responsible for their execution (Perechen' poruchenii 2009).[21] This concretization of guidance from Russia's central leader is uncannily similar to the directives to lower party organs that were generated by the authoritative speeches and documents issued by the central leadership of the Communist

Party. The final stage in this ritual is a monitoring process that measures the extent to which the directives have been carried out.

As during the Soviet era, political plans in postcommunist Russia are often scuttled by incompetence, corruption, bureaucratic resistance, and changing circumstances. A cable published by Wikileaks noted that in 2006, 60 percent of President Putin's assignments remained unimplemented by the bureaucracy (Chivers 2010, A1). What is important for us, however, is not the effectiveness of this form of rule, but the continuation of a method of executive governance grounded in detailed directives that emanate from a guiding document or speech presented by the central leader. There are vestiges here of "the correct line," which Jowitt describes as "a modern program encompassed and understood in neosacral terms" (1992, 10).

Many rituals in the everyday life of Russian officialdom have roots in the Soviet era, though whether these represent thin or thick legacies remains open to debate. Among such rituals are the regular public berating of subordinates by leaders, apparently designed to illustrate the authority of the ruler and his intolerance of wrongdoing or incompetence, and the requirement that legal drafts and key decisions adopted in the executive receive the signatures, or "visas," of all interested officials (Postanovlenie Pravitel'stva 1997; Administrativno-pravovoi status 2002). Referencing the work of Joseph Berliner on the Soviet economy, Paul Gregory offered the following explanation for the staying power of the system of *vizirovanie*:

> Berliner showed that the Soviet system did not provide adequate rewards for risk taking. There was an asymmetry between risks and rewards. Risky decisions that turned out poorly were punished. Risky decisions that turned out well were not rewarded. Decision making processes which reduced the risks to decision makers became ingrained. One such process, which survived into the post 1991 period was the process of *vizirovanie* – the fact that all parties affected by a decision would have to sign off on that decision. *Vizirovanie* is a version of governance by unanimity, which is cumbersome and practically unworkable. (Gregory 2002)

That the practice of issuing visas has been maintained in spite of its dysfunctionality owes something to an uncritical acceptance of work routines from the old regime as well as the continuing asymmetry between risks and rewards in executive decision making.

Conclusion

Several steps are required to construct a convincing argument that patterns of practice and belief in the postcommunist era represent legacies from the old regime. The first two of these may be dispensed with summarily. If one accepts the definition of legacy used by Kotkin and Beissinger, which holds that "practices and beliefs embedded by an earlier regime find new or renewed meaning over the long term, within a different macrohistorical context," it is first necessary to show that there has been a fundamental break or disruption in regimes. This precondition for a legacy argument is not in dispute. In the Soviet case, there was the collapse of the state itself; of its ruling organization, the Communist Party; of its legitimating ideology; and of the command economy. Although scholars disagree about how to characterize the successor regime, there is little doubt that a new institutional context emerged.

The second precondition for an argument that legacies matter is that sufficient time has passed between the end of the old regime and the present to ensure that similar institutional patterns in the new order are not merely fading remnants from the old. In the case of Russia and other postcommunist states, we are now two decades removed from the collapse of the old regime, a point at which similarities are likely to reflect what Kotkin and Beissinger have termed the "reproduction, recombination, resurrection, and redeployment" of older practices in a new environment rather than simply short-term spillover from the old order. As we saw in the case of elite recruitment patterns in the executive, specifically the cadres reserve system and the geographic rotation of cadres, Soviet institutional patterns were revived in the Russian executive after a hiatus during the early postcommunist period when they had been fully or partially rejected.

The most difficult step in the identification of legacies is assuring that similarities across the regime divide are the product of institutional persistence rather than conditions specific to the new environment alone (Wittenberg 2010, 2). In several cases discussed in this chapter, such as those relating to the continued prominence of personalism and organizational redundancy in executive institutions, similar patterns of practice and belief across the regime divide result from what has been termed "constant causes," that is "a common set of factors [that] is responsible for both the production and the reproduction of an institution" (Mahoney 2001, 8). For example, both the Soviet and postcommunist executive have relied on a multiplicity of checking mechanisms because of the absence in both regimes of more subtle means of monitoring and disciplining the agents of state, such as the rule of law. Thus, although the overall environments changed from the Soviet to the postcommunist eras, particular causal features remained.

There are many instances, however, when the original Soviet-era conditions giving rise to the phenomena examined earlier were not altogether different from conditions in other developing countries, yet the institutions created in response to these conditions were novel. It is our assumption that the maintenance of these unusual practices and beliefs, when functional alternatives were available under the new regime, is a confirmation of the power of Soviet executive legacies. Such novel institutions include the proliferation of deputy ministers, the maintenance of a state-run business empire to provision the elite, the use of *vizirovanie*, and the cadres reserve system. Once in place under Soviet rule, these institutions became part of the habitus that conditioned the choices that elites on either side of the regime divide viewed as available, or unavailable, to them. As Bachrach and Baratz argued decades ago, certain alternatives to the existing order are never considered because of the "mobilization of bias" (1962).[22]

What of the legacies that failed? Why did certain practices and beliefs relating to executive institutions fail to travel across the regime divide? By examining these failed implants, these departures from previous practices and beliefs, we may gain an understanding of the features of the inheritance or of postcommunist circumstances that contribute to the vitality of legacies. One notable departure from the Soviet era is the Russian executive's preference for a demobilized rather than a mobilized society. Instead of encouraging the population to participate actively in ritualized institutions (for example, the elections, demonstrations, or spring cleaning days of the Soviet era), the current leadership has welcomed the retreat of citizens from the public square. This preference reflects not only the greater difficulty in the current climate of controlling the effects of political participation – demonstrations are, after all, no longer simply rituals – but also the complete lack of a mobilizing ideology in postcommunist Russia. Presidents have called at times for the creation of a new unifying Russian idea, but that project has gone nowhere. The legacy of the mobilized society failed in part, then, because postcommunist leaders lacked the discursive and organizational tools to channel extensive popular participation into system-enhancing rather than system-destabilizing directions. Yet in one sense this legacy failure also rests on the persistence of a common mental framework, which Jowitt described as the elite's "distrust of an ideologically 'unreconstructed' population" (1992, 289).

As we have seen, institutional persistence depends in some measure on the continuation in the new order of some of the conditions that gave birth to and sustained these practices and beliefs in the old regime. Remove these conditions and many of the legacies will wither. Thus, a more democratic Russia may be able to retain the awkward organizational redundancy of presidency and government or even a president with certain monarchical qualities, but executive institutions like the cadres reserve system and the ritualized directives to regional governments need an authoritarian environment to survive. If Russia develops vibrant political parties and a rule of law, there will be little need for a socializing institution like the presidency to school mid-career cadres in the lessons of governance. Likewise, it is difficult to sustain neo-patrimonialism as a basis of regime legitimacy in a system with competitive elections and a free press. These points are perhaps embarrassingly obvious, but they should serve as reminders that a heightened interest in historical legacies in the Russian case seems to depend as much on the recent consolidation of authoritarianism in that country as on a recognition of the limits of ahistorical explanations in the social sciences.

Notes

1. Among the many recent works that consider the power of legacies in postcommunist development are Beissinger and Young (2002); Bunce (2005); and Ekiert and Hanson (2003). For a general assessment of how and why institutions change, see Campbell (2007).

2 Much of Brubaker's work considers the power of discursive or cultural legacies in France and Germany on matters of citizenship. One might have imagined that "the inertial weight and normative dignity of tradition" would be less imposing in the postcommunist era than in, say, contemporary France, but the legacies in the ways of thinking and acting in the Russian executive indicate that the rejection of the Soviet inheritance was quite limited in this sphere.
3 Kopstein notes that it is important to identify which past is affecting the present, and further research would be needed to understand the relative influence of tsarist versus Soviet traditions and early versus mid- and late Soviet-era traditions (2003, 233).
4 Before the Bolshevik Revolution, Karl Kautsky noted that "the capitalist class rules but does not govern."
5 The decision of Vladimir Putin, the "national leader," to step down from the presidency in 2008 and assume the role of prime minister may appear to complicate the comparison of the Russian state executive across the communist/postcommunist divide. However, during his years as prime minister Putin did not seek to diminish the institutional prominence of the Russian presidency. Although he made a few structural changes to the prime minister's office to enhance its role (such as the formation of a presidium and the merger of the offices of prime ministerial chief of staff and head of the governmental apparatus), Putin was careful in public to respect the logic of the super-presidential system, deferring to President Medvedev when protocol dictated. In short, the tenure of Medvedev as caretaker president did not disrupt the pattern of executive rule carried forward from the Soviet era, and of course Putin reclaimed the presidency in 2012.
6 Stephen Hanson speaks of this as a "legacy of communism" (1997, 242), but in reality both models were communist legacies.
7 One could argue that the adoption of the presidential model by Gorbachev reflected in part the influence of individuals within his entourage who were inspired as much by the French example as by Soviet tradition, yet the semi-presidential structure put in place in the USSR and Russia accorded far greater power and authority to the president, to the point that the option of *cohabitation* – the power sharing between president and prime minister – was never on the table in the Russian case.
8 For an official history of this committee, see Istoriia sozdaniia.
9 The range of organizational subsidiaries of the Business Office is provided at http://www.udprf.ru/Subordinated_structures.
10 See the presidential hotels at http://www.udprf.ru/podvedomstvennye-struktury/gostinichnyi-kompleks/fgup-gostinichnyi-kompleks-prezident-otel/fgup-gostinichnyi-kompleks-prezident-otel/50. There have also been repeated accusations that the Business Office has been involved in illicit activities, especially related to kickbacks for renovations to the Kremlin and other government properties.
11 For the website of the Kremlin Trading House, see http://www.udprf.ru/podvedomstvennye-struktury/obshchestvennoe-pitanie-i-torgovlya/fgup-torgovyi-dom-kremlevskii/fgup-torgovyi-dom-kremlevskii/226.
12 Figures drawn from the Web site of the Russian government in May 2008. On the movement of high-ranking officials across presidency, government, and large economic enterprises during the postcommunist era, see Huskey (2010).

13 See, for example, the description of the program in Tomsk (Kadrovyi rezerv, Tomskii regional'nyi).
14 Note that the federal cadres reserve system maintained by the president has proved something of a disappointment to its enrollees, many of whom have been passed over for key appointments.
15 This paragraph draws from Huskey (2009, 262).
16 This argument is developed in Huskey (2012).
17 The language here was used to describe technocracy in Latin America in earlier decades.
18 On the persistence of family circles in Russian life, see Yaney (1965, 379–90).
19 In the run-up to the 2009 state of the union address, President Medvedev invited the population to submit its suggestions for inclusion in the address. See Medvedev (2009).
20 The presidential assignments that followed the November 2009 address may be read in Dmitrii Medvedev (2009). The document is known as the List of Presidential Assignments Relating to the Implementation of the State of the Union Address. Unlike the message itself, this document is not required by the constitution.
21 Among the many institutional legacies not discussed here is ethno-federalism.
22 In a few cases, such as the reproduction of a variant of the party/state model, in which the presidency mimicked in many respects the Central Committee, the costs of reversing the Soviet-era tradition were high, to use the language of path dependency. However, most other executive institutions inherited from the Soviet era could have been replaced at a relatively modest cost, suggesting that other factors besides path dependence were at work.

References

Bachrach, Peter and Morton Baratz. 1962. "Two Faces of Power." *American Political Science Review* 56(4): 947–52.

Beissinger, Mark R. and Crawford Young. 2002. "Convergence to Crisis: Pre-Independence State Legacies and Post-Independence State Breakdown in Africa and Eurasia." In *Beyond State Crisis? Postcolonial Africa and Post-Soviet Eurasia in Comparative Perspective*. Ed. Mark R. Beissinger and Crawford Young, 19–50. Washington, DC: Woodrow Wilson Center Press.

Brubaker, Rogers. 1992. *Citizenship and Nationhood in France and Germany*. Cambridge, MA: Harvard University Press.

Bunce, Valerie. 2005. "The National Idea: Imperial Legacies and Post-Communist Pathways in Eastern Europe." *East European Politics and Societies* 19(3): 406–42.

Campbell, John L. 2007. "Institutional Reproduction and Change." Unpublished paper, August.

Centeno, Miguel Angel. 1993. "The New Leviathan: The Dynamics and Limits of Technocracy." *Theory and Society* 22(3): 307–35.

Chivers, C. J. 2010. "Beneath Surface, US has Dim View of Putin and Russia," *New York Times*, December 2, A1.

"Dmitrii Medvedev dal riad poruchenii po realizatsii Poslaniia Prezidenta Federal'nomu sobraniiu." 2009. [http://www.kremlin.ru/acts/6001].

Ekiert, Grzegorz and Stephen E. Hanson, eds. 2003. *Capitalism and Democracy in Central and Eastern Europe: Assessing the Legacy of Communist Rule*. Cambridge: Cambridge University Press.
Gregory, Paul R. 2002. "Should Soviet Specialists Have Been Consulted? Or: Was Experience in Latin America or Africa Good Enough?" Paper Prepared for the Havighurst Symposium in Economics, "Russia Ten Years Later: Taking Stock," Miami University of Ohio, April 7–8.
Hanson, Stephen E. 1997. "Leninist Legacy, Institutional Change, and Post-Soviet Russia." In *Liberalization and Leninist Legacies: Comparative Perspectives on Democratic Transitions*. Ed. Beverly Crawford and Arend Lijphart, 228–52. Berkeley, CA: International and Area Studies.
Hill, Ronald J. 1980. "Party-State Relations and Soviet Political Development." *British Journal of Political Science* 10(2): 149–65.
Huskey, Eugene. 1999. *Presidential Power in Russia*. Armonk, NY: M. E. Sharpe.
    2004. "Nomenklatura Lite? The Cadres Reserve in Russian Public Administration." *Problems of Post-Communism* 51(2): 30–39.
    2009. "The Politics-Administration Nexus in Post-Communist Russia." In *Russian Bureaucracy and the State: Officialdom from Alexander III to Vladimir Putin*. Ed. Don K. Rowney and Eugene Huskey, 253–72. London: Palgrave Macmillan.
    2010. "*Pantouflage a la russe*: The Recruitment of Russian Political and Business Elites." In *Russian Politics from Lenin to Putin: Essays in Honour of T. H. Rigby*. Ed. Stephen Fortescue, 185–204. London: Palgrave Macmillan.
    2012. "Legitimizing the Russian Executive: Identity, Technocracy, and Performance." In *Power and Legitimacy: Challenges from Russia*. Ed. Per-Arne Bodin, Stefan Hedlund, and Irina Sandomirskaja, 46–58. Routledge.
Istoriia sozdaniia Sledstvennogo komiteta Rossiiskoi Federatsii i ego sovremennyi pravovoi status. http://www.sledcom.ru/history/.
Jowitt, Ken. 1992. *New World Disorder: The Leninist Extinction*. Berkeley: University of California Press.
Kadrovyi rezerv Prezidenta Rossii. http://www.re-serve.ru/people/stat/.
Kadrovyi rezerv, Tomskii regional'nyi resursnyi tsentr. http://rrc.tomsk.ru/rrc/kadr_rezerv/.
Kozlov, A. E., ed. 1997. Konstitutsionnoe pravo: uchebnik. Moscow, Izdatel'stvo BEK. http://pravouch.com/page/kozlovp/ist/ist-1--idz-ax267--nf-61.html.
Kopstein, Jeffrey. 2003. "Postcommunist Democracy: Legacies and Outcomes." *Comparative Politics* 35(2): 231–50.
Kryshtanovskaya, Olga and Stephen White. 2003. "Putin's Militocracy." *Post-Soviet Affairs* 19(4): 289–306.
Mahoney, James. 2001. *The Legacies of Liberalism: Path Dependence and Political Regimes in Central America*. Baltimore, MD: Johns Hopkins University Press.
Medvedev, Dmitrii. 2009. "Rossiia, vpered!" Gazeta.ru, September 10. http://www.gazeta.ru/comments/2009/09/10_a_3258568.shtml.
Moses, Joel. 2010. "Russian Local Politics in the Putin-Medvedev Era." *Europe-Asia Studies* 62(9): 1427–52.
    Forthcoming. "The Political Resurrection of Russian Governors." *Europe-Asia Studies*.

Ogushi, Atsushi. 2011. "From the CC CPSU to Russian Presidency: The Development of Semi-Presidentialism in Russia," 5–7. Hokkaido. http://src-h.slav.hokudai.ac.jp/coe21/publish/no21_ses/01ogushi.pdf.

Perechen' poruchenii Prezidenta RF, nakhodiashchikhsia na ispolnenii v sub'ektakh RF i obespechivaiushchikh realizatsiiu osnovnykh polozhenii Poslaniia Prezidenta Rossiiskoi Federatsii na 2009 god (Prilozhenie 2), Karelia. http://www.gov.karelia.ru/gov/Leader/Work/090615.html.

"Postanovlenie Pravitel'stva Rossiiskoi Federatsii ot 13 avgusta 1997 g. N 1009." 1997. In *Pravila podgotovki normativnykh pravovykh aktov federal'nykh organov ispolnitel'noi vlasti i ikh gosudarstvennoi registratsii; Konstitutsionnoe pravo: uchebnik.* Ed. A. E. Kozlov. Moscow, Izdatel'stvo BEK. http://pravouch.com/page/kozlovp/ist/ist-1--idz-ax267--nf-61.html.

"Prem'er Rossii otchital ministrov za nedistsiplinirovannoe ispolnenie poruchenii Putina." 2005. Novosti, May 12. http://palm.newsru.com/russia/12may2005/fradkov.html.

"Prezident obnarodoval perechen' poruchenii po realizatsii Poslaniia." 2008. Kreml.org, December 3. http://www.kreml.org/other/198808088.

Prilepina, Oksana. 2006. "Zachem biznesmeny idut v chinovniki." *Ogonek* 11: 22.

Raeff, Marc. 1979. "The Bureaucratic Phenomena of Imperial Russia, 1700–1905." *American Historical Review* 84(2): 399–411.

Sobolevskii, I. B. (2002). "Administrativno-pravovoi status Prezidenta Rossii." Kandidat dissertation, VNII MVD RF, Moscow. http://law.edu.ru/book/book.asp?bookID=1170777.

"Upravlenie delami prezidenta Rossii nachinaet vypusk konfet 'Kremlevskaia belochka.'" 2012. Gazeta.ru, March 16.

"Vtoroi prizyv." 2010. *Vedomosti*, November 26. http://profkomanda.edinros.ru/article/32300.

Wittenberg, Jason. 2010. "What is a Historical Legacy?" Paper presented to the Annual Meeting of the American Political Science Association. Washington, DC. September 2–5.

Yaney, George L. 1965. "Law, Society and the Domestic Regime in Russia in Historical Perspective." *American Political Science Review* 59(2): 379–90.

7

From Police State to Police State? Legacies and Law Enforcement in Russia

Brian D. Taylor

Over the past twenty-five years, the Russian state has apparently come full circle. The Soviet Union was "the world's largest-ever police state" (Kotkin 2001, 173). Reflecting on Vladimir Putin's first two terms as president, C. J. Chivers (2008; see also Easter 2008) declared that Putin's "signature legacy" was the rebuilding "of a more sophisticated and rational police state than the failed USSR." If Russia has traveled the long road from police state to police state, what happened to the police during that journey? And does the historical legacy of the Soviet past explain the outcome?

Legacies abound in the study of postcommunist law enforcement. Louise Shelley contends that communist, Soviet, and (in some cases) colonial legacies of Russian rule "will continue to weigh heavily on law enforcement in these nations for years to come" (1999, 85). Rasma Karklins observes that "a concrete legacy of the Soviet system" is the ability of officials to "use their investigative and judicial powers to intimidate citizens and political rivals" (2002, 30). Similarly, according to Andrei Soldatov and Irina Borogan (2010), the "enduring legacy of the KGB" lives on in the FSB, the Federal Security Service.

This chapter, in keeping with the spirit of this volume, turns a critical eye on the notion of legacy as an explanation for both the organizational format and behavioral practices of Russian law enforcement organs. The approach is critical, not because the notion of legacy is necessarily wrong – indeed, I will argue that legacies are important in several ways – but because it can be applied too liberally, invoked without reflection or detailed evidence. Obviously, much of what happens in social and political life has roots in the past. For the purposes of this chapter, locating a past practice or institutional form that is similar to present day ones is insufficient evidence for a legacy, which, following Kotkin and Beissinger, involves "a durable causal relationship between earlier institutions and practices and those of the present in the wake of a macrohistorical rupture." A more persuasive case for a legacy involves an investigation of the mechanisms by which it came to be reproduced in the new historical period, how it may have changed in the process, and whether there are plausible alternative explanations for the current institution or practice other than a legacy explanation.

In this chapter, I argue that there are several legacies that meet these evidentiary standards and that seem important in Russian law enforcement. Specifically, the organizational mandate and power of the Procuracy, the status and cultural reputation of "Chekists" (former KGB personnel), and several features of everyday policing are definitely important aspects of Russian law enforcement, and ones that seem to be, at least in part, legacies from the Soviet past. At the same time, these legacies are not simply transplants from the Soviet past into the present. Instead, the greater openness of the new order – politically, internationally, and especially economically with the transition to capitalism – has fundamentally changed the way Russian law enforcement works, despite the persistence of these legacies.

What Counts as a Legacy?

In this chapter, I follow Kotkin and Beissinger in terms of the definition of legacy and the different types of legacies, but two general points seem appropriate before proceeding to specific legacies.

First, how recent does something have to be to be a legacy? The question itself seems wrongheaded, because legacies are by definition remnants of the past. But in the case of Russian law enforcement, some common organizational forms and behavioral practices are not decades old, but centuries old. A few examples should clarify the point.

1) The secret (high) police. The origins of the FSB and its Soviet predecessor, the KGB, are often traced back deep into the tsarist past. Some historians see roots of the KGB in Ivan the Terrible's *Oprichniki*, a secret police force whose brutal repressions of real and perceived enemies is compared to the repressive *Cheka* and NKVD of Lenin and Stalin, or the Third Section created under Nicholas I in 1825 and its successor, the *Okhrana*, created in 1880, which had mandates to counter subversion and revolution (Andrew and Gordievsky 1990, 17–37; Murawiec and Gaddy 2002).

2) The regular (low) police. Both the organizational forms and everyday behavior of the Soviet militia also were said to have deep roots in the tsarist past. For example, the tendency toward centralized organizational control of the regular police in the Ministry of Internal Affairs (MVD), as opposed to local control, has been a recurrent pattern in Russia (Bayley 1985, 60–61). Similarly, Shelley saw behavioral legacies from the imperial past in Soviet police practice, observing that "the tsarist legacy remained: the militia was part of the political control apparatus of the state" (1996, 21).

3) The Procuracy. Created by Peter the Great in 1722, throughout most of imperial and Soviet history the Procuracy has been the "eyes of the state," responsible for upholding legality in the country. The functions of the Procuracy have generally been considerably more expansive than those of public prosecutors in other countries, with a broad mandate of "general oversight" to enforce compliance with the law. Given this centuries-old history, Inga Mikhailovskaya states, the current Procuracy can only be understood in light of "its remote precommunist context" (1999, 98).

What does it mean that the three main Russian law enforcement agencies – the FSB, the MVD, and the Procuracy – seem to have significant tsarist roots, in terms of organizational structure, general functions, and standard practices? To put it differently, can something be a communist legacy if it predates communism? In several instances we may be talking about traditional Russian institutional forms or practices. To the extent I discuss features of Russian law enforcement that may have pre-Soviet roots, I will only treat them as a legacy if a specific connection to the late Soviet past can be found, and I can trace how it continued into the present era, including how it may have changed as a result of the institutional rupture caused by the end of communism.

A legacy argument should not only be able to connect to a specific trait from the recent past, but it should also not be overly universal outside the Russian, or at least the postcommunist, context. What do I mean by "overly universal?" If some institution or practice is relatively common in a specific functional area – in this case, law enforcement – then a legacy argument has a higher burden of proof. For example, the division between "high" (political) and "low" (criminal) police, which has often – although not always – characterized Russian and Soviet police over the past one hundred eighty-five years, is quite common in many countries (Andreas and Nadelmann 2006, 61–64). Many aspects of Russian law enforcement might not persist because they are legacies, but because they are functional for law enforcement agencies more generally. In other words, the Russian police and secret police might be organized the way they are, or behave the way they do, not because they are *Russian* or *postcommunist*, but because they are *police*.

Saying that the burden of proof is higher should not mean it is insurmountable. Some institution or practice may still be a legacy, even if it is present elsewhere in the world, if one can show how it persisted in specific form, and why the form it takes is not simply functional or isomorphic, but has indigenous characteristics, especially ones that reflect an imprint from the communist experience. For example, I will argue later that both the high and low police in Russia have historically tended to privilege service to the state over service to the population, and that this behavior is in some sense a legacy. But because the police in many countries, particularly but not exclusively authoritarian ones, have a similar feature, I will need to show in what way the specific form this

TABLE 7.1. *Legacies in Russian Law Enforcement*

	Formal	Informal
Fragmentation		
Translation	*Procuracy Mandate* (but changing in recent years)	*Chekist Culture*
Bricolage		*Passport and Registration System Everyday Policing*
Parameter Setting	*Centralization of MVD* (partial legacy)	

behavior takes in Russia qualifies it as a legacy. Where possible, comparisons to other postcommunist countries may help clarify what is a legacy and what is not.

With these caveats in mind, let us proceed to examine some of the most obvious candidates for legacy influence in Russian law enforcement. I first examine possible legacies at the formal level, in terms of laws and organizations, and then turn to the informal level, in terms of culture and everyday practice. Following the legacy forms set out by Kotkin and Beissinger, I argue that there are examples of "translation" (redeploying old institutions/practices in a new way), "bricolage" (elements of past intermixed with the present), and "parameter setting" (limits set by past institutions). Table 7.1 summarizes the key legacy types in Russian law enforcement.

Organizational Legacies in Russian Law Enforcement

In this section on formal organizational legacies in the Russian law enforcement realm, I consider the structure and functions of the three most important agencies – the FSB, the MVD, and the Procuracy. I conclude that the continued high degree of centralization of the MVD is a partial legacy, and that the broad mandate of the Procuracy was an important legacy, but one that has changed in recent years because of a series of organizational reforms.

FSB

Clearly, the biggest attempt to disrupt previous structures and create a new look for law enforcement was the dismantling of the KGB and breaking it into five separate structures, a process that coincided with the Soviet breakup (Albats 1994, 294–359; Knight 1996, 29–61; Soldatov and Borogan 2010, 12–14). Such a change was justified on functional grounds, to rationalize the responsibilities of the KGB's diverse components, and on political grounds, to reduce its political weight. On the first point, it made sense to separate foreign and domestic intelligence, border security from internal security, and leadership security from law enforcement. Indeed, the split between foreign and domestic intelligence to a certain extent already existed within the KGB, especially because the directorate responsible for foreign intelligence moved from KGB headquarters to the Moscow suburbs during the 1970s.[1]

On the second point, the reduction in the political weight of the secret police was less substantial than advertised. Many personnel were kept on in their same or similar roles, few outsiders with more democratic credentials were brought in, and the secret police continued to monitor a wide range of public figures (journalists, parliamentarians, etc.). Most important, the political confrontation between Yeltsin and his opponents, including the parliament and opposition parties and movements, meant that Yeltsin was determined to maintain control over the new Ministry of Security as a reliable political weapon on the side of the president. Yeltsin balked at taking the more radical step of disbanding the KGB and starting over. Timothy Colton, based on an interview with one of Yeltsin's closest political allies, Gennadiy Burbulis, contends that Yeltsin believed that "the CPSU [Communist Party of the Soviet Union] had been the country's brain and the KGB was its spinal cord" and, in Burbulis's words, "he clearly did not want to rupture the spinal cord now that the head had been lopped off" (2008, 259). Rather than eliminating it, Yeltsin sought to keep it under his control. Vadim Bakatin, the last head of the KGB, also thought it would be too dangerous either to eliminate the KGB entirely or to leave it basically as it was, and thus took the middle path of breaking it up into multiple parts (1999, 283–84).

The partial nature of this organizational change becomes evident when compared to other postcommunist states. In some countries, most notably the Czech Republic and the Baltic states, the communist-era security police were abolished and their personnel, as well as collaborators, were banned from positions in the new security services or other high government bodies as part of the process of lustration. In most other Central and Eastern European postcommunist countries, the old secret police were dismantled and new ones were created; the degree of continuity in terms of structure and personnel has varied, but generally change has gone further than in Russia (Welsh 1996; Stan 2008). In other countries, such as Belarus and most Central Asia states, the republic KGB generally survived the Soviet collapse and carried on as before, albeit usually under a new name (National Security Committee, National Security Service, etc.); in Belarus, even the name remained the same – State Security Committee (Knight 1996, 147–63). Thus, in organization terms, the reform of the KGB in Russia lagged considerably behind most Central and Eastern European states, but was more far-reaching than in some post-Soviet states.

This conclusion must be qualified, however, because of the 2003 decision of President Putin to partially reverse the fragmentation of the former KGB. The Federal Border Service was returned to the FSB, as was most of the Federal Agency for Government Communications and Information (Soldatov and Borogan 2010, 19–21). This step is probably more readily explained on political grounds than functional ones – Putin clearly did not fear the secret police the way that Yeltsin did, and restoring some of his old agencies' former functions and bureaucratic heft probably appealed to his Chekist identity. At the same time, he resisted proposals to recreate the structure of the KGB in toto, leaving foreign intelligence (SVR, the Foreign Intelligence Service) and leadership security (FSO, Federal Guard Service) as separate entities. Such a decision likely had both functional and political rationales, similar to those that motivated the breakup of the KGB in 1991.

Overall, the current organizational structure of the FSB is not in itself a legacy. The multiple organizational changes from 1991 to 2003 were more a product of the political calculations of Yeltsin and Putin than of the stickiness of past organizational forms, although those obviously played some role. The most important KGB legacy was not formal but informal, a cultural legacy of "elite Chekism" that influenced Yeltsin, Putin, and many other political elites.

MVD

The Ministry of Internal Affairs (MVD), in contrast to the KGB/FSB, continued relatively unchanged. The biggest formal organizational change was the 1998 removal of control over prisons from MVD jurisdiction and prisons' transfer to the jurisdiction of the Ministry of Justice, a move pushed by the Council of Europe. Several other major changes were repeatedly rejected; most important, efforts by reformers both within and outside government to formally decentralize the MVD have repeatedly failed. Such efforts have been pushed under all three presidents – Yeltsin, Putin, and Dmitrii Medvedev.

Decentralizing the MVD would involve the transfer of complete responsibility for the public order police to the regional or local level. The most basic functional division within the MVD is between the criminal police and the public order police. The criminal police include those units responsible for tasks such as criminal investigation, fighting economic crime, and combating terrorism and extremism. The criminal police are centrally financed and are not required to wear a uniform. The public order police, by contrast, are sometimes referred to as the "local police" and include beat cops and traffic police, and its personnel are required to wear uniforms on duty. Seventy percent of Russian police are in the public order police, and a significant share of their funding came from local and regional governments, although with the 2011 adoption of the new Law on the Police, all police financing, including for the local police, now comes from the federal budget (*Federal'nyy Zakon "O Politsii"* 2011, Article 47).

The issue of decentralizing the Russian police is a persistent debate among Russian law enforcement experts. Indeed, in the Soviet Union under Nikita Khrushchev, the entire central MVD was dismantled, and policing was transferred to the republics – a move reversed under Leonid Brezhnev (Shelley 1996, 41–47). Debates about decentralizing the police reemerged under Mikhail Gorbachev. His minister of internal affairs from 1988–1990, Vadim Bakatin (2003), argued for greater regional and local control over the public order police, but Gorbachev resisted this idea. Similarly, under Yeltsin, reformers such as his legal adviser Mikhail Krasnov (2003) pushed a similar proposal, which would have transferred the MOB to governors or mayors while leaving the criminal police under the federal MVD. One of Putin's top officials, Dmitriy Kozak, indicated in 2002 (Babayeva 2002) that legislation to turn control over public order policing to municipalities was soon to be introduced, but nothing came of this proposal. Finally, under Medvedev, with a new Law on the Police under consideration, multiple voices, including a think tank with close ties to Medvedev (INSOR 2011: 277–84), argued for decentralization of the MVD. Instead, Medvedev opted to keep the current MVD structure while centralizing financing of the local police (Ovchinskiy 2011).

What does it mean that the efforts of reformers to decentralize the MVD continually lose out to those who prefer to maintain the current structure? In particular, can this continuity be considered a legacy? There is no straightforward answer to this important question. The literature on institutional change and path dependence suggests several reasons for organizational continuity, including the costs (political and economic) of change, the taken-for-granted nature of existing arrangements, and existing power relations that favor the status quo (Campbell 2010). Even in Central and Eastern European states, where police reform has progressed further than in Russia, experts maintain that a communist policing legacy exists that makes these forces more centralized and militarized than in the West (Caparini and Marenin 2004, 321). This suggests there is an element of postcommunist legacy to the current organizational format.

On the other hand, after the major rupture of the communist collapse, there was an opening for substantial change. There was a significant decentralization of political power in the Russian Federation in the 1990s that could have bolstered arguments for organizational decentralization of the police. Further, in a super-presidential political system, a decision of the chief executive could bring about major change. Police reformers could have won.

In this case, it seems that a combination of "parameter setting" and functional logic led to the maintenance of the existing structure. Kotkin and Beissinger note that parameter setting as a legacy puts "limits on how individuals think and behave," including limits "imposed by the inertia of past practices or institutions." This type of parameter setting is evident in this case. But there were also functionalist reasons why these parameters proved so resilient.

For centuries, Russia has tended to have centralized policing. David Bayley maintains that a strong degree of path dependence endures in police organization, a pattern that holds true across many countries, including Russia. Bayley states, "The administrative practices established early in state histories persist, despite enormous changes in social structure, economic forms, and political character" (1985, 61). This finding leads Bayley to probe further into how these varying national traditions arise, and his answer is straightforward: "violent resistance to state demands," especially from the periphery, lead to centralized policing (1985, 70).

Bayley's argument is about the founding of national police systems, which then persist in a path-dependent fashion, but it offers a fairly compelling explanation for why arguments in favor of centralization of policing have repeatedly carried the day in post-Soviet Russia. Indeed, one former high-ranking police official remarked in 2003 that the decentralization of control over the local police to regional governments would lead to the creation of "89 armies of Dudayev," a reference to the former Chechen separatist leader. "Violent resistance to state demands" was not simply a feature of the distant past, but is a current phenomenon in post-Soviet Russia. Coupled with the fear that regional leaders had been allowed to swallow too much sovereignty under Yeltsin, the prospect of formally decentralizing control and financing of the bulk of the police was rejected not just by MVD officials, but by national leaders, particularly Putin, who wanted to recreate the "power vertical" that had been seriously weakened under Yeltsin (Taylor 2011, 112–55).

Further, what Americans see as a natural affinity between federalism and decentralized policing is far from a universal pattern. Indeed, among existing federations there is an almost even three-way split among those that have centralized policing, those that have decentralized policing, and those that treat policing as a shared or concurrent power. Other multiethnic federations, such as Nigeria and Malaysia, that fear separatist challenges rely on centralized police forces to help hold the country together (Taylor 2007). Democratic, federal, and multiethnic India has generally decentralized police forces, but several safeguards, such as centralized officer training and placement, the constitutional provision allowing for "President's rule" in case of emergency, and a Central Reserve Police Force able to supplement state forces in the event of civil unrest, are also in place to bolster the power of the central government in the law enforcement realm, although in practice state governments often successfully pressure the police to do their bidding (Wilkinson 2004, 65–79; Kumar 2005).

Thus, the centralized and militarized organization of the Russian MVD should be seen as not simply a legacy of the Soviet past, but also one that arguably has a functional basis, particularly given the reality of violent conflict on the periphery, specifically in the North Caucasus, since the Soviet collapse. The centralized organizational structure of the MVD is a partial legacy. The status quo has both a bureaucratic and cultural advantage, and is not only a communist tradition, but a long-standing Russian one. It also is far from unique in comparative terms, including for large, multiethnic federations. Efforts to decentralize the police will remain on the agenda, but will likely continue to lose out unless at some point in the future Russia becomes a genuine democratic federation, in which both political and economic power are more decentralized.

Finally, one further organizational continuity that affected both the FSB and the MVD was the continued split between "high" (political) and "low" (criminal) police. Such a division has roots both in the Soviet and tsarist periods, but because this division of law enforcement responsibilities is fairly common around the world, it would be hard to contend that this division is simply a legacy of the past. There was an abortive effort by Yeltsin in December 1991/January 1992 to erase this division between high and low policing and combine the MVD and the remaining KGB elements in a Ministry of Security and Internal Affairs (MBVD). Yeltsin's decree on this issue, which was promulgated without much consultation, was met with public outcry from liberal circles and the media, accusing Yeltsin of seeking to recreate a "Stalinist" NKVD (for much of the Stalin era high and low policing were combined). The parliament rejected the move, and the Constitutional Court ruled that the decree was unconstitutional (Waller 1994, 101–09; Knight 1996, 33–34). In this case, the public reaction to the proposal may have been the more important communist legacy, rather than the organizational one. In hindsight one wonders whether such a merger, if properly implemented, might have ended some of the functional overlap and bureaucratic competition between the two agencies, as well as helped root out the cultural legacies of the KGB that contributed to the FSB's rejuvenation.

The Procuracy
Continuity was also the order of the day with the Procuracy. It maintained its wide mandate and multiple functions from the Soviet period. These functions included criminal prosecution, criminal investigation for certain crimes, general oversight (*nadzor*) over all government agencies to ensure their compliance with the law, and coordination of the law enforcement organs (Smith 1996, 104–28; Mikhailovskaya 1999; Burger and Holland 2008).

Russian legal reformers in the early 1990s fought to strip the Procuracy of its general oversight functions and limit its role to criminal investigation and prosecution, but they lost that battle (Smith 1996). The legal reformers did succeed in pushing through the parliament a "Concept of Judicial Reform" in October 1991 that would have weakened the Procuracy and expanded the powers of the courts, but the Procuracy fought back against these efforts. In 1992–93, Procurator General Valentin Stepankov opposed any major changes and succeeded in pushing a new "Law on the Procuracy" through the Supreme Soviet in January 1992. This law preserved many of the existing powers of the Procuracy. The Procuracy successfully argued that the major upheaval in the country, including skyrocketing crime, made it an inopportune time to weaken the powers of the country's central law enforcement agency. For Yeltsin, legal reform issues were "peripheral" to the political battle between the president and the parliament at the time (Baturin et al. 2001, 390–95). Once this opportunity was lost in the early 1990s, no major legal or organizational changes for the Procuracy were forthcoming until the late 2000s.

A 2011 study (Institut Problem Pravoprimeneniya 2011, 46–77) comparing the formal powers of the Procuracy in ten former communist countries concluded that the powers of the Russian Procuracy were the widest among the group. At the same time, the considerable divergence among this previously more homogenous group of countries, which had imported the Soviet Procuracy model after the imposition of communism, suggests that there is no general postcommunist organizational legacy for the Procuracy. In some countries the Procuracy is an independent organ, in some countries it is part of the executive branch, and in other countries it is considered part of the judicial branch. In some countries it has a relatively narrow mandate related to criminal investigation and prosecution (the Czech Republic, Estonia, Latvia), whereas in other countries it has a broad range of functions similar to those in Russia, including general legal oversight (Hungary, Poland, Slovakia, Ukraine), and other countries fall somewhere in the middle (Bulgaria, Lithuania).

Was the continuation of a powerful Procuracy in Russia a legacy, and, if so, what kind? Some of the same "parameter setting" reasons for organizational continuity in the MVD – powerful interests, the costs of change, and so forth – were at work with the Procuracy as well. At the same time, it is important to remember how the political and economic environment has changed for the Procuracy, which makes this more a case of "translation" than "parameter setting." Translation refers to the deployment of an old institution in a new way. In two very important ways, the collapse of communism actually elevated and empowered the Procuracy and made it a valuable weapon that could be wielded in new ways. The first important change was the end of communist rule. While the Soviet Constitution affirmed the "leading and guiding" role of the Communist Party, the Russian Constitution declares in its first article that Russia is a "rule of law state" (*pravovoye gosudarstvo*). Because the Procuracy is tasked with general oversight of legality, it has a sweeping mandate that competing political forces seek to wield for their own advantage. A second key change was the introduction of capitalism and private property. As several of Yeltsin's former advisers noted (Baturin et al. 2001, 395), the general oversight power was a convenient "club" that commercial structures could use to attack their rivals. One journalist compared the Procuracy's powers to that of an "assault cannon, capable of destroying any walls" (Shleynov 2007).

Because of these two important contextual changes, the Procuracy ceased being a reliable weapon of CPSU domination, becoming a tool that multiple forces sought to control. During both Yeltsin's and Putin's second terms, as the succession contest heated up, major battles took place between so-called clans (informal networks of political and economic elites) for control over the Procuracy (Burger and Holland 2008; Taylor 2011, 65–66, 103–04, 174–75). The extensive formal legal powers of the Procuracy, combined with an instrumental approach to the law by political elites, made it too valuable a resource to leave unattended. At the same time, these skirmishes were usually much more about informal relationships and groupings than formal organizational responsibilities.

The continuation of the Procuracy's broad powers across the institutional rupture of the communist collapse was an organizational legacy with important consequences for Russian politics. At the same time, however, the Procuracy's standing stimulated battles for control that ultimately are undermining its position, although perhaps not strengthening the rule of law. In 2007, the Investigative Committee of the Procuracy was made semiautonomous from the rest of the General Procuracy, with a new head appointed directly by the president. The first (and to date only) head, Aleksandr Bastrykin, went to law school with Putin. In 2011, this reform was taken further, with the Investigative Committee (SK) entirely separated from the Procuracy. The separation of the Procuracy and the SK induced more or less open warfare between the two structures, resulting in several prominent corruption scandals (Novoye obostreniye 2011; Sakwa 2013). Although the Procuracy's substantial role in Russian politics over the past two decades has been at least in part a legacy from the past, the multiple reforms undertaken with respect to this organization since 2007, not to mention the more substantial changes in other postcommunist states, suggest that formal organizational legacies may be "sticky," but they are hardly immutable.

Organizational Legacies: Summary
This section has highlighted two organizational legacies in Russian law enforcement: a centralized MVD and a powerful Procuracy. I argued that maintaining a centralized MVD was a partial legacy in which parameter setting played an important role, but this organizational continuity could also be explained on functional grounds. In contrast, I claimed that the persistence of a powerful Procuracy was an example of translation, because the old structure was used in fundamentally new ways because of the radically different political and economic environment. Further, this legacy may be a waning one because of reforms in the 2000s that weakened the Procuracy.

Cultural and Behavioral Legacies

Legacies at the level of practice and culture are likely to be both more enduring and harder to observe. Still, there are some generally accepted attributes of law enforcement practice from the Soviet period that might well qualify as legacies if they persist. These include:

- the primacy of serving the state and political demands in law enforcement activity, as opposed to service to the citizenry;
- enforcement of party-defined standards for personal activity among the population;
- institutional rivalry among the main law enforcement agencies;
- the elite status of the KGB and KGB agents, particularly as compared to the militia; and
- a goal-oriented approach to policing, both in terms of party-diktat and in terms of plan-like targets for police performance set by the party and the police leadership, combined with weak legal consciousness and training.

In the rest of the section, I discuss the extent to which these more behavioral and cultural tendencies have persisted since the Soviet collapse and, if so, to what extent they may be considered legacies. Not only do I ask what is old, but also what is new and significant in Russian policing. Only by looking for new practices as well as examining old ones can we see whether legacies get us very far in understanding the evolution of law enforcement since 1991.

Policing and Personal Freedom
A key change for Russian citizens since the late 1980s is the much greater freedom they have in terms of where they go, how they dress, what they read, and so forth than they had in the past. Not only the KGB but also the regular police had a mandate to impose Communist Party standards of behavior. Networks of informers among the general population helped the police maintain social control (Shelley 1996, 128–61, 178–92; Light 2010). An effective system of "low-intensity coercion" (Levitsky and Way 2010) helped ensure an adequate (from the authorities' point of view) degree of social control. This system has by and large broken down, although clearly not everywhere and for everyone – for example, dressing and praying the "wrong way" can be a hazard for Muslims, especially in some North Caucasus republics (Myers 2005).

One potential law enforcement legacy for average citizens in their daily lives, despite greater personal freedom, is the continuation of an internal passport and registration system. Although the Russian Constitution (Article 27) guarantees freedom of movement and freedom to choose where one lives, many legal and administrative restrictions still exist. The most important change from the Soviet period is that permission for residence in a particular place, the so-called *propiska* system, has been replaced with registration based on notification. Residents in Russia (citizens and noncitizens alike) are required to notify the police both where they live (residence), as well as where they are staying away from their permanent residence when they travel within the country. The police and local governments frequently abuse this registration system to harass migrants, not only from other countries (usually other post-Soviet states), but also from other regions of Russia (Light 2010; Krepostnaya Rossiya 2013).

Matthew Light (2010) has shown that the way the Moscow police enforce these regulations and directives from the Moscow city government is not simply a legacy of the past. The old way of enforcing movement to Moscow, using state control over employment and housing (including building managers who ratted out suspicious activity), has completely broken down. Instead, the police now rely much more heavily on public document checks and sweeps, especially at transportation points and in workplaces likely to employ migrants (construction sites, markets, etc.). These public checks are not simply – although they certainly are in part – about corruption and "predatory policing" (Gerber and Mendelson 2008; Taylor 2011, 161–85). They are a fundamental piece of the Moscow city government's efforts to control who comes into the city and on what terms, given that the old controls no longer work.

The current registration system and how it is policed is a case of institutional "bricolage" – a legacy that combines elements from the past with new, post-communist elements. Specifically, a new economic context – private ownership of business and housing, and economic migration from former Soviet states in a more globalized economy – combined with the old, albeit modified, internal registration system has introduced important changes to law enforcement practices. For migrants and minorities, in particular, Light observes, "the collapse of the Soviet police state has actually created more anarchy and violence in the day-to-day enforcement activities of the police" (2010, 303).

Institutional Rivalry and Elite Chekists

Institutional rivalry among the different law enforcement agencies was a key feature of the law enforcement realm during the Soviet period. These institutional conflicts existed both at the macro-level of bureaucratic politics and at the micro-level of everyday interactions between officials from different agencies. Considerable animosity existed, in particular, between the MVD and the KGB. A young Vladimir Putin took great offense when someone suggested that he was headed toward a career in the police, retorting, "I won't be a cop (*ment*)!" Putin noted that "those of us in the Cheka never liked the police" (Gevorkyan, Timakova, and Kolesnikov 2000, 25, 128–29).

There is widespread agreement that this rivalry, especially between the MVD and the FSB, has persisted in Russia (e.g., Siloviki snova stali sil'nymi 2004). It would be hard to claim that this enmity is some kind of communist legacy, however, because disputes between bureaucracies with overlapping jurisdiction is a near-universal feature of modern states, as is rivalry between high and low policing agencies. However, in this subsection I suggest that the specific form of this rivalry intersects with a more important broader and cultural legacy of Soviet rule, the elite "blue blood" status of the Chekists from the secret police, allegedly loyal and incorruptible servants of the state.

The MVD/KGB rivalry sharpened in the early 1980s. When Yuriy Andropov, the longtime KGB head, became the head of the Communist Party and leader of the Soviet Union in 1982, he launched a purge within the MVD. Police corruption clearly had increased under Brezhnev and MVD head Nikolay Shchelokov, a longtime Brezhnev crony; Brezhnev's son-in-law Yuriy Churbanov was named first deputy head of the MVD in 1979, and he and his wife, Galina, were later implicated in a string of corruption scandals. Andropov sought to clean house and transferred his successor as head of the KGB, Vitaliy Fedorchuk, to the MVD. Over the next three years, many police officials at all levels were dismissed, and Fedorchuk brought other high-ranking KGB officials into the MVD to help him gain control over the agency. Shchelokov was ousted from the Party in 1984, was stripped of his medals and rank, and committed suicide to avoid trial on corruption charges (Knight 1990, 91–93; Shelley 1996, 46–52).

Andropov also broadened the Soviet policy of promoting the exploits of the KGB and the incorruptibility and superior abilities of its agents (Soldatov and

Borogan 2010, 11). Earlier propaganda films and books had the desired effect on a teenage Putin, who was inspired by romantic notions about foreign intelligence to seek a career in the KGB; he was, he later admitted, a "successful product" of such patriotic influences (Gevorkyan et al. 2000, 39). Survey data from the last years of the Soviet Union suggest that, even at a time of enormous publicity about the historic crimes of the KGB, it remained one of the most trusted institutions in Soviet society (Popov 1992, 329–30; Waller 1994, 247–48, 259).

It is difficult to know how widespread these romantic notions about the KGB are today. It seems clear that secret police officials themselves hold such ideas. Russian journalists Andrei Soldatov and Irina Borogan note that FSB officers today see themselves as the "intellectual elite," "the best and the brightest," and "the saviors of [the] nation," wryly observing that this view is perhaps "a legacy of old Soviet propaganda films" (2010, 5). Top Chekist allies of Putin also have articulated this perspective. Nikolay Patrushev, the head of the FSB throughout Putin's 2000–08 presidency, referred to FSB agents as "the new nobility." Viktor Cherkesov (2004, 2007), like Patrushev and Putin a native Leningrader who served in the KGB, held several top posts under Putin and set out what amounted to a "Chekist manifesto" in two extraordinary newspaper articles. He declared that Chekists had to assume responsibility for the country: "History has arranged it that the burden of upholding Russian statehood has to a considerable extent fallen on our shoulders." Indeed, Cherkesov asserted that the Chekists were a "hook" that society was clinging to to avoid plunging into an abyss; Putin and the Chekists were preventing Russia from falling to its death.

The image of KGB/FSB agents as pure and exemplary state servants is apparently held not only by Chekists, but also by many members of the political elite and the general population. Public opinion surveys over the past two decades show that the FSB is one of the more trusted state institutions, lagging behind the army but well ahead of the other law enforcement structures (police, Procuracy, courts), as well as the Duma and regional governments. The percentage of those expressing full or some confidence in the state security organs has tended to hover between 50–60 percent, with the percentage expressing no confidence around the 20–25 percent level. For Russia, at least, these numbers are comparatively high (Levada Tsentr 2009, 73; Taylor 2011, 206). Putin's campaign aides in 2000 saw his Chekist background as a plus, noting that "he had managed to exploit the legend that our services were still one of the only effective, uncorrupted elements of Soviet and post-Soviet society" (Baker and Glasser 2007, 61). Although Russians in 2007 rated secret police personnel as more "professional" than civilian officials, however, they did not rate them as any less corrupt (Levada Tsentr 2007, 90).

Most significant for Russian politics, it seems that Yeltsin also somewhat believed in this myth of the KGB as a repository of elite and honest state servants. The evidence on this point is circumstantial, but telling. Yeltsin's last three prime ministers – Yevgeniy Primakov, Sergey Stepashin, and Putin – had all headed one of the KGB successor organizations under Yeltsin: Primakov the Foreign Intelligence Service and Stepashin and Putin the FSB. Second, the general expansion of *siloviki* (power ministry personnel), especially Chekists, throughout the government started in Yeltsin's second term before accelerating under Putin (Kryshtanovskaya and White 2003). For example, former KGB officer Nikolay Bordyuzha headed both the Security Council and the Presidential Administration in 1998–99. Third, Yeltsin himself made clear in his memoirs that his consideration of Bordyuzha and Stepashin as potential successors, as well as his eventual choice of Putin, was influenced by his belief that society was yearning for a leader who was not only a "new-thinking democrat," but also a "strong, military man" (2000, 254).

Once Putin became president, the expansion of Chekists (and other *siloviki*) throughout the Russian government accelerated. He also followed in Andropov's footprints by appointing former KGB officers to head not only the MVD (Rashid Nurgaliyev), but also the Ministry of Defense (Sergei Ivanov). KGB veterans also filled second-tier positions in both of these ministries (Kryshtanovskaya and White 2003; Taylor 2011, 57–64, 68–69). There was also an effort to promote the old notion of the secret police as the repository of capable and upright officials, including, in particular, Andropov himself, whose allegedly sensible reforms were tragically cut short by his untimely death (Murawiec and Gaddy 2002; Soldatov and Borogan 2010, 91–97, 101–05). At the same time, it is clear that Putin as president elevated the FSB, not the other way around. The argument is not that the secret police took over the state, but that a certain image of the KGB, held certainly by Putin and seemingly also by Yeltsin and other elites and citizens, created the conditions for the FSB to dominate the other power ministries and play a central role in domestic politics.

This apparent belief in incorruptible elite Chekists is contradicted by reality. There is ample evidence that FSB officials have been involved in a wide range of corrupt and predatory behavior, such as providing protection services for businesses ("roofing," in Russian parlance) (e.g., Soldatov and Borogan 2007). Further, they are hardly a unified collective. Indeed, the second of Cherkesov's manifestos was part of a spirited battle between opposing *siloviki* clans that led to the arrest of Cherkesov's deputy at the Federal Service for the Control of Narcotics, apparently at the behest of a rival clan affiliated with FSB head Patrushev (Taylor 2011, 65–66). Cherkesov's 2007 article, entitled "Warriors Should Not Become Traders," made it clear that they had become exactly that.

Institutional rivalry between law enforcement agencies, especially those with many overlapping functions like the MVD and the FSB, is not unusual and is certainly not simply a communist legacy, even though such competition existed during the Soviet period. This rivalry is structural. Differing power and status between rival agencies also is not unique. What does seem to have some legacy aspects is the enduring image of the Chekists as the elite of the law enforcement community, particularly when compared to the low police, who were singled out for their corrupt ways by Andropov and the KGB in the 1980s. Further, in comparative terms the role of the security services seems particularly elevated. In Latin America, Africa, and Asia, the military has been much more likely to dominate politics than the secret police. Even in the Middle East, where the secret police have considerable political power, the military usually has the upper hand, and the security services do not enjoy the cultural reputation that the KGB and FSB seem to command (Springborg 2010). This feature of Russian politics does seem to be at least in part a legacy from the communist past, and if so it is a very important one.

The elite Chekist legacy is best thought of as a case of translation. An old set of cultural beliefs has been deployed in a new way. During the Soviet period, the Party promoted a myth of elite Chekists to strengthen its political control and domestic legitimacy. This elite status successfully translated into political power and economic gain during the post-Soviet period. Many top state positions are occupied by Chekists. Moreover, some Chekists used their political power to "become traders," in Cherkesov's phrase. Old KGB allies of Putin occupy or occupied important roles in many state companies, including Igor Sechin (Rosneft), Sergey Ivanov (United Aircraft Construction Corporation), Vladimir Yakunin (Russian Railways), Sergey Chemezov (Russian Technology), Nikolay Tokarev (Transneft), and Viktor Ivanov (Aeroflot, Almaz-Antei). Daniel Treisman (2007) dubbed these figures *silovarchs* – silovik plus oligarch. In the more open political and economic environment of postcommunism, Chekists were able to translate their elite status into political and economic power in a way they never would have been able to when they were under Party control.

Everyday Policing: Serving the Plan and One's Pocket
It is at the level of everyday practice for ordinary police that we see the most interesting combination of old and new. Regular police in the Soviet Union were guided most of all in their daily work by controls and tasks imposed from above, with adherence to the law or service to citizens of relatively minor importance. Although this basic behavioral orientation persists, it has combined with opportunities provided by the new capitalist economic system to create a different form of policing, yet one that retains elements from the past.

Policing on behalf of the "powers that be" rather than ordinary citizens is, if not ubiquitous, then quite common worldwide. Indeed, some approaches to policing contend that all policing, by definition, is designed to serve state and elite interests. However, most policing experts (e.g., Bayley 2006) do recognize that in many developed states a model of "democratic policing" has been created in which there is some degree of public accountability, the police generally exhibit a commitment to civil rights, and police see themselves not just as state officials, but as public servants – "to serve and protect," as the motto goes. Assessments of efforts to democratize postcommunist police have found that in all of these countries significant problems remain with changing the norms and behavior of the police, but that the countries of Central Europe have been more successful generally than those in the Balkans or the former Soviet Union (Caparini and Marenin 2004).

At the rhetorical level, the Russian police are also moving toward a model of democratic policing. In both the 1991 "Law on the Militia" and the 2011 "Law on the Police," the very first article states the police's responsibility to "defend the life, health, rights, and freedoms" of inhabitants of Russia (citizens or otherwise). Police leaders frequently state the commitment of the MVD to openness to citizens and working to raise the level of popular trust in the police. Yet most experts have noticed little real progress toward these rhetorical commitments and contend that the police tend to work either for the state or for their own interests, to the neglect of the general public (Gerber and Mendelson 2008; Gladarev 2009; Volkov, Paneyakh, and Titov 2010).

Because Russia is not a democracy, it is not surprising that it does not have democratic police. And the types of pathologies common among the Russian police – corruption, poor training, a tendency toward excessive violence, up to and including torture, and so forth – are quite common among police in states with authoritarian, hybrid, or recently democratic regimes (e.g., Davis 2006). At this general level, the evident similarities between Soviet and Russian policing may bear some legacy aspects, but even if Russia had not experienced communism at all, but was still a middle-income country with a semiauthoritarian regime, police behavior would be roughly similar.

Probing more closely into the details of everyday policing, however, shows us an important mechanism by which this neglect of service to citizens has persisted. The Soviet system of "quotas" and "plans" for police activity have carried over into Russia. The effect of this quota system has been to prioritize the gathering and manipulation of statistics by the police. Rather than constraining police activity, in actual practice the heavy reliance on these indicators has allowed police considerable autonomy to pursue their own economic gains once they have fulfilled their quotas through various standard schemes.

Evaluating and supervising police is a problem for police supervisors everywhere. This is because policing as a bureaucratic type is what James Q. Wilson called a "coping" organization, in which it is difficult for supervisors both to watch what the average cop is doing and to assess whether the cop's activities contribute to public order and crime reduction (1989, 158–71). One solution many police forces use in an attempt to monitor police performance is a set of quantitative indicators meant to track police activity. Common measures include crime rates, crime clearance rates (percentage of recorded crimes solved), average response times, street time per officer, citizen and crime victim surveys, and so forth. Like in Russia, there are incentives to manipulate statistics to increase one's rating (Eterno and Silverman 2012). In this respect, Russia fits the common pattern.

Often these statistical indicators are used as performance assessment and management tools. Russia is the same in this respect also. Where Russian policing differs from many countries is the way these quantitative indicators are set by a central ministry as a series of quotas and plans, and the use of campaigns to target priority crimes. In this respect, the Russian approach to crime is very much like the Soviet command economy. And, as with the plan during Soviet times (Berliner 1957), clever agents at lower levels have figured out how to "shirk" rather than "work," and indeed, to profit from the system.

The Soviet MVD adopted the use of planning and a quota system for fighting crime.[2] A series of indicators were passed down from the center. The targets were often absurdly precise (a certain number of firearms arrests per month, a specific number of traffic violations, another target for passport infringements, etc.) as well as impossibly high (such as clearance rates of more than 90 percent). There was considerable pressure to meet these targets, which led officers to cook the books to meet their quotas. This could be done in several ways. One common method was the failure to record crimes for which there was little prospect of a successful case. Another technique was to force someone to plead guilty to multiple offenses as a way of clearing unsolved crimes. If necessary, cases and suspects could be invented. This quota system was often combined with centrally directed "campaigns" to suddenly achieve high results for specific crimes, which further increased incentives to manipulate statistics. Even when police actually tried to solve crimes, the incentive was to solve easy crimes that met certain performance parameters, rather than more complicated cases (Shelley 1996, 164–67; Favarel-Garrigues 2010, 4–6, 57–68, 84–89).

This quota system has persisted with only minor changes into the post-Soviet period (Gladarev 2009; Favarel-Garrigues 2010). Police officers call it the "stick" (*palka*) system, in reference to the hash marks on a form. As before, the quotas are often both very precise and completely unrealistic, and particularly divorced from local conditions. According to one report, a 2010 attempt to reform the system actually increased the number of "control indicators" from sixty-five to seventy-two (Volkov et al. 2010, 10). Often these indicators are set with respect to the previous year. So, for example, if in one small village the police were supposed to arrest three people for selling narcotics, the next year they might have to arrest four. What if all dealers in this small village are already in jail, and there is no one else left to arrest? In the best case, this village police officer might make a deal with his boss to falsify the report, but it might also be necessary, for example, to coerce someone arrested for petty theft to plead guilty to drug trafficking. As should be obvious, preventing crime in this system before it happens is a bad thing, because the system requires a specific number of arrests for specific offenses for every reporting period. And with the tendency to set criteria based on the previous year, the whole system is actually premised on a continual increase in crime. Experts have rightly classified this system as "fictitious" and leading to the construction of a "virtual reality" world for the police (Novikova 2011). As during the Soviet period, it creates incentives to cook the books and direct one's efforts not at fighting real crime or helping actual citizens, but at adhering to norms and plans imposed from above and manipulating actual crime data to meet the requirements set by centralized staffs.

Changing the police quota system is often discussed, and some changes have been introduced to how it works. Overall, however, this institution has proved resistant to change. Its initial persistence can probably be explained by the taken-for-granted nature of the practice. More recently, a fear of the unknown has seemed to stymie efforts to do away with or radically reform the system. Police officials recognize the perverse outcomes generated by the system, but they fear a loss of control over their subordinates without this monitoring and control mechanism. Vadim Volkov (2010) notes, "the quota system is the most important institution of organizational control inside the police agency, without which there would be a complete privatization of its activity."

In a perverse way, however, the quota system also has the effect of giving officers greater license to freelance while on work time. Once one has met the quantitative performance criteria – and there are tried and true methods to fulfill one's targets – officers have considerable license to enrich themselves on work time. This practice actually began during the Soviet period. Gilles Favarel-Garrigues (2010) shows that with the growth of the second economy during the Brezhnev period, police responsible for policing economic crime were able to use the standard methods to meet their quotas, and then use their remaining time to exploit their access to the second economy for their own personal gain. When the quota system continued into the post-Soviet period almost unchanged but the command economy was replaced with the early capitalism of the so-called wild '90s, the opportunities for personal enrichment multiplied exponentially. The new market economy (including the market for force exploited by "violent entrepreneurs"), combined with the legacy of a planned approach to law enforcement, created a system in which the police were substantially privatized (Kolesnikova et al. 2002; Volkov 2002). One police sergeant colorfully summarized the consequences:

Those of us working in the Patrol-Guard Service [beat cops] have tough yet simple work. We work on "blacks" [minorities from the Caucasus and Central Asia], winos, drug addicts, bums, and such trash. First we collect the required number of "sticks," then we can work for ourselves. Anything above the quota is for me. (Quoted in Gladarev 2009)

The tendency of Russian law enforcement officials (and it is not just the police) to be guided by commercial motives is arguably the most fundamental aspect of their current practice. This behavior has some legacy aspects, but ultimately it is more a consequence of the introduction of a market economy and private property than it is of the Soviet past. It also connects to a different legacy – the neglect of citizen service as a key orientation. During the Soviet period, the demands and interests of the Party-State took precedence over societal concerns, so law enforcement was predominately a repressive organization. That repressive component of behavior has lessened but persisted, while the predatory (economically self-interested) element has grown but is not entirely new. What remains the case is that protection of citizens is often a secondary or even tertiary concern of law enforcement personnel. This is hardly a postcommunist phenomenon alone, but the particular form in which it persists does seem to be a Soviet legacy. In particular, this is another example of institutional bricolage, in which elements of the past are intermixed with the present.

Cultural and Behavioral Legacies: Summary
The rupture of the Soviet collapse brought about important changes in the behavior of Russian law enforcement personnel. In particular, the end of Communist Party domination in politics and daily life and the introduction of capitalism have created both new challenges and new opportunities for the Russian high and low police. Nikolay Bukharin's injunction to peasants during the New Economic Policy of the 1920s – "enrich yourselves!" – has been taken to heart (quoted in Cohen 1971/1980, 177). But the institutions that structure this behavior, such as the citizen registration system and the quota system used in crime reporting, are communist legacies. In these examples, a process of bricolage has combined these legacies with new features of the socioeconomic order. In the case of cultural beliefs in elite Chekism, this artifact has been translated into the new political and economic order, deployed not to bolster the power and legitimacy of the Party, but strategically deployed to capture the state and access to state resources.

Conclusion

Legacies – organizational, cultural, behavioral – matter for Russian law enforcement. But rarely, if ever, is it the case that something from the past crossed the institutional rupture of the end of communism unscathed. Instead, we find that the major changes of 1991 mix with these Soviet remnants. The three most important changes – the end of Communist Party domination, the end of the planned economy, and the collapse of the Soviet state and its civilizational autarky – created new challenges and opportunities for Russian law enforcement.

The most consequential organizational legacy was the broad powers of the Procuracy. These powers have been used and abused by executives (state and business) at all levels, but they have been divided and eroded in recent years. The MVD remains a super-centralized structure, but this is not simply a legacy, although parameter setting played some role – it may also be functional for the Russian state. The most powerful policing agency, the KGB, was split into multiple parts to weaken its influence, although this breakup was later partially reversed.

Not surprising, informal institutions and practices have proven more resistant to change than formal organizational structures, and arguably are more consequential. The formal end to the KGB did not mean the death of certain myths about the attributes of its agents. Greater personal freedoms for average citizens did not end their need to account for their whereabouts to the police, a persistent power that both local governments and the police themselves exploit, especially to harass migrant workers in the new global economy. Finally, the death of the planned economy did not mean the end of planned policing; the advent of private property and the market radically changed the extent to which cops work for themselves, even if it did not change the fact that service to society remains a low priority.

Legacies matter, but legacy arguments can only get us so far in understanding Russian law enforcement today. Cops, Chekists, and prosecutors are shaped not just by the past, but also by general pressures faced by law enforcement officials everywhere, and by a broader social and institutional environment that is a complicated mix of old and new. Attention to these cross-national institutional similarities and to how a changing environment leads to institutional change gives us a more nuanced but ultimately more compelling understanding of legacies.

Notes

1 FSB is the third name of the post-Soviet secret police, after Ministry of Security (1992–93) and Federal Counter-Intelligence Service (1994–95).
2 I have been unable to pinpoint a specific decision or year in which this system was adopted, but Peter Solomon's (1987) research on the Procuracy suggests that it happened during the late Stalin period.

References

Albats, Yevgenia. 1994. *The State within a State: The KGB and Its Hold on Russia – Past, Present, and Future*. New York: Farrar, Strauss, and Giroux.
Andreas, Peter and Ethan Nadelmann. 2006. *Policing the Globe: Criminalization and Crime Control in International Relations*. Oxford: Oxford University Press.
Andrew, Christopher and Oleg Gordievsky. 1990. *KGB: The Inside Story*. New York: Harper Collins.
Babayeva, Svetlana. 2002. "Dmitriy Kozak: 'Eto – vlast', a ne samodeyatel'nost'." *Izvestiya*. November 19.
Bakatin, Vadim. 1999. *Doroga v proshedshem vremeni*. Moskva: Dom.
    2003. (former minister of internal affairs and director of KGB, Soviet Union). Interview by author. April.
Baker, Peter and Susan Glasser. 2007. *Kremlin Rising*, updated ed. Dulles, VA: Potomac Books.
Baturin, Yu. M. et al. 2001. *Epokha Yel'tsina: Ocherki politicheskoy istorii*. Moskva: Vagrius.
Bayley, David H. 1985. *Patterns of Policing*. New Brunswick, NJ: Rutgers University Press.
    2006. *Changing the Guard: Developing Democratic Police Abroad*. Oxford: Oxford University Press.

Berliner, Joseph S. 1957. *Factory and Manager in the USSR*. Cambridge, MA: Harvard University Press.

Burger, Ethan S. and Mary Holland. 2008. "Law as Politics: The Russian Procuracy and Its Investigative Committee." *Columbia Journal of East European Law* 2(2): 143–94.

Campbell, John L. 2010. "Institutional Reproduction and Change." In *The Oxford Handbook of Comparative Institutional Analysis*, ed. Glenn Morgan et al. 87–116. Oxford: Oxford University Press.

Caparini, Marina and Otwen Marenin. 2004. "Process and Progress in the Reform of Policing Systems." In *Transforming Police in Central and Eastern Europe: Process and Progress*, ed. Marina Caparini and Otwen Marenin, 321–39. Munster, Germany: Lit Verlag.

Cherkesov, Viktor. 2004. "Moda na KGB?" *Kom'somolskaya Pravda*. December 29.

2007. "Nel'zya dopustit', chtoby voiny prevratilis' v torgovtsev." *Kommersant"-Daily*. October 9.

Chivers, C. J. 2008. "Power. The Vladimir Putin Story." *Esquire*, October 1.

Cohen, Stephen F. 1971/1980. *Bukharin and the Bolshevik Revolution: A Political Biography, 1888–1938*. Oxford: Oxford University Press.

Colton, Timothy J. 2008. *Yeltsin: A Life*. New York: Basic Books.

Davis, Diane E. 2006. "Undermining the Rule of Law: Democratization and the Dark Side of Police Reform in Mexico." *Latin American Politics and Society* 48(1): 55–86.

Easter, Gerald. 2008. "The Russian State in the Time of Putin." *Post-Soviet Affairs* 24(3) (Jul.–Sep.): 199–230.

Eterno, John A. and Eli B. Silverman. 2012. *The Crime Numbers Game: Management by Manipulation*. Boca Raton, FL: CRC Press.

Favarel-Garrigues, Gilles. 2010. *Policing Economic Crime in Russia: From Soviet Planned Economy to Privatization*. London: Hurst.

Gerber, Theodore P. and Sarah E. Mendelson. 2008. "Public Experiences of Police Violence and Corruption in Contemporary Russia: A Case of Predatory Policing?" *Law and Society Review* 42(1): 1–43.

Gevorkyan, Natal'ya, Natal'ya Timakova, and Andrey Kolesnikov, eds. 2000. *Ot pervogo litsa: Razgovory s Vladimirom Putinym*. Moskva: Vagrius.

Gladarev, Boris. 2009. "Mutatsiya dyadi Styepy: Sotsiologicheskiy ocherk." *Neva*, No. 1.

Institut Problem Pravoprimeneniya. 2011. "20 let reform sudebnoy sistemy: komparativnyy analiz postsotsialisticheskikh stran." Sankt Peterburg: European University at St. Petersburg. Unpublished manuscript.

Institut Sovremennogo Razvitiya (INSOR). 2011. *Obreteniye budushchego. Strategiya 2012*. Moskva.

Karklins, Rasma. 2002. "Typology of Post-Communist Corruption." *Problems of Post-Communism* 49(4) (July/August): 22–32.

Knight, Amy W. 1990. *The KGB: Police and Politics in the Soviet Union*. Boston, MA: Unwin Hyman.

1996. *Spies Without Cloaks: The KGB's Successors*. Princeton, NJ: Princeton University Press.

Kolesnikova, O. et al. 2002. *Ekonomicheskaya aktivnost' rabotnikov pravookhranitel'nykh organov postsovetskoi Rossii: Vidy, masshtaby i vliyaniye na obshchestvo*. Moskva.

Kotkin, Stephen. 2001. *Armageddon Averted: The Soviet Collapse 1970–2000*. Oxford: Oxford University Press.
Krasnov, Mikhail (former legal adviser to Boris Yeltsin). 2003. Interview by author. April.
Krepostnaya Rossiya. 2013. *Lenta.ru.* January 11.
Kryshtanovskaya, Olga and Stephen White. 2003. "Putin's Militocracy." *Post-Soviet Affairs* 19(4): 289–306.
Kumar, Pramod (Indian Police Service). 2005. Interview by author. November.
Levada Tsentr. 2007. *Obshchestvennoye mneniye – 2007: Yezhegodnik.* Moskva: Levada Tsentr.
  2009. *Obshchestvennoye mneniye – 2009: Yezhegodnik.* Moskva: Levada Tsentr.
Levitsky, Steven and Lucan A. Way. 2010. *Competitive Authoritarianism: Hybrid Regimes after the Cold War*. Cambridge: Cambridge University Press.
Light, Matthew. 2010. "Policing Migration in Soviet and Post-Soviet Moscow." *Post-Soviet Affairs* 26(4): 275–313.
Myers, Steven Lee. 2005. "Growth of Islam in Russia Brings Soviet Response." *New York Times*. November 22.
Mikhailovskaya, Inga. 1999. "The Procuracy and Its Problems: Russia." *East European Constitutional Review* 8(1/2) (Winter/Spring): 98–104.
Murawiec, Laurent and Clifford C. Gaddy. 2002. "The Higher Police: Vladimir Putin and His Predecessors." *The National Interest* 67 (Spring): 29–36.
Novikova, Asmik. 2011. "Sistema upravelniya v militsii: konstruirovaniye virtual'nnoy real'nosti s real'nymi postradavshimi." *Vestnik obshchestvennogo mneniya* 2 (April–June): 38–46.
Novoye obostreniye v silovykh strukturakh. 2011. *NEWSru.com*. October 13.
Ovchinskiy, Vladimir (retired MVD general). 2011. Interview with author. July.
Popov, Nikolai P. 1992. "Political Views of the Russian People." *International Journal of Public Opinion Research* 4(4): 321–34.
Sakwa, Richard. 2013. "Investigator Bastrykin and the Search for Enemies." *Open Democracy*, April 10.
Shelley, Louise. 1996. *Policing Soviet Society: The Evolution of State Control*. London: Routledge.
  1999. "Post-Socialist Policing: Limitations on Institutional Change." In *Policing Across the World*, ed. R. I. Mawby, 75–87. London: Routledge.
Shleynov, Roman. 2007. Donoschiki snaryadov. *Novaya Gazeta*. April 26.
Siloviki snova stali sil'nymi. 2004. *Vremya Novostey*. March 11.
Smith, Gordon B. 1996. *Reforming the Russian Legal System*. Cambridge: Cambridge University Press.
Soldatov, Andrei and Irina Borogan. 2007. Sokrytiye pokazhet. *Novaya Gazeta*. May 7.
  2010. *The New Nobility: The Restoration of Russia's Security State and the Enduring Legacy of the KGB*. New York: Public Affairs.
Solomon, Peter H., Jr. 1987. "The Case of the Vanishing Acquittal: Informal Norms and the Practice of Soviet Criminal Justice." *Soviet Studies* 39(4): 531–55.
Springborg, Robert. 2010. Civilian Control of Arab Armed Forces: Lessons from Non-Arab Democracies. Paper prepared for delivery at the International Studies Association 51st Annual Convention, New Orleans, February.

Stan, Lavinia, ed. 2008. *Transitional Justice in Eastern Europe and the Former Soviet Union: Reckoning with the Communist Past*. London: Routledge.
Taylor, Brian D. 2007. "Force and Federalism: Controlling Coercion in Federal Hybrid Regimes." *Comparative Politics* 39(4) (July): 421–40.
   2011. *State Building in Putin's Russia: Policing and Coercion after Communism*. Cambridge: Cambridge University Press.
Treisman, Daniel. 2007. "Putin's *Silovarchs*." *Orbis* 51(1): 141–53.
Volkov, Vadim. 2002. *Violent Entrepreneurs: The Use of Force in the Making of Russian Capitalism*. Ithaca, NY: Cornell University Press.
   2010. "Palochnaya sistema: Instrument upravleniya." *Vedomosti*. February 19.
Volkov, V. V., E. L. Paneyakh, and K. D. Titayev. 2010. *Reforma MVD v Rossii: chetyre problemy i vosem' mre po ikh resheniyu*. Sankt-Peterburg: Institut Problem Pravoprimeneniya.
Waller, J. Michael. 1994. *Secret Empire: The KGB in Russia Today*. Boulder, CO: Westview Press.
Welsh, Helga A. 1996. "Dealing with the Communist Past: Central and East European Experiences after 1990." *Europe-Asia Studies* 48(3) (May): 413–28.
Wilkinson, Steven I. 2004. *Votes and Violence: Electoral Competition and Ethnic Riots in India*. Cambridge: Cambridge University Press.
Wilson, James Q. 1989. *Bureaucracy: What Government Agencies Do and Why They Do It*. New York: Basic Books.
Yeltsin, Boris. 2000. *Prezidentskiy marafon*. Moskva: ACT.

8

How Judges Arrest and Acquit

Soviet Legacies in Postcommunist Criminal Justice

Alexei Trochev

> I hope that every year we will have more and more acquittals because this is absolutely correct. We should not be shy in issuing them.
> Dmitry Medvedev, president of Russia, April 26, 2012

> The times in the past, when the acquittals were issued in 2–3 percent of cases, are gone.
> Viktor Yanukovych, president of Ukraine, October 2, 2012

If someone fell asleep in the late 1980s in a courtroom in Sofia, Moscow, or Tbilisi and suddenly awoke in 2010, she or he would notice many differences. Courtrooms would have become larger and equipped with computers, microphones, and video cameras. Courthouses would no longer have posters about socialist legality and the guiding role of the Communist Party. Instead, their hallways would be full of people talking to their lawyers about all kinds of new legal rules and rights. Judges dressed in dark-colored robes would be busily hearing countless cases about these rights. They would often rule against the government authorities of all levels in various kinds of disputes.

However, postcommunist judges would also behave in some very familiar ways. In addition to keeping the trials soporific, they would be systematically biased in favor of state prosecution in the criminal justice system. Similar to the period of "developed socialism," the first twenty years of postcommunism demonstrate that judges consistently show the Soviet-era "accusatory bias" and side with the state prosecutors in both pretrial and trial stages of criminal proceedings. This cozy relationship between judges and prosecutors has been remarkably stable across postcommunist countries. These countries vary in terms of politics, composition of judicial and prosecutorial corps, funding of the judiciary and of the law enforcement system, crime rates, and court caseloads. Yet this variation does not seem to affect the nature of the friendly relations between judges and prosecutors. Despite serious expansion of judicial discretion, a more vibrant bar, and the introduction of adversarial court proceedings, postcommunist judges continue to strengthen two late socialist legacies of criminal justice systems: near universal approval of detention of the accused, and avoidance of acquittals. Postcommunist judges from Warsaw to Astana have the newly acquired exclusive power to detain the accused, yet they consistently approve nine out of ten detention requests and nearly all (96 percent) requests for extension of detention proposed by state prosecutors. They acquit defendants in criminal trials extremely rarely (with no higher than 3 percent rates of acquittal) – much like socialist-era judges did in the 1980s when they acquitted less than 2 percent of the defendants. In other words, if the socialist-era judicial chiefs were to wake up in 2010, they would award postcommunist judges with bonuses and holiday trips for an excellent performance simply on the basis of these two indicators.

Why does this attractiveness of detentions and avoidance of acquittals persist and (in many cases) proliferate in postcommunist democracies and nondemocracies alike? Why do postcommunist judges almost always say yes to the state prosecution in criminal cases the same way they did under late socialism, yet the same judges often say no to other government officials in a way unimaginable during the 1980s (Hendley 2002; Solomon 2004; Trochev 2010, 2013)?

The answer to these questions lies in a mix of different types of legacy relationships, as identified by Kotkin and Beissinger in the introduction to this volume. Like during the 1980s, judges today face a host of formal and informal pressures and expectations, which discourage acquittals and denials of detention requests. In some countries (Belarus and Uzbekistan, for example), these pressures and expectations persist because of a Soviet legacy of fragmentation, to use the terminology of Kotkin and Beissinger. Here, the old guard remains in charge: courts have been renamed, and the word "socialist" no longer precedes "legality," but the essential task of judges in criminal cases remains the same: to support the Procuracy. In other countries (Russia and Moldova, for instance), the Soviet legacy plays out as a process of translation (in Kotkin and Beissinger's terms), in which judges gain the power to detain the accused yet use this power the same way that Soviet-era procurators did. Finally, the Soviet legacy of friendly relations between judges and procurators persists as bricolage in countries like Bulgaria, Latvia, and Saakashvili's Georgia. These countries clearly rejected the communist past, purged the judiciary, and enlisted massive Western financial aid to reform the criminal procedure. But rulers demand that judges remain tough on crime and continue to treat them as if the latter are lieutenants of the ruling political party and assistants to state prosecutors. The fourth type of the legacy relationship, an embedded way of thinking and behaving, is clearly present in criminal justice of all postcommunist countries and remains a backbone of the mechanism of conserving and reproducing judicial deference to law enforcement agencies. As Dmitry Medvedev openly explained, the avoidance of acquittals was the problem of the consciousness of judges who were ashamed of acquitting an innocent person and challenging the law enforcement agencies (*Neue Zürcher Zeitung*, January 26, 2013). Even though a new generation of judges and prosecutors who never worked during the Soviet era enters the scene, old habits of mutual agreements and cover-ups among them persist. True, presidents insist on raising the number of acquittals, and judges frequently and openly criticize the poor quality of the job of state prosecutors. Yet when it comes to deciding criminal cases, judges tend to cover it up or to give law enforcement officials a second chance, thus rejecting the very idea that the acquittal rates could serve as legitimate indicators of judicial performance.

The actual practices, informal institutions, and strong linkages between postcommunist judges and prosecutors within the criminal justice system remained insulated from the shocks of new nationhood, new statehood, multiparty politics, and market economy. Despite constitutional promises of separation of powers and judicial independence, judges are part and parcel of the law enforcement world both in practice and in the view of the public. State prosecutors, whose powerful status has withstood attacks from the Council of Europe and the European Union, still view denials of arrests and acquittals as unacceptable failures. They do their best to overturn them on appeal and often succeed. Appellate judges overturn a much higher proportion of acquittals than convictions, and themselves acquit a very small number of defendants. The message to the trial-level judges is clear: convict or have your Soviet-era indicator of "stability of sentences" lowered with potential dismissal from the bench.

Moreover, the postcommunist transformation added new pro-accusation incentives to the mix. One of them is the need to protect one's career on the bench, as the job of a judge becomes better paid and more prestigious. Unlike during the socialist period, when judges often switched professions, generous salaries and retirement benefits are now too attractive for them to change their careers. Judges who disagree with state prosecutors over detention or conviction are blamed for incompetence, suspicious leniency, and for selling judicial decisions to the accused, all of which are bases for potential dismissal and criminal charges from the very same state prosecutors. Facing widespread general public distrust in the judiciary, politicians' haste to blame someone else for corruption, and the media's sensationalism over judicial bribery, recalcitrant judges have nowhere to turn for protection against unfounded accusations. Appellate judges who preserved their power to overturn acquittals thanks to the massive lobbying efforts of law enforcement elites do not praise judges who acquit as heroes protecting judicial independence. As a result, trial judges engage in risk-averse behavior by strengthening their already existing relationships, loyalties, and friendships with state prosecutors and appellate judges. Court chairs, who remain important figures in the judicial system, tend to recruit judicial candidates from the pool of trusted court clerks and judges' assistants – insiders in the judicial system who are already imbued with the sense of conformity to the orders of judicial bosses and state prosecutors in criminal proceedings.

To be sure, the formal and informal context in which postcommunist judges practice their deference to state prosecutors varies from country to country and from court to court. The next section of this chapter explores how frequently postcommunist judges defer to the state prosecutors when the former decide whether to arrest a person accused of crime. I then lay out evidence of how the mix of old and new incentives within the law enforcement world deepens accusatorial bias by encouraging judges and state prosecutors to find new ways of avoiding acquittals. I conclude that the actual power map of administering criminal justice in the post-Soviet world discourages judges from disagreeing with state prosecutors.

Wholesale Approval of Pretrial Detention

The continuity of informal relationships between judges and state prosecutors during postcommunism is remarkably stable. The criminal justice system during the last years of the USSR witnessed both the domination of the Procuracy (the centralized state agency in charge of both state prosecution and supervision of legality in the work of the judiciary) and the increasing role of appellate-level courts in maintaining judicial discipline. Procurators detained accused persons and prosecuted them in criminal proceedings. Trial-level judges were subject to the sanctions of the higher-level courts. In 1985, 11 percent of all judges in Soviet Russia had been disciplined for making bad decisions that had been overturned on appeal (Foglesong 1997).

The collapse of communism and of the Soviet Union did little to break this structure of incentives – the Soviet-era quantitative indicator of stability of sentences remains the key tool of assessing judicial performance. This is despite the fact that all postcommunist constitutions embraced the judiciary as a separate branch of government in charge of protecting due process rights, removed Communist Party cells from the judiciary and Procuracy, transferred the power to detain and key decision-making prerogatives from procurators to judges, declared judicial independence, and granted judges long terms on the bench and even life tenure. Reforms of criminal procedure declared judges to be impartial referees in the contest between the state prosecution and defense attorneys, yet most postcommunist judges seem to avoid confronting the prosecution. These judges received more powers, higher wages, and stronger career protections, yet they continue to side with procurators when it comes to detentions and convictions of the accused. The Communist Party's line to detain and convict is gone, yet judges follow it consistently and play on the team of the procurators.

Legacy as Fragmentation
The collapse of the communist system and the breakup of the USSR triggered the rise of crime rates, and new ruling elites felt the need to ensure the functioning of the criminal justice system. One way to do this was to ensure continuity

in the ranks of top judges. This is why many judges who sat on the bench of the supreme courts in the countries of the Eastern Bloc during late socialism kept their positions after 1991.

Soviet legacy as fragmentation is clearly at work in the pretrial detention patterns in Kazakhstan and Uzbekistan, countries in which judges and procurators have close affinity in the criminal justice system. Prior to August 30, 2008, Kazakhstani procurators approved about 94 percent of detentions requested by law enforcement officials. After that date, only judges in Kazakhstan were authorized to approve detention requests in a separate hearing with the accused, the defense attorney, and the state procurator present. This transfer of detention power did not result in change on the ground. According to the official court statistics, in 2012, judges approved 94.5 percent of detention requests (12,930 persons) – the same proportion procurators had approved a decade earlier, even though the number of arrested persons halved. In 2010, Kazakhstani judges approved 96 percent of detention requests (19,457 persons), though in that year prosecutors released and dropped criminal charges against 30 percent of those detained. None of the judges and procurators faced any sanctions for detaining these 30 percent (*Kazakhstanskaia Pravda*, January 15, 2011). Monitoring of detention hearings showed that in one out of three cases, law enforcement officials did not even try to justify the arrests – judges approved them automatically (OSCE ODIHR 2011). Rather, according to the chair of the Aktobe Oblast Court, Erlan Aitzhanov, judges who release the accused from custody are automatically punished via disciplinary proceedings initiated by law enforcement officials if the accused are nowhere to be found (Merkulova 2011).

In 2008, Uzbekistan implemented habeas corpus (President Karimov repeatedly used this phrase in his speeches) guarantees by granting its judges the exclusive prerogative to approve pretrial detention. That year judges received 16,610 detention requests from state procurators, but dared to deny only 248, resulting in a 98.5 percent approval rate (UzMetronom.com, March 13, 2009). Between 2009 and 2010, judges in Uzbekistan disagreed with the Procuracy even less often: they denied a total of 330 or 1 percent of detention requests. Appellate judges cancelled 4.4 percent of detention orders in 2008 and 7.5 percent in 2009 (Uzbekistan 2011).

The Soviet legacy of cozy relationship between judges and state prosecutors in both countries persists because the old guard is in charge of both countries, making the criminal justice system work for the maintenance of these political regimes. Indeed, Kazakhstan and Uzbekistan's judicial chiefs learned from other postcommunist countries that engaged in a more drastic break with the Soviet past that empowering postcommunist judges would not necessarily result in their disapproval with the prosecutorial requests.

Legacy as Translation
The Soviet legacy in law plays out as translation, in Kotkin and Beissinger's terms, in countries where judges gain the power to detain the accused yet they

use this power the same way that Soviet-era procurators did. On paper, judges are to be impartial referees in the adversarial-style contest between the accused and procurators. But in practice, judges automatically approve almost all detention requests, replicating Soviet-era practice. Ukraine and Russia, in which a 90 percent detention approval rate and a 97 percent detention extension rate persist, demonstrate this pattern very clearly. Even though the job of a judge is more prestigious and better paid than the job of a procurator in both countries, judges still routinely approve procurator detention requests and apply the same Soviet-era criteria, like the gravity of the criminal charges and the refusal of the accused to cooperate with the police, in the process of deciding whether to place the accused in custody until the trial. In both countries, judges openly and frequently criticize the quality of work done by state prosecutors, even though the latter do not prioritize pretrial detention (PublicPost.Ru 2012).

Until July 2001, procurators in Ukraine had the unilateral prerogative to detain the accused, and used it more often than not to secure confessions by locking the accused up in thirty-two overcrowded detention facilities, many of which were built during the pre-Soviet period. The accused, in turn, had the right to appeal against illegal detention in court and to ask for release from custody. In the mid-1990s, by which time the number of criminal defendants had increased by 230 percent compared to 1990, courts released from custody every third prisoner (877 out of 2,648 in 1998) who contested the legality of his pretrial detention (Foglesong and Solomon 2001). Since July 2001, Ukraine's judges have held the exclusive right to detain the accused in an adversarial hearing with the procurator, the accused, and her attorney present. In the wake of the transfer of this detention prerogative to judges, the number of detention requests filed by procurators steadily dropped until 2006, when it stabilized at around forty-five thousand (see Table 8.1).

One reason for the drop is that procurators are not allowed to ask for detention in criminal cases for which the punishment is less than a three-year imprisonment. Another reason is bribery of procurators – the accused pay their way out of detention. Finally, procurators may weed out weak and sloppy cases and do not prioritize pretrial detention. Between 2008 and 2010, about 17 percent of all criminal suspects were kept in custody (Centre of Judicial Studies 2011). Yet the analysis of the detention requests shows that most of them have the same boilerplate wording: detention is requested on the basis of the severity of the alleged crime alone. Judges consistently approved all but 2–3 percent of procurators' requests to prolong detentions. Add to this the excessively lengthy criminal trials, which may last several years, during which the accused are also held in custody. Between 2007 and 2010, the number of detainees awaiting trial in Yushchenko's Ukraine steadily grew from 13,157 to 18,148 (Centre of Judicial Studies 2011). Following the Soviet-era practice (discussed in the next section) judges, then, hand out prison sentences equal to the length of pretrial detention. As a result, many convicts finish serving their prison sentences while still waiting for their actual sentencing (Human Rights Ombudsman of Ukraine 2011, 18).

TABLE 8.1. *Judge-Approved Detentions in Ukraine*

	2002	2003	2004	2005	2006	2007	2008	2009	2010	2011
Detention requests received	66,160	62,098	52,917	50,215	44,967	44,190	44,543	45,300	—	—
Detention requests reviewed	66,176	62,062	52,872	50,140	44,734	44,005	44,600	45,127	45,975	45,700
Detentions approved	60,708	55,647	47,838	44,881	39,537	38,607	38,400	39,107	40,445	39,700
Percent of detentions approved (%)	91.7	89.6	90.5	89.5	88.4	87.7	86.3	86.7	88	86.9

Source: Official court statistics, http://www.scourt.gov.ua.

TABLE 8.2. *Procurators' Appeals against Denied Detentions in Ukraine*

	2003	2004	2005	2006	2007	2008	2009
Detentions denied	6,415	5,034	5,259	5,197	5,398	6,200	6,000
Denied detentions reviewed	1,400	2,100	2,200	2,340	2,527	3,003	3,600
Procurator appeals approved	–	690	682	715	795	–	914
Successful appeals (%)	–	33	31	31	31	–	25

The Supreme Court of Ukraine repeatedly advised judges to consider release on bail as a viable alternative to detention. However, Ukrainian judges use bail extremely rarely (between 63 and 161 persons are released on bail every year), even though nine out of ten persons released on bail do not violate its conditions (Lehmann 2000; Pizyk 2007). Similarly, Justice Ministry officials in charge of detention facilities estimate that one out of every five kept in pre-trial detention are released to serve their sentences outside of prisons (6,527 in 2008, 5,942 in 2010). Moreover, procurators release from custody about nine thousand detained persons every year, nearly one out of four detainees (Kislov 2011). All in all, Justice Ministry officials estimate that in order to bring Ukrainian jails, some of them are called "gates to hell" because of the growing number of deaths (227 deaths in 2010) in jails, to European human rights standards, judges must reduce the use of detention by 40 percent, a figure similar to that in Kazakhstan (Lyska 2010; Amirkhanian 2011).

As in Kazakhstan, Ukrainian judges who dare to disagree with prosecutors face punishment via disciplinary proceedings. The High Judicial Qualification Commission, a body consisting of top-level judges, conducts these proceedings, which can be initiated by the prosecutors, and reprimands judges or recommends them for dismissal from the bench. In 2011, at the request of the prosecutors, the Commission punished at least two judges (Serhyi Anipko and Tamara Trusova) for denying detention requests. Both judges defended their denials by citing the lack of supporting evidence in the prosecutors' detention requests (*Zakon i Biznes*, July 29, 2011; *Zakon i Biznes*, November 26, 2011). Clearly, prosecutors are not detaining only those against whom they have strong incriminating evidence.

Moreover, judges also refuse to say no to procurators when it comes to detention, in part because appellate courts encourage them to do so. Procurators increasingly file appeals against denied detention requests in the appellate courts and win at least a quarter of appeals (see Table 8.2). Defense attorneys also increasingly appeal against detentions, yet they are less successful than state prosecutors. As Table 8.3 shows, between 2002 and 2010, the proportion of appealed detentions doubled from 5 percent to 11 percent of all detentions.

TABLE 8.3. *Detainees' Appeals against Judge-Approved Detentions in Ukraine*

	2002	2003	2004	2005	2006	2007	2008	2009	2010
All detentions	60,708	55,647	47,838	44,881	39,537	38,607	38,400	39,100	40,445
Appeals reviewed	2,966	2,887	2,770	3,200	3,100	3,200	3,700	4,300	4,400
Detentions canceled	533	608	535	554	482	532	628	674	693
Successful appeal rate (%)	18	21	19	17	16	17	17	16	16
% of all detentions canceled	0.9	1.1	1.1	1.2	1.2	1.4	1.6	1.7	1.7

Source: Official court statistics, http://www.scourt.gov.ua.

TABLE 8.4. *Judge-Approved Detentions in Russia*

	2003	2004	2005	2006	2007	2008	2009	2010
Detention requests reviewed	231,149	228,000	284,000	272,000	247,500	230,269	208,416	165,323
Detentions approved	211,526	207,024	259,576	248,608	225,498	207,456	187,793	148,689
Percent of detentions approved (%)	91.5	90.8	91.4	91.4	91	90	90.1	89.9
Detentions appealed	–	24,200	27,500	28,600	21,900	20,545	20,220	17,417
Detentions canceled on appeal	–	2,700	2,800	2,800	1,400	1,187	1,129	1,053
Successful appeal rate (%)	–	11.2	10.8	9.8	6.4	5.8	5.6	6

Source: Official court statistics, http://www.cdep.ru

The success rate of the accused in the appellate courts, however, remained stable and well below the success rate of procurators: the accused consistently won one out of six appeals against detention. Overall, appellate courts canceled less than 2 percent of all detentions in Ukraine between 2002 and 2010 but approved many more appeals of prosecutors. In sum, the appellate courts encourage cooperation of judges and the Procuracy when it comes to detention, even if it means rubber-stamping detention requests.

Russia's experience with judge-ordered pretrial detentions further demonstrates how and why the appellate courts encourage the amicable relationship between judges and prosecutors. In Russia, judges received the exclusive power to detain the accused persons in July 2002, a year later than in Ukraine. Prior to that, as in Ukraine, Russia's procurators detained and judges had the power to hear appeals against the illegality of pretrial detention. In 1994 and 1995, the success rate of those appeals stood at 20 percent (as compared to 33 percent in Ukraine), with about half of the persons accused of crimes placed in custody (Foglesong 1995, 549). By 1999, the success rate of appeals against prosecutorial detentions declined to 11 percent (Petrukhin 2003, 166). Since 2002, Russia's patterns of judge-ordered detention have followed the pattern of 90 percent approval found in Ukraine (see Table 8.4). As in Ukraine, Russia's judges prolong 97 percent of detentions. Human Rights Ombudsman Vladimir Lukin openly complained to President Medvedev that judges automatically approved detention requests (Kremlin.Ru 2008). As in Ukraine, the accused persons and their attorneys appeal about one-tenth of detentions. However, their success rate is three times lower than that of their Ukrainian counterparts and even lower than that in Uzbekistan. As in Ukraine, Russia's procurators have a much higher chance of having the denied detentions overturned by appellate courts. Procurators win about 20 percent (585 out of 2,696 in 2010) of appeals in this category of cases.

As in Ukraine, Russian judges avoid granting bail despite the fact that some judicial chiefs encourage bail instead of detentions, and despite the fact that very few accused violate bail conditions. Russia's judges are also very reluctant to place the accused under house arrest, an option they have had since 2002. Between 2008 and 2010, judges placed merely 921 persons under house arrest, even though the Justice Ministry estimated that some 20,000 persons were eligible for this measure instead of custody (*Rossiiskaia gazeta*, November 13, 2008). Clearly, judges and law enforcement officials do not wish to be blamed if the accused who is released on bail or placed under house arrest is at large (Melnikov 2007).

Data on the backgrounds of the chairs of appellate courts in Russia reveal why these courts encourage the Soviet-era practice of deferring to state prosecutors in criminal justice. Every other chair of appellate courts received his law degree during the 1970s, with only 10 percent of them graduating from law school during the 1990s. Every other chair of the appellate court has worked in the court as a judge or a court clerk prior to becoming a chair. Meanwhile, only a quarter of them worked in the Procuracy or in the police force prior to appointment to the bench. Eight out of ten chairs of appellate courts had their initial appointment as a judge prior to 1990 (Sukhovei 2011). These seasoned career judges carry over the legacy of deference to the procurators, even though the former now hold much higher status within the legal system. For example, in November 2008, Chair of the Volgograd Oblast Court Sergei Potapenko succeeded in dismissing Marianna Lukianovskaia, the judge of the same court, from the bench for refusing to extend the detention of a person accused of extorting five thousand rubles ($190 U.S.). She ordered the accused released on the grounds that the latter was unlawfully deprived of the right to an interpreter during the detention hearing. The procurator, however, arrested the accused again and wrote to Potapenko that Lukianovskaia had to extend the detention. She was fired from the court, and the Russian Supreme Court, the court in which Potapenko served as a judge between 2002 and 2005, confirmed her dismissal in the fall of 2009 (Kasparov.Ru 2009; Lukianovskaia 2012).

Moreover, even when the procurators uncover wrongful detentions and release illegally detained persons from custody, the perpetrators are rarely criminally prosecuted. The official number of registered unlawful arrests and detentions (criminal offenses under Article 301 of the Russian Criminal Code) is minimal and declining from the record high of seventy-three in 1997 to fourteen in 2006. By contrast, experts estimate the number of wrongful detentions in Russia in the thousands (Mirzabalaev 2005; Dadaev 2007). In short, strong ties between prosecutors and judges make it quite safe for judges to approve detention requests: they are encouraged from above to arrest criminal suspects and face virtually no risk of being punished for automatic approval of detention requests even when some criminal cases are clearly fabricated (Firestone 2010).

Legacy as Bricolage

More puzzling is that the 90 percent detention approval rate persists even in those countries that rejected many of the Soviet-era practices and institutions, purged judiciary and law enforcement agencies from personnel linked with the Communist Party, and joined the European Union as consolidated democracies. Here, judges portray themselves as the builders of the rule of law, champions of judicial independence, and protectors of individual rights – all of which were supposed to embody the means and ends of transition from the socialist era. For example, Poland transferred the power to detain from state prosecutors to judges in 1996. As in Russia and Ukraine, state prosecutors no longer prioritize pretrial detention (police supervision of accused persons is the most widespread practice). And as in Russia and Ukraine, when state prosecutors ask judges to detain the accused prior to trial, they succeed 90 percent of the time (see Table 8.5).

Similarly, the wholesale judicial authorization of detention persists in those post-Soviet democracies in which state prosecutors prioritize pretrial detention.

TABLE 8.5. *Judge-Approved Detentions in Poland*

	2001	2002	2003	2004	2005	2006	2007	2008	2009	2010	2011
Detention requests received	42,185	36,230	41,157	38,712	38,519	38,032	36,079	28,200	27,918	25,688	25,452
Detention requests approved	38,331	33,171	37,207	34,475	35,142	34,291	31,722	24,848	24,967	23,060	22,748
Percent of detentions approved	90.9	91.6	90.4	89.1	91.2	90.2	87.9	88.1	89.4	89.8	89.4

Sources: Justice Ministry of Poland, http://bip.ms.gov.pl/pl/pl/dzialalnosc/statystyki/statystyki-2010/download,731,2.html. Statistics for 2010–11 are from the Procuracy General of Poland, http://www.pg.gov.pl/bip/index.php?o,813.

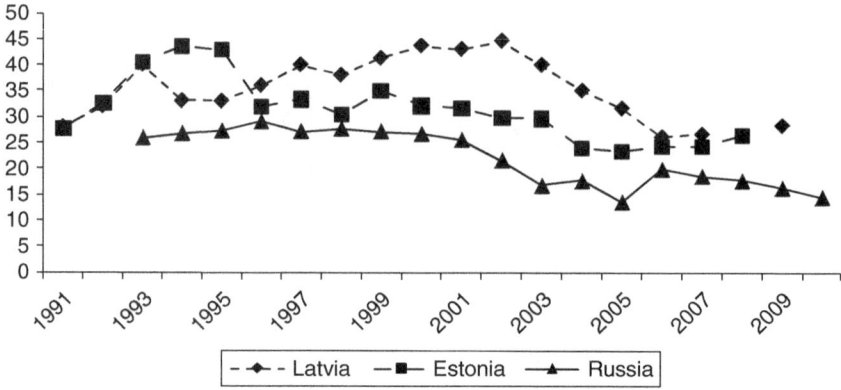

FIGURE 8.1. Share of pre-trial detainees in the total prison population in Estonia, Latvia, and Russia.
Sources: Van Kalmthout and colleagues (2009, 301); Latvian Centre for Human Rights; "World Prison Brief: Latvia"; Federal Service of Execution of Punishments of Russia; A. M. van Kalmthout, M. M. Knapen, and C. Morgenstern, eds., *Pre-trial Detention in the European Union* (Wolf Legal Publishers, 2009), 301; Annual reports "Human Rights in Latvia" by Latvian Centre for Human Rights, http://www.humanrights.org.lv; "World Prison Brief: Latvia," http://www.prisonstudies.org/info/worldbrief/wpb_country.php?country=149; Federal Service of Execution of Punishments of Russia, http://www.fsin.su.

For example, as Figure 8.1 illustrates, if someone fell asleep reading pretrial detention statistics in Estonia and Latvia at the time of the breakup of the USSR and suddenly awoke in Tallinn in 2008 or Riga in 2009, she would probably fall asleep again, because so little changed in the number of detainees as a proportion of the total prison population in Estonia (27.7 percent in 1991 against 26.4 percent in 2008) and Latvia (28 percent in 1991 against 28.3 percent in 2009). Although the prison population as a whole is shrinking in both Estonia and Latvia, even as judges learn to use alternatives to imprisonment, they have not changed their ways of handling pretrial detention, continuing to defer to state prosecutors. Consider the first two decades of postcommunist democratic Latvia. Unlike in Poland, they featured nearly total use of pretrial detention in dilapidated and disease-infected jails and prisons. Although Latvia's judges had been exercising the exclusive power to arrest since the mid-1990s (several years earlier than judges in the other former Soviet republics), they used this newly acquired power only to rubber-stamp the flood of detention requests of law enforcement officials (Naimark-Rowse 2008, 164). An unpublished survey of police officers and state prosecutors conducted between 2002 and 2004 indicated that they often try to receive the judge's approval for pretrial detention because it makes the job of investigating criminal cases easier. In the media as well as in the public's view, the prevailing opinion is that criminals should wait for their trial in custody (Van Kalmthout, Knapen, and

Morgenstern 2009, 589). Judges rarely refuse. As late as the end of 2002, an average judge in Latvia still was "the functionary expediting 'telephone justice' as it originates in prosecutors' offices" (*Baltic Times*, December 12, 2002). Numerous cases against Latvia's excessive use of detention in the European Court of Human Rights revealed that Latvian judges used computerized forms for authorizing and prolonging detentions in which they simply filled in the blanks with the names and charges of the accused without providing any reason for arresting them.[1]

To deal with this international shaming, and in the wake of its admission into the European Union, in 2005 Latvia abolished these computerized detention forms and introduced a new position of investigating judge, an officer of the court in charge of authorizing detentions and monitoring the observance of human rights in the pretrial phase of criminal procedure. However, as Figure 8.1 shows, this formal institutional change did not make much difference. Like judges in Russia and Ukraine, investigating judges defer to procurators and extremely rarely use alternatives to detention (such as house arrest and, more recently, release on bail). In 2006, investigating judges released detainees on bail only twice (thirty times – in 2007) and placed the accused under house arrest thirteen times (twice – in 2007) (Van Kalmthout et al. 2009, 592). Meanwhile, Latvia's procurator general remained extremely skeptical about improving the quality of pretrial investigation (*Baltic Course*, February 8, 2013). In sum, democratization in Latvia has so far strengthened judicial deference to state prosecutors and has failed to produce greater respect for due process rights in the criminal justice system, contrary to the established wisdom that democracy and human rights go together and that negative rights are easily enforceable (see, e.g., Sung 2006).

The experience of postcommunist Georgia, which does not prioritize pretrial detention, also confirms this pattern. The Republic of Georgia was among the first non-Baltic post-Soviet republics to grant judges the monopoly to arrest the accused. Since 1999, the Procuracy or the police was allowed to detain persons for forty-eight hours, and judges were given an additional twenty-four hours to approve or refuse the detention. However, both the poor recordkeeping of underpaid law enforcement agencies and judges (who did not hesitate to sell the release of detainees) and strong informal communications between procurators and judges (Waters 2004) preserved the practice of holding detainees in custody for days without the approval of a judge. In 2003, a year that ended with the Rose Revolution and the ouster of President Shevardnadze, Georgian courts approved 88 percent of detention requests filed by procurators (Freedom House 2008, 292).

Saakashvili's Georgia saw a dramatic change in many aspects of the criminal justice system – except in the collusion between procurators and judges. As Table 8.6 clearly shows, while the total number of detentions fluctuated, the success rate of procurators in detention hearings steadily grew and stabilized at around 94 percent. Many domestic and international observers note the

TABLE 8.6. *Judge-Approved Detentions in Georgia, 2005–2011*

	2005	2006	2007	2008	2009	2010	2011
Detention requests reviewed	9,042	11,761	9,559	8,197	8,713	8,761	6,948
Detention requests approved	7,159	10,358	8,929	7,806	8,199	8,109	6,558
Percent of approved detentions	79%	88%	93%	95%	94%	93%	94%

Source: Official court statistics, Supreme Court of Georgia, http://www.supremecourt.ge.

domination of the Procuracy vis-à-vis judges, even though the Procuracy was repeatedly purged, the police were halved in size, and many judges resigned or were forced to leave the bench (American Bar Association 2005, 2009; Transparency International Georgia 2010). Newly hired judges, young and inexperienced, look up to the Procuracy, which has been the primary instrument of President Saakashvili's "zero-tolerance" approach to fighting crime and petty corruption (Saakashvili 2006). Procurators view the denial of detentions as a sign of failure and do not hesitate to telephone judges with orders on how to decide cases. Neither the purge of the judiciary nor higher pay for judges empowered them to say no to state prosecutors. Saakashvili's regime reactivated the Soviet legacy of cooperation between judges and law enforcement officials in which prosecutors are in the driver's seat. This legacy was responsible for the increasing use of release on bail at the request of procurators, something that procurators and judges in other post-Soviet countries remain very reluctant to use. When it comes to detention or release on bail, judges in Saakashvili's Georgia agree with state prosecutors 94 percent of the time – at the same rate as judges in Kazakhstan do. The analysis of judges' detention orders or releases on bail shows that in most cases judges, similar to their Latvian colleagues, use ready-made templates, in which they change only the names, dates, and places of the alleged crimes. Unfortunately, there are no statistics about the success rate of defense attorneys in bail or detention-related hearings. But the anecdotal evidence suggests that judges ignore most of the motions filed by the defense (Waters 2004).

In sum, postcommunist judges systematically agree with the state prosecutors when they decide whether to detain the accused. In Latvia and Georgia, the new rulers rejected the Soviet era and purged the judicial corps. Yet the rulers demanded close cooperation between judges and law enforcement officers as a way of combating crime. Responding to these demands, new judicial bosses as bricoleurs reinvigorate the Soviet legacy of tight cooperation between law enforcement officials and judges in the area of pretrial detention, even if it means international embarrassment over "telephone justice" and the inhumane conditions of detention facilities. In Russia and Ukraine, the highly stable 90 percent pretrial detention rate is a symptom of the Soviet legacy as translation: Soviet-era judges and procurators continue to dominate the criminal justice system and adapt their close partnership to the new challenges of judicial independence and due process rights. Meanwhile, in Kazakhstan and Uzbekistan, the Soviet legacy results from fragmentation: many judges and procurators simply continue treating the accused and enforcing criminal law like they did twenty years ago because their version of postcommunism has not changed the structure of incentives in their job performance. The following section on avoidance of acquittals in criminal trials provides further evidence of these patterns.

Avoidance of Acquittals in Postcommunist Criminal Justice

Unlike the newly acquired monopoly over approving pretrial detentions, the power of judges to acquit in criminal trials existed during the Soviet era. During late socialism, judges, who depended for their salaries and careers on the Justice Ministry and Communist Party bosses, were strongly encouraged to convict the accused and strongly discouraged from acquitting by procurators, court chairs, and appellate judges. In cases where procurators did a poor job of assembling incriminating evidence, judges were expected to convict on less harsh criminal charges or to return cases to procurators for supplementary investigation at the end of the trial, in effect giving the prosecution a second chance. Acquittals were extraordinary events considered equal to a failure of the prosecution, with potentially serious repercussions for the careers of procurators. Acquittals were also extraordinary for judges, who, in the event of an acquittal, fulfilled the role of whistleblowers in a closed law enforcement system. Many acquittals would be overturned on appeal by cassation courts at the request of the procurators, who had a much stronger influence on Communist Party bosses. Meanwhile, cassation courts acquitted extremely rarely. The incentives for trial-level judges were clear: a working relationship with the procurators, avoiding acquittals, and keeping stably high conviction rates were the keys to maintaining performance bonuses and obtaining promotions, as much as regular attendance at Communist Party meetings. Acquittal rates in the USSR at the end of the Soviet era dropped to less than 1 percent, down from 9 percent in 1945 (Solomon 1987, 1996). Postcommunist criminal justice did not change this pattern much, as judicial chiefs kept the Soviet-era indicator of "stability of sentences" as the key indicator of judicial performance and rejected acquittal rate as a legitimate indicator of judicial quality.

Legacy as Fragmentation
This legacy of avoiding acquittals is most visible in those countries that did not have a clear break with the communist past and kept the old guard in charge. For example, the Criminal Procedure Code of Uzbekistan (article 419) allows judges to return cases twice to the procurators for supplementary investigation.

TABLE 8.7. *Outcomes of the Jury Trials in Kazakhstan, 2007–2012*

Year (total number of jury trials)	2007 (36 cases)	2008 (44 cases)	2009 (59 cases)	2010 (270 cases)	2011 (355 cases)	2012 (288 cases)
Persons convicted	57	72	101	334	461	355
Persons acquitted	5	6	15	43	30	24
Percent of acquitted persons to the total number of tried persons	8%	7.7%	12.9%	11.4%	6.1%	6.3%

Source: Official court statistics, http://www.pravstat.kz.

There, courts acquitted seven persons in 2003 and thirteen in 2004 (*Vechernii Tashkent*, June 23, 2005). Only in November 2011 did the chair of the Supreme Court of Kazakhstan propose to eliminate this Soviet-era judicial mechanism of avoiding acquittals (*Tengri News*, November 11, 2011). Indeed, between 2007 and 2009, Kazakhstani judges returned about 1.2 percent of all cases for supplementary investigation (about twelve hundred accused persons). State prosecutors brought back for trial only half of those cases. Meanwhile, acquittal rates in Kazakhstan steadily grew from 0.5 percent in 1998 to 1.25 percent (about four hundred tried persons) in 2010. This growth is largely due to acquittals in criminal cases of private prosecution, like libel or battery, in which state prosecutors do not participate and judges seem to avoid accusatorial bias. Indeed, in 2012, Kazakhstani judges heard three hundred eighty-three cases of private prosecution, in which they convicted one hundred seventy-eight persons and acquitted three hundred eighteen persons – two-thirds of tried persons.

The outcomes of jury trials, which have been judging grave crimes like rape and murder since 2007, also show that it is possible to overcome accusatorial bias. As Table 8.7 shows, even though jurors in Kazakhstan deliberate the verdict together with a professional judge, the acquittal rate in jury trials has never been below 6 percent. On average, jury acquittals make up about one-third of all acquittals in the criminal trials of public prosecution where a procurator is present. Drug-related crimes, a category of crimes police often use to fabricate criminal charges, constituted the largest share of acquittals in 2010. These crimes together with white collar crimes like fraud and abuse of power composed the majority of acquittals in 2011 and 2012.

Acquittals in Kazakhstan can be reversed on appeal – an opportunity that the state prosecutors pursue with vigor. This is because the appellate courts are much more likely to reverse acquittals than convictions. In 2007, acquittals of twenty-five persons (8 percent of the total number of acquitted persons) were overturned, in 2008, thirty-six persons (11 percent), and in 2009, nineteen persons (5 percent). Compare this to the total of 0.5 percent of overturned sentences in these three years. Judges are clearly discouraged from handing down acquittals, and there is an informal rule: three overturned sentences in a year leads to dismissal from the bench.

In most cases, judges have to justify acquittals personally in front of appellate courts and the Supreme Court. As one judge put it, "the most important concern for a judge is that his decision not be overturned" (American Bar Association 2004, 18, 33–35). For example, in 2012, judge Aliya Zhumasheva from Pavlodar Oblast received a reprimand for acquitting two persons in the case of a stolen fridge. She complained that appellate judges had told her not to scrutinize the evidence of the prosecution and had insisted that good relations with procurators were a key to her successful judicial career (*Uralskaia nedelia*, October 19, 2012). A judge of the Supreme Court confirmed her complaints: "Unfortunately, there are judges who unconditionally trust the prosecution" (*Kazakhstanskaia Pravda*, July 2, 2011). Yet none of them faced any negative consequences.

Legacy as Translation
The legacy of low acquittal rates persists two decades after the breakup of the Eastern Bloc. The former republics of the USSR that attempted to break from the Soviet past show that this legacy is well entrenched in both practice and public perception. Russia's courts have not acquitted more than 1 percent of defendants in the past two decades – the same proportion of acquittals as in the 1980s in the USSR (Petrukhin 2009). The proportion of acquitted doubled from 0.4 percent to 1 percent between 1992 and 2009. The number of acquitted persons also doubled: 4,183 persons were acquitted in 1994, and 9,179 persons were acquitted in 2009. As in Kazakhstan, more than two-thirds of these acquittals (6,568 persons in 17,600 completed cases) have been the outcomes of minor criminal cases of private prosecution (libel, battery, etc.), in which state prosecutors are not required to take part and there is no pretrial investigation. This means that judges can and do hand out acquittals in these minor criminal cases in which state prosecutors are not involved without accusatorial bias (see Paneiakh et al. 2010 for the detailed analysis of the 2008 data).

Russia's jury trials, which handle criminal cases in which the penalty is longer than ten years of imprisonment, provide another benchmark for assessing the accusatorial bias of judges. As in Kazakhstan, Russia's jury trials handle a tiny proportion of crimes (murder, corruption, etc.), yet they are a site that champions adversarial judicial procedure and protects judges from allegations of leniency. For example, in 2009, jury trials reached verdicts in 555 cases concerning 1,311 defendants and ended up acquitting 244 of them. This 18.6 percent acquittal rate suggests that state prosecutors send weak cases to courts much more often. This stably high acquittal rate (by postcommunist standards) has been so unusual that Russia removed terrorism and organized crime cases from the jurisdiction of jury trials at the end of 2009.

When state prosecutors are involved, they see each and every acquittal as a failure, accuse judges of being too lenient or on the take, and appeal every acquittal even if they have a weak case against the defendant (Churilov 2010). The 2002 Russian Criminal Procedure Code allows unlimited appeal of acquittals. State prosecutors know that they have a chance, just as they appeal denials of their detention requests. On average, between 1996 and 2007 procurators won one out of three appeals against acquittals they had filed, as compared to the 2.4 percent success rate of appeals filed by convicted defendants. In 2009, appellate-level courts overturned the acquittals of a total of nine hundred eighty-one persons (10.7 percent of all acquitted persons), including ninety-nine persons in cases of private prosecution, and forty-seven persons acquitted by juries. This sent a clear message to trial-level judges: do not hurt your "stability of sentencing" indicator, inherited from the Soviet era, by issuing acquittals.

In the absence of support from the appellate-level courts, judges who choose to acquit draw on the support of the European Court of Human Rights (ECtHR), the most popular court in Russia today (Trochev 2010). For example, in 2006, the Prokhladnenskii District Court in the Kabardino-Balkariya Republic acquitted the accused in six "fake" drug-trafficking cases (cases in which undercover law enforcement officials provoked the sale of illicit substances) and blasted the police for not combating real traffickers (Guseinov 2007). The court announced the first two of these acquittals without knowing about the European Court's judgment in the *Vanyan v. Russia* case, in which such provocations by Moscow police officers were found to be in violation of the 1950 European Convention on Human Rights.[2] The chair of the Prokhladnenskii Court admitted that it was very difficult to acquit innocent people in these fake crimes without knowing about this ECtHR judgment because his court was criticized for being too soft on drug traffickers. He stressed that the *Vanyan* judgment was very helpful to judges for overseeing the legality of law enforcement agencies (Guseinov 2007).

The return of criminal cases to procurators for supplementary investigation by judges – another Soviet legacy of avoiding acquittals and giving state prosecutors a second chance – does not show signs of extinction. In the late 1980s, judges in the USSR returned some 4–5 percent of criminal cases for supplementary investigation instead of handing down acquittals (Solomon 1987). In 2000, Russian judges returned the cases of 22,827 persons, while in 2004, judges returned cases to the prosecutors for 38,913 persons while acquitting only 4,100 persons. In 2009, Russia's judges returned to the procurators 21,325 cases (2 percent of all completed criminal cases) involving 27,763 persons – three times the number of those acquitted. Although judges return most cases before the opening of a criminal trial, they are clearly more comfortable giving a second chance to the prosecution than proceeding to acquittal.

TABLE 8.8. *Crime Rates, Convictions and Acquittals in Ukraine*

Year	Registered Crimes	Convicted Persons	Acquitted Persons	Percent of Acquitted Persons to the Total Number of Tried Persons
1990	369,809	104,199	–	
1991	405,516	108,553	820	0.76
1992	480,478	115,260	901	0.78
1993	539,299	152,878	756	0.49
1994	572,147	174,959	829	0.47
1995	641,860	212,915	908	0.43
1996	617,262	242,124	797	0.33
1997	589,208	257,790	950	0.37
1998	575,982	232,598	884	0.38
1999	558,716	222,239	774	0.35
2000	567,795	230,903	755	0.33
2001	514,597	201,627	–	–
2002	460,389	194,212	539	0.28
2003	566,350	201,081	524	0.26
2004	527,812	204,794	592	0.26
2005	491,754	176,934	898	0.46
2006	428,149	160,865	910	0.52
2007	401,293	165,459	689	0.41
2008	384,424	168,300	559	0.33
2009	434,678	146,450	284	0.19
2010	500,902	–	–	0.2

Source: Bukalov 2007, 28. Official court statistics, http://www.scourt.gov.ua.

The late Soviet-era legacy of vanishing acquittals stays strong in Ukraine, a country in which the number of registered crimes did not skyrocket as it did in Russia, yet acquittal rates actually declined from 0.8 percent to 0.2 percent in the past two decades (see Table 8.8). Like in Russia, minor criminal cases of private prosecution, which can be launched only by the victims of the crime, account for at least a half of the acquittals. Like Russia, there is a significant variation across regions and time periods in terms of frequency of acquittals.

Like in Russia, appellate courts in Ukraine overturn a much larger share of acquittals compared to convictions. Like their Russian counterparts, Ukrainian judges are much more willing to return criminal cases to state prosecutors for supplementary investigation and to allow procurators to recall the case from trial instead of acquitting the defendants – around 4 percent of the total completed criminal cases. This rate would be very familiar to Soviet judges, who on average returned 4–5 percent of criminal cases for supplementary investigation during the late 1980s. But Soviet judges would surely envy Ukraine's current judges for handing down so few acquittals – 0.2 percent in 2009 and 2010!

Legacy as Bricolage

If someone fell asleep in 1989 in Sofia, after reading Bulgaria's acquittal statistics (370 persons or 1.8 percent that year), and woke up in 2004 (670 persons or 2.1 percent acquitted) or in 2009 (870 persons or 2.1 percent acquitted), this person would not notice much difference in the way Bulgarian judges avoid acquitting defendants in criminal trials. Conviction rates are also stable. In 1989, Bulgarian judges convicted 92.8 percent of defendants, while in 2009, they convicted 89 percent of defendants, despite the fact that the number of criminal trials doubled from 20,720 to 42,032 during those twenty years.[3] Judges are assessed on the basis of the "stability of sentences" indicator inherited from the socialist era. Konstantin Penchev, the chair of the Supreme Administrative Court, publicly admitted that there was a certain "fear" among judges to acquit (Alegre, Ivanova, and Denis-Smith 2009, 34). Moreover, prosecutors are considered a part of the judicial system and "serve on the panels and commissions when they are appointing, evaluating, promoting and disciplining not only prosecutors but also judges. The public prosecutors operate in a tightly-knit hierarchy, in which the actions of lower-level prosecutors are controlled by and reported to their superiors up the chain. A judge ruling for the defendant in a criminal case does so knowing that the prosecutor who just lost the case may someday be in a position to influence the judge's career advancement, and almost certainly reports directly or indirectly to another prosecutor who will." Moreover, "judges and prosecutors within a given court meet frequently to address court administrative, procedural and sometimes substantive issues and developments, giving the impression of a 'team' working together to serve the needs of justice." Learning this team concept and the "creation of team spirit and collegiality between" judges and prosecutors is an important part of the initial training curriculum for junior judges (American Bar Association 2006, 52).

The same pattern of avoiding acquittals is true of Polish judges. In 1990 and 2008, they convicted the same proportion (90.5 percent) of persons in criminal trials, despite the fact that the number of tried persons nearly quadrupled. In 1990, judges acquitted 1.9 percent (2,474) of the tried persons. Two decades later, in 2008, they acquitted 2.3 percent (10,600) of the tried persons.[4] The consolidation of democracy, heavier court caseloads, and a stronger defense bar in Poland do not seem to have disrupted the legacy of cooperative relationship between judges and state prosecutors in the criminal justice system.

However, Soviet judges would be most envious of the nearly extinct acquittal rate of 0.04 percent (a total of seven cases involving eight persons, with one acquittal overturned on appeal) reached in Georgia in 2010 (see Table 8.9). This is nearly ten times lower than the acquittal rate (0.36 percent) achieved by judges in Belarus in 2010.

Even in Moldova, which seems to have the highest acquittal rate among former Soviet republics (see Table 8.1), judges, especially those who are up for reappointment for life, complain about phone calls and pressure to avoid

TABLE 8.9. *Acquittal Rates in Lithuania, Moldova, Kazakhstan, and Georgia*

	Lithuania	Moldova	Kazakhstan	Kyrgyzstan	Georgia
1996	–	–	–	–	2.2%
1997	–	–	–	–	2.9
1998	–	–	0.5%	1.1%	2
1999	–	3%	–	1.2	–
2000	–	3.2	–	1.6	2.7
2001	–	3.4	–	1.5	–
2002	–	2.8	0.6	1.3	4
2003	–	–	0.8	–	0.7
2004	2.3%	2.7	0.7	–	0.4
2005	2.1	–	0.8	1.8	0.8
2006	2.2	–	0.8	1.8	0.2
2007	2.3	–	0.8	2.1	0.1
2008	2	3.1	0.8	–	0.1
2009	1.8	3.2	0.8	1.7	0.1
2010	2.4	–	1.3	–	0.04
2011	3.1	–	–	–	0.4
2012	3.2	–	–	–	–

Source: Author's calculations based on official court statistics.

acquittals, as they fear accusations of corruption. While criticizing the bad job of state prosecutors, judges often admit inadmissible evidence and ignore procedural violations made by procurators. Moldova's procurators are rewarded for the quick filing of criminal cases in court and for the absence of acquittals. Procurators are required to write long explanations for why judges handed down the acquittals or imposed a punishment lighter than the one the procurators requested. Procurators tend to appeal every acquittal regardless of how weak their case is, a pattern that exists in most post-Soviet states. Judges, in turn, are rewarded for the low number of appealed, contested, and annulled judgments, using the Soviet-era indicator of "stability of sentence" as a reference basis (Soros Foundation-Moldova 2009). Meanwhile, defense attorneys complain about their underdog status in the criminal justice system. In sum, the structure of incentives that judges face encourages a friendly relationship with procurators and appellate courts. Allegations of judicial corruption in the post-Soviet countries function as a substitute for the party discipline once used to push judges to avoid acquittals in the Soviet Union.

Finally, are these acquittal rates different from those in the civil law countries in Western Europe? As Table 8.10 shows, the answer is yes. Caution must be taken in interpreting these results because national criminal justice systems may vary with regards to the outcomes of criminal proceedings and the mechanisms of weeding out sloppy cases prior to the stage of sentencing (Barclay 2000).

TABLE 8.10. *Convictions and Acquittals in Selected EU Member States, 2004*

State	Convicted Persons	Acquitted Persons	Percent of Acquitted to the Sum of Acquitted and Convicted Persons (%)
Finland	54,018	3,486	6
France	1,115,823	47,800	4.1
Germany	442,356	37,243	7.7
Netherlands	126,174	6,353	4.8

Source: European Commission for the Efficiency of Justice (CEPEJ) (2006, 100). *European Judicial Systems* (Brussels: Council of Europe, 2006), 100.

Conclusion

Two decades of reforms of criminal procedure in postcommunist countries clearly show that implementing the right to a fair trial and cultivating judicial independence is an arduous task that goes well beyond separating powers and raising judicial salaries. In administering criminal justice, postcommunist judges, in democracies and nondemocracies alike, remain junior partners to law enforcement agencies, which dominate:

1) in the pretrial phase when they get approval for detentions in nine out of ten cases
2) during criminal trials when they succeed in avoiding acquittals;
3) in appellate proceedings when they have their appeals against denied detentions, lenient sentences, or acquittals confirmed at a much higher rate than defense attorneys do.

The Soviet-era treatment of acquittals as failures of state prosecutors and trial-level judges drives the unwillingness of judges to acquit because judges know that acquittals have a much higher chance of being overturned. The Soviet-era indicator of "stability of sentences" is still one of the most important job performance indicators for a judge in any postcommunist country, no matter how long this country lived under communism. Add to this the ability of the law enforcement agencies to allege that recalcitrant judges are selling their decisions and to influence judicial careers even where judges have life tenure. As a result, judges are strongly expected both to detain and to convict, yet are unable to convince the public that bails, house arrests, and acquittals are good for society. Indeed, this Soviet-era informal judge-procurator relationship, as shown by surprisingly stable detention and acquittal rates, is so strong that it resists any changes in international shaming, formal institutions, political regimes, crime rates, and court caseloads. Its strength lies in the blend of trust, mutual understanding, and fellow feeling between judges and law enforcement officials, who exert occasional pressure against recalcitrant judges, judges who dare to disagree with the wishes of prosecutors. In the cases of Russia, Ukraine, Kazakhstan, and Uzbekistan, this close relationship is preserved by the old guard – appellate judges who made their careers by deferring to the Procuracy during Soviet times. In Bulgaria, Poland, Latvia, and Georgia, the new rulers rely on the Procuracy, reconstruct its domination, and encourage newly appointed judges to detain and to convict to save their country from crime. It is through these mechanisms of preservation and reconstruction that Soviet legacies define the meanings of law and order, shape the functioning of the law enforcement system, and reinforce existing power hierarchies in postcommunist countries twenty years after the fall of communism. Legacies determine that the rule-of-law innovations are likely to take root in the criminal justice system as long as they reinforce or do not hurt the amicable relationship between judges and prosecutors.

Notes

1. See, for example, *Svipsta v. Latvia* (66820/01), Judgment (Third Section), March 9, 2006.
2. *Vanyan v. Russia* (appl. no. 53203/99), Judgment (First Section), December 15, 2005.
3. Official court statistics are available at the Web site of the National Statistics Institute of Bulgaria at http://www.nsi.bg/otrasal.php?otr=25.
4. Data for 1990 are only about tried adults, http://www.bip.ms.gov.pl/pl/dzialalnosc/statystyki/ download,33,0.html. Data for 2008, http://www.bip.ms.gov.pl/Data/Files/_public/bip/statystyki/prokur_dzial_2008.pdf.

References

Alegre, Susie, Ivanka Ivanova, and Dana Denis-Smith. 2009. "Safeguarding the Rule of Law in an Enlarged EU: The Cases of Bulgaria and Romania," *CEPS Special Report* April. http://www.ceps.eu/ceps/download/1655.

American Bar Association. 2004. *Judicial Reform Index for Kazakhstan*. http://apps.americanbar.org/rol/publications/kazakhstan-jri-2004.pdf.

    2005. *Judicial Reform Index for Georgia*. http://apps.americanbar.org/rol/publications/georgia-jri-2005-eng.pdf.

    2006. *Judicial Reform Index for Bulgaria*. http://apps.americanbar.org/rol/publications/bulgaria-jri-2006.pdf.

    2009. *Judicial Reform Index for Georgia, 2008*. http://apps.americanbar.org/rol/publications/georgia_judicial_reform_index_volume_iI_2009_En.pdf.

Amirkhanian, Natalia. 2011. "Pochti vse SIZO Ukrainy – postroeny do 70-kh godov." 24.*Ua*, November 6. http://24.ua/news/show/id/19206.htm.

Barclay, Gordon C. 2000. "The Comparability of Data on Convictions and Sanctions: Are International Comparisons Possible?" *European Journal on Criminal Policy and Research* 8(1): 13–26.

Bukalov, A. 2007. *Ugolovnye nakazaniia v Ukraine*. Donetsk: Memorial.

Centre of Judicial Studies. 2011. "Analiz stanu zastosuvannya zapobizhnykh zakhodiv ta dotrymannya rozumnykh strokiv provadzhennya po kryminal'nym spravam (2008–2010 rr.)." Kyiv: CJS. Unpublished document. http://www.judges.org.ua/article/zvit_08-10.PDF.

Centre for Liberal Strategies. 2006. *The Judiciary: Independent and Accountable. Indicators on the Efficiency of the Bulgarian Judicial System*. Sofia: CLS. http://www.cls-sofia.org/download.php?id=52.

Churilov, Iurii. 2010. *Aktual'nye problemy postanovleniia opravdatel'nogo prigovora v rossiiskom ugolovnom sudoproizvodstve*. Moscow: Wolters Kluwer Russia.

Dadaev, Khamzat. 2007. "Ugolovnaia otvetstvennost' za nezakonnoe zaderzhanie, zakliuchenie pod strazhu ili soderzhanie pod strazhei." Unpublished dissertation of the candidate of legal sciences. Kuban State University. Krasnodar. http://law.edu.ru/book/book.asp?bookID=1268275.

European Commission for the Efficiency of Justice (CEPEJ). 2006. *European Judicial Systems*. Brussels: Council of Europe.

Firestone, Thomas. 2010. "Armed Injustice: Abuse of the Law and Complex Crime in Post-Soviet Russia." *Denver Journal of International Law & Policy* 38: 555–80.

Foglesong, Todd. 1995. "Habeas Corpus or Who Has the Body – Judicial Review of Arrest and Pre-Trial Detention in Russia." *Wisconsin International Law Journal* 14: 541–78.

    1997. "The Reform of Criminal Justice and Evolution of Judicial Dependence in Late Soviet Russia." In *Reforming Justice in Russia, 1864–1996: Power, Culture, and the Limits of Legal Order*, ed. Peter H. Solomon, Jr., 282–324. Armonk, NY: M. E. Sharpe.

Foglesong, Todd S. and Peter H. Solomon, Jr. 2001. *Crime, Criminal Justice, and Criminology in Post-Soviet Ukraine*. Washington, DC: NIJ.

Freedom House. 2008. *Nations in Transit, 2007*. Lanham, MD: Rowman & Littlefield.

Guseinov, Oleg. 2007. "Sprovotsirovali opera." *Gazeta Iuga*, January 25. http://www.gazetayuga.ru/archive/2007/04.htm.

Hendley, Kathryn. 2002. "Suing the State in Russia." *Post-Soviet Affairs* 18(2): 122–47.

Human Rights Ombudsman of Ukraine. 2011. *2010 Annual Report*. April 5 http://www.ombudsman.gov.ua/images/stories/07022011/Dopovid_7.pdf.

Kasparov.Ru. 2009. "Osnovanie naidetsia." *Kasparov.Ru*, August 31. http://www.kasparov.ru/material.php?id=4A9B7E0CA226A.

Kislov, O. I. 2011. "Dovidka pro kil'kist' osib yaki buly zvil'neny iz slydchykh yzolyatorov derzhavnoj penytencyarnoj sluzhby Ukrayny." *Argument*. October 31. Unpublished document. http://argumentua.com/stati/sledstvie-bez-predela-ukrainskii-sizo-kak-rudiment-gulaga-dokumenty.

Kremlin.Ru. 2008. "Nachalo vstrechi Prezidenta RF s Upolnomochennym po pravam cheloveka Vladimirom Lukinym." *Kremlin.Ru*. December 15. http://www.kremlin.ru/appears/2008/12/15/1739_type63376_210577.shtml.

Lehmann, Christopher. 2000. "Bail Reform in Ukraine: Transplanting Western Legal Concepts to Post-Soviet Legal Systems." *Harvard Human Rights Journal* 13: 191–227.

Lukianovskaia, Marianna. 2012. "My dolzhny verit' ne dokazatel'stvam, a silovikam na slovo." *PublicPost.Ru*. May 25. http://publicpost.ru/theme/id/1495/my_dolzhny_verit_ne_dokazatelstvam_a_silovikam_na_slovo.

Lyska, Volodymyr. 2010. "Zastosuvannya vzyattya pid vartu yak krajn'oho zapobizhnoho zakhodu." December 24. Unpublished document. http://www.minjust.gov.ua/0/33155.

Melnikov, Viktor. 2007. "Problemy primeneniia domashnego aresta kak mery presecheniia." *Zhurnal rossiiskogo prava* 3: 72–80. http://www.juristlib.ru/book_2934.html.
Merkulova, Svetlana. 2011. "Khvatit plodit' arestantov!" *OKO*. November 9. http://oko.kz/uridicheskiy-klub/chvatit-plodit-arestantov.
Mirzabalaev, Mirzabala. 2005. "Nezakonnye zaderzhanie, zakliuchenie pod strazhu ili soderzhanie pod strazhei: Ugolovno-pravovoi i kriminologicheskii analiz." Unpublished dissertation of the candidate of legal sciences. Dagestan State University. Makhachkala. http://www.lib.ua-ru.net/diss/cont/220373.html.
Naimark-Rowse, Benjamin, Martin Schönteich, Mykola Sorochinsky, and Denise Tomasini-Joshi. 2008. "Studies in Reform: Pretrial Detention Investments in Mexico, Ukraine, and Latvia." *Justice Initiatives* Spring: 152–71. http://www.opensocietyfoundations.org/sites/default/files/Justice_Initiati.pdf.
OSCE ODIHR. 2011. *Judicial Authorization of Pre-trial Detention in the Republic of Kazakhstan*. Warsaw: OSCE ODIHR. http://www.osce.org/odihr/77357.
Paneiakh, Ella, Kirill Titaev, Vadim Volkov, and Denis Primakov. 2010. "Obvinitel'nyi uklon v ugolovnom protsesse: factor prokurora." *Analiticheskie zapiski po problemam pravoprimeneniia*. Saint Petersburg: Institut problem pravoprimeneniia. http://www.enforce.spb.ru/wp-content/uploads/pm1003_obvinit_uklon.pdf.
Petrukhin, Igor. 2003. *Sudebnaia vlast'*. Moscow: Prospekt.
    2009. *Opravdatel'nyi prigovor i pravo na reabilitatsiiu*. Moscow: Prospekt.
Pizyk, Iryna. 2007. "Suddi, ne bijtesya zastosovuvaty zastavu!" *Yurydychna Gazeta*. March 1. http://www.yur-gazeta.com/article/948.
PublicPost.Ru. 2012. "Sud'i o pravosudii." *PublicPost.Ru*, May 25. http://publicpost.ru/theme/id/1496/sudi_o_pravosudii.
Saakashvili, Mikheil. 2006. "Annual Address to Parliament." February 14. Unpublished document. http://www.president.gov.ge/index.php?lang_id=ENG&sec_id=231&info_id=2485.
Solomon, Peter H., Jr. 1987. "The Case of the Vanishing Acquittal: Informal Norms and the Practice of Soviet Criminal Justice." *Soviet Studies* 39(4): 531–55.
    1996. *Soviet Criminal Justice under Stalin*. New York: Cambridge University Press.
    2004. "Judicial Power in Russia: Through the Prism of Administrative Justice." *Law & Society Review* 38 (Fall): 549–82.
Soros Foundation-Moldova. 2009. *Criminal Justice Performance from a Human Right Perspective*. Chisinau: Soros Foundation-Moldova. http://www.soros.md/en/publication/criminal_justice_performance.
Sukhovei, Oksana. 2011. "Sovetskie sud'i vo glave rossiiskikh sudov." *Pravo.Ru*. March 14. http://www.pravo.ru/info_graph/view/49943/28947.
Sung, Hung-En. 2006. "Democracy and Criminal Justice in Cross-National Perspective: From Crime Control to Due Process." *Annals of the American Academy of Political and Social Science* 605 (May): 311–37.
Transparency International Georgia. 2010. "Plea Bargaining in Georgia: Negotiated Justice." December 15. Unpublished document. http://transparency.ge/en/post/report/plea-bargaining-georgia-negotiated-justice.
Trochev, Alexei. 2009. "All Appeals Lead to Strasbourg? Unpacking the Impact of the European Court of Human Rights in Russia." *Demokratizatsiya* 17(2): 145–78.
    2010. "Suing Russia at Home." *Problems of Post-Communism* 59(5): 18–34.

2013. "Fragmentation? Defection? Legitimacy? Explaining Judicial Roles in Post-Communist 'Colored Revolutions.'" In *Consequential Courts: Judicial Roles in Global Perspective*, ed. Diana Kapiszewski, Gordon Silverstein, and Robert A. Kagan, 67–92. New York: Cambridge University Press.

Uzbekistan. 2011. "Fourth Periodic Report of the Republic of Uzbekistan on the Implementation of the Convention against Torture and Other Cruel, Inhuman or Degrading Treatment or Punishment." Unpublished document. http://www2.ohchr.org/english/bodies/cat/docs/CAT.C.UZB.4_en.doc.

UzMetronom.com. 2009. "Sazhat' budut men'she. No chashche." *UzMetronom.com*. March 13. http://www.uzmetronom.com/2009/03/13/sazhat_budut_menshe_no_chashhe.html.

Van Kalmthout, A. M., M. M. Knapen, and C. Morgenstern, eds. 2009. *Pre-trial Detention in the European Union*. Nijmegen: Wolf Legal Publishers.

Waters, Christopher P. M. 2004. *Counsel in the Caucasus: Professionalization and Law in Georgia*. Leiden: Martinus Nijhoff.

9

Historical Roots of Religious Influence on Postcommunist Democratic Politics

Anna Grzymala-Busse

How do religious authorities gain political power and influence public policy? Among postcommunist democracies, we see deeply Catholic countries where the Roman Catholic Church has gained moral authority and exerted extensive sway over policy (Poland), and those where the Church has accomplished far less (Croatia). In mixed Catholic-Protestant countries, religion has influenced politics in Slovakia far more than in similarly heterogeneous Hungary.

One answer advanced to explain church influence is the historical fusion of national and religious identities tout court (Stark and Iannaccone 1996; Stark 1999; Burleigh 2007). Such fusion means that religious and political identities have become conflated over time. Political arguments are justified in religious terms, and religious authorities successfully use the nation as both a religious category and a justification for incursion of religion into politics. Observable aspects include a popular and elite consensus that equates national and religious identities, historical and national myths that explicitly refer to religion, and mutual references between religion and nation in songs, symbols, and icons. Religious values become national norms, and churches gain moral authority. As a result, the prevailing view goes, this historical legacy means that churches easily influence public policy and obtain their preferred outcomes as politicians scramble to fulfill their obligations to the "nation."

This chapter argues that explaining religious influence on postcommunist politics necessitates a more nuanced view of both historical legacies and the fusion of nation with religion. It demonstrates that historical legacies have to be sustained and reproduced over time, as Kotkin and Beissinger argue. The sustained reproduction of this fusion allowed its translation into democratic practice, and the survival of the churches' policy-making access. These mechanisms of reproduction and influence have been (at best) assumed by the extant literature. At the same time, I emphasize that important legacies need not be traceable to historically distant developments. Late-era legacies proved as important as the more temporally remote factors in the translation of national-religious fusion into democratic political influence.

Thus, the fusion of national and religious identities itself does not guarantee political influence. It grants the churches a diffuse and indirect moral authority, but one that is insufficient for post-1989 impact on democratic politics. Under certain circumstances, however, fusion of national and religious identities can foster the institutional access that *is* the critical and direct channel by which churches shape public policy both under authoritarian and subsequently democratic regimes. Specifically, where churches act as national representatives and politics are unstable, churches can become guarantors of social peace for political actors from all sides. These secular authorities then grant the churches direct access to governance in exchange for compliance by including clergy in policy formulation, allowing church discretion in naming secular officials, and naming church representatives to secular institutions. As result, churches gain enormous policy influence during times of potential instability (such as regime transitions) – precisely when institutional and policy frameworks can be transformed. Once the political situation stabilizes and church guarantees are no longer needed, however, their direct policy influence quickly wanes. There is thus a distinct temporal dynamic to religious influence on politics: churches have their greatest influence in moments of regime crisis, and then have to act quickly to spend the political capital accrued.

Differences in Policy Influence across Postcommunist Democracy

The translation of the fusion of religion and nation into democratic policy influence is not straightforward. Table 9.1 summarizes the patterns of church influence on policy debates and outcomes across five contentious domains where secular states and religious authorities have clashed.

In three predominantly Catholic countries, where the nation and the Church were closely identified with each other, we observe different patterns of religious influence on politics. The Roman Catholic Church in Poland has been the most influential. After the fall of communism in 1989, the Catholic Church in newly democratic Poland successfully and publicly lobbied for a ban on abortions and the introduction of religious education into the public school system, and continues to denounce stem cell research, same-sex marriage, and no-fault divorce as immoral and unacceptable, finding considerable political purchase. Among postcommunist democracies, the Polish fusion of national and religious identities is said to have deep historical roots – reinforced by decades of communist repression – and to directly promote powerful church influence on secular democratic politics. Yet precisely because this case is so familiar, it is all the more important that we examine how exactly organized religion could influence policy. For one, other cases with national-religious fusion show different patterns of influence. The church in equally Catholic Croatia failed to eliminate abortion, restrict stem cell research, or forestall civil unions for gays.

TABLE 9.1. *Church Success in Public Policy Outcomes*

	Poland	Croatia	Lithuania	Slovakia	Hungary	Czech Republic
Abortion restricted?[3]	Yes	No	No	Yes	No	No
Divorce restricted?	Yes	No	No	No	No	No
Religion in schools?[4]	Yes	Yes	Opt.	Yes	Opt.	No
Stem cell research restricted?	Yes	No	Yes	Yes	No	No
Same-sex marriage restricted?	Yes	No	Yes	Yes	No	No
Summary score	5	1	2.5	4	.5	0

Note: The churches' efficacy in achieving policy gains is measured by whether policy changes were (a) compatible with Church teachings, and (b) justified by the politicians passing them as having a Christian character, to avoid coding an accidental coincidence as influence.

Lithuania is in between the two, with the church succeeding more than in Croatia (restricting stem cell research and same-sex marriage), but less than in Poland (failing to restrict divorce or abortion).

In three mixed Protestant-Catholic countries, the tie between national and religious identities under communism varied, as did policy outcomes after 1989. Ironically, the Slovak church had greater success in achieving policy outcomes than in framing public debates and had its preferences enacted in abortion policy, religion in schools, stem cell research restrictions, and same-sex marriage restrictions. Despite a similar religious profile and similar efforts, the churches in Hungary have had limited rhetorical and policy success. Finally, the Czech Catholic Church, never closely associated with the nation, failed to exert any influence on politics after 1989.

This variation is not attributable to religiosity and the demand it creates for church influence. As Table 9.1 shows, the Church influenced politics in very Catholic countries such as Poland, but failed to do so in similarly religious Croatia. Slovakia and Hungary share religious profiles, but not levels of church influence on policy, which is clearly higher in Slovakia.

Nor is it the case that religiosity creates demand for church influence on politics. Norris and Inglehart (2004), for example, argue that greater levels of social and economic deprivation increase religiosity, because they lead individuals to seek comfort in religion and thus increase the demand for religious influence over policy. Given religion's traditional concern with morality, such constituencies should be especially receptive to religious incursion into public policy issues framed as "moral." Two predictions follow. First, lower economic

TABLE 9.2. *Religious Profiles*

	Poland	Lithuania	Croatia	Slovakia	Hungary	Czech Republic	European Mean (SD)
Percent believing in God (%)	96.9	70	93.2	82.5	68.5	33.1	73.4% (17.6)
Percent belonging to a religious denomination (%)	95.5	81	88.4	76.9	57.1	34	77.6% (19.1)
Percent attending services > 1/month (%)	77.8	31.5	53	81.3	59.3	11.7	31.9% (19)
Percent stating religious leaders should *not* influence politics (%)	77.6	75.7	74.1	67.4	64	74	72.3% (8.9)
Percent Catholic (%)	96	80	91	75	77	25	

development should correlate with higher participation and belief. Yet there is little significant correlation between the relatively constant levels of postcommunist economic development and the variety of religious belief, belonging, and participation. Second, religious participation and belief should correlate with a greater demand for religious influence in politics and with higher levels of such influence. However, religion influences politics whether or not mass publics want it to.[1] There is no relationship between the *demand* for the influence of religion on politics and its *supply*. Desired influence is not correlated to policy efficacy (–.11 correlation at .72 *p* level).[2] If churches can influence politics even when an overwhelming majority of the faithful prefers they stay out of politics, we need an account of both religion's ability to retain adherents in face of their disapproval and its ability to influence policy in spite of popular preferences.

Communist Legacies, Religion, and National Identities

In contrast to prevailing conceptualizations of national-religious fusion, I argue that it comprises two distinct effects: a diffuse moral authority that arises over decades and even centuries, and a concrete and immediate institutional access to policy making that is made possible (but not determined) by the churches' moral authority. In effect, national-religious fusion operates at two temporalities and with two distinct mechanisms. It is historically conditioned, and reproduced by the interaction between a contentious society, a repressive state, and a church that takes risks to protect the nation against the state. The question then is how, when, and to what extent this synthesis of nation and religion took place – and how it then translated into political influence.

Where the administrative state and an existing nation historically opposed each other, churches could serve as protectors of national identity against the state. They could do so through informal education, sheltering the opposition, providing physical and spiritual space for opponents to gather, and by imbuing religious symbols (such as icons and saints' relics) with national meaning. Public religiosity became a political act, and patriotism blurred with religious loyalty (Martin 1991). By contrast, some churches *opposed* national aspirations and the nation-state project. The Roman Catholic Church and the papacy, for example, explicitly and vigorously battled liberal or nationalist revolutions in the Czech Lands, Italy, and France. The nation-state and the Church in these countries had a subsequently uneasy relationship: private religious beliefs coexist with secular political identities, but the Church has only a tenuous claim to moral national authority.

As a result, we cannot take for granted the "nation-state" as a coherent entity: the state may oppose national aspirations, as communist states were accused of doing. The formation of *states* tended to be a secular process, often at odds with established churches. Both states and churches attempted to create a hierarchy of control, and their claims often competed. In contrast, *nation* building can be imbued with religious meaning and the active participation of religious authorities. Religion can then become a protector of the nation, closely aligning religious and national identities – and providing resonance to subsequent political claims by religious authorities (Grzymala-Busse 2012).

Both religious and political implications follow. The relationship between nation and religion matters for church vitality – and state oppression can strengthen the church. Religious bodies can symbolically infuse the nation with religious significance, and physically protect important national symbols and representatives. Conversely, national myths can serve to fuel religious belief and participation. Another implication is that movement between religions is no longer devoid of transaction costs: instead, the costs of conversion will vary directly with the degree of national-religious fusion. Apostasy or conversion can be perceived as betraying the nation. Natural monopolies not only exist – but they can flourish. A homogenous nation can more easily sustain (and be sustained by) one dominant church. Above all, churches can now enter the political arena, and find that their claims resonate.

Two mechanisms reproduce fusion of national and religious identities over time and through institutional contexts. The first is repeated conflict with the secular state. Across East Central Europe, communism was seen as an alien and unwelcome imposition: but only in some countries did the Church and the anticommunist opposition form an alliance. The more the communist authorities tried to repress societal protest, and the more the Church stood in defense of the opposition, the more opportunities for the fusion of nation and religion. Here, education and indoctrination within the family and religious community, often in the face of considerable political repression from the state (Darden and Grzymala-Busse 2006; Wittenberg 2006), also reproduced the equation of nation with religion as part of the resistance to communist rule. Another mechanism is religion's unique ability to withstand secular onslaught. Religious organizations are much harder to repress than unions, newspapers, political groups, or student organizations (Sahliyeh 1990, 13). The clergy often have little to lose: for them, the benefits of participation are far greater than the costs of inaction, because the latter means they stand to lose their congregations. This may be why the more public the protest of local clergy under communism, the greater their authority and legitimacy (Wittenberg 2006). And, if the church(es) represent *the nation*, rather than a specific constituency, they make secular "divide and conquer" strategies even more difficult. If a domestic national movement is under church protection, eradicating such movements means crossing over into the sphere of the sacred: a move even Stalin was reluctant to make. Thus, fusion of nation and religion is reproduced through conflict with a hostile secular actor, whether a repressive state (as in the communist cases) or a colonial power (as in Ireland).

For us to identify national-religious fusion (or any other historical legacy), it must be clear and sustained: that is, we need to be able to identify a consistent and empirically demonstrable set of conditions, actors, resources, institutions, attitudes, or relationships and their persistence over time. As suggested previously, we also need to identify mechanisms of reproduction. Finally, changes in the exogenous context allow the impact of these legacies to be visible – if a pattern persists despite upheaval, we can be more certain it exerts an independent influence beyond the conditions that gave rise to it. Note that the impact of the legacies does not follow from their duration under the previous regime: powerful historical legacies may have begun decades or centuries ago. These standards are empirically quite demanding, and mean that we overlook relevant legacies such as the effects of long-ago cultural conflicts or subtle changes. However, because the fusion of religious and national identities is hypothesized to have such powerful effects, a false negative (Type II error) is preferable to a false positive (Type I error).

Fusing Nation and Religion in East Central Europe

Such caution allows us to place the origins of a given legacy with greater precision, by elucidating the conditions that gave rise to the patterns in question and demonstrating how they were sustained. For example, some analysts have placed the origins of the fusion of Polish national identity and Roman Catholicism in the national partitions that began in the late eighteenth century.

The church protected expressions of Polish national identity, and in effect allowed a nation without a state to survive with its identity intact (Ramet 1998; Froese and Pfaff 2001). Church and nation were said to first become closely identified with each other during the eighteenth and nineteenth centuries, when Poland was repeatedly partitioned among Prussia, Austria, and Russia. Catholic clergy repeatedly opposed the foreign influence, siding with local notables in resisting Prussian initiatives in education, for example, and subsequently supporting Polish-language instruction with a Catholic curriculum. As a result, "linguistic and educational conflict became part of a national struggle which in this century formed an issue in two succeeding world wars" (de Swaan 1988, 78).

Yet these arguments fail to take into account that Poland before World War II was a multinational and multidenominational entity, and that the Church often sided with the Austrian or Prussian (though not Russian) imperial administrations rather than with the populace. Catholicism was only one strand of Polish national identity, and one that began in earnest only in the late nineteenth century (Zubrzycki 2006, 53–54). Interwar Poland saw massive anticlericalism and the contestation of the "Pole=Catholic" equation by important political forces, including the man who dominated interwar politics, General Józef Piłsudski. Anticlerical parties gained in popularity as the Church began to side with successive interwar governments (Chrypiński 1990, 125). Neither an elite nor a popular consensus existed about either the content of "Pole" or its link to Catholicism, despite a strong National Democratic wing that equated the two.

In short, the fusion of nation and religion in Poland is a relatively new phenomenon. It was the ethnic and religious homogenization of Poland, the result both of the devastation of World War II and the population transfers that followed, that made possible the full fusion of national and religious identities. Postwar Poland became a homogenous Catholic nation – one where communism was seen as an alien imposition that violated tenets both of sovereignty and faith. The result was a renewed consensus about a "conflation of the ideas, institutions, and so to speak, behavioral displays of religion with nationality in Poland ... the Roman Catholic Church has provided the means for the emergence and preservation of a modern national consciousness among the Poles" (Morawska 1995, 51).

Yet even this fusion of nation and religion did not become politically salient until the Church sided with the nation against the communist state in the 1960s and 1970s. The Church repeatedly resisted state incursion into its affairs during the communist era, and tried to recast this as resistance to the communist imposition on the Polish nation (Morawska 1995, 55). But only in the 1970s did the Church move beyond self-defense and begin to speak out more forcefully in favor of human rights (Anderson 2003, 144). It became more closely identified with the "true" Polish nation as a result of the rise of anticommunist mobilization and of two other events: the pilgrimage of the Black Madonna around Poland in the late 1970s, and the triumphal return of Pope John Paul II to Poland in 1979. These reinforced the notion that Polish identity was inextricably linked to Catholicism and served as the basis for a political awakening. Subsequently, in the 1980s, especially after the collapse of the opposition trade union Solidarity and the military crackdown, this identification strengthened, because churches offered physical protection for individual dissidents and broader opposition activity. The Church became the protective umbrella for anticommunist opposition, and attending Mass became a political act.

Both the Communist Party and the opposition recognized the Church's authority and legitimating power: while Solidarity sought the Church's shelter, the communist party repeatedly entered into negotiations with the Church, easing restrictions in exchange for the Church exercising its capacity to stabilize the political situation. Church representatives were invited to a special joint church-state commission, which acted as a forum for policy consultation and coordination. By the late 1980s, the Church's moral authority meant it had become the fulcrum in the political scales: and its support was critical to the success of both the Round Table negotiations between Solidarity and the communist regime in 1989 and the transition that immediately followed. Its representatives participated in the Round Table negotiations and acted to mediate between the two sides. Throughout the transition, the joint commission was in place – and became a vocal voice for policy in the new democratic parliament. Such institutional access made possible the Church's remarkable subsequent inroads in abortion, education, and church-state relations policy, as the Church "used Solidarity's advances to obtain more and more concessions" (Luxmoore and Babiuch 1999, 229).

In many ways, Lithuania resembles Poland. As one analyst argued, "the Catholic Church in Lithuania was vital to sustaining a sense of national identity, especially in preserving the language" (Bruce 2000, 41). During the interwar period, the Catholic Church under communism increasingly served as a site for nationalist mobilization, "propagating nationalism and democracy in questions of regime, and clericalism in the sphere of worldly relations" (Ochmański 1982, 313). The Church was the antithesis of Russian Orthodoxy and Soviet domination, and thus became a focal point for nationalist sentiment. It also consistently acted to defend national and democratic (if not liberal) interests, both under the authoritarian Voldemaras regime, when it became the "only organized, legal force that could oppose the actions of the government" (Ochmański 1982, 314), and subsequently under communism.

Both the Church's own earlier persecution by the communist regime and its embrace of the 1968 law that allowed petitions to government authorities (which resulted in an avalanche of petitions on behalf of religious freedoms and human rights) lend credibility to its support of the dissident movement culminating in Sajudis. When the Vatican moved to appoint bishops willing to appease the communist regime, the local clergy protested vehemently, "as it would dilute the church's support and legitimacy" (Luxmoore and Babiuch

1999, 189–90). By the 1970s, the anticommunist movement blended appeals in defense of the Church and the rights of believers with its advocacy of national rights and self-determination. Two-thirds of all protests in the 1970s were religious in nature (Vardys and Sedaitis 1997, 84–85). A 1989 survey showed that 91 percent of Lithuanians polled believed that religion "fostered the development of national consciousness" (Vardys and Sedaitis 1997, 116).

Much as in Poland, nation and religion became fused, although the protective umbrella of the Church was much more of a physical safety net for Solidarity than for Sajudis (partly for lack of opportunity: the latter had emerged in 1988, eight years after Solidarity). By the late 1980s, "the church came out of the ordeal of almost half a century of suppression strong enough to command attention. Both Sajudis and [the] Communist party found it advisable to vie for its support" (Vardys and Sedaitis 1997, 117). Accordingly, the communist leadership sought and obtained meetings with the church hierarchy in late 1987 and participated actively in the Sajudis dissident movement. Sajudis, for its part, reserved a number of seats for the clergy at its founding meeting in October 1988. The Lithuanian Church thus became a "guardian of [the] nation's cultural heritage" (Girnius 1989, 109) – and just as importantly, gained direct access to the top echelons of both communist and opposition decision makers.

The fusion of nation and religion was not seamless. Earlier national movements in Lithuania had traditionally had an anticlerical and secular wing (Kilp 2005), and the Church had been earlier associated with Polish dominance and imperial ambitions during the fifteenth through eighteenth centuries (Vardys and Sedaitis 1997, 13). Catholicism implied Polish clergy and secular rule, which tainted its link to Lithuanian national consciousness. Not until the mid-nineteenth century did tsarist anti-Polish and anti-Catholic policies in Lithuania lead to a greater tie between Lithuanian national identity and Catholicism (Vardys and Sedaitis 1997, 16; Kilp 2005). And Sajudis itself emphasized that the Lithuanian movement did not develop around the Church, but instead, the Church "came to the movement" (Vardys and Sedaitis 1997, 188).

Similarly, the Roman Catholic Church in Croatia was closely identified with the Croatian nation within Yugoslavia, and maintained a moral and political distance from the communist regime. During the nineteenth century, the Catholic Church actively backed the struggle for national autonomy and fought Magyarization efforts under the Dual Monarchy. Subsequently, until the 1920s the Church was divided between advocates of a more liberal vision of a union with Serbia, and the proponents of a more exclusivist and nationalist version that "was loath to bind Catholic Croatia to Orthodox Serbia" (Ramet 1998, 155). The latter view won, and the Church helped to found Croatian language newspapers, a national organization (Matica Hrvatska), the Croatian National Museum, and even the first Croatian savings bank (Ramet 1998, 155). Religion was part of Croat national identity, and Catholicism was explicitly contrasted with Serbian Orthodoxy or Bosnian Islam. Under communism, the Church was initially prosecuted in the immediate postwar period. During the Croatian Spring of 1967–71, the Church defended the nation against the League of Communists of Yugoslavia. The post-crackdown repression of Croatian nationalist organizations only strengthened the Church's position as the chief guardian and defender of the Croat national interests (Ramet 1998, 157).

Yet even as the stage was set for church influence on postcommunist politics, two critical points emerged. First, the collapse of Yugoslavia attenuated the conflict between the communist party and the nation. Unlike in Lithuania or Poland, the Church would not play a mediating role. Instead, conflict with Serbia quickly emerged, and party and nation stood on the same side. Second, while the Church continued to claim to represent the Croat nation after 1990, it allowed itself to be embraced by a particular party (the HDZ), which undermined its claims to speak for the entire nation (Lovrenovic 1998; Gruenfelder 2000). The Tudman-led HDZ government repeatedly emphasized the strong link between the Church and the Croatian people; by the time the Church criticized the autocratic tendencies of the HDZ in 1997, it had become identified with a specific partisan option.

Turning to the mixed Protestant-Catholic cases, we find even starker variation. Czech anti-Catholicism, and the explicit rejection of a Catholic identity, has its roots in the seventeenth-century loss of sovereignty at the Battle of White Mountain, and the subsequent imposition of a politicized Catholicism by the Habsburgs. The Catholic Church became synonymous with Austrian imperial rule and the defeat of an independent Czech national project (Agnew 1993; Hamplová and Nešpor 2009). During the interwar period, Czech Catholicism rebounded to an extent; as one observer noted, "no longer subjected to the pressures of the Habsburg state, the church witnessed the emergence of significant intellectual forces and a desire to maintain a suprapolitical stance" (Reban 1990, 142). Yet despite its new independence, and the interwar democratic republic's association with the governing Christian Democrats, no church assumed the mantle of national prophet or defender of national identities.

Given communist oppression of the churches (and the latter's acquiescence), the communist era did little to rehabilitate their image. Irreligiosity and antipathy persisted throughout the communist era and cannot be attributed to the communist regime itself. Churches did not participate in the 1968 Prague Spring, nor did they shelter the few dissidents (Kepel 1995, 91). The result was that public opinion polls conducted in the 1990s show churches to be one of the least trusted and most poorly evaluated Czech institutions, ranking lower than the media, president, various parties, unions, the army, and so forth (Misovic 2001, 140). This was not a communist legacy, but an antagonism inherited centuries earlier and deepened by communist-era acquiescence and passivity.

Slovak nationalism and national independence, in contrast, was much more tightly tied to the Roman Catholic Church. If the Czechs associated the Roman Catholic Church with Habsburg domination, the Slovaks linked it to a defense of the nation against forced (Protestant) Magyarization under the Dual Monarchy. The brief period of Slovak sovereignty in World War II was directly associated with the Catholic Church: a Catholic clergyman, Monsignor Jozef Tiso, was the president. Scholars have emphasized the nation-building aspect of the independent wartime Slovak state (Leff 1988, 90; see also Jelínek 1976).

However, the Tiso government collaborated with the Nazis, and the popular 1944 Slovak National Uprising fought against this regime. As a result, the Church could not unequivocally claim the mantle of a moral representative of Slovak national interests (Reban 1990, 143). Further, under communism, the Slovak church never mobilized society or served as an opposition umbrella. This was due partly to a more oppressive communist policy in Czechoslovakia, but the policy was possible because the Church was not as powerful a social actor as it was in Poland. While some Catholic activism began in the 1970s (with an elite strand of intellectuals around Ján Čarnogurský, the founder of the democratic Christian Democratic Party in Slovakia), and public activities began in earnest in the 1980s with petitions and pilgrimages, these were never as widespread as in Poland, nor were they supported by church authorities. In contrast to the 10 million members of Solidarity, the most visible Slovak prayer meeting in March 1988 gathered around ten to fifteen thousand (Cohen 1999, 63). As a result, the Church had less symbolic capital and national moral authority than in Poland, even if it commanded a narrower but very loyal constituency.

Finally, in Hungary, the bloody conflicts of the Reformation meant that no church could fully identify itself with the Hungarian nation, even if the Catholic Church dominated the Protestants, both numerically and politically (Enyedi 2003, 159). The Catholic Church played little historical role in preserving national consciousness (Schanda 2003), so that "Catholicism never became equated with Hungarian patriotism" (Eberts and Torok 2001, 131). The liberal governments of the nineteenth century, backed by the Protestant churches, moved toward church-state separation, but Church and state grew closer during the interwar period, sharing the same antiliberal views. Under communism, the Roman Catholic Church did not serve as a symbol of national independence, nor as a source of protection for the opposition; with a few notable exceptions such as Cardinal Mindszenty, "the communist regime succeeded in co-opting the Church leaderships and a portion of the local priesthood" (Wittenberg 2006, 43). Even as village priests sustained some political identities, the Church as a whole did not have the symbolic or political capital of its Polish or even its Slovak counterparts. More than thirty church officials were elected to parliament and national councils in 1985, further implicating the Hungarian churches in communist rule. If the Church remained neutral in Slovakia, it was effectively neutralized in Hungary.

The Policy Consequences of National-Religious Fusion

Even if it is sustained, the fusion of national and religious identities does not automatically translate into policy influence. First, religious influence is highest in the "right" issue domains – that is, those that are plausibly relevant to both doctrine and to the nation. For example, the U.S. Bishops' Conference antinuclear stance was neither and thus failed to influence policy. Even more critically, the *reproduction* of national-religious fusion, and its translation into influence, relies on the church representing the nation rather than identification with a particular demographic cleavage or political party. The narrower the churches' political alliances or the greater the internal elite conflict within the religious organization, the less credible their fusion with the *nation*. If a church ties itself closely to a particular government or subnational group rather than the defense of the nation, its claims of universal morality and national protection are immediately suspect (Gill 1998). Paradoxically, to sustain their political success, churches have to maintain the appearance of being above the political fray. Yet such isolation is difficult to achieve for a church with democratic policy ambitions. As a result, some churches dallied with political parties, and paid the price in lowered moral authority and influence on politics.

How, then, did fusion between religious and national identities translate into policy influence? Religious organizations do not legislate directly, and rarely have formal political representation. Instead, fusion influenced postcommunist politics in two ways: translating moral authority into electoral threat, and by direct access to policy making. First, the more religious and national identities overlap, the more all politicians are wary of offending churches for fear of losing fragile electoral support. Churches frame policy domains they consider important. This framing is successful when existing levels of participation and belief are high and the church can reinterpret opposition as antipatriotic, given the double bind of betraying the nation by defying the religion. The definition of "heresy becomes a national definition of treachery" (Martin 2005, 131). Politicians, meanwhile, are uncertain of electoral preferences, and worry about offending a powerful societal actor. As a result, once the churches frame issues as moral imperatives, politicians tend to comply.

Second, fusion between religion and national identity increases the likelihood of direct church access to policy making. Where *both* the communist regime and the opposition saw the Church's moral authority in its role as a national representative as critical to maintaining social stability, the Church could exploit that position. In exchange for maintaining social peace, it could gain access to joint state-church parliamentary commissions, negotiations over policy proposals, vetting of government officials, and significant policy concessions. Much of this direct (and critical) access was covert: neither Church nor governments called attention to it. Importantly, the threat of destabilizing social conflict or backlash came immediately after the regime transition – at precisely the moment when entire swathes of policies could be reevaluated and reformulated. If the Church was in a position to take advantage of this timing, it could win enormous policy concessions early on.

The channels of institutional access took several different forms. Church officials actively participated in policy-making discussions (special episcopal commissions, for example, formulated the abortion law in Poland and in Lithuania), took part in national negotiations during regime transitions (Poland and to a lesser degree, Lithuania), and influenced personnel and organizational decisions within ministries (Poland) (see Torańska 1994). Vulnerable politicians felt they had no choice but to go along with Church demands if they were to preserve the new democratic order – even when the Church prioritized its interpretation of natural law over democratic rule (Gowin 1995). The fusion of national and religious identities empowered churches not just as moral authorities, but as guarantors of social peace. Policy concessions were a small price for secular actors to pay.

At lower levels of alignment between nation and religion, there are fewer costs to offending religious sensibilities, both because the church has fewer supporters and because noncompliance with the demands of religion is no longer seen as an act of national betrayal. Elites thus have greater opportunity to pursue anticlerical claims and constituencies. The looser the alignment between nation and religion, the harder it is for churches to frame policy as a moral or religious issue, and the lower the risks for secular politicians of offending the churches. Church support is no longer critical to ensuring social stability or political order, and many politicians see no point in exchanging church support for policy concessions. To obtain their preferred policies, churches have to seek out specific secular allies, and their policy leverage is a function of the coalitions they form (and the allied party's status). Thus, at lower levels of fusion, churches do not either claim the moral high ground or gain direct institutional access to decision making, and rely instead on more tenuous coalitions with specific political parties, as in Slovakia or Hungary. Finally, where national and religious identities are orthogonal, as in the Czech Republic, politicians have little to fear from offending a weak church and pursue their own policy preferences, knowing that offending religious authorities carries no widespread or high costs. Churches become marginal political players, with no moral authority, alliances, or access.

Thus, the Polish Church translated the political capital earned under the communists into political influence in a sovereign democracy. It did so by using its moral authority, and by exploiting democratic institutions. First, as it pushed for changes in the laws regarding abortion, divorce, and education, "it also felt morally authorized to insult and scold in public those who dared to contest these provisions," denouncing opponents as "the sons and daughters of Russian officers" (Morawska 1995, 62). The Church's authority was so great that few parliamentarians dared to risk its disapproval; across the spectrum, for example, politicians adopted the Church's language of "protecting the unborn" rather than "abortion rights." Even as the Church's popular support dropped over the first three years of democracy, bill after bill legislated the Church's preferences into law. Moreover, even when the communist successor SLD won the 1993 elections partly on the strength of its secular credentials, it did not roll back any of the Church's legislative gains in abortion, religion in schools, or material privileges for the Church.

Second, the church relied on its institutional access and clerical representation in key secular bodies. The Episcopal Commission for Family Affairs put forth an extremely restrictive abortion bill in the communist parliament in May 1989, a month before the semi-free elections that brought an end to the communist regime in Poland. The proposal would not only eliminate abortion under any circumstances (including threat to the mother's life), but would also punish the mother and any medical personnel with unspecified jail terms. This extreme proposal became the basis for subsequent parliamentary discussion unchallenged by public dialogue (the public was preoccupied with the elections, and no consultation was invited). The Bishops' Conference further sent an open memorandum to parliament, and Church officials pressed for a full prohibition, arguing that the principle "'Thou shall not kill' does not allow any exceptions"(Morawska 1995, 63). In response, some parliamentarians pushed for societal consultation and a referendum. The Church's reaction was to flood parliamentary offices with thousands of letters and petitions against abortion signed after masses at local churches (Gowin 1995, 108). Within a year, in 1991, not only was abortion criminalized, but with very little debate in some legislative quarters (Casanova 1994, 111).

At no point did legislators propose a return to the liberal communist-era laws. The Church itself vehemently (and successfully) opposed the possibility of a public referendum on the issue, fearing the results. (Public opinion polls showed that majorities both disapproved of abortion on demand, and rejected many of the proposed restrictions.) Mild modifications were made in 1993 only in exchange for assurances to the Church that abortion law would not be subject to a popular referendum. The changes proposed by the SLD government in 1996, which would have allowed for early abortions for hardship reasons (and with the approval of two doctors), were quickly scuppered. The Constitutional Tribunal effectively did away with these amendments, and the Chief Justice called this decision a "present for the Holy Father" in anticipation of the papal visit to Poland. A new center-right government reinvigorated the 1993 restrictions in December 1997.

The Church's stance on religion in schools was similar: it introduced the issue through the joint commissions in the summer of 1990, and it was quickly ratified into law by fiat in August 1990 under the implicit threat of the Church withdrawing its support for the compromise government. The Church's unequivocal advocacy of religion in schools was justified by national survival and "repairing the damage society incurred from the totalitarian regime, which aimed to exclude God from human life and thus to dilute national identity" (Gowin 1995, 140–41). Finally, on divorce, the Episcopate and its partisan

Historical Roots of Religious Influence

allies halfheartedly pushed for greater constraints on divorce, but these debates were neither as controversial nor as successful.

To obtain these policy concessions, the Church did not rely either on referenda (which it explicitly avoided) or on mobilizing electoral forces (it did sway the electorate in 1991 and in the 1995 presidential elections, but such efforts were met with backlash in 1993). Instead, it reframed issues as moral ones and thus falling within its domain, resorting to the language not only of religion, but also of the nation – and the need to protect the moral health and stable development of the (now) sovereign Polish nation. More important, the Church not only presented specific versions of bills, but also frequently intervened in ensuring that civil servants and officials favorable to its views would be in charge of sensitive ministries and offices, as well as in charge of church-state dialogue (Torańska 1994; Gowin 1995). Critically, its greatest push was in the immediate aftermath of 1989 – both when its support was most needed to preserve social peace and consolidate democracy, and when society's attention was turned away from the details of policy making. All sides of the political spectrum acceded to these demands for fear of destabilizing Polish democracy and newly found sovereignty.

In Lithuania, both the communists and the opposition relied on the Church to keep social peace. The Church itself relied both on rhetorical moves similar to those in Poland (equating Church demands with the continued flourishing of the nation) and on similar tactics of ensuring its presence on sensitive government commissions and as advisors within ministries. The critical difference is that many of its efforts came considerably later than in the Polish case – in the late 1990s–2000s instead of 1989–91. By that point, even though the Church still claimed moral authority, its support was no longer necessary for democracy and independent statehood, and its guarantees that it could ensure social peace no longer seemed credible.

The decade-long delay by the Church proved critical – and undermined the Church's efforts to influence politics. Ten years after the collapse of the communist regime, Church support was no longer needed to stabilize the political situation. The electoral threat the Church posed was neither widespread (only center-right and right-wing politicians had to fear the Church) nor deep (withdrawing support for democracy would damage the Church's position and its claims of national interests more than it would destabilize Lithuanian democracy). For example, the Church objected vociferously to Soviet-era abortion laws, and its representatives sat on committees that put forth bills to restrict abortion access in the late 2000s. A 2008 bill would limit abortion to situations where pregnancy was a risk to the life or health of the mother, or a consequence of a criminal act. The bill was justified by both "the low moral level of society and a critical demographic situation" in Lithuania. However, it failed in parliament: the bill, and several others were declared unconstitutional by the parliamentary legal affairs committee. The Church also pushed unsuccessfully for the inclusion of religion in the public schools: it was offered only if the parents actively petitioned for it. Finally, the Church in Lithuania did not set the terms of debate on same-sex marriage: parliamentarians who opposed these policies did so on the basis of *secular* social conservatism.

In Croatia, the fusion of nation and religion did not translate into policy influence because the Church could not exchange policy concessions for ensuring social stability. Both the communist party and the opposition represented the nation, and the threat came not from social instability, but from the burgeoning conflict with Serbia. Further, Croatia illustrates how the fusion of religion and identity is dependent on the Church remaining nonpartisan and credibly "national." The Church initially lent its support to the Croatian Democratic Union (Hrvatska Demokratska Zajednica, or HDZ). The Church saw the HDZ as akin to Solidarity or Sajudis – a national movement that posed the critical alternative to the communist party, and the main guarantor of Church rights. This error was largely the result of the HDZ's self-representation as a national force rather than a narrow party, which justified its subsequent monopolization of Croatian political competition (Mojzes 1994, 132). Unlike Solidarity or Sajudis (or the Slovak KDH), the HDZ arose independently of the Church, and with an autonomous power base it saw little reason to give the Church formal access to policy making.

Nonetheless, the fusion of nation and religion made the Church a useful ally for the HDZ. Church leaders opened the parliamentary meetings, politicians and clergy were frequently portrayed together in the media, and both sides reinforced the notion that Church, nation, and the newly independent Croat state were symbiotically linked (Mojzes 1994, 132). Tuđman "never fail[ed] to bring up another of the church's virtues: its strong link with the Croatian people ... interlacing the church with the very idea of Croatian statehood and nationhood" (Lovrenovic 1998). As Croatia entered the wars of Yugoslav succession (1991–98), this embrace became increasingly stifling for the Church. Cardinal Franjo Kuharić attempted to maintain a distance from the party beginning with the Bosnian war in 1993, and his successor, Josip Bozanić, criticized Tuđman in his inaugural Christmas address of 1997. Even so, the Church and the state promoted the cult of Cardinal Alojzije Stepinać, a wartime Croat nationalist, and high-ranking clergy continued to bless political and military events. The church "rarely ... expressed its disapproval, and not even when the government was accused of crimes against humanity, violation of human rights, and war crimes" (Gruenfelder 2000).

In return, the Church obtained some policy concessions. The HDZ government introduced Catholic instruction as an optional subject in public schools. The HDZ also concluded four agreements in 1996–97 between Croatia and the Holy See (On Legal Questions, On Economic Issues, On Spiritual Care in Military and Police Forces, and On Co-operation in the Field of Education and Culture). In 1998, the government signed an agreement with the Croatian Bishops' Conference as part of its treaties with the Vatican, stating that the schooling system "must take into account the deeply rooted Catholic tradition in the Croatian cultural heritage" and undertake "appropriate religious and cultural initiatives and programs" (Lovrenovic 1998). Financial support for the Church mandated by the same treaties, however, proved too costly and controversial to be implemented.

Nor was the Church's institutional access to policy making strong and pervasive enough to successfully promote its policy agenda. Policy concessions were less than what either the Polish or the Lithuanian Churches achieved – partly because of the Church's more limited institutional access as a result of the HDZ's independent authority, and partly because its embrace of a particular party made it dependent on the HDZ rather than vice versa. One ironic result of the HDZ government embrace was that the Church lost its policy influence. Once its old ally, the HDZ, lost power in 2000, the Church was seen as having discredited itself through its support for the HDZ, and was largely unable to affect either the rhetoric or the substance of policy. Major political parties distanced themselves from the Church, with even the HDZ eventually severing the close links as part of its campaign to reinvent itself as a fully democratic party. The Church then tried to exert greater policy pressure, but instead further lost leverage. A 2004 controversy over a ban on trade on Sundays pitted the HDZ, the Catholic Church, and their allies against the Croatian People's Party (HNS) and the Social Democratic Party (SDP). The Church also opposed sex education in public schools, much as in Poland and in Slovakia. In 2005, it called for a ban on abortion. However, it was unable to affect either public debates or policy outcomes, and political parties rejected its proposals (Loza 2007).

Turning to the mixed Catholic-Protestant countries, the Slovak Catholic Church was initially "studiously neutral" in politics (Tancerova 2002), despite the courting of the Christian Democratic Party to form closer ties. The efforts of the dominant governing party, the Movement for a Democratic Slovakia (HZDS), largely stopped at the October 1993 restitution law (*Transition*, April 5, 1996; Haughton 2005, 38). Already very popular, the HZDS had little to gain from being closely identified with the Church. As a result, the Catholic Church became publicly involved in politics only in 1995, when it came out in support of President Michal Kováč in his conflict with the increasingly authoritarian Prime Minister Vladimír Mečiar (*Transition*, April 5, 1996). Subsequently, after considerable debate and repeated Church efforts, the Concordat treaty with the Vatican was signed in late 2000. However, it failed to address abortion, divorce, or registered partnerships. It was not until 2002 that "important issues were gradually being introduced into the public discourse ... including reproductive rights, representation of women in the public sphere, and the role of the church in society, among others" (*Transitions Online* 15, 2003).

This belated entry would have had little impact were it not for the exigencies of party politics. The Slovak Church tended to *follow* rather than set the terms of the debate, as illustrated by the issue of abortion. The battles over abortion that raged were initiated by the Christian Democrats rather than Church pressure and did not invoke Church support initially. As late as 2001, when the

Slovak Christian Democratic Party (KDH) attempted to regulate the liberal abortion provisions, the Church itself did not want to take a public stance for fear of scuppering other constitutional reforms (*Transition*, February 12–18, 2001). However, after two years of increasingly successful Christian Democrat Party efforts (and with no other political allies), the emboldened Church declared in 2003 that supporters of abortion would be excommunicated. In 2002, the KDH went to the Constitutional Court to argue that Slovakia's liberal abortion law was unconstitutional, causing a coalition crisis with one of its partners, the Alliance for a New Citizen (ANO). ANO pushed through the amendment in parliament with the help of the opposition, and KDH declared it would leave the coalition if the law passed. Finally, in December 2007, the Constitutional Court declared abortion on demand up to the twelfth week constitutional, and abortion for genetic reasons thereafter.

As the KDH split into conservative and more liberal factions, the conservatives sought Church support by legislating Church preferences on abortion, religion in schools, stem cell research restrictions, and same-sex marriage regulations, and then seeking the Church's imprimatur. There was little broader consensus about the role of the Church in politics, and not even its moral authority was taken for granted. Church actions were met with considerable backlash. When Archbishop Jan Sokol criticized the SMER Party's political advertising (which featured "unchristian" nudity), party leader (and after 2006, Prime Minister) Jan Fico immediately lashed out that "this is unprecedented interference by the church into politics ... Instead of interfering in this way, Mr. Sokol should say how much property the church got back through restitution" (Tancerova 2002) – a pointed allusion to the return of lucrative Church property after the collapse of communism. Similarly, the papal visit in 2003 met with controversy over the costs of providing security and accommodations (Tancerova 2003); by contrast, *all* Polish politicians remained silent on the costs of the repeated papal visits to Poland and did not castigate Church officials. In short, the Slovak Church had to rely on specific political allies to make any gains rather than on popular authority and the direct and immediate political repercussions that it could bring.

If the Church achieved its policy goals in Slovakia belatedly, it was entirely dependent on the good graces of its political allies in Hungary. Here, the churches were not able to frame political debates, and their policy achievements were incidental to their efforts. The Hungarian Church attempted to frame policy in terms that fused religious and national concerns once democratic politics returned. After 1989, both the conservative government and the Hungarian Church raised objections to abortion and same-sex marriage in national terms: abortion would threaten the integrity and continuation of the Hungarian nation by lowering the number of Hungarians. In the words of the Catholic priest who headed the Hungarian League for the Defense of the Unborn, "the number of Hungarians is dropping every year" (*New York Times*, January 5, 1992, accessed January 11, 2009). Subsequently, the Church opposed same-sex marriage on the grounds that it would "undermine society's health" in addition to violating natural law (*Catholic Online*, December 29, 2007, accessed February 2, 2011).

Yet these attempts to frame political debates met with little resonance. Actual policy proposals came *before* the Church began to agitate: the Church was reiterating the terms of the debate initially set by the Hungarian Democratic Forum (MDF), the senior governing party. Proclerical and anticlerical camps continued their conflict, and no ready champion of Church interests could be found despite the 1990–94 government participation of the Christian Democratic Party (KDNP), formally allied with the Catholic Church. The 1994–98 socialist government openly advocated the separation of church and state, further undermining Church policy efforts. By 1998, most proclerical initiatives came not from the clergy, but from Viktor Orban, the prime minister and leader of the conservative-nationalist Fidesz party. Fidesz did so for two reasons: first, the Christian Democratic KDNP had earlier fallen apart, and many of its members joined Fidesz, strengthening pro-Church currents within Fidesz. Second, Fidesz elites gained both legitimation and an arena for political mobilization, as open-air masses were held for Orban and his family, for example. Nonetheless, few public policy changes resulted, thanks both to an activist Constitutional Court and to the lack of support within Fidesz ranks for what were seen as controversial policy initiatives. In short, both the Slovak and the Hungarian Churches were dependent on political parties to achieve their goals. The Slovak Church found an eager ally in the Christian Democrats, a party keen on exploiting the Church's political capital (the best the small party could do under its circumstances). Meanwhile, the Hungarian Church could rely only on the incidental mercies of conservative parties eager to pursue their own political goals.

Finally, the Czech story illustrates how the conflict between Church and nation, and the continuing failure to symbolically protect the nation, can have far-reaching consequences. Rather than pushing a moral agenda or a claim of national representation, the Church focused on defending its own interests after 1989 (and specifically, unsuccessfully demanding the restitution of its property). Its protests against same-sex marriage in 2006 had no impact, and it failed to establish any policy issues as lying within its moral authority.

In short, the different levels of fusion between nation and religion were sustained by years of clashes between state and society and the Church's response to these. Yet, if long-term communist repression turned some churches into national representatives, state-society crises turned them into legislative players as well. Two distinct historical processes unfolded. One – a gradual development of moral authority as the Church proved itself time and again a defender of the nation against communist state repression – took decades. By contrast, the other – institutional access – was a rapid and contingent outcome of both state and society turning to the Church and its moral authority to maintain social peace, and emerged only periodically and in the period of late communism and in the wake of the transition.

Conclusion

The historical fusion of nation (not state) and religion occurred in both communist and precommunist guises. Yet this is only one strand of the story of historical legacies in the relationship between religion and the state in postcommunist states, and by itself an insufficient explanation for policy influence. The fusion of national and religious identities resulted in two distinct legacies: a) a diffuse but fairly robust moral authority; and b) a direct but far more short-lived institutional access. While both survived the rupture of the regime collapse in 1989, it was the latter – the churches' pragmatic and direct insinuation into opposition movements and government policy-making institutions – that was critical to translating fusion into influence on public policy. The institutional access was a legacy of the very late communist period, the 1980s – yet it was indubitably a communist inheritance, not a post-1989 creation. This was the hidden side of the fusion of nation and religion, as all political forces relied on the churches to ensure political stability. The result was that the churches could retain influence (and adherents) even as they advocated highly unpopular policies, and even as ever-growing majorities denounced church influence on politics.

In effect, the fusion of nation and religion functioned in two temporalities: one that developed and sustained the moral authority of the churches over decades of interacting with society, and another, far more recent one, where societal crises led to the churches' direct institutional access to policy making. Both the older legacy of moral authority, and the more recent legacy of church institutional access, were powerful forces in influencing public policy, but operated in different levels of society and on distinct timelines.

Notes

1. These results hold across countries, see Grzymala-Busse, forthcoming. An average 50 percent of respondents wanted the Church to have less influence on politics throughout the 1990s and 2000s in Poland, and 78 percent of respondents did not wish the Church to be politically active. *CBOS*. 2007. "*Opinie o dzialalnosci Kosciola*," Komunikat z Badan, Warsaw, March 2007. In the United States, 70 percent of respondents do not want churches to endorse political candidates (Pew Forum on Religion and Public Life, 2002, "Americans Struggle with Religion's Role at Home and Abroad," available at http://people-press.org/reports/pdf/150.pdf, accessed August 7, 2008). Majorities believe it is wrong for churches to speak out on politics (51 percent) and for clergymen to address politics from the pulpit (68 percent) (Pew Forum on Religion and Public Life, 2000, "Religion and Politics: The Ambivalent Majority," available at http://people-press.org/reports/pdf/32.pdf, accessed August 7, 2008).
2. Survey measures of desired influence are from the World Values Survey and the International Social Survey Programme, correlated with log GDP per capita from the Penn World Tables.

3 Abortion is defined as "unrestricted" if abortion is available freely up to 12 weeks of pregnancy, as was the case under Soviet-era laws. It is "restricted" if access is more constrained than it was under the communist era.
4 Either the state funds religious schools, or mandatory religion/ ethics classes are taught in public schools.

References

Agnew, Hugh LeCaine. 1993. *Origins of the Czech National Renascence*. Pittsburgh, PA: University of Pittsburgh Press.

Anderson, John. 2003. "Catholicism and Democratic Consolidation in Spain and Poland." In John T. S. Madeley and Zsolt Enyedi, eds., *Church and State in Contemporary Europe: The Chimera of Neutrality*. London: Frank Cass, 137–56.

Bruce, Steve. 2000. "The Supply-Side Model of Religion: The Nordic and Baltic States," *Journal for the Scientific Study of Religion*, 39(1): 32–46.

Burleigh, Michael. 2007. *Sacred Causes*. New York: MacMillan.

Casanova, Jose. 1994. *Public Religions in the Modern World*. Chicago, IL: University of Chicago Press.

Chrypiński, Vincent. 1990. "The Catholic Church in Poland, 1944–1989." In Pedro Ramet, ed., *Catholicism and Politics in Communist Societies*. Durham, NC: Duke University Press, 117–41.

Cohen, Shari. 1999. *Politics Without a Past*. Durham, NC: Duke University Press.

Darden, Keith and Anna Grzymala-Busse. 2006. "The Great Divide: Literacy, Nationalism, and the Communist Collapse," *World Politics*, 59(1): 83–115.

de Swaan, Abram. 1988. *In Care of the State: Health Care, Education and Welfare in Europe and the USA in the Modern Era*. New York: Oxford University Press.

Eberts, Mirella and Peter Torok. 2001. "The Catholic Church and Post-Communist Elections: Hungary and Poland Compared." In Irena Borowik and Tomka Miklós, eds., *Religion and Social Change in Post-Communist Europe*. Krakow: NOMOS, 125–47.

Enyedi, Zsolt. 2003. "The Contested Politics of Positive Neutrality in Hungary." In John T. S. Madeley and Enyedi, Zsolt, eds., *Church and State in Contemporary Europe: The Chimera of Neutrality*. London: Frank Cass, 157–76.

Froese, Paul and Steven Pfaff. 2001. "Replete and Desolate Markets: Poland, East Germany, and the New Religious Paradigm." *Social Forces* 80(2): 481–507.

Gill, Anthony. 1998. *Rendering Unto Caesar: The Catholic Church and the State in Latin America*. Chicago, IL: University of Chicago Press.

Girnius, Kestutis. 1989. "Catholicism and Nationalism in Lithuania." In Pedro Ramet, ed., *Religion and Nationalism in Soviet and East European Politics*. Durham, NC: Duke University Press, 109–37.

Gowin, Jaroslaw. 1995. *Kosciol po Komunizmie*. Krakow: Znak.

Gruenfelder, Anna Maria. 2000. "The Church and Croats," *Central European Review* May 15.

Grzymala-Busse, Anna. 2012. "Why Comparative Politics Needs to take Religion More Seriously." *Annual Review of Political Science*, 15, 421–42.

   Forthcoming. *States and Sinners: How Religion Influences Democratic Policy*. Book ms. University of Michigan.

Hamplová, Dana and Zdenek R. Nešpor. 2009. "Invisible Religion in 'Non-believing' Country: The Case of the Czech Republic." *Social Compass* 56(4): 581–97.
Haughton, Timothy. 2005. *Constraints and Opportunities of Leadership in Post-Communist Europe*. Aldershot, Hants: Ashgate.
Htun, Mala. 2003. *Sex and the State*. Cambridge: Cambridge University Press.
Jelínek, Yeshayahu. 1976. *The Parish Republic: Hlinka's Slovak People's Party, 1939–1945*. Boulder, CO: East European Monographs.
Kepel, Gilles. 1995. *The Revenge of God*. University Park: Pennsylvania State Press.
Kilp, Alar. 2005. "Catholicism and Democracy in Post-Communist Europe," Paper prepared for the 3rd ECPR Conference, September, Budapest.
Leff, Carol Skalnik. 1988. *National Conflict in Czechoslovakia: The Making and Remaking of a State, 1918–1987*. Princeton, NJ: Princeton University Press.
Lovrenovic, Ivan. 1998. "Sympathy for the Devil." *Transitions* December 15.
Loza, Tihomir. 2007. "Strange Bedfellows." *Transitions* November 20.
Luxmoore, Jonathan and Babiuch, Jolanta. 1999. *The Vatican and The Red Flag*. London: Geoffrey Chapman.
Martin, David. 1991. "The Secularization Issue: Prospect and Retrospect." *British Journal of Sociology* 42(3): 465–74.
  2005 *On Secularization: Towards a Revised General Theory*. Aldershot: Ashgate.
Misovic, Jan. 2001. *Víra v Dejinách Zemí Koruny Ceské*. Prague: Slon.
Mojzes, Paul. 1994. *The Yugoslav Inferno*. New York: Continuum.
Morawska, Ewa. 1995. "The Polish Roman Catholic Church Unbound." In Stephen Hanson and Willfried Spohn, eds., *Can Europe Work?* Seattle: University of Washington Press.
Norris, Pippa and Ronald Inglehart. 2004. *Sacred and Secular: Religion and Politics Worldwide*. Cambridge: Cambridge University Press.
Ochmański, Jerzy. 1982. *Historia Litwy*. Wroclaw: Ossolineum.
Ramet, Sabrina. 1998. *Nihil Obstat: Religion, Politics, and Social Change in East-Central Europe and Russia*. Durham, NC: Duke University Press.
Reban, Milan. 1990. "Catholic Church in Czechoslovakia," in Pedro Ramet, ed. *Catholicism and Politics in Communist Societies*. Durham, NC: Duke University Press, 142–55.
Sahliyeh, Emile, ed. 1990. *Religious Resurgence and Politics in the Contemporary World*. Albany, NY: SUNY Press.
Schanda, Balazs. 2003. "Religion and State in the Candidate Countries to the European Union: Issues Concerning Religion and State in Hungary." *Sociology of Religion* 64(3): 333–48.
Stark, Rodney. 1999. "Secularization, RIP." *Sociology of Religion* 60(3): 249–73.
Stark, Rodney and Laurence Iannaccone. 1996. "Recent Religious Declines in Quebec, Poland, and the Netherlands: A Theory Vindicated." *Journal for the Scientific Study of Religion*, 33(3): 431–44.
Tancerova, Barbora. 2002. "State vs. Church?" *Transitions Online*, September 20.
Tancerova. Barbora. 2003. "Catholic yet Liberal?" *Transitions Online*, September 11, 2003.
Torańska, Teresa. 1994. *My*. Warsaw: Most.
Vardys, Stanely and Judith B. Sedaitis. 1997. *Lithuania: The Rebel Nation*. Boulder, CO: Westview Press.

Wittenberg, Jason. 2006. *Crucibles of Political Loyalty.* Cambridge: Cambridge University Press.

Zrinščak, Siniša. 2001. "Religion and Social Justice in Post-Communist Croatia." In Irena Borowik and Tomka Miklós, eds., *Religion and Social Change in Post-Communist Europe.* Krakow: NOMOS, 181–94.

Zubrzycki, Genevieve. 2006. *The Crosses of Auschwitz.* Chicago, IL: University of Chicago Press.

10

Soviet Nationalities Policies and the Discrepancy between Ethnocultural Identification and Language Practice in Ukraine

Volodymyr Kulyk

One of the peculiar consequences of Soviet nationalities policy in Ukraine is a large-scale discrepancy between ethnic identification and language use.[1] This discrepancy is the result of the interaction between, on the one hand, policies promoting the use of Russian as a language of social mobility and interethnic integration and, on the other, policies promoting identification with primordially conceived ethnic groups and their eponymous languages. While the former policies gradually increased the number of ethnic Ukrainians and members of non-Russian minorities speaking mainly Russian in their everyday life, the latter policies impeded a change of ethnic and linguistic identity in alignment with language practice. Although the discrepancy was to be found in many other parts of the former USSR, in Ukraine its scale was larger than in most of the other union republics that became independent in 1991 (and comparable to patterns found in the lower-level autonomous units within the Russian Federation), primarily because of the more aggressive linguistic Russification of the late Soviet decades. Remarkably, this discrepancy persists in post-Soviet Ukraine, even though its policies with regard to ethnicity and language differ significantly from those of the Soviet regime. The continuation of this phenomenon in a radically different political and cultural context warrants its classification as a legacy of the communist decades, in the sense of "a durable causal relationship between earlier institutions and practices and those of the present in the wake of a macrohistorical rupture" as proposed by Kotkin and Beissinger in their introduction to this volume.

My inquiry into the emergence and persistence of a discrepancy between ethnolinguistic identity and language practice does not stem from a normative belief that the two should necessarily be congruent, but rather from an empirical observation that in most countries they tend to be, suggesting that there must be some reasons why Ukraine and some other post-Soviet societies stand apart. In the following sections, I will examine the origins of this mismatch and the reasons for its persistence in post-Soviet Ukraine. But first it is worth describing in some detail the phenomenon itself, both in Ukraine and elsewhere.

The Phenomenon of Discrepant Ethnic and Linguistic Markers

A lack of correspondence between ethnicity and language was first discussed by scholars in the 1970s as a widespread phenomenon in Soviet society after the censuses of 1959 and 1970 had shown an increasing percentage of non-Russians who declared Russian as their native language. The interpretation of this percentage as a measure of linguistic assimilation was facilitated by the finding that the share of those claiming Russian as their native language was considerably higher among populations with more interest in and exposure to the Russian language, such as urban residents, youth, and Slavs. Moreover, it generally increased with every census as more people grew affected by Russification processes (Silver 1974). But the overall level of Russification seemed rather modest: according to the 1970 data, even in cities the share of those whose declared native language differed from their ethnic identification did not exceed a quarter of the population in any union republic. The figures for those residents of Ukraine identifying as Ukrainians and claiming Russian as their native language (second highest among union republics after Belarus) were 17 percent in the cities and 23 percent in the capital (Silver 1975, 592–97). The situation did not change significantly during the two following decades: the last Soviet census of 1989 revealed the level of acceptance of Russian as the native language among those claiming Ukrainian nationality to be 12 percent in Ukraine as a whole and 19 percent in the cities. In all but two other union republics, the proportion of those urban residents claiming the titular ethnicity of the republic but declaring Russian as their native language was below 4 percent (Kaiser 1994, 273, 276).

It was the obvious discrepancy between these modest figures for titulars claiming Russian as their native language and the observed linguistic practice in many big cities of Ukraine and some other republics (i.e., the actual predominance of Russian on the streets) that made Soviet scholars and their Western colleagues begin to reconsider the meaning of the census declaration of native language. Most scholars came to believe that this declaration reflected not so much communicative competence or linguistic practice as loyalty to the ethnic group associated with the language. Pointing to this "psychological and self-identificatory content of the 'native tongue' category" in the Soviet census, Rasma Karklins challenged the "frequently encountered argument that the generally high percentage of non-Russians regarding the language of their name-giving nationality as their native tongue indicates a low level of linguistic assimilation." Rather, she argued, "it indicates a high level of ethnic self-assurance" (1980, 421).

This conceptual decoupling of native language and language of everyday use led scholars to realize that there was a much wider gap between language practice and ethnic identification than measured in the census (that is, a much greater presence of Russian-language usage in the non-Russian republics, particularly Ukraine, than the census data indicated). This gap was fully revealed by the mass surveys that became routine only after the breakup of the USSR. According to an annual series of surveys by the Kyiv International Institute of Sociology (KIIS), in terms of the language people prefer to use in communication with a supposedly bilingual and accommodating interviewer, the share of Ukrainian speakers in the country's population as a whole is less than half (44 percent, according to the aggregated data of the surveys between 1991 and 1994) – a huge difference from almost two-thirds (65 percent in the 1989 census) who considered Ukrainian their native language. The survey data also showed a sharp regional differentiation in language preference patterns, with preference for using Ukrainian ranging (according to 2003 data) from an overwhelming 95 percent in the west to only 16 percent in the east and 8 percent in the south (Khmelko 2004).

While it is debatable how much this "language of convenience" reflects the respondents' everyday preference as distinct from their perception of the appropriate language for interaction with an institutionally empowered stranger (in this case, the survey canvasser), other data show that even in the most intimate and unconstrained context of the family, Ukrainian by no means predominates. An annual survey series by the Institute of Sociology (IS) of the National Academy of Sciences of Ukraine has revealed that the Ukrainian language was exclusively used in family communication by slightly more than a third of respondents (37 percent in 1992). The share of people exclusively speaking Russian in the home was not much smaller (29 percent), and the remaining portion of the population used both of these languages (32 percent). Remarkably, the preference for Ukrainian in the family communication has not become much stronger in the years since Ukraine became an independent state and Ukrainian was granted the status as the country's sole official (state) language. At the same time, the use of Russian in the home significantly increased by the 2000s at the expense of the use of both languages (Resul'taty 2006, 482). Similarly, the supposed language of convenience during these years shifted only slightly toward Ukrainian, which was, according to the aggregate data of 2000–03, preferred by 48 percent of respondents, as opposed to 52 percent preferring Russian (Khmelko 2004).

Russian thus did not become less prominent in the language practice of Ukraine's residents. Nor did their identification with Ukrainian nationality or Ukrainian language weaken. In the IS annual surveys, the share of respondents declaring Ukrainian as their native language oscillated between 59 percent and 64 percent, not much lower than the level indicated by the 1989 Soviet census (Resul'taty 2006, 482). In the first post-Soviet census of 2001 (All-Ukrainian n/d), this share even slightly increased to 68 percent, although the increase was twice as small as that of self-declared ethnic Ukrainians (to 78 percent, mostly at the expense of those who identified themselves as Russians). Some scholars argued that the retention of Ukrainian as native language confirmed the tautological nature of this characteristic vis-à-vis ethnicity (nationality) and therefore considered it redundant (Arel 2002a), while others disregarded this characteristic in view of its conceptual ambiguity, that is, the varied interpretations that respondents were likely to have made of the census question (Shul'ga 2009). However, focus group discussions administered by the Hromadska Dumka (HD) center in 2006 in five Ukrainian cities showed that while participants did attach different meanings to the notion of native language, it was nonetheless meaningful, important, and stable for almost all of them (even though some tried to reconcile their ethnocultural attachment and language practice by declaring both Ukrainian and Russian languages as native). Moreover, a regression analysis of the results of a survey conducted by the same center in 2006 revealed that native language had at least as strong an impact as everyday language on the respondents' preferences with regard to various aspects of language policy – and even more remarkably, with regard to other identity-related matters such as foreign policy and historical memory (Kulyk 2011).

The relative stability of both ethnocultural identity and language practice since independence means that a discrepancy between them remains roughly as large as it was at the end of the Soviet period. While most surveys did not inquire about all relevant characteristics or did not measure them on commensurate scales, the Hromadska Dumka survey of 2006 enables comparisons of the distributions by the ethnic and linguistic dimensions of identity on the one hand and by language identity and practice on the other. To be sure, these distributions differ from those obtained in censuses and many surveys using census-like categories, as the HD survey also allowed mixed identities and complex language repertoires (e.g., both the Ukrainian and Russian languages as native or using both of them "equally" in one's everyday life). However, the use of the same scale for all three variables makes it possible to compare not only the exclusive "flanks" but also the hybrid "middles" and the relative strengths of hybrid choices. Table 10.1 presents the distributions for declared nationality, native language, and the main language of everyday use. As differences between the figures in adjacent columns show, the two gaps turn out to be almost identical – in each of them the loss in the Ukrainian part being transformed into roughly equal gains for the Russian and hybrid components. With few hybrid responses to the nationality question, the share of ethnic Ukrainians matches the census result, while the considerable hybridity in native language responses comes exclusively at the cost of Ukrainian ones, with the figure for Russian being even higher than in the census. The hybridity is the greatest in the distribution by everyday language, which also corresponds to the results of the KIIS surveys in that the Ukrainian speakers are somewhat fewer than the Russian speakers.

While it is clear from Table 10.1 that most of the people having ethnolinguistic characteristics at variance with one another are ethnic Ukrainians

TABLE 10.1. *The Distribution of Respondents in the 2006 Survey in Ukraine by Nationality, Native Language and Everyday Language (in Percentage)*

	Nationality	Native Language	Everyday Language
Ukrainian	77.0	55.5	35.3
Both	0.7	11.1	23.5
Russian	20.3	32.0	40.3
Other	2.0	1.4	0.9

who use mainly Russian in everyday life, statistical analysis of the survey data also reveals the spatial and social distribution of this group. By comparing the mean values of the nationality, native language, and everyday language variables (ordered on the three-point scale from Ukrainian to both to Russian, with other identities/languages excluded) for various subsamples, I have ascertained that the discrepancy between ethnicity and language is the largest in the eastern and southern regions and in large cities. These linguistic environments contributed to the predominant use of Russian by people who, at the same time, usually retained their Ukrainian linguistic and/or ethnic identity. Moreover, a comparison of mean values for different age categories shows that younger respondents are more likely than older ones to *both* identify as Ukrainians and speak primarily Russian. The discrepancy between ethnocultural identity and language practice is thus larger among the younger generation, and hence is unlikely to shrink in the immediate future.

A similar discrepancy can be found in a number of other parts of the former USSR. The late Soviet censuses and post-Soviet sociolinguistic studies indicate that the largest share of those claiming the titular nationality but considering Russian as their native language and/or speaking primarily Russian in everyday life is to be found in Belarus, Kazakhstan, and (even more so) in Russia's "national" autonomies (Kaiser 1994, 273; Brown 2005; Smagulova 2008). Not in all cases is there enough data to convincingly demonstrate a discrepancy and examine its relation to demographic characteristics, as censuses do not usually inquire about language practice, and language-related surveys are relatively rare and limited in what they ask. The best evidence has been provided by the so-called Colton-Hough survey, which was conducted in sixteen autonomous republics of the Russian Federation in 1993 and thus, as far as ethnolinguistic categorizations and language practices were concerned, reflected the impact of Soviet policies as modified by late Soviet nationalist mobilizations (cf. Gorenburg 2001). This survey differed from the 2006 Ukrainian one in that it limited the list of options that the respondents could choose to census-like exclusive categories and did not ask a question on the language(s) of everyday use in general, but rather inquired about the respondents' communication with their parents, spouses, and children. Table 10.2 presents the data for nationality, native language, and two aspects of language use for eight

TABLE 10.2. *The Distribution of Respondents in the 1993 Survey in Russia's Autonomies by Nationality, Native Language and Two Aspects of Language Use (in Percentage; N/A Responses Excluded)*

	Nationality		Native Language		Language Spoken to Mother		Language Spoken to Children	
	Titular	Russian	Titular	Russian	Titular	Russian	Titular	Russian
Chuvashia	68.8	23.0	61.6	31.8	59.5	34.1	40.4	56.1
Tuva	65.3	30.7	64.9	32.1	63.0	34.6	59.4	40.0
Kalmykia	50.5	47.9	47.9	43.8	23.6	69.9	11.0	85.4
Tatarstan	47.3	44.2	46.9	47.8	40.5	54.8	30.6	67.5
Sakha	38.1	46.8	38.2	54.0	36.4	55.6	33.0	65.3
Mari El	35.4	53.8	31.2	61.8	27.7	66.1	17.8	80.4
Buriatia	23.8	69.9	22.3	75.6	18.9	79.2	13.8	85.9
Karelia	20.4	63.7	12.4	81.7	13.8	79.9	3.8	94.7

republics. Despite a large variation in the degree of discrepancy between ethnic identification and language use that cannot be explained by differences in the share of the titular nationality relative to Russians, the direction of the discrepancy is the same in all republics. Moreover, in most republics the discrepancy is considerably larger in cities than in villages and among younger respondents than among older ones.

At the same time, discrepancies between ethnicity and language are by no means limited to the former USSR. Two kinds of ethnolinguistic situations seem to be particularly likely to produce such discrepancies. On the one hand, migration to other countries rapidly changes the communication repertoires of people who find themselves in a different linguistic environment, but does not necessarily deprive them of distinct ethnic identity; hence societies with large numbers of recent migrants are often characterized by considerable ethnolinguistic mismatch. For example, while 35 million people asserted Hispanic ethnicity in the 2000 U.S. survey, only 28 million reported speaking Spanish at home, either as the only language or along with others (Grieco and Cassidy 2001; Shin and Bruno 2003). On the other hand, in many societies local languages were largely abandoned in favor of those of foreign rulers, but the descendants of their former speakers retain "autochthonous" ethnic identity and even try (usually with limited success) to "revive" their perceived group languages. Thus the eponymous languages of Ireland and Basque Country are spoken by a clear minority of those who identify themselves as Irish and Basque, respectively. However, these two types of situations are different from that found in the post-Soviet states in that they lack the kind of institutionalized linguistic and ethnic identities with which language practice could be juxtaposed. Hardly any state in the world contributed as much to the formation of a discrepancy between ethnocultural identities and language practices through its long-term policies aimed at pushing these identities and practices in opposite directions as did the USSR.

Origins of the Legacy: Soviet Nationalities and Language Policies

I turn now to examine more thoroughly Soviet policies with regard to ethnic and linguistic identity on the one hand and to language practices on the other, focusing first and foremost on their specific features and their consequences in Ukraine. The origins of these policies lay in the 1920s, when the Soviet leadership responded to the power of non-Russian nationalisms – which had been vividly demonstrated during the revolution and civil war – by "systematically promoting the national consciousness of its ethnic minorities and establishing for them many of the characteristic institutional forms of the nation-state" (Martin 2001, 1). The best-known manifestations of this establishment were the creation of a multilayered structure of national territories, the promotion of national elites into positions of leadership in the respective territories, and support for the development and wider use of non-Russian languages. Moreover, as Martin emphasizes, the instillation of national consciousness also included "the aggressive promotion of symbolic markers of national identity" such as folklore, classic literature, commemoration of historical events, and so on (2001, 13). While initially meant as a response to already existing national feelings of the non-Russians, the indigenization policies of the 1920s and early 1930s quickly expanded to include the *creation* of mass-level national consciousness among those groups where it had previously been limited to parts of the elites. The state ascription of ethnonational identity to all its citizens was complete with the inclusion of the nationality question in the first Soviet general census of 1926 and the introduction of the respective entry in internal passports in 1932. Originally meant to be a matter of individual consciousness and thus choice, nationality was transformed into an inheritable and virtually unchangeable characteristic, at least from the point of view of the state (Zaslavsky and Luryi 1979; Hirsch 1997).

Although the Bolsheviks considered language one of the most important traits of nationality, they ascribed linguistic identity separately from ethnic identity. While introducing the census category "nationality," the Soviet leaders, upon the recommendation of ethnographers, retained the question on native language, with the purpose of registering the extent of tsarist assimilation which, they believed, should be undone by teaching all citizens the languages of "their" nationalities (Hirsch 1997; Arel 2002b). The promotion of acquisition and use of numerous non-Russian languages, first and foremost the titular languages of the union republics and lower-level units, was a crucial component of the indigenization policy. The promotion was designed to include the codification of languages, making the indigenous and nonindigenous populations literate and professionally competent in them, bringing these languages to the workplace on both the elite and mass levels, and establishing cultural facilities for the (re)production of the languages' knowledge, use, and legitimacy.

For less than a decade during its relatively determined implementation, this policy brought truly impressive results, even though it failed to achieve some of its goals. In Ukraine, while more than a dozen languages were used in education, the media, and administrative bodies of various levels, the main result of the policy was an increasing use of the titular language in those domains where Russian had dominated during the tsarist rule. Not only did literacy in Ukrainian increase drastically, but Ukrainian also became the main language of primary and secondary education, so that even ethnic Russians were partly schooled in Ukrainian. Even more impressive was the change in the media, with an overwhelming majority of books and newspapers published in Ukrainian by the end of the 1920s (Krawchenko 1985, 86–98; Martin 2001, 106–10). Moreover, the titular language was gradually introduced in most institutions of higher education in what Martin called "the most successful effort to Ukrainize a recalcitrant Russian urban island" (2001, 112).

At the same time, two other crucial urban domains of language use – the factory and the office – remained predominantly Russian-speaking, despite a considerable influx of ethnic Ukrainian villagers in the course of industrialization. Martin argues that "a Ukrainian peasant arriving in a major Ukrainian city in 1932 would most likely be compelled to adopt Russian as his workplace language" (2001, 122). In his view, the main reason for the failure of comprehensive linguistic Ukrainianization lay in the combination of the passive resistance of the Russian and russified urban population and the party leadership's refusal to pursue a hard-line approach similar to that pursued in areas that were its top priorities, collectivization and industrialization. Instead of the titular language becoming dominant in all domains of public life, a bilingual environment emerged in Ukraine where "Russian would be the dominant language in the economic, industrial, and hard-line political spheres, whereas Ukrainian would predominate in the cultural, rural, and soft-line political spheres" (2001, 123).

Since 1933, a rather radical change in the regime's priorities brought about rapid strengthening of the Russian-language component of public life at the expense of Ukrainian and minority languages. Not only were educational and cultural facilities in languages other than Ukrainian and Russian mostly abolished, but the share of facilities working in the titular language decreased considerably during the 1930s. By the end of the decade, the share of Ukrainian-language book titles dropped by half. The educational changes were particularly perceptible in the eastern and southern cities where instruction in Ukrainian had drastically expanded only several years earlier. However, as of 1937, 83 percent of all school students in the republic were still learning in Ukrainian, which exceeded by 10 percent the share of ethnic Ukrainians in the population as a whole. At the same time, Russian was made a mandatory subject in all schools of the USSR regardless of the language of instruction to ensure general competence in the language that was seen as a unifying force within the multiethnic society. De-Ukrainianization of education was reinforced by the arrests or dismissal of thousands of teachers, scholars, administrators, and even college students during the Great Purge, which hit ethnic Ukrainians disproportionally hard. The same was true for creative intelligentsia, white-collar staff, and the communist party membership (Krawchenko 1985, 132–52). This asymmetrical terror signaled the regime's changed priorities to the elites and masses no less clearly than official statements.

Notwithstanding some oscillations in state policies between the aggressive promotion of Russian and the moderate support for Ukrainian, the decades after World War II were characterized by a gradual expansion of the former language and shrinking of the latter. The large-scale immigration from Russia and other republics, which the state encouraged and at times imposed, strengthened the role of Russian as a lingua franca, particularly in the cities where most migrants worked and lived. Moreover, the increasing subordination of Ukraine's industry to the union ministries imposed Russian as the language of documentation and thereby contributed to its spread in higher education and managerial communication. In turn, this pressured lower-level staff (largely consisting of Ukrainian-speaking migrants from the countryside) to accommodate their superiors' language preferences. At the same time, higher education also came to be largely subordinated to the union authorities and thus progressively russified, leading to an influx of students from outside of Ukraine (Krawchenko 1985, 222–26). Although these process affected all parts of Ukraine, in the western regions that had been incorporated by the USSR during World War II and experienced large-scale nationalist resistance, the regime tolerated a high level of national awareness and thus allowed the continued prevalence of Ukrainian in education, the media, and many other domains (Szporluk 2000).

This mutual reinforcement of various mechanisms of Russification was primarily characteristic of the cities, with their big factories, universities, and high-level offices. This was all the more so in the east and south where Russian had predominated in urban public and private life since tsarist times. Although Ukrainian continued to be used in many cultural and symbolic practices, its presence diminished steadily, as illustrated by book publishing, where in 1988 the share of Ukrainian-language titles was more than three times lower than the proportion of ethnic Ukrainians in the population (Kaiser 1994, 259). At the same time, the public use of Ukrainian in other domains could well be perceived in the cities outside the west as a sign of rural backwardness or a manifestation of nationalist opposition to the regime. This perception was once again reinforced in the 1960s to the early 1980s by the repression and public denunciation of hundreds of Ukrainian-speaking cultural elites protesting against what they viewed as comprehensive Russification of Ukraine (Krawchenko 1985, 250–53).

Although school education remained one of the most Ukrainian-speaking of public practices, it was also subject to Russification pressures from both

Soviet Nationalities Policies

the government and citizens, the latter influenced by the increasing use (and therefore usefulness) of Russian. A major shift in the education policy was introduced in 1958 by a new law on education that replaced the principle of instruction in the child's native language – usually understood in this regard as the language of his/her nationality – with the principle of free parental choice. Moreover, the law made the languages of the republics' titular nationalities an optional subject in Russian-language schools while retaining Russian as a mandatory subject in schools with other languages of instruction. This shift brought about a drastic decline in urban titular-language education in Ukraine from the 1960s through the mid-1980s, except for the western regions (Bilinsky 1962; Krawchenko 1985, 229–35). In the late 1970s, the regime made a more determined effort to increase knowledge of Russian in the "national" republics, which was primarily caused by its inadequate knowledge among non-Slavic populations, but nevertheless ended up having the most perceptible ramifications for knowledge and use of the titular languages in Ukraine and Belarus (Solchanyk 1982). As a result, 60 percent of ethnic Ukrainians in the 1989 census declared knowledge of Russian as a second language, but only 33 percent of Ukraine's Russians claimed knowledge of Ukrainian. Moreover, even among ethnic Ukrainians, 5 percent admitted to not knowing the language of their putative ethnic group (Natsional'nyi 1991, 78–79; Kaiser 1994, 290, 294).

These changes in language competence and use were not, however, accompanied by a commensurate change in linguistic and ethnic identities. Apart from cultural inertia, the predominant retention of these identities was made possible by public discourses and practices recognizing and supporting the existence of separate nations distinguishable first and foremost by "their" languages, even if individual members of the nations were not necessarily expected to speak these languages. Even at the times of the most active promotion of Russian language, glorification of the Russian nation, and prosecution of any forms of perceived non-Russian nationalism, the "continued existence of nationally defined communities and the legitimacy of their claims to particular cultural, territorial, economic and political identities ... was never in doubt" (Slezkine 1994, 441). Moreover, the revision of nationalities policy in the 1930s included, as Martin put it, "a dramatic turn away from the former Soviet view of nations as fundamentally modern constructs and toward an emphasis on the deep primordial roots of modern nations" (2001, 443). This primordialism was a consequence of a shift in emphasis from class to ethnically conceived people as a principal unit of social organization. The registration of nationality in passports (compounded with the prohibition of free choice and change of nationality) both reflected and reinforced the perception of ethnicity as a permanent hereditary characteristic, which, in turn, found its reflection in the continuity of census declarations.

However, not only did Soviet state policies reproduce the dominant perception of the existence of nations and individual belonging to one of them, but they also made this existence and belonging symbolically prominent and socially meaningful. The primordialist understanding was also manifested in official discourse and cultural policy by the increased attention to the national cultures of the Soviet peoples and glorification of their achievements, which, however, also had to be reconciled with the emphasis on multinational unity and the primacy of Russian culture as an asset of all "brotherly" peoples (Martin 2001, 443–57). It was these "internationalist" achievements of the Soviet nations that were featured in education, the official calendar, toponymy, and other domains. Moreover, nationality continued to be used as a criterion for affirmative action in many spheres, from the party leadership to university enrollment (although in Ukraine such use was not as pervasive as in some other republics). With some geographical and chronological variation, this promotion of ethnonational identities persisted until the very end of the USSR and paved the way for nationalist mobilization of many Soviet peoples, eventually resulting in the dissolution of the union.

As for the predominant declaration by the non-Russians in general and the Ukrainians in particular of their respective group languages as native (whether or not they actually spoke the language), it was facilitated by the presentation of languages as the most natural and valuable attributes of nations. This presentation continued in public discourse long after the promotion of the *use* of "national" languages ceased to be a priority within Soviet nationalities policy. It was supported by administrative, educational, media, and other institutions in the republics using their titular languages, usually along with Russian, whereby the former language appeared to be that of the republic and the latter that of the union (since independence, Russian has been dropped or replaced by English as the supposed international language). Even in the cities of eastern and southern Ukraine, where Russian fully dominated in public communication, Ukrainian continued to perform important symbolic functions in public signage, official documentations, and so forth (the only exception was Crimea, which had not acquired a Ukrainian ethnolinguistic dimension after its transfer from the Russian Federation to Ukraine in 1954). By declaring Ukrainian their native language, Russian-speaking Ukrainians – to the extent their choice was based on reflection rather than sheer inertia – displayed their support for its limited use by the state, even after they had ceased using that language in their own everyday life.

Mechanisms of the Legacy's Reproduction

The policies of the independent Ukrainian state regarding ethnicity and language differed considerably from Soviet policies, but the differences have not altered the inherited discrepancies between the citizens' ethnocultural identities and language practices. While the Ukrainocentric orientation of public discourse on ethnolinguistic matters strengthened Ukrainian ethnic and (to a lesser extent) linguistic identities, the policy with regard to language use did not really precipitate a Ukrainian language "revival" among Russian-speaking

Ukrainians. Therefore, the discrepancy was not only reproduced, but actually grew larger, as suggested by patterns of language use and ethnic identification within the younger generation.

The proclamation of Ukraine's independence resulted from nationalist mobilization, which in turn was instigated by public discourse emphasizing ethnocultural and economic grievances of ethnic Ukrainians and, by extension, other residents of the republic. In addition to the neglect of history and culture, degradation of the environment, and economic exploitation by Moscow, one of the main grievances pertained to the marginalization of the Ukrainian language, which nationalists considered the only appropriate means of communication and self-expression for ethnic Ukrainians. They thus lamented the discrepancy between language and ethnicity and, accordingly, the perceived deviation of Ukraine's ethnolinguistic structure from that of European nation-states that were considered as models for independent Ukraine. Viewed as the product of the Russification policies of the Soviet regime, this "deviation" was to be undone by the post-Soviet Ukrainian state by means of the "de-Russification" of Russian-speaking Ukrainians and members of non-Russian minorities (Kulyk 2001).

However, the nationalist opposition to the Soviet regime was defeated in the parliamentary and presidential elections of 1990–91 and thus denied a chance to engage in the full-fledged implementation of this agenda. The victorious *nomenklatura* headed by President Leonid Kravchuk took over some of the opposition's slogans and suggestions to legitimize the new state and to promote the loyalty of its citizens, but it avoided radical measures capable of provoking social division and unrest. Kravchuk's ethnocultural policy continued the Soviet glorification of the national, except that it was no longer constrained by the primacy of the Russian and could overtly oppose it. Official discourse sought to implant in public consciousness Ukrainian nationalist myths, traditions, and symbols, particularly those relating to the history of Ukraine in its allegedly incessant resistance to Russia's imperial policies. Kravchuk's policy promoted a form of nation building that featured the Ukrainian ethnic core but seemed inclusive enough to engage minorities (including Russians), because discursive "othering" was supposedly directed against Russian imperialism rather than the Russian people. However, a severe economic crisis broke popular faith in the president and his nation-building policy, which his opponents could present (particularly in the east and south) as "nationalism" and "forcible Ukrainianization" (Motyl 1995; Kulyk 2001).

Leonid Kuchma was elected president in 1994 largely because of the support of Russian speakers from the east and south. He emphasized friendly and mutually beneficial relations with Russia (while not abandoning Kravchuk's effort to build a partnership with the West) and downplayed anti-Russian themes in public discourse. Moreover, while promoting the integrity of the Ukrainian state, he allowed and even encouraged regional authorities in the east and west to feature symbols and traditions favored by their respective populations. His successor, Viktor Yushchenko, who came to power in the wake of the Orange Revolution of 2004, revived and strengthened anti-Russian themes in public discourse (the most prominent of them being Soviet/Russian responsibility for the Great Famine of 1932–33) and reemphasized a pro-Western foreign policy orientation, thereby provoking deterioration of the relations with Russia (Kulyk 2001; Portnov 2010, 40–90). In turn, the fourth President Viktor Yanukovych mostly reverted to Kuchma's ambiguity in both foreign policy and identity discourse. Notwithstanding these obvious oscillations, there has been a remarkable continuity in the promotion of national identity featuring the Ukrainian ethnocultural core. It has resulted from the common view of all presidents (and many other prominent statesmen) that such promotion constitutes an important element of state building. A contributing factor has been the parliamentary confrontation between the supporters of this view and those preferring a less Ukrainocentric orientation (such as Yanukovych's Party of Regions), which has hindered considerable changes in many domains.

The continuity of nation-building policies was most noticeable in education, whose subject structure and content consistently prioritized Ukrainian culture and history defined primarily in ethnic terms. In particular, history textbooks featured the Ukrainian "liberation struggle" largely directed against Russia, although teachers did not always transmit the prescribed message, particularly in predominantly Russian-speaking regions (Wanner 1998, chap. 4; Janmaat 2000, chap. 3, 4; Rodgers 2007). Ethnic Ukrainian culture and history was also featured in other state-controlled practices such as museums, the official calendar, and public monuments, except for the east and south, where local authorities sought to assert the legitimacy of the Russian and Soviet tradition. This assertion was particularly prominent under Yushchenko, when it played an important role in the political confrontation between Orange and anti-Orange forces (Wanner 1998, chap. 6, 7; Portnov 2010, 90–98; Zhurzhenko 2011).

While recognizing ethnocultural rights and occasionally acknowledging specific cultural achievements of minorities, the state was otherwise not inclined to differentiate between the civic nation and its titular ethnic core, thereby contributing to the popular confusion of these two identities. The confusion was also facilitated by the abolition of passport registration of nationality (allegedly in order to bring Ukrainian practice in conformity with European standards). This was not, however, accompanied by the abandonment of the discourse of nationalities as the constituent units of Ukrainian society, even though this discourse became much less prominent than it was in the USSR. Not only was the nationality question retained (albeit with a somewhat different wording) in the post-Soviet census of 2001, but its results also were presented by statisticians and journalists (in accordance with the ingrained Soviet tradition) as reflecting the actual sizes of objective groups. Given the continuation of the accustomed understanding of nationality, the discontinuation of its unchangeable ascription did not lead to any noticeable re-identification of

Russian-speaking Ukrainians so as to make their nationality match their everyday language. Quite the contrary, the census registered a clear increase in the share of self-declared Ukrainians. Moreover, the reported "disappearance" of about a quarter of Ukraine's Russians did not provoke any visible protests against the census results or the situation it supposedly reflected, so that the increasing identification with the titular group was mostly perceived as normal (Arel 2002a; Kulyk 2010, chap. 6).

The increase partly had to do with the more pronounced Ukrainian identification of the youth, who inherited the predominant understanding of nationality as primordial and, therefore, viewed it as entirely distinct from language practice. At the same time, many young people raised in independent Ukraine could interpret their declared Ukrainian identity not so much as an ethnic identity as a civic one. A survey conducted by KIIS in 2012 confirmed that while 75 percent of respondents defined their nationality by that of their parents (or one of their parents), 16 percent defined it by the country they lived in and 4 percent by the language they spoke. Remarkably, the youngest adult cohort (18 to 29 years) demonstrated both the strongest Ukrainian identification and the strongest tendency to define it in civic terms (by the country of residence). However, the youth was no more inclined than older respondents to view their nationality as defined by language practice.

Both change and continuity were also characteristic of policy with regard to language use. All presidents sought to promote the knowledge and use of Ukrainian without antagonizing Russian speakers and endangering social stability. However, Kravchuk and Yushchenko prioritized the promotion, and Kuchma and Yanukovych stability (which, after the period of perceived Ukrainianization, meant offering some reassurances to Russian speakers). Moreover, the confrontation between supporters of the dominance of Ukrainian and proponents of formal equality between the two languages often resulted in a legislative stalemate best illustrated by the longevity of the ambiguous language law of 1989, which neither party was able to change in its favor until as late as 2012. The confrontation became particularly heated after the Orange Revolution, when anti-Orange elites presented the Russian language as a crucial element of the distinct identity of the east and south and vehemently opposed attempts by the Orange regime to expand the use of Ukrainian at the expense of Russian. This opposition was supported and partly instigated by the Russian government's effort to ensure the continued prevalence of Russian in Ukraine as a means of keeping Ukraine under Moscow's influence. At the same time, there was an impressive heterogeneity in terms of regions and social domains, which both reflected and shaped popular preferences. While in the west Russian was quickly marginalized in the public sphere, in the east and south it retained its dominance in most practices, even those controlled by the state. The expansion of Ukrainian in education continued throughout the years of independence and brought the share of Ukrainian-language schools above that of ethnic Ukrainians (and back to the level of the late 1920s). In contrast, the use of the titular language in print media has actually decreased in comparison with the last Soviet decades, and in cinemas Ukrainian was not at all present until 2007. Notwithstanding the rather aggressive promotion of Ukrainian in the broadcast media under Yushchenko, Russian continued to dominate prime-time television on all major nationwide channels (Kulyk 2006, 2009, 2013).

Whatever their specific preferences, there was a clear limit to what policy makers believed could be done in the language domain because of expected resistance on the part of elites and masses to more radical changes. For example, none of the presidents dared or deemed it necessary to impose strict requirements regarding the mastery of the state language by state employees or even high-ranking officials. Therefore, while Ukrainian gradually replaced Russian in official documents, in their oral interactions with visitors most public servants speak whatever language they prefer (given that both Ukrainian and Russian are widely believed to be comprehensible to all residents of the country) rather than reciprocating the visitors' preference. Actually, most Ukrainians believe that public servants should respond in Ukrainian to those citizens addressing them in that language. Fifty-seven percent of respondents in the KIIS survey of 2012 applied this principle to the entire Ukraine and a further 21 percent limited it to those territories where Ukrainian speakers constitute a majority of the population (even in the east and south, 36 percent supported the former option, while 34 percent preferred the latter). However, citizens rarely stand up for their language rights – or even consider them to be violated. In the 2006 survey of Hromadska Dumka, only 6 percent of respondents declared having fairly often encountered instances of discrimination against Ukrainian speakers, and 8 percent admitted similar encounters involving Russian speakers (for the members of the respective language groups as defined by the main everyday language, the figures were 5 percent and 12 percent, respectively). This means that the failure of public servants to reciprocate the language choice of citizens addressing them is usually not perceived as violation of citizens' rights. At the same time, these and other survey data (particularly those pertaining to the media consumption) demonstrate that Russian speakers are more likely to perceive any imposition of the unaccustomed and less-known Ukrainian as violating their rights than Ukrainian speakers are to complain about the continued use of the more familiar and well-known Russian (Kulyk 2013). This asymmetry of grievances is another factor hindering the adoption of more resolute Ukrainianization policies by the state.

As a result, most Russian speakers can rely on their language in virtually all contexts and can even impose their preferred linguistic environment on those who would prefer Ukrainian but are ready to use Russian. In the 2006 survey, 83 percent of those speaking mostly Russian at home said they also used it in their place of work or study; this exceeded the analogous figure for Ukrainian speakers (78 percent), which means that the higher status of Ukrainian does not necessarily translate into more favorable conditions for its use. Russian continues to dominate the workplace in big cities, where it was identified as the main language of work by 58 percent of respondents (versus 20 percent indicating that they use mostly Ukrainian). Therefore, as during the Ukrainianization of the 1920s, a Ukrainian-speaking migrant from the countryside is likely to have to use Russian in the workplace. Although education in Ukrainian ensures better *knowledge* of Ukrainian among the younger generation in comparison with older generations, the younger generation *uses* Russian as much as older generations in cities, and significantly more in towns and villages. Accordingly, societal bilingualism with the predominance of Russian is likely to be reproduced in the next generation, because Russian speakers intend to raise their children mainly in Russian, even if they are more willing to let them combine the two languages than they themselves do (Kulyk 2007, 298–305).

Many people see no contradiction between the state promotion of Ukrainian and their own predominant use of Russian. A majority of Russian speakers, however, would like the state to bring its policy in conformity with popular preferences by legalizing the use of Russian in all social domains alongside of Ukrainian, so that everyone would supposedly speak whichever language they want. Of those respondents in the 2006 survey who defined their nationality as Ukrainian but reported speaking mostly Russian in their everyday life, 61 percent supported an upgrade of the status of Russian, and 59 percent called such an upgrade the most important task confronting the state's language policy. On the eve of the parliamentary election of 2012, Yanukovych and his party decided to fulfill these wishes to please their largely Russian-speaking constituency. This change in the legal framework both reflected and encouraged the curtailment of state efforts to overcome the consequences of Soviet Russification by bringing language practice into line with ethnic and linguistic identities.

Conclusion

In post-Soviet Ukraine, the persistence of the discrepancy between ethnolinguistic identity and language practice results from two separate processes that continue, albeit in a modified form, those processes set in motion under communist rule. In terms suggested by Kotkin and Beissinger, the legacy relationship in both cases is best characterized as what they refer to as translation (an old practice finds new purpose and is redeployed in a different way), although elements of what they call parameter setting are also noticeable. On the one hand, the ethnocultural policies of the Ukrainian state continue the Soviet glorification of the national in general and of the titular nation in particular. The main difference is that the latter no longer has to concede primacy to Russian culture, but instead is constrained by pressures from international minority rights organizations and the kin states of sizable minorities within Ukraine. Rather than emphasizing the Ukrainians' distinctiveness among the brotherly Soviet peoples, the policies of independent Ukraine came primarily to serve as a means for building a Ukrainian civic nation with an eponymous ethnocultural core. The new practice retains a fundamental parameter of the old one: while categorization by nationality ceased to be a pervasive and influential social practice, the category itself remains legitimate and meaningful to both elites and masses in their thinking about the composition and organization of society, even though the Ukrainian identification has acquired a civic overtone that implicitly challenges the perceived primordialism of ethnic groups.

On the other hand, policies in the language domain reproduce societal bilingualism with considerable heterogeneity of practices in different regions and social domains and varying combinations of the two languages in individual language repertoires. Contrary to the Soviet regime's primary preoccupation with the knowledge and use of Russian, the Ukrainian state promotes first and foremost the titular language both as the language of the supposed core ethnonation and as a factor (or at least an attribute) of state independence. However, this promotion is constrained not only by pressures from European organizations and kin state governments (particularly Russia), but also by the potential discontent of constituencies who care about language practices much more than ethnocultural symbols. Moreover, the inherited advantage of Russian over Ukrainian is reinforced by increasing globalization in the media, trade, tourism, and other domains, which facilitates knowledge and use of Russian (alongside or instead of English) as the regional lingua franca. In terms of parameters set during the Soviet decades, Russian continues to be viewed by many members of both language groups as better known among Ukraine's population and better suited for certain communicative practices. While learning and speaking Ukrainian by those accustomed to Russian is no longer considered unreasonable, it has by no means become inconceivable for Ukrainian speakers to use Russian in institutional or everyday communication.

A discrepancy between ethnolinguistic identities and language practice can be found in many societies around the globe, but it is not always as perceptible and measurable as it is in the post-Soviet countries, which continue employing Soviet categories of nationality and native language. Among comparable countries, the persistence of this ethnolinguistic discrepancy varies. Restoring the conformity between ethnicity and language has been easier in countries like Moldova, where even after Soviet Russification Russian remained the main language of a relatively small number of titulars, and thus of a minority of the general population. At the same time, the lack of strong political contestation in Kazakhstan contributed to a remarkable success of the state's relatively mild promotion of the knowledge and use of Kazakh within the eponymous group, particularly in the younger generation, leading to the gradual curtailment (although by no means elimination) of the discrepancy between ethnic identity and language use. In Ukraine, by contrast, Russian is too pervasive to recede without state pressure, and politics is too competitive to leave such pressure unopposed. In the still more russified Belarus, even the refusal of the authorities to apply such pressure is resolutely contested, although contestation is muted by the authoritarian nature of the political regime. Whatever the differences between these two countries, they are similar in that the continued prevalence of Russian in language practice coexists with the increasing identification with the titular group.

Notes

1 I am grateful to Mark Beissinger for his comments on earlier drafts of this text and to participants in the conference on "Historical Legacies of Communism" at Princeton University in April 2011 for their responses to my presentation. The 2006 survey in Ukraine was part of a collaborative project supported by the International Association for the promotion of cooperation with scientists from the New Independent States of the former Soviet Union (INTAS). The Ukrainian survey of 2012 was funded by a grant awarded to me by the Shevchenko Scientific Society in America from the Natalia Danylchenko Endowment Fund. Timothy Colton and Dmitry Gorenburg kindly made the data of the 1993 survey in Russia's autonomies (the Colton-Hough survey) available to me. Unless indicated otherwise, the survey results reported throughout the text are based on my processing of the raw data.

References

All-Ukrainian Population Census 2001. No date. http://2001.ukrcensus.gov.ua/eng/.
Arel, Dominique. 2002a. "Interpreting 'Nationality' and 'Language' in the 2001 Ukrainian Census." *Post-Soviet Affairs* 18(3): 213–49.
  2002b. "Language Categories in Censuses: Backward- or Forward-Looking?" In *Census and Identity: The Politics of Race, Ethnicity and Language in National Censuses*, ed. David I. Kertzer and Dominique Arel, 92–120. Cambridge: Cambridge University Press.
Bilinsky, Yaroslav. 1962. "The Soviet Educational Laws of 1958–59 and Soviet Nationality Policy." *Soviet Studies* 14(2): 138–57.
Brown, N. Anthony. 2005. "Language and Identity in Belarus." *Language Policy* 4(3): 311–32.
Gorenburg, Dmitry. 2001. "Nationalism for the Masses: Popular Support for Nationalism in Russia's Ethnic Republics." *Europe-Asia Studies* 53(1): 73–104.
Grieco, Elizabeth M. and Rachel C. Cassidy. 2001. "Overview of Race and Hispanic Origin." *Census 2000 Brief*, C2KBR/01-1 (March). http://www.census.gov/prod/2001pubs/cenbr01-1.pdf.
Hirsch, Francine. 1997. "The Soviet Union as a Work-in-Progress: Ethnographers and the Category *Nationality* in the 1926, 1937, and 1939 Censuses." *Slavic Review* 56(2): 251–78.
Janmaat, Jan Germen. 2000. *Nation-Building in Post-Soviet Ukraine: Educational Policy and the Response of the Russian-Speaking Population*. Amsterdam: University of Amsterdam.
Kaiser, Robert J. 1994. *The Geography of Nationalism in Russia and the USSR*. Princeton, NJ: Princeton University Press.
Karklins, Rasma. 1980. "A Note on 'Nationality' and 'Native Tongue' as Census Categories in 1979." *Soviet Studies* 32(3): 415–22.

Khmelko, V. Ye. 2004. *Lingvo-etnichna struktura Ukraïny: regional'ni osoblyvosti ta tendentsiï zmin za roky nezalezhnosti.* http://www.kiis.com.ua/txt/pdf/ing-ethn.pdf.
Krawchenko, Bohdan. 1985. *Social Change and National Consciousness in Twentieth-Century Ukraine.* New York: St. Martin's Press.
Kulyk, Volodymyr. 2001. "The Politics of Ethnicity in Post-Soviet Ukraine: Beyond Brubaker." *Journal of Ukrainian Studies* 27(1–2): 197–221.
  2006. "Normalisation of Ambiguity: Policies and Discourses on Language Issues in Post-Soviet Ukraine." In *History, Language and Society in the Borderlands of Europe: Ukraine and Belarus in Focus,* ed. Barbara Törnquist-Plewa, 117–40. Malmö: Sekel Bokförlag.
  2007. "The Demography of Language Practices and Attitudes in Ukraine." *Harvard Ukrainian Studies* 29(1–4): 295–326.
  2009. "Language Policies and Language Attitudes in Post-Soviet Ukraine." In *Language Policy and Language Situation in Ukraine: Analysis and Recommendations,* ed. Juliane Besters-Dilger, 15–55. Frankfurt am Main: Peter Lang.
  2010. *Dyskurs ukraïns'kykh medii: identychnosti, ideolohiï, vladni stosunky.* Kyiv: Krytyka.
  2011. "Language Identity, Linguistic Diversity, and Political Cleavages: Evidence from Ukraine." *Nations and Nationalism* 17(3): 627–48.
  2013. "Language Policy in the Ukrainian Media: Authorities, Producers and Consumers." *Europe-Asia Studies* 65(7): 1417–43.
Martin, Terry. 2001. *The Affirmative Action Empire: Nations and Nationalism in the Soviet Union, 1923 – 1939.* Ithaca, NY and London: Cornell University Press.
Motyl, Alexander J. 1995. "The Conceptual President: Leonid Kravchuk and the Politics of Surrealism." In *Patterns in Post-Soviet Leadership,* ed. Timothy J. Colton and Robert C. Tucker, 103–21. Boulder, CO: Westview Press.
Natsional'nyi sostav naseleniia SSSR. Po dannym Vsesoiuznoi perepisi naseleniia 1989 g. 1991. Moscow: Finansy i stattistika.
Portnov, Andrei. 2010. *Uprazhneniia s istoriei po-ukrainski.* Moscow: OGI, Polit.ru, Memorial.
"Rezul'taty natsional'nykh shchorichnykh monitorynhovykh opytuvan' 1992–2006 rokiv." 2006. In *Ukraïns'ke suspil'stvo 1992–2006: Sotsiolohichnyi monitorynh,* ed. V. Vorona and M. Shul'ha, 419–569. Kyiv: Institute of Sociology, National Academy of Sciences of Ukraine.
Rodgers, Peter. 2007. "Compliance or Contradiction? Teaching 'History' in the 'New' Ukraine: A View from Ukraine's Eastern Borderlands." *Europe-Asia Studies* 59(3): 503–19.
Shin, Hyon B. and Rosalind Bruno. 2003. "Language Use and English-Speaking Ability: 2000." *Census 2000 Brief,* C2KBR-29 (October). http://www.census.gov/prod/2003pubs/c2kbr-29.pdf.
Shul'ga, Nikolai. 2009. "*Rodnoi iazyk: nadumannyi konstrukt ili real'nost'.*" http://odnarodyna.com.ua/topics/1/252.html.
Silver, Brian. 1974. "Soviet Mobilization and the Russification of Soviet Nationalities." *The American Political Science Review* 68(1): 45–66.
  1975. "Methods of Deriving Data on Bilingualism from the 1970 Soviet Census." *Soviet Studies* 27(4): 574–97.

Slezkine, Yuri. 1994. "The USSR as a Communal Apartment, or How a Socialist State Promoted Ethnic Particularism." *Slavic Review* 54(3): 414–52.
Smagulova, Juldyz. 2008. "Language Policies of Kazakhization and Their Influence on Language Attitudes and Use." *International Journal of Bilingual Education and Bilingualism* 11(3–4): 440–75.
Solchanyk, Roman. 1982. "Russian Language and Soviet Politics." *Soviet Studies* xxxiv(1): 23–42.
Szporluk, Roman. 2000. "West Ukraine and West Belorussia: Historical Tradition, Social Communication, and Linguistic Assimilation." In Roman Szporluk, *Russia, Ukraine, and the Breakup of the USSR*, 109–38. Stanford, CA: Hoover Institution Press.
Wanner, Catherine. 1998. *Burden of Dreams: History and Identity in Post-Soviet Ukraine*. University Park: Pennsylvania State University Press.
Zaslavsky, Victor and Yuri Luryi. 1979. "The Passport System in the USSR and Changes in Soviet Society." *Soviet Union* 6(2): 137–53.
Zhurzhenko, Tatiana. 2011. "'Capital of Despair': Holodomor Memory and Political Conflicts in Kharkiv after the Orange Revolution." *East European Politics and Societies* 25(3): 597–639.

11

Pokazukha and Cardiologist Khrenov
Soviet Legacies, Legacy Theater, and a Usable Past

Jessica Pisano

This chapter addresses not so much legacies themselves as the production of the appearance (or perception) of such legacies, and the work that such perception does in the world. Through an analysis of an episode of *pokazukha*, or political window dressing, that captured Russian media at the end of 2010, this chapter suggests two alternative lenses through which we might regard elements of the Soviet past that are still present today: legacy theater – evocations of the past that deliberately create an impression of continuity, even as they may disguise new aims; and usable pasts – social and linguistic repertoires of the past from which contemporary actors deliberately draw. The former seeks to recreate elements of the past in the present; the latter serve as a resource for interpretation of the present. Both legacy theater and usable pasts represent ways political, social, and economic actors reintroduce elements of Soviet experience into today's landscape. In contrast to legacies, which primarily express the structural residue of past regimes (here, state socialism), these two concepts permit us to understand the recurrent presence of certain elements of the Soviet past in terms that more explicitly recognize the agency of contemporary actors.

Historical legacies, understood as persistent institutional effects, do seem real and observable in many areas of postcommunist politics, economics, and society.[1] However, it is also the case that not all apparent legacies derive from the meaningful and unconscious integration of elements of the past into present practices. Not all legacies are true palimpsests. Instead, some "legacies" are the product of deliberate political maneuvering in the present: at times, political actors write the past onto the surface of the present, integrating elements of earlier historical experience into their organizational and symbolic repertoires to enhance their legitimacy and to consolidate power over political and material resources. From there, they pursue agendas and behaviors that may share little in common with the pasts they have invoked. Such institutions and practices are legacies in a sense, as they incorporate elements of the past, but above all they are theater. Often, they are performances intended to invoke a sense of continuity with the past. In Eurasia, they often serve ends ideologically and practically at odds with the communist-era institutions, practices, ideas, and symbols they imitate. These performances are what this chapter calls legacy theater.

Still other invocations of Soviet-era experience might be usefully understood as a "usable past" or, given the changing character of Soviet rule over time, usable pasts (Brooks 1918; see also Commager 1967). This term, first used in early twentieth-century literary movements in the United States, has recently gained currency in Russian and Soviet studies as a general term for the conscious creation of a historical and literary canon (Britlinger 2000; Brandenberger 2009). In analyzing post-Soviet politics, this chapter suggests we might use the term in a way that more closely approaches its original meaning. For Van Wyck Brooks, who coined the phrase, and his circle, a "usable past" was not only a body of history and cultural production from which contemporary intellectuals could draw, but also a way of consciously and selectively reaching into the past to identify the sources of present challenges. Before Depression-era writers took up the idea a decade later, conceiving a "usable past" as more objectively construed historical work, the term was an instrument for critique of the past, designed, in Alfred Haworth Jones's words, "to justify a preconceived indictment of the present" (1971, 715). In applying this term to the post-Soviet present, this chapter identifies elements of Soviet cultural and political repertoires that may appear to reiterate or in some cases reaffirm Soviet vocabularies but serve instead as vehicles of criticism of the Soviet past and its apparent legacies in the present.[2]

Why is it important to distinguish among different ways the Soviet past is with us? One problem in the study of legacies is that phenotypical similarities between contemporary and historical political, economic, and social phenomena sometimes belie underlying shifts that have taken place. Interpreting elements of the past or formal similitude as persistence, we risk misreading actors' intentions: we may see people as simply repeating the past, even as they incorporate new practices in the service of entirely novel aims. Further, if we see only structure where there is also agency, we limit our political imaginations, our capacity to envision and anticipate change. If we fail to distinguish instances of persistence from legacy theater or usable pasts, we risk ossifying analytical paradigms – even as tectonic changes may be taking place. This chapter suggests that we require a framework that allows us to distinguish between historical residue and conscious uses of the past.

This chapter centers on a single instance of *pokazukha*: a call-in show on Russian national television in December 2010, in which a young doctor from Ivanovo confronted Vladimir Putin with an account of how officials and workers in his city staged a performance of well-funded health care in a hospital wing for the premier's visit. The event prompted a broad national discussion about political façades. This chapter examines this episode of *pokazukha* from multiple angles, considering how the event was described and interpreted by various actors – national media, regional officials, cultural workers, and inhabitants of virtual space – and how these various actors used Soviet and other repertoires to advance their points of view. These various angles permit a focused discussion of legacies, legacy theater, and usable pasts: the form and content of the call, and media responses to it, illuminate different ways social and political actors reproduced aspects of the Soviet past in the present.

Without access to the intentions of social and political actors, it is not possible to untangle all the pathways by which characteristics of past institutions appear in the present. However, this chapter does introduce two important distinctions: between continuities that represent persistence (legacies) from performances of the past that advance distinctly contemporary aims (legacy theater); and between efforts to stage elements of the past (legacy theater) and uses of language and practices associated with the past to comment on the present (usable pasts).

The following text begins with a brief discussion that places *pokazukha* in broader global and historical contexts, following with an account of the episode at the center of this text. The following section examines elements of the episode that seem to resonate with Soviet-era practices and considers whether we can conclusively identify them as "legacies." Next, this chapter discusses the role of legacy theater in the context of specific historical repertoires involved in the production of this iteration of *pokazukha*.[3] This section analyzes the nested set of state-orchestrated illusions that together constitute the episode, what those illusions were meant to conceal, and why what looks "Soviet" may not always be so. The final section examines usable pasts in the context of Russian print commentary and radio broadcasts about the episode. The conclusion considers the role of laughter and derision in evocations of the Soviet past, addresses what Vladimir Putin's administration may have been up to in the production of the *pokazukha* at the center of this chapter, and returns to some of the epistemological and methodological implications of studying how, today, the Soviet Union is with us.

Pokazukha

Pokazukha, a Russian term that approximates "window dressing," denotes performances or displays, often state-sponsored, that are just for show and meant to create positive impressions of economic or political development.[4] *Pokazukha* is endemic in contemporary Russian politics and is widely understood as a social fact; to use the language borrowed by anthropology from psychoanalysis, *pokazukha* is an experience-near concept – one that has salience for the people whose politics are the object of discussion (Geertz 1974). Even more than other façade institutions, *pokazukha is* theater. With it, all of the Russian Federation's a stage: state actors recruit ordinary people as players, and elaborate productions are rehearsed and then executed. Actors and audience alike often are aware that what they are doing and seeing is a performance.⁵

Some elements of *pokazukha* have clear roots in the Soviet past – even as others are reminiscent of earlier practices. Presentations of model farms, factory production lines, schools, stores, and many other institutions were staples of Soviet-era performances for delegations from Moscow and foreign audiences alike. The form of the practice was the presentation of successful results. Among the purposes of the practice were to disguise flawed results, attract resources and praise, and deflect punishment from the center. The concept was officially acknowledged as well as practiced: *pokazukha*, while itself critical to the maintenance of Soviet power, was also used in official language to critique (supposed) ideological opponents: some performances of *pokazukha* were cast as efforts to conceal less than full participation in state projects.

Much popular discourse about contemporary Russia and other states of the former Soviet Union explicitly or implicitly conceptualizes phenomena such as *pokazukha* as Soviet residue, or what Ken Jowitt (1992) called Leninist legacies, here resurrected by Vladimir Putin in his reassertion of a long historical tradition of Russian authoritarianism. Other approaches see *pokazukha* and related practices as part of an even longer tradition in the political culture of the region – a tradition that has been present in Russia not only during the Soviet and imperial periods (Seifrid 2001), but even as far back as fifteenth-century Muscovy (Kollman 1987).

However, while contemporary *pokazukha* shares some features with Soviet-era and earlier forms in Russia, it also shares characteristics of related practices elsewhere in the world. Similar ideas have other names in other contexts: contemporary *pokazukha* is not a phenomenon specific to post-Soviet space, or even to postsocialism. In Lusophone Africa and Brazil, people speak of laws that exist "só para inglês ver" – "just for the English to see," in reference to nineteenth-century pro forma Portuguese efforts to stamp out the slave trade in the face of British criticism. In the Arab world, people refer to *dimuqratiyya shakliyya* (formal democracy) and *al wajiha al dimuqratiyya* (the democratic façade). In Emmanuel Terray's (1986) work on Côte d'Ivoire, he introduces a similar duality in the politics of *la véranda* and *le climatiseur*. And in the United States, we have Astroturf lobbyists who pay PR firms to create campaigns that resemble grassroots political movements – as well as a powerful "populist" political movement with origins and financial backing from American oligarchs (Mayer 2010).

The existence of similar practices in imperial and pre-Petrine Russia, as well as the presence of related phenomena elsewhere, suggests that claims of cultural particularity, or of Soviet residue, may require reexamination: we need to be careful about understanding or explaining present developments in terms that take for granted continuities with the past and the durability of institutions or culture. This is of particular importance in this case: unlike other aspects of Soviet-era political and social life that seemed to disappear for years and then resurface during the Putin era, the concept of *pokazukha* remained more or less present (if not uniformly prevalent) in official and media speech during the 1990s.⁶ However, its appearance in different periods is not in itself prima facie evidence of continuity: morphological similarity does not mean that today's and yesterday's façades or imitations are, to use the language of evolutionary biology, homologous structures, or structures with a common origin.

Rather than attempting to establish elusive genealogical links between contemporary and past political behavior, this chapter offers two, alternative optics that allow us to analyze different ways people use the past. Today's *pokazukha* involves a mix of persistence, evocation and reference, ironic recycling, and instrumental use. None of these categories can be said to stand entirely apart from one another. This chapter does not seek to demonstrate all of the ways examples of legacy theater and usable pasts are interrelated. Rather, it uses these concepts to analyze the form, content, and purpose of elements of Soviet experience that are present in contemporary politics. In the following section, we begin to examine an episode that offers an opportunity to draw such distinctions.

Vladimir Vladimirovich and the Doctor from Ivanovo

In mid-December 2010, the prime minister of the Russian Federation held one of his regular television call-in shows, in which citizens from all over Russia could phone the studio to ask questions – a practice he had begun years before as president of the Federation. This time, something unusual happened: a young cardiology intern from the town of Ivanovo called Vladimir Putin live on air and told a truth instantly recognized across the country: "Vladimir Vladimirovich," he said, "in November you were in our town on a working visit. You were evaluating the development of health care in the region. So, I think to date there has never been such a *pokazukha* in our town. Hospitals quickly were prepared for your visit, and a lot of equipment was temporarily brought into the regional hospital for your visit and brought out afterwards." The doctor went on to say that employees had been given fake slips that showed their salaries were more than twice what they were in reality, and that hospital workers had even been recruited to dress up as patients and lie in hospital beds as the prime minister's entourage passed through the wing.⁷

As the doctor spoke, the moderator for the studio audience, Maria Sittel' – a newscaster on state television familiar to all Russian viewers – grew visibly uncomfortable. When he finished speaking, the studio audience broke into applause, prompting the apparently nonplussed Putin to ask, "I don't understand what you're applauding – the artfulness of the local leader or the physician's courage." The young people on whom the camera trained at that moment responded in unison, "the courage." Putin then responded at length to the question and assured the audience that the matter would be investigated.⁸

In the aftermath of the call, Russian media space was filled with discussion of the cardiologist's phone call to Putin. In the days that followed, it became a subject of heated debates as well as jokes on television shows, radio debates, blogosphere commentary, Twitter, YouTube, and so on. Everywhere one turned in Russian media and virtual space, the phone call was the focus of discussion.

The response of the Ivanovskaia regional administration, as reported in the "Ivanovo blogosphere,"[9] was swift: local politicians immediately questioned the veracity and reliability of the doctor's narrative, and television and newspapers dissected the elements of his story to identify factual errors or find any way to discredit him. The speaker of the regional assembly, Sergei Pakhomov, suggested that "competent organs" should deal with the doctor (Lenta.ru 2010). The doctor was called to the local prosecutor's office, and rumors flew on television and in print media that he would be fired. The head doctor of the Ivanovo regional hospital called the phone call a "provocation" (Karmazin 2010).

Several days afterward, the doctor received a call that the prime minister's press secretary later confirmed to have come from the prime minister himself. In it, Putin reportedly offered the doctor his protection (Sazonov 2010): "We won't leave you in the lurch. We'll help you, we know the whole situation. Don't worry" (Petrov 2010). Some ultimately came to see the episode as a public relations coup for Putin, who in the end came across as a sympathetic character supporting an honest doctor who had dared to tell on dishonest local bureaucrats.

This was not the first time such an event had occurred, in which an ordinary person publicly voiced a broad social complaint to Vladimir Putin and in so doing, received his sympathy – and a redirection of responsibility toward mid-level professionals or bureaucrats. At a February 2008 press conference, a female university student who appeared to be either extremely nervous or under the influence of a controlled substance asked Putin about stipends for students, noting that, "students have to work, and that affects how we study. So we work, we earn money, we give [money] to teachers – those are the kinds of specialists we produce." The student's frank recognition of bribes to educators – a widely known and discussed social phenomenon related to low teachers' salaries – was met with joking dry complicity on the part of the president: "What are you saying about the teachers?" to which the audience responded with laughter.[10]

We might think that such moments of truth telling, like the Ukrainian sign language broadcaster who broke with the script of a 2004 newscast to sign that the reported results of a presidential election were "lies," thus helping to unleash what came to be known as the Orange Revolution (see Boustany 2005), could have acted as a catalyst to bring people into the streets of the Russian Federation. Instead, official media and virtual space alike responded with furious but short-lived debates. The following sections discuss those debates, consider "Soviet" elements of this iteration of *pokazukha*, and show how legacy theater and usable pasts help to interpret this episode and the debates it provoked.

Soviet Legacies? Interpreting the Doctor's Crimes

Before examining ways political actors consciously draw on past repertoires and participate in the reproduction of past practices and institutions, it makes sense to consider what we mean by "legacies" in this context and whether and how we are able to positively identify them. First, in the absence of open acknowledgment of political strategies and tactics, how can we distinguish palimpsests from legacy theater? An example from Putin-era politics crystallizes the epistemological and methodological challenge of differentiating persistence from deliberate performance: the "Brezhnevization" of the Putin government.

To the extent that political and social actors choose Soviet vocabularies to communicate meaning in this and other episodes in the present, those vocabularies have tended to date from a particular period in Soviet history. Arguably, what we see in Putin-era Russia are not resurrections of the entire Soviet period generally, but of Brezhnev-era ways of thinking and talking. In 2011, this connection came to dominate public discourse when Vladimir Putin's press secretary, Dmitrii Peskov, commented on the usefulness of the Brezhnev period in a widely discussed television interview.[11]

Many agree on striking similarities between the political leadership of that time and contemporary Russian politics, including the prevalence of imitations in politics.[12] In a 2010 performance, Mikhail Zadornov, wearing a Pioneer neckerchief "to put everyone in a good mood," made reference to parallels between the Brezhnev and Putin eras:

> I'll suggest the next sentence in a whisper, because otherwise they'll cut it out, but such that only he who can hear it will hear it. In a whisper: they say that the stenographers of the United Russia congress did a little hack work – they took the material from the twenty-fifth congress of the CPSU and simply changed the last names where necessary. They'll kick me out of the Pioneers after that phrase. (Zadornov 2011)

Despite evident similarities between the two periods, what is not as clear is to what extent people evoke the 1960s and 1970s primarily because governance in the contemporary period happens to remind people of those days, and to what extent politicians do so because they wish to improve perceptions of contemporary realities by association, evoking the nostalgia some people feel for that period (Pelevin 1999; Boym 2001, 1995; Yurchak 2005). In other words, is this broadly agreed upon resemblance a case of persistence, or a performance of elements of that period for political gain?

Second, how do we establish genealogical relationships between practices, when first, they are separated by two or more decades and second, they are not unique to the period or region under study? Several aspects of the situation described in the doctor's phone call to Vladimir Vladimirovich, as well as certain elements of the reaction to it, appear recognizably "Soviet." Most obviously, the liturgy in which hospital staff participated – "local physicians awaiting the *vozhd*'" (Karmazin 2010) – appeared to draw on Soviet repertoires of political behavior, performances of economic development having been the stock in trade of Soviet-era delegations' visits to enterprises of any sort. However, that resemblance demonstrates nothing more than a perception of resonance. To illustrate this analytical problem, here we consider another aspect of the episode, namely, the furious response of Ivanovo bureaucrats in the aftermath of the call.

After the episode, the doctor wondered publicly about what had caused such reaction from members of the regional administration: "I didn't reveal any horrible secrets. I simply described a *pokazukha* that constantly is going on here and there. Everyone admits to me: they say, well, we know about that, it's common knowledge. So why did the functionaries react so sharply to those words?" (Sazonov 2010). The young doctor was not alone in the view that he "didn't reveal any secrets." When the hosts of a radio show asked callers about a milder version of the phenomena the doctor had described – namely, whether they adjust figures or reports for their bosses' sake when evaluators come – the response from one Muscovite was rapid: "It's an absurd question. It's everywhere in our country" (Radio Maiak 2010).

If the doctor was simply stating what everyone already knew, what explains the reaction to his phone call – on the part of both the regional authorities, who panicked, and the rest of the country, which followed the story with great interest? Here, Soviet norms of communication may help us understand why and how certain parties responded the way they did. In Yurchak's interpretation, in Soviet discourse pragmatic categories of meaning tended to matter to participants more than semantic ones: Yurchak writes of unanimous voting at Komsomol meetings, "to participants this was usually an act of recognition of how one must behave in a given ritualistic context in order to reproduce one's status as a social actor rather than as an act conveying 'literal' meaning" (2003, 486). In this example, as in many other instances of Soviet-era unanimous voting, the content of the proposition at hand was not what was significant. Rather, it was the fact of participating in an expression of unanimity that held meaning.

In the case of the call-in show, the young doctor declined to follow the normal "rules of the game." From this perspective, it was not the content of his critique that mattered so much as his decision to break a particular social rule.[13] The significance of the information lay in its public verbalization, not its content: the challenge to authority in the doctor's phone call, and the reason for the furor it caused, lay not in the situation he described, but in his decision to describe it.

In other words, calling a *pokazukha* by its name was a direct challenge to the regional administration not because the information revealed was particularly surprising to anyone, but because in so doing, the doctor challenged a means by which the state expresses its power. The truth is beside the point; it was participation in the ritual that was expected. When Ivanovo hospital staff writing anonymously noted that, "All kinds of big cheeses from the local administration have come to the regional hospital and are deciding how to remove the stain of shame" (Karmazin 2010), the shame in question was not the pretense. Rather, here shame arguably lay in the poverty of a health care system compelled to put on a show for visitors from Moscow or in local authorities' seeming inability to control a particular employee.

The apparent persistence of both a Soviet-era discursive convention and underlying patterns of social and political expectations, brought into relief by the reactions that the doctor's call provoked, would seem to suggest a relationship, perhaps even a direct line of descent, between late Soviet practices of communication and interpretations of the doctor's phone call. However, such an inference is complicated by the existence of similar practices in other places and times: to the extent that such practices are present across national contexts, there may be other reasons why they happen to arise in contemporary politics. Lisa Wedeen offers a useful parallel in the context of Syrian politics. As she has argued in the case of the al-Asad cult, the performance of ritual itself constituted state power. She writes, "the idea being reproduced in the specific practice of uttering patently spurious statements or tired slogans is not the one expressly articulated – Asad is in no meaningful literal sense the 'premier pharmacist.' Rather, Asad is powerful because his regime can compel people to say the ridiculous and to avow the absurd" (1999, 12). There, as in Soviet and post-Soviet Russia, some people may participate in a political charade by acting "as if" they supported a regime, and the fact of participation may supersede whatever people may privately think or say about that charade (Wedeen 1998).

Further, without a reliable way to observe directly and trace the reproduction of discursive norms – and without systematic consideration of the various other influences that may contribute to the production of norms that appear to echo Soviet-era ones – it may be difficult in this case to demonstrate the presence of "legacy" with any degree of either precision or accuracy.[14] *Post hoc, ergo propter hoc* arguments are not helpful for conclusively identifying the complex ways people may, deliberately or unconsciously, reproduce past practices. We can, however, begin to consider the ways actors in contemporary politics may manipulate, draw on, and perform elements of the Soviet past.

Legacy Theater: A *Pokazukha Matrioshka*

What had happened during the prime minister's visit to Ivanovo? We know from the doctor's phone call that regional authorities in Ivanovo sought to present an image of economic progress in the health sector to the prime minister and his entourage. Having received specially allocated funds for regional development, they hoped to show – or at least believed they were expected to show – that hospital staff members were well paid, certain wings of the hospital were well equipped, and patients were cooperative and appreciative of the care they were receiving. Additionally, as others later reported, they hoped to show that roads were freshly covered with asphalt, hospital buildings had roofs that protected patients from rain, and infrastructure in the city was well cared for. Implicit in Khrenov's account was the notion that funds for regional development had not made their way to their intended destinations.

What was the actual material state of affairs in the health care system in Ivanovo at the time? Notwithstanding the performance that had been staged for the Moscow delegation, conditions at the regional hospital where the *pokazukha* occurred were far better than in other health care facilities in the region. In investigating the call-in incident, *Komsomol'skaia pravda* reported on conditions in the first municipal hospital in Ivanovo. That facility is housed in a pre-revolutionary former stable, in which rooms are arranged shotgun style: "you open a door – and you end up in the dressing room, next – the toilet, behind it, the hall. That is, the toilet is a walk through" (Suprycheva 2010, 10). The journalist went on to describe some of the conditions there:

The walls are chipped and flaking. Enterprising patients paste wallpaper on them at the level of their beds, so that pieces of plaster don't fall on their heads. Besides, they stick them with improvised means – pieces of sticking plaster. It's a picturesque scene, particularly in combination with the black moss on the ceiling – it's impossible to remove it, since the ceilings are four meters high. But the most interesting thing happens here starting at 8 o'clock in the morning. From departments that are not connected with each other by corridors – they're isolated – they bring through the sheets and mattresses for disinfection. (Suprycheva 2010, 10)

After the phone call to Putin, local newspapers were bombarded with letters from people anxious about the quality and accessibility of health care in the region. A journalist for *Argumenty i fakty* wondered at the phenomenon: "It's true that, surprisingly, before … [the] speech it turns out that no one noticed the ruin. And he, the young specialist, having announced it to the whole country, is now being made to offer his apologies at length" (Boiarkina 2011, 40).

According to the prime minister, the regional hospital in Ivanovo had received 130 million rubles from the federal budget. Such an influx of cash represented a special privilege, not only for the region, but also for the hospital itself. Most hospitals in the region were struggling with multiple challenges, including huge shortages of qualified personnel – in one hospital, only half of all shifts were staffed, and almost half of all staff worked double shifts (Smol'iakova and Gritsiuk 2010, 1). Most often, this left patients' families to care for and feed loved ones, as well as to take turns mopping hospital floors. Further, amidst gross infrastructural decay, there were limited resources for paying hospital staff – if the national minimum monthly salary was 4,300 rubles, nurses in Ivanovo were being paid 2,660 rubles, and doctors' starting salaries were 3,560 rubles (Suprycheva 2010, 10).

In an interview after the incident, the doctor explained his actions by saying that people were afraid and that he had simply "voiced the mood in the city." What were people afraid of? In his view, unemployment, layoffs, economic distress (Alalykin 2010). He sought to call attention to two things: the low pay of health care workers and the political behavior required by their precarious economic positions. The participation of hospital staff in the show for the Moscow delegation had been, in all likelihood, motivated by concerns about their personal economic situations.[15]

It may be the case that such performances, which may remind people of Soviet-era practices – and Soviet-era fears of the state – inspire a climate of social anxiety, and that politicians stand to gain something from that anxiety. However, in this case Soviet morphology conceals a logic rooted not in a fear of political violence (which might be said to have played a role in some, though not all, Soviet iterations of *pokazukha*), but rather of economic vulnerability – vulnerability in a system in which social welfare provisions have been all but entirely eroded, and in which the social contract underlying the final decades of Soviet citizens' participation has been broken.

The hospital was not the only theatrical space in this episode. As became apparent later, the preparations for Vladimir Putin's visit to the Ivanovo regional hospital were only one of two iterations of *pokazukha* that were part of the doctor's call. *Pokazukha* was a basic mechanism of communication not only in the events described in the doctor's phone call, but also in the organization and presentation of the televised phone call itself. As media commentary on the event later revealed, both the hospital visit and the phone call itself were examples of *pokazukha*: the phone call itself was, in certain respects, staged. Further, the orchestration of the entire episode appears to have been meant to provide an illusion of openness and responsiveness on the part of the Putin government.

What had happened during the show? The organizers of the show ensured that from the audience's perspective, it appeared that the doctor's phone call had been both serendipitous and anonymous. During the show, toll-free telephone numbers and addresses for text messages were announced and flashed across the screen, giving the impression that a lucky caller could reach the premier simply by dialing or texting. During the call, Sittel' simply identified the caller as "a cardiologist from Ivanovo": he did not introduce himself, and the premier noted that he hadn't caught the caller's name.

It emerged later that, suggestions to the contrary by members of the Ivanovo regional government and some national media notwithstanding, the cardiologist from Ivanovo was a real person, he had a name, and he was known to the show organizers in advance. His name was Ivan Khrenov (that his last name happens to carry obscene connotations in Russian slang could not have been lost on the public, and was not lost on those who subsequently sought to use derision as a political tool to discredit the young doctor). In media investigations of Khrenov, it further came to light that the young doctor had not himself dialed the call center. Rather, as he explained in a televised interview, after receiving his parents' blessing, he had submitted a letter in advance to the prime minister. That letter was chosen from among about 2 million others to perhaps be presented to Putin: several days before the show, a technician had come, presumably to verify that his phone line was working properly (Khrenov wondered if the technician had been from the FSB); during the show, the television studio had called him.

That Khrenov had managed to get through to Vladimir Putin and ask such a question thus was no accident, but rather part of the theater: "everyone accepts the rules of the game, and even the truth-lover Khrenov has no way of leaping across the barrier if not for a higher will" (Petrovskaya 2010, 8). The staging of the phone call about the staging of the hospital visit thus differed in important respects from the *pokazukha* in Ivanovo: the phone call revealed an economic reality – things are not as rosy as they may have appeared – even as the illusion of the phone call concealed a political one – ordinary people cannot, in fact, simply get through to the prime minister's line with a confrontational question.

Note that not only Soviet, but also imperial repertoires were present in the overall narrative that emerged in the week following the performance. As Khrenov's story unfolded, it came increasingly to resemble a central trope in imperial history, in which the benevolent tsar is insulated from knowledge of what troubles the country by selfish boyars – played here by today's power-hungry bureaucrats, or *chinovniki*. Khrenov's letter to Putin follows the form of an appeal to the autocrat; the author presumes that the information contained therein is unknown to the leader and suggests confidence that he will take action, once he is informed. Finally, in this narrative, trouble comes from the regional authorities, not from the tsar himself. Putin, by contrast, is meant to be Khrenov's protector. Even Khrenov's mother reproduced this trope: "If they're really going to drive him out, of course he'll appeal to Putin. Maybe he'll go to Moscow" (Lenta.ru 2010).

Upon closer examination, Khrenov's phone call appears to be part of a broader strategy on the part of the Putin government: to present a façade of what Matthews and Nemtsova call a "highly controlled version of liberalization from above that will include more freedom of expression, a friendlier face toward the West, and inviting former liberal critics to act as Kremlin advisers. He and his advisers hope that allowing a degree of free speech and creating the appearance of responsive government will keep voters happy" (2010; also see Whitmore 2010). As a journalist for *Izvestiia* noted at the end of 2010, that year had seen "a new genre of links between the people and the authorities – the voice 'from Potemkin villages,'" noting further Moscow's Center for

Political Technologies Alexei Makarkin's description of the government's uses for the phenomenon – as a rather "vivid method of communication between the authorities and society. You know, rather than discussing this or another theme, you can take a concrete story ... a concrete Doctor Khrenov unmasks falsifiers and those who would varnish the truth" (Beluza 2010, 2012). Elements of illusion present in the televised call to the premier concealed other aspects of contemporary political realities and suggest different aspects of the complex relationships between contemporary politics and their Soviet progenitors. Here, the staged disruption of a Soviet politico-theatrical form was the vehicle for the idea that contemporary Russian politics are democratic, and that the government is responsive to citizens' concerns.

Like other pressure valves currently permitted in Russian media and virtual space, such performances themselves together thus partake in a third, broader *pokazukha*: in this instance, Khrenov called to report on a performance that was Soviet in form but that expressed the anxieties of a neoliberal economic present, in the context of a performance of responsiveness meant to reassure the Russian public of the liberal politics of an increasingly authoritarian regime. Here, paradoxically, performances of the past are not Soviet continuities as such, but props that support an impression of just enough freedom of expression to ensure continued support for the Putin government.

Usable Pasts: Murzilki Salute Pioneer Ivan

If the televised *pokazukha* provides an illustration of legacy theater, public reception of the event on radio demonstrates how the concept of "usable pasts" may be useful for understanding other "Soviet" elements of this episode. In the days that followed Khrenov's phone call, parody was an important tool for political and social actors commenting on the episode, as they deliberately chose and performed elements of Soviet culture to achieve particular ends – in this case, to discredit the young cardiologist.

A few days after the call, a popular musical parody and morning show on a nationally syndicated radio station made Khrenov the subject of a song. The show was *Murzilki International*, named for a children's literature and art magazine published throughout most of the Soviet period and into the present day. The song drew explicitly on numerous musical, gestural, and verbal tropes associated with the Soviet past as they described, contextualized, and commented on Khrenov's action.

Here, Soviet tropes were used not to create an illusion of historical continuity, but to ridicule the young doctor. The Soviet past furnished tools with which to critique the present: the Murzilki parody used children's vocabularies of the late Soviet period to mock and discredit Ivan Khrenov – and, by association, everyone who had appreciated the content of his phone call to Putin. The parody began with a pioneer salute: "dress to Khrenov, the country's [Young] Pioneer! (*ravniais' na Khrenova, pionir strany!*)"[16] The tone of the song is facetious: the refrain hails the doctor as honest and brave and observes how quickly he achieved fame:

> Khrenov the cardiologist! F#@%ing cardiologist!
> You're honest and courageous, and young!
> Khrenov the cardiologist! F#@%ing cardiologist!
> The path to the heights of glory was not long,
> Cardiologist Khrenov! Cardiologist Khrenov!
> He called! He informed! He reported the facts!
> Cardiologist Khrenov! Cardiologist Khrenov!
> On TV! On the radio! Became known to everyone!
> (Lomovoi 2011)

The critique embedded in this musical rendition of the doctor's truth telling carried serious overtones. In this interpretation, Khrenov is not a brave individualist but a friend of power.[17] Here was an accusation of collaboration, using Soviet-era language associated with informers: *nastuchal, fakty soobshchal*. Khrenov's critique is cast as an appeal from within the system, using the language of the system – not an attempt to overturn it. The Soviet police state provides the language with which to level such an accusation.

At the same time, in the context of the parody's particular musical accompaniment, Khrenov's zeal appears naïve and idealistic: the verse was set to the music of a Soviet-era children's song about multiplication tables, *Dvazhdy dva – chetyre* ("Two times two is four").[18] Even more than an informant, Khrenov is a tattletale:

> All around they divide the budgets,
> Divide!
> There's nothing you can do,
> Do!
> But to whom can an honest mind tell about it?
> How, to whom? To Putin!
> How, to whom? To Putin!
> That's absolutely right!
> (Lomovoi 2011)

Through its sarcasm, the message here was that resistance is useless; telling the truth only made the speaker look naïve and foolish. Normal behavior meant participating in the charade.

Other comments about the phone call followed a similar pattern, drawing on Soviet tropes to critique Khrenov's action – expressing not so much solidarity with the local functionaries who directed the *pokazukha* in Ivanovo, but rather dissatisfaction with Khrenov's seemingly having broken ranks. In particular, the idea that Khrenov was enacting a Soviet heroic children's trope in the service of a political regime could be found elsewhere in media space. Writing in *Komsomol'skaia pravda*, Elena Suprycheva dryly observed, "The glory of Pavlik Morozov has been eclipsed. A new hero is on the stage: a cardiologist, that same guy who gave up, wholesale, all of the functionaries of his native Ivanovo" (2010, 10). Here, Khrenov is portrayed as taking up a central role in an enactment of a Soviet morality tale: the son who turns on (and in) his father to maintain his fidelity to the values of the communist state.

The use of the Pavlik Morozov trope is curious; in Khrenov's case, his loyalty appears to lie with the people around him who are struggling to make ends meet, rather than with an ideology promulgated by the state. However, Suprycheva's "clever boy" (*soobrazitel'nyi mal'chik*) Khrenov is the object of derision not because he challenges the performance of the central state, but because he is viewed as complicit in it. In other words, if regional authorities publicly smeared Khrenov after the phone call, calling the young doctor psychologically unstable (*nevmeniaemyi*), parts of the national media moved to discredit him with implicit accusations of "acting Soviet" – specifically, being a good communist. Khrenov's own words likewise may have contributed to this perception: in his televised interview, he tried to legitimize one of his arguments by making reference to a statement by Stalin (Alalykin 2010).

Such critiques, while using Soviet characters and vocabularies of morality to make a point, approached the Soviet past as a disparate set of tools with which to comment on the present. Amidst a wide variety of possible shared social metaphors that could have been used to interpret the situation, and given the eclectic and sometimes contradictory character of the references people used to comment on it, critiques of Khrenov's actions may be said not to reflect mere reproduction of Soviet discourse, but rather deliberate, and ironic, recycling. In these examples, the Soviet period functions not so much as a constraint framing present action as a reservoir of usable pasts.

Conclusion

After the call-in show, state-owned media moved to manage perceptions of the entire episode. The morning after Khrenov's phone call to Putin, Radio *Maiak*, one of the five radio stations held by the All-Russian State Television and Radio Broadcasting Company, held a call-in show to discuss the phenomenon of *pokazukha* in contemporary Russian society (Radio Maiak 2010). The program began with laughter and a series of jokes about the doctor's last name, followed by a summary of the episode and a question to listeners about their participation in *pokazukha*. The atmosphere was of carnival in Bakhtin's sense – only the apparent aim, or at least result, of the performance seemed to be to normalize the interventions of the imitating state.

Callers to the show spoke openly about a variety of different episodes of *pokazukha*, at times describing their own roles, and at others enumerating various outrageous and hilarious tactics employed by other people in their entourage or city: ground painted green to simulate grass[19]; road repair paid for but undone (a staple of budgetary misdirection nearly everywhere); and a host of other diversions. A private businessman who said he had been personally involved in preparations for the visit to Ivanovo of the man to whom he referred on air as "our respected [leader]" recounted how a child had hung around the work crew, curious about what they were doing. When the child started to get in the way, irritating the crew, the foreman had joked, "Don't touch the child! He's probably an officer of the FSB."

The episode on *Maiak* included a great deal of laughter – primarily laughter at descriptions of various iterations of *pokazukha*. What was the meaning of that laughter? Soviet traditions of subversion – and post-Soviet nostalgia for such subversion[20] – might suggest social critique and a virtual circle of intimates created in the audience through the program. However, another meaning, one consistent with the tone of other re-descriptions of Khrenov's action, also emerges.

First, in successfully encouraging others to share tales of *pokazukha* on the airwaves, the program hosts managed to dilute one aspect of the doctor's phone call to Putin: here, others also were talking openly about political secrets on the airwaves. The discussion was not part of a wave of protest that, in another national context, might have followed an event such as Khrenov's phone call. Rather, it served to render banal the seemingly extraordinary event of the evening before: How brave was the doctor, really, if others could talk about the same things, publicly?

Second, it normalized and underlined widespread complicity in such performances as the Ivanovo *pokazukha*. The message seemed to be that we are all in on this together: participation meant neither false consciousness nor, precisely, an expression of the fragmented self or double consciousness.[21] Rather, participation in *pokazukha* expressed a version of ideological fantasy, an inversion of Marxist false consciousness: "they know very well what they are doing, but still, they are doing it."[22] Khrenov emerges from the episode as a *chudak*, an eccentric – an oddity for having come forward.

Further, to the extent that Soviet tropes are present in the discussions of Khrenov's phone call, they are used to criticize him for his supposed ideological enthusiasm. Ultimately, if all of the parts of this episode are taken together, we see that performances of and references to Soviet repertoires serve primarily to discredit persons (here, Khrenov) associated with them, to normalize both administrative incompetence and participation in the political theater that conceals it, and to cast Putin in a positive light. In the end, state and media management of the event produce a complex narrative with complicated relationships to the Soviet era: here, the Soviet Union is very much with us, but there is no direct line connecting the past and present, nor any single valence attached to the various elements of the Soviet past that make their appearance in this multilayered episode of political theater.

This chapter has identified different ways political actors encounter, articulate, and use historical residue. I have here sought to go beyond the rubric of "legacies" because without conceptual refinement, we take certain analytical risks. Those risks include, first, misreading contemporary politics through lenses that may exaggerate the importance of the past in determining the present. To whatever degree certain elements of the past remain relevant today, whether in administrative practices, infrastructure, or other ways, historical repertoires are not the only tools of which contemporary actors avail themselves. As we see in the case of Khrenov's letter and phone call, complaints articulated using language and forms associated with the past often reflect concerns about contemporary political and economic arrangements. Second, without considering the role of legacy theater and usable pasts, we are unable to account for historical consciousness or agency on the part of political actors. This seems risky indeed, for in such a case, the past becomes the sole actor, and we are left with a vision of historical destiny that leaves little room for the possibility of contingency, irony, or the solidary change prompted by movements of individual citizens (Rorty 1989) – a vision that would constitute a more precise recapitulation of some Soviet ontologies than any of the Leninist residue that may be present in contemporary Russian politics.

Notes

1   "Historical legacy" and "legacy" often are used interchangeably. This chapter will use the term "legacy" rather than the pleonasm "historical legacy."
2   The use of a "usable past" here thus contrasts with other approaches to conscious cultural recycling, such as the idea of "restorative nostalgia" elaborated by Boym (2001) or the complex forms described by Oushakine (2007).
3   *Pokazukha* and "legacy theater" both denote performances. However, they have different functions in this analysis: *pokazukha* is a category of practice, whereas legacy theater is a category of analysis. On distinctions between the two, see Brubaker and Cooper (2000).
4   G. A. Solganik provides the following definition: "Pokazukha, -i (*f*). *Neg.* Anything affected; activities calculated for an outward effect, in order to create a favorable impression" (2008, 488).
5   *Pokazukha* was widely discussed in 2010. See, for example, a December episode of Roman Gerasimov's Channel 5 program *Otkrytaia studiia*, entitled "Pokazukha." In introducing the program, Gerasimov notes, "You can agree, this phenomenon is commonplace for our country, dammit, we know that before every visit of the higher authorities they lay fresh asphalt and one could make a list of all that they do, sometimes they steal, oops, I mean they paint the grass (*inogda kradut ... fu, travu krasiat*). All that is outrageous and unfortunately it's become a tradition." Video at http://rutube.ru/tracks/3914531.html?v=68c136a55b5027036f646a18fef63dof. Accessed June 10, 2013.
6   An Eastview search for January 1992–December 1999 finds 603 matches.
7   "The nurses were ordered to say that their salary is twelve thousand [rubles per month], and doctors were given receipts for the sum of thirty thousand, which is not true. Several of the sick were dispersed [*razognali*] and hospital workers in hospital gowns were put there [in their beds]. My understanding is that this is how the situation was presented to you: everything is going according to plan; the money is being used. What can you say about this?" Video at http://www.youtube.com/watch?v=mr9RX_qnwFA&feature=grec_index. Accessed June 10, 2013.

8   That night's show was long, lasting four and a half hours. The moderator seated with Putin opened the program by characterizing the Russian Federation as "in crisis." In the course of the program, Putin was asked questions not only about the state of the economy, health care, and other social matters, but also about riots in Moscow, ethnic tension, and violence. In a question framed by a query about his dogs, one woman asked him about Khodorkovsky's most recent trial. Video at http://www.youtube.com/watch?v=Um4PgVZG3xg. Accessed June 10, 2013. The doctor's call came later, during a relative lull in the program, in the context of a discussion of health care in the Russian Federation. During his call, a medical team from Cheboksary appeared on the television screen.
9   This interesting spatial locution comes from Karmazin (2010).
10 The video of this episode, entitled "Putin i obkurennaia devushka" ("Putin and the stoned girl"), has been watched more than 6.6 million times on YouTube: http://www.youtube.com/watch?v=RlCrAmQEUdk&feature=related. Accessed June 10, 2013.
11 See, for example, "Peskov: rassuzhdaiushchie o brezhnevizatsii Putina nichego ne znaiut o genseke, on byl pliusom dlia strany," 2011. *Gazeta.Ru*, October 4. http://www.gazeta.ru/news/lenta/2011/10/04/n_2037898.shtml#p2. Accessed June 10, 2013.
12 On the Brezhnev era, see a joke cited in Krylova that catalogs characteristics of various periods in Soviet history: "in Brezhnev's time, they would have started rocking the train and announcing train stations in order to create the illusion of movement" (1999, 252).
13 On the "rules of the game" in post-Soviet Russia, see Ledeneva (2006).
14 Further complicating interpretation of the episode as a Soviet legacy, some commentary on the Ivanov *pokazukha* situated the performance not in Soviet traditions, but in contemporary global technologies. Imitating a style of writing popularized in the postmodern fantasies of Viktor Pelevin, an article in *Izvestiia* evoked Tatarsky, the protagonist of Pelevin's *Generation "P"*, describing television as the "main emperor and *pokazushnik* of our days, running from real life like the devil from incense, and inspirationally creating a parallel reality, where handmade scandals become simply the engine of advertisement and where, in the final analysis, everyone gets along with everyone" (Petrovskaya 2010, 8). Here, the performance and references to it are understood as part of the massive PR constructions that, together with commercial interests, constitute contemporary politics. See Wilson (2005).
15 For an explication of some of the underlying motivations driving participation in similar political rituals in post-Soviet space, see Allina-Pisano (2010).
16 "Ravniais'" is a military drill command that in this usage has no precise equivalent in Western contexts (where soldiers may be asked to "dress right" on parade, for example, but not to dress to a specific person, as here). Here, the radio audience is being asked, facetiously, to look toward or align themselves with Khrenov, who is portrayed as exemplifying good Pioneer behavior.
17 This impression deepens in the third stanza of the parody, in which Putin "arranges" those who are dishonest.
18 In one rendition of the song, which was written by M. Pliatskovskii and V. Shainskii, Eduard Khill leads members of Bolshoi Detskii Khora in a staged classroom performance. Video at http://www.youtube.com/watch?v=u5DPEg1lp3s. Accessed June 10, 2013.

19 Also see Lacey (2011) on similar practices in suburban Arizona.
20 As well as for, as Krylova puts it, "the lost position of the Soviet subject," for whom the workings of power were understood (1999, 249).
21 As many authors writing on forms of marginality and totalitarian societies suggest. Wedeen advances a version of the argument that Bakhtin and others suggest in Eastern European contexts. Ellison (1952) and DuBois (1997) describe a related phenomenon in American life.
22 As Žižek notes, following Sloterdijk's *Critique of Cynical Reason* (1989, 33).

References

Alalykin, Oleg. 2010. *Aktual'no: Dialogii v studii*. Interview with Ivan Khrenov, December 17. Video http://www.youtube.com/watch?v=twsyrZP5u5w. Accessed June 10, 2013.
Allina-Pisano, Jessica. 2010. "Social Contracts and Authoritarian Projects in Post-Soviet Space: The Use of Administrative Resource." *Communist and Post-Communist Studies* 43(4): 373–82.
Beluza, Aleksandra. 2010."Potemkinskie golosa," *Izvestiia* December 29, 12.
Boiarkina, Natal'ia. 2011. "Chto vy nas 'lechite'?" *Argumenty i fakty* 10, March 9, 40.
Boustany, Nora. 2005. "As Ukraine Watched the Party Line, She Took the Truth into Her Hands." *The Washington Post*, April 29, A19.
Boym, Svetlana. 2001. *The Future of Nostalgia*. New York: Basic Books.
   1995. *Common Places: Mythologies of Everyday Life in Russia*. Cambridge, MA: Harvard University Press.
Brandenberger, David. 2009. "A New *Short Course*? A. V. Filippov and the Russian State's Search for a 'Usable Past.'" *Kritika* 10(4) (Fall): 825–33.
Britlinger, Angela. 2000. *Writing a Usable Past: Russian Literary Culture, 1917–1937*. Illinois: Northwestern University Press.
Brooks, Van Wyck. 1918. "On Creating a Usable Past." *Dial* 64 (April 11): 337–41.
Brubaker, Rogers and Frederick Cooper. 2000. "Beyond 'Identity.'" *Theory and Society* 29: 1–47.
Commager, Henry Steele. 1967. *The Search for a Usable Past and Other Essays on Historiography*. New York: Knopf.
Du Bois, W. E. B. 1997. *The Souls of Black Folk*. David W. Blight and Robert Gooding-Williams, eds. Boston, MA: Bedford-St. Martin's.
Ellison, Ralph. 1952. *The Invisible Man*. New York: Random House.
Geertz, C. 1974. "'From the Native's Point of View': On the Nature of Anthropological Understanding." *Bulletin of the American Academy of Arts and Sciences* 28(1): 26–45.
Jones, Alfred Haworth. 1971. "The Search for a Usable American Past in the New Deal Era." *American Quarterly* 23(5) (December): 710–24.
Jowitt, Ken. 1992. *New World Disorder: The Leninist Extinction*. Berkeley: University of California Press.
Karmazin, Igor'. 2010. "Pravdorub Khrenov." *Moskovskii komsomolets* 281, December 18, 1.
Kollmann, Nancy Shields. 1987. *Kinship and Politics: The Making of the Muscovite Political System, 1345–1547*. Stanford, CA: Stanford University Press.

Krylova, Anna. 1999. "Saying 'Lenin' and Meaning 'Party': Subversion and Laughter in Soviet and Post-Soviet Society." In Adele Marie Barker, ed. *Consuming Russia: Popular Culture, Sex, and Society since Gorbachev*, 243–65. Durham, NC: Duke University Press.

Lacey, Marc. 2011. "Spraying To Make Yards Green...but With Paint, Not Water," *New York Times*, April 9, A1.

Ledeneva, Alena. 2006. *How Russia Really Works: The Informal Practices that Shaped Post-Soviet Politics and Business*. Ithaca, NY: Cornell University Press.

Lenta.ru. 2010. "'Zloveshchego' kardiologa iz Ivanova vyzvali v prokuraturu," published online on December 27. Subsequently posted by numerous other news sites. http://lenta.ru/news/2010/12/17/procur/. Accessed June 13, 2013.

Lomovoi, Oleg. 2011. "Kardiolog Khrenov rasskazal vsiu pravdu Putinu." Lyrics to parody of *Dvazhdy dva chetyre*. Original text and video may be viewed at: http://www.avtoradio.ru/?an=ml_parody_page&uid=142960. Accessed June 10, 2013.

Matthews, Owen and Anna Nemtsova. 2010. "Moscow's Phony Liberal," *Newsweek*, February 25.

Mayer, Jane. 2010. "Covert Operations: The Billionaire Brothers Who Are Waging a War against Obama," *The New Yorker*, August 30.

Oushakine, Serguei Alex. 2007. "'We're Nostalgic but We're Not Crazy': Retrofitting the Past in Russia." *Russian Review* 66(3) (July): 451–82.

Pelevin, Viktor. 1999. *Generation 'P'*. Moscow: Vagrius.

Petrov, Vitalii. 2010. "Obratnyi zvonok." *Rossiiskaia gazeta* 287, December 20, 2.

Petrovskaya, Irina. 2010. "Tvortsy vselenskoi pokazukhoi." *Izvestiia* 242, December 24, 8.

Radio Maiak, 2010. "Pokazukha v Rossii," December 17. Video at http://www.youtube.com/watch?v=jygrov-aYmA. Accessed June 10, 2013.

Rorty, Richard. 1989. *Contingency, Irony, and Solidarity*. Cambridge: Cambridge University Press.

Sazonov, Evgenii. 2010. "Kardiolog Ivan Khrenov: 'Tol'ko posle razgovora ia ponial, chto mne zvonil glava pravitel'stva!" *Komsomol'skaia pravda* 189, December 20, 5.

Seifrid, Thomas. 2001. "'Illusion' and Its Workings in Modern Russian Culture." *Slavic and East European Journal* 45(2): 205–15.

Smol'iakova, Tat'iana and Marina Gritsiuk. 2010. "Ivanovo deistvo." *Rossiiskaia gazeta* 294, December 28, 1.

Solganik, G. A. 2008. *Tolkovyi slovar'. Iazyk gazety, radio, televideniia*. Moscow: AST: Astrel'.

Suprycheva, Evgeniia. 2010. "Korrespondent 'KP' proveril: Mnogo li pravdy v tom, chto rasskazal Putinu doktor Khrenov." *Komsomol'skaia pravda* 194, December 28, 10.

Terray, Emmanuel. 1986. "Le Climatiseur et la Véranda." In *Afrique Plurielle, Afrique Actuelle. Homage à Georges Balandier*, Emmanuel Terray, ed. Paris: Karthala, 37–46.

Wedeen, Lisa. 1998. "Acting 'As If': Symbolic Politics and Social Control in Syria." *Comparative Studies in Society and History* 40(3) (July): 503–23.

   1999. *Ambiguities of Domination: Politics, Rhetoric, and Symbols in Contemporary Syria*. Chicago, IL: University of Chicago Press.

Whitmore, Brian. 2010. "The Pokazukha Liberalization." RFE/RL, March 8.

Wilson, Andrew. 2005. *Virtual Politics: Faking Democracy in the Post-Soviet World.* New Haven, CT: Yale University Press.
Yurchak, Alexei. 2003. "Soviet Hegemony of Form: Everything Was Forever, Until It Was No More." *Comparative Studies in Society and History* 45(3) (July): 480–510.
    2005. *Everything Was Forever, Until It Was No More: The Last Soviet Generation.* Princeton, NJ: Princeton University Press.
Zadornov, Mikhail. 2011. "Bud' gotov!" Video, March 2011. http://www.webtelek.com/media/rutube.php?v=6881e7994c184fecbadc55bdof36dcca. Accessed June 10, 2013.
Žižek, Slavoj. 1989. *The Sublime Object of Ideology.* London: Verso.

Index

Albania, 71t4.1
Alekperov, Vagit, 94, 96
Alliance for a New Citizen (ANO) (Slovakia), 196
Amsden, Alice, 75, 79
Andropov, Yuriy, 140, 142, 143
apparatchiks, 98
Armenia, 71t4.1
Aslund, Anders, 95, 100
authoritarianism, 123, 225
Azerbaijan, 71t4.1, 101

Baibakov, Nikolai, 93
Bakatin, Vadim, 132, 133
Balkan states, 10, 30, 35, 73, 144
  See also Albania; Bosnia and Herzegovina; Bulgaria; Croatia; Macedonia; Romania; Slovenia; Serbia; Montenegro
Baltic states, 2, 10, 11, 15, 70, 73–74, 76–79, 80, 83, 132. See also Estonia; Latvia; Lithuania
Bastrykin, Aleksandr, 138
Bayley, David, 134, 135
Beissinger, Mark, 115
Belarus, 10, 12, 13, 35, 71t4.1, 132, 153, 172, 203, 206, 211, 218
Berliner, Joseph, 121
Beslan massacre, 119
Bogdanov, Vladimir, 96
Bohle, Dorothee, 69
Bolshevik Revolution, 54, 56, 58
Bordyuzha, Nikolay, 142
Borogan, Irina, 128, 141

Bosnia and Herzegovina, 187, 194
Bozanić, Josip, 194
Brezhnev, Leonid, 2, 119, 133, 140, 146, 228
bricolage, 12, 14, 16, 75, 131, 131t7.1, 140, 147, 153, 162–66, 172–73
Brooks, Van Wyck, 223
Brown, David, 76
Bukharin, Nikolay, 147
Bulgaria, 35, 45, 69, 70, 71t4.1, 72t4.2, 73t4.3, 74, 76, 77, 78, 80, 86t4.4, 137, 153, 172, 175
Burbulis, Gennadiy, 132

cadres
  cadres reserve list, 16, 117–18, 122, 123
  geographic rotation of, 119, 120, 122
capitalism, 18, 43, 55–56, 68, 69–74, 78, 81–82, 83, 87, 129, 137, 143, 146, 147
Cardiologist from Ivanovo. See Khrenov, Ivan
Čarnogurský, Ján, 189
Caucasus, 10, 11, 135, 139, 146
Central Asia, 10, 11, 30, 55, 75, 116, 119, 132, 146. See also Kazakhstan; Kyrgyzstan; Tajikistan; Turkmenistan; Uzbekistan
Central Europe, 10, 14, 35, 69–87, 72t4.2, 73t4.3, 86t4.4, 132, 134, 144, 183
central planning. See command economy
centralization, 93, 131, 135
Cheka, 13, 129, 131, 133, 140–43, 147, 148
Cherkesov, Viktor, 141, 142–43
Chernomyrdin, Viktor, 95, 96
chernyi piar, 13
chinovniki (bureaucrats), 118, 233

Chivers, C.J., 128
Christian Democratic Movement (KDH) (Slovakia), 195, 196, 197
Christian Democratic Party (KDNP) (Hungary), 197
Churbanov, Yuriy, 140
climate, 15, 21, 52–65
 temperature per capita, 60–62
Coase, Ronald, 53
collectivization, 31, 32, 44, 209
colored revolutions, 35, 119. See also Orange Revolution; Rose Revolution
Colton, Timothy, 132
COMECON, 85
command economy, 9, 10, 17, 21, 32, 60, 90–106, 122, 145, 146, 147, 148
Committee for State Security. See KGB
Commonwealth of Independent States (CIS), 73
communism, 1, 2, 3, 4, 5, 6, 7, 9, 10, 11, 12, 13, 16, 17, 18, 19, 20, 21, 22, 29, 30, 31, 32, 33, 34, 35, 38, 39, 40, 44, 45, 46, 56, 64, 115, 130, 137, 144, 147, 155, 174, 175, 180, 181, 183, 184, 185, 186, 187, 189, 196, 197
Communist Party of the Soviet Union, 9, 42, 111, 112, 114, 116, 120, 121, 122, 132, 137, 138, 139, 140, 143, 146, 147, 152, 155, 162, 167, 186, 187, 210
 Central Committee, 112, 114, 115, 116, 117
Communist Party of Yugoslavia, 188, 194
competition
 bureaucratic, 136, 140, 142
 economic, 53, 75, 77, 78, 95
 elite, 119
 media, 13
 political, 1, 9, 194
Congress of People's Deputies, 113
corruption, 103, 104, 105, 115, 121, 138, 139–40, 144, 154, 166, 169, 173
Cost of the Cold Project, 56, 58, 59, 60, 62
Council of Europe, 133, 154
criminal justice systems, 21, 152–75
Croatia, 45, 71t4.1, 179, 180, 181, 181t9.1, 182t9.2, 187, 188, 194–95
Croatian Democratic Union. See HDZ
cultural schemata, 12, 15–16, 28, 30, 40
Czech Republic, 30, 69, 70, 71t4.1, 72t4.2, 73t4.3, 76, 82, 83, 86t4.4, 132, 137, 181, 181t9.1, 182t9.2, 183, 188, 191, 197
Czechoslovakia, 70, 76, 81, 83, 189
 See also Czech Republic; Slovakia

decentralization of the MVD, 133–35
democracy, 6, 16, 18, 28, 29, 30, 32, 35, 38, 39, 40, 44, 45, 46, 100, 144, 165, 172, 186, 191, 192, 193, 225.
 See also democratization
democratic deficit, 15, 28–46
Democratic Left Alliance (SLD) (Poland), 192
democratization, 2, 28, 29, 30–31, 34, 35, 38, 39, 44, 45, 165
Dudayev, Dzhokhar, 135

Eastern Europe, 1, 2, 3, 4, 7, 8, 10, 21, 28, 30, 31, 32, 39, 44, 45, 69, 76, 80, 81, 82, 83, 85, 132, 134
education, 7, 9, 14, 16, 21, 28, 31, 32, 33, 34, 34t2.2, 35, 38, 39, 40, 41t2.4, 44, 45, 46, 85, 117, 180, 183, 184, 185, 186, 191, 195, 209, 210, 211, 212, 214, 215, 217
 non-democratizing effects, 41–44
energy sector, 17, 20, 21, 63, 90–106
 privatization, 92, 94, 95, 96, 97, 98, 106
 renationalization, 91, 97, 98, 99, 106
Estonia, 69, 71t4.1, 72t4.2, 73t4.3, 74, 76, 78, 82, 84, 86t4.4, 137, 164
Eurasia, 2, 3, 4, 6, 10, 22, 28, 30, 34t2.2, 36t2.3, 38, 39, 41t2.4, 223
European Bank for Reconstruction and Development (EBRD), 98
European Convention on Human Rights, 170
European Court of Human Rights, 165, 170
European Union, 1, 2, 35, 69, 73, 76, 82, 154, 162, 165, 174t8.10

Favarel-Garrigues, Gilles, 146
Federal Guard Service (FSO), 133
Federal Security Service. See FSB
Fedorchuk, Vitaliy, 140
Fico, Jan, 196
Fidesz (Hungary), 197
foreign direct investment (FDI), 73, 73t4.3, 74, 76, 77
Foreign Intelligence Service (SVR), 133, 142
fragmentation, 12–13, 16, 28, 131t7.1, 132, 153, 155–56, 167–69
Frye, Timothy, 100
FSB, 13, 128, 129, 130, 131–33, 135, 136, 140–43, 233, 237

Gaidar, Yegor, 95
Gazprom, 90, 94–96, 97–98, 100–06
geography, 2, 15, 52–65, 74, 212
Georgia, 15, 45, 71t4.1, 153, 165–66, 166t8.6, 172, 173t8.9, 175

Index

Glassman, Maurice, 82
globalization, 2, 6, 218
Gorbachev, Mikhail, 113, 133, 134
Gosplan, 92, 93
Gregory, Paul, 121
Greskovits, Béla, 69, 76
Gulag system, 55
Guriev, Sergei, 99
Gustafson, Thane, 52, 93

Haggard, Stephan, 87
HDZ, 188, 194–95
Hillygus, D. Sunshine, 43
historical legacies, 1–22, 29, 53, 91, 106, 121–23, 129–31, 179–80, 222–23
   as a concept, 7–11
   definition, 7
   forms of, 11–16. (*see also* fragmentation; translation; bricolage; parameter-setting; cultural schemata)
   methods for robust arguments, 17–20, 223
   revivals, 16, 212
human capital, 64, 69, 70, 75, 76, 77, 85
Hungarian Democratic Forum (MDF), 197
Hungary, 6, 42, 69, 71t4.1, 72t4.2, 73t4.3, 74, 76, 78, 81, 83, 86t4.4, 137, 179, 181, 181t9.1, 182t9.2, 189, 191, 196–97

identity
   ethnic identity, 15, 21, 38, 185
   ethnolinguistic identity, 202–19
   fusion of religious and national, 179–98
industrialization, 30, 31, 32, 44, 52, 68–87, 209
inequality, 31, 35, 38
Inglehart, Ronald, 181
Ivanovo, 223, 226, 227, 230–33, 235, 236, 237
   regional administration, 227, 229, 230, 232

Janos, Andrew, 8
Jánossy, Ferenc, 81
Jones, Alfred Haworth, 223
Jowitt, Ken, 1, 2, 9, 115, 121, 123, 225

Karimov, Islam, 156
Karklins, Rasma, 128, 203
Katzenstein, Peter, 83
Kazakhstan, 12, 71t4.1, 101, 114, 156, 159, 166, 167, 168–69, 168t8.7, 173t8.9, 174, 206, 218
KGB, 12, 128, 129, 131–33, 136, 138, 139, 140–43, 147

Khasbulatov, Ruslan, 113
Khodorkovsky, Mikhail, 98
Khrenov, Ivan, 226–27, 231, 232–38
Khrushchev, Nikita, 133
Kirienko, Sergei, 97
Kornai, János, 87
Kováč, Michal, 195
Kozak, Dmitriy, 134
Krasnov, Mikhail, 134
Kravchuk, Leonid, 213, 215
krysha (client protection), 119, 142
Kryshtanovskaya, Olga, 118
Kuchma, Leonid, 213, 214, 215
Kuharić, Franjo, 194
Kulcsár, László, 76
Kyrgyzstan, 71t4.1, 116, 119, 173t8.9

Laar, Mart, 82, 84
Lagovskii, Andrei, 56
Lane, David, 6
language, 11, 15, 21, 81, 112, 185, 186, 187, 191, 193, 202–19
Latvia, 69, 71t4.1, 72t4.2, 73t4.3, 74, 76, 78, 84, 86t4.4, 137, 153, 164–65, 166, 175
law enforcement, 19, 20, 128–48
Lazarev, Valery, 55
legacy theater, 17, 21, 222–23, 224, 226, 228, 234, 238
legal institutions, 18, 21, 76, 103, 136, 137, 138, 139, 152–75, 193, 217
Lenin, Vladimir, 129
Leopold, Lajos, 81
Lerner, Daniel, 45
Light, Matthew, 139
Lipman, Masha, 1
literacy, 4, 31, 33, 34, 209. See also education
Lithuania, 69, 71t4.1, 72t4.2, 73t4.3, 76, 78, 86t4.4, 137, 173t8.9, 181, 181t9.1, 182t9.2, 186–87, 188, 191, 193, 194, 195
loans for shares, 95
loans for shares auctions, 94
Lukin, Vladimir, 161
Lukoil, 94, 96
Lustick, Ian, 18, 19

Macedonia, 71t4.1
Malamud, Ofer, 42
Martin, Terry, 208, 209, 211
Mečiar, Vladimir, 195
media, 13, 45, 103, 114, 136, 154, 164, 188, 194, 209, 210, 212, 216, 218, 222, 224, 226, 227, 232, 233, 234, 235, 236, 237

Medvedev, Dmitriy, 97, 114, 118, 119, 133, 134, 161
Mencinger, Joze, 83
middle class, 16, 21, 28, 44, 45
Mikhailovskaya, Inga, 130
Ministry of Internal Affairs. *See* MVD
Ministry of the Gas Industry, 92–93, 94, 95
Ministry of the Oil Industry, 92–93, 95
MOB, 133, 134, 135
mobilization, 10, 28, 42, 43, 44, 45, 46, 79, 122, 123, 185, 186, 189, 193, 197, 206, 212, 213
modernization, 20, 28, 30, 31, 33, 34, 34t2.2, 35, 36t2.3, 38, 39, 40, 44, 45, 46, 75, 80, 81. *See also* socio-economic development
Moldova, 71t4.1, 153, 172–73, 173t8.9, 218
Mongolia, 31
Movement for a Democratic Slovakia (HZDS), 195
MVD, 129, 130, 131, 133–36, 137, 138, 140, 142, 144, 145, 147

National Security Committee (KNB) (Kazakhstan), 12
nationalities policy, 15, 21, 202, 211, 212
NATO, 1
neo-patrimonialism, 116, 119, 123
New Economic Policy, 147
NKVD, 129, 136
nomenklatura system, 98, 99, 117, 213
Norris, Pippa, 181

October Revolution. *See* Bolshevik Revolution
Okhrana, 129
Oprichniki, 129
Orange Revolution, 214, 215, 227
Orban, Viktor, 197

parameter-setting, 12, *14–15*, 16, 28, 30, 40, 131, 131t7.1, 134, 137, 138, 147, 217
Patrushev, Nikolay, 141, 142
PEMEX (Mexico), 103–06
People's Party (HNS) (Croatia), 195
Peter the Great, 130
Piłsudski, Józef, 185
pokazukha (political window-dressing), 17, 222–38
Poland, 6, 11, 42, 69, 71t4.1, 72t4.2, 73t4.3, 76, 83, 85, 86t4.4, 137, 162, 163t8.5, 164, 172, 175, 179, 180, 181, 181t9.1, 182t9.2, 184–86, 187, 188, 189, 191–93, 195, 196
Polanyi, Karl, 82

policing
    quota system, 144–47
    in the Russian Federation, 20, 21, 144–47
    in the USSR, 21, 143
Pop-Eleches, Cristian, 42
Pop-Eleches, Grigore, 43, 44, 99
post-communism, 1, 2, 3, 38, 39, 40, 90, 143, 152, 155, 167, 179, 190
    post-communist development, 182
post-communist development, 1, 2, 4, 5, 10
    development-democracy link, 28–46
Presidency (Russian), 13, 101, 111–23
    Business Office, 13, 115–16
    state of the union address, 120–21
Primakov, Yevgeniy, 142
privatization, 76, 83, 90, 91, 92, 94, 95, 96, 97, 98, 99, 106, 146
Procuracy, 13, 130, 153, 155, 156, 161, 165, 166, 175
    of the Russian Empire, 130
    of the Russian Federation, 115, 130, 131, 136–38, 141, 147, 162
    of the USSR, 111, 129, 130, 155, 175
property rights, 17, 53, 90–106
propiska system, 139
Public Order Police. *See* MOB
Putin, Vladimir, 13, 16, 98, 101, 113, 114, 115, 117, 118, 119, 121, 128, 132, 133, 134, 135, 137, 138, 140, 141, 142, 143, 223, 224, 225, 226–29, 231, 232, 233, 234, 235, 236, 237

Raeff, Marc, 119
religion, 7, 11, 14, 21, 179–98
    Catholic Church, 14, 179–98
    Protestant churches, 179, 181, 188, 189, 195
resources, 68, 75, 76, 80, 93, 101, 118, 147, 222, 225, 231
    spatial misallocation, 15, 21, 52–65
Revenue Watch Institute (RWI), 101, 102
Romania, 42, 43, 45, 69, 70, 71t4.1, 72t4.2, 73t4.3, 74, 76, 77, 78, 80, 86t4.4
Romanov, Nicholas I, 129
Romanov, Peter I. *See* Peter the Great
Rose Revolution, 165
Rosneft, 94, 97
rule of law, 7, 18, 114, 122, 123, 137, 138, 162
Russia, 9, 10, 13, 15, 17, 19, 20, 21, 35, 58t3.1, 60t3.2, 61f3.2, 62f3.3, 63f3.4, 64f3.5, 70, 71t4.1, 85, 131t7.1, 153, 155, 157, 160t8.4, 162, 165, 166, 171, 174, 185, 202, 206, 207t10.2, 210, 212, 213, 214, 215, 218
    acquittals in criminal justice, 169–70

Index

law enforcement, 128–48
pokazukha (political window-dressing), 222–38
pre-trial detentions in criminal justice, 161–62
property rights in the energy sector, 90–106
spatial misallocation of economic resources, 52–65
state executive, 111–23
Russian Empire, 7, 15, 17, 19, 21, 55, 56, 111, 112, 113, 114, 118, 119, 129, 130, 135, 187, 208, 209, 210, 233
Russian Far East, 52–65

Saakashvili, Mikheil, 153, 165, 166
Sajudis, 186–87, 194
Serbia, 46, 187, 188, 194
Shchelokov, Nikolay, 140
Shelley, Louise, 128, 129
Shevardnadze, Eduard, 165
Siberia, 15, 52–65, 92
Sibneft, 94, 98
Sidanco, 94
siloviki, 118, 141–43
Slovakia, 69, 70, 71t4.1, 72t4.2, 73t4.3, 86t4.4, 137, 179, 181, 181t9.1, 182t9.2, 188–89, 191, 194, 195–96, 197
Slovenia, 69, 70, 71t4.1, 72, 72t4.2, 73, 73t4.3, 74, 75, 76, 77–79, 80, 83, 86t4.4
Sobianin, Sergei, 117
Social Democratic Party (SDP) (Croatia), 195
socialism, 14, 21, 56, 68, 69, 70, 71, 72, 75, 76, 79, 80, 82, 83, 84, 87, 152, 153, 156, 167, 222
socio-economic development, 16, 21, 28, 29, 30, 32, 35, 38, 46
Sokol, Jan, 196
Soldatov, Andrei, 128, 141
Solidarity, 186, 187, 189, 194
Soviet bloc, 29, 30, 31, 34, 41, 46, 156, 169
Soviet propaganda, 13, 69, 141
Soviet Union, 1, 2, 7, 10, 15, 17, 19, 21, 32, 39, 52, 53, 54, 55, 56, 92, 101, 118, 128, 133, 140, 141, 143, 144, 211, 224, 225, 237
  collapse of, 2, 4, 12, 35, 147, 155
Stalin, Joseph, 55, 129, 136, 184, 236, 240n22
State Duma (Russia), 105, 141
Stepankov, Valentin, 136
Stepashin, Sergey, 142
Stepinać, Alojzije, 194
Surgutneftegaz, 94, 96

Tajikistan, 71t4.1
technocracy, 118, 119
Tiso, Jozef, 189
Tocqueville, Alexis de, 9
transitions theories, 4, 5, 7, 29, 84
translation, 12, 13–14, 16, 28, 131, 131t7.1, 137, 138, 143, 153, 156–62, 167, 169–71, 179, 180, 190, 217
Transneft', 92
transparency, 53, 101, 102, 117, 119
Treisman, Daniel, 143
tsarist regime. *See* Russian Empire
Tuđman, Franjo, 188, 194
Turkmenistan, 13, 46, 71t4.1, 101

Ukraine, 10, 13, 15, 21, 71t4.1, 137, 157–61, 158t8.1, 159t8.2, 160t8.3, 162, 165, 166, 171, 171t8.8, 174, 202–19, 206t10.1, 227
United Russia party, 117, 228
urbanization, 7, 28, 31–32, 31f2.1, 33, 34, 34t2.2, 39, 41, 44, 45, 55
usable past, 17, 22, 222, 223, 224, 226, 228, 234, 238
Uzbekistan, 71t4.1, 153, 156, 161, 167, 174

Vanyan v. Russia, 170
Vassilev, Rossen, 35
Vernon, Raymond, 75
Victor, Nadejda, 100, 101, 102
Visegrád states, 70, 72, 73, 74, 75, 76, 77–79, 80, 83. *See also* Czech Republic; Hungary; Poland; Slovakia
vizirovanie, 121, 122
Volkov, Vadim, 146

Wedeen, Lisa, 230
White, Stephen, 6, 118
Wilson, Andrew, 13
Wilson, James Q., 144
Wittenberg, Jason, 12
World Bank, 74, 85, 102
World War II, 6, 30, 32, 39, 79, 92, 185, 189, 210

Yanukovych, Viktor, 214, 215, 217
Yeltsin, Boris, 94, 95, 105, 113, 132, 133, 134, 135, 136, 137, 141, 142
Young, Crawford, 115
YUKOS, 94, 97–98
Yurchak, Alexei, 229
Yushchenko, Viktor, 157, 214, 215, 216

Zadornov, Mikhail, 228
Zhirinovsky, Vladimir, 97